D1232284

Applied Microsoft Power BI

Bring your data to life!

Second Edition

Teo Lachev

Prologika Press

Applied Microsoft Power BI
Bring your data to life!
Second Edition

Published by:
Prologika Press
info@prologika.com
http://www.prologika.com

Printed in the United States of America

ISBN 13	978-0-9766353-7-6
ISBN 10	0-9766353-7-2

Author:	Teo Lachev
Editor:	Edward Price
Cover Designer:	Zamir Creations

The manuscript of this book was prepared using Microsoft Word. Screenshots were captured using TechSmith SnagIt.

contents

preface

To me, Power BI is the most exciting milestone in the Microsoft BI journey since circa 2005, when Microsoft got serious about BI. Power BI changes the way you gain insights from data; it brings you a cloud-hosted, business intelligence and analytics platform that democratizes and opens BI to everyone. It does so under a simple promise: "five seconds to sign up, five minutes to wow!"

Power BI has plenty to offer to all types of users who're interested in data analytics. If you are an information worker, who doesn't have the time and patience to learn data modeling, Power BI lets you connect to many popular cloud services (Microsoft releases new ones every week!) and get insights from prepackaged dashboards and reports. If you consider yourself a data analyst, you can implement sophisticated self-service models whose features are on a par with organizational models built by BI pros.

Speaking of BI pros, Power BI doesn't leave us out. We can architect hybrid organizational solutions that don't require moving data to the cloud. And besides classic solutions for descriptive analytics, we can implement innovative Power BI-centric solutions for real-time and predictive analytics. If you're a developer, you'll love the Power BI open architecture because you can integrate custom applications with Power BI and visualize data your way by extending its visualization framework.

From a management standpoint, Power BI is a huge shift in the right direction for Microsoft and for Microsoft BI practitioners. Not so long ago, Microsoft BI revolved exclusively around Excel on the desktop and SharePoint Server for team BI. This strategy proved to be problematic because of its cost, maintenance, and adoption challenges. Power BI overcomes these challenges. Because it has no dependencies to other products, it removes adoption barriers. Power BI gets better every week and this should allow us to stay at the forefront of the BI market. As a Power BI user you're always on the latest and greatest version. And Power BI has the best business model: most of it it's free!

I worked closely with Microsoft's product groups to provide an authoritative (yet independent) view of this technology and to help you understand where and how to use it. Over more than a decade in BI, I've gathered plenty of real-life experience in solving data challenges and helping clients make sense of data. I decided to write this book to share with you this knowledge, and to help you use the technology appropriately and efficiently. As its name suggests, the main objective of this book it so to teach you the practical skills to take the most of Power BI from whatever angle you'd like to approach it.

Trying to cover a product that changes every week is like trying to hit a moving target! However, I believe that the product's fundamentals won't change and once you grasp them, you can easily add on knowledge as Power BI evolves over time. Because I had to draw a line somewhere, *Applied Microsoft Power BI (Second Edition)* covers all features that were that were released by early January 2017.

Although this book is designed as a comprehensive guide to Power BI, it's likely that you might have questions or comments. As with my previous books, I'm committed to help my readers with book-related questions and welcome all feedback on the book discussion forums on my company's web site (http://bit.ly/powerbibook). Consider also following my blog at http://prologika.com/blog and subscribing to my newsletter at http://prologika.com to stay on the Power BI latest.

Bring your data to life today with Power BI!

Teo Lachev
Atlanta, GA

acknowledgements

After seven books and starting from scratch every time, I finally got to write a revision! It was definitely easier but not by far. The book added 20% new content and probably that much content was rewritten to keep up with the ever changing Power BI. Writing a book about a cloud platform, which adds features weekly, is like trying to hit a moving target. On the upside, I can claim that this book has no bugs. After all, if something doesn't work now, it used to work before, right? On the downside, I had to change the manuscript every time a new feature popped up. Fortunately, I had people who supported me.

The book (my eight) would not have been a reality without the help of many people to whom I'm thankful. As always, I'd like to first thank my family for their ongoing support.

The main personas mentioned throughout the book, as imagined by my 13-year old son, Martin, and 16-year old daughter, Maya.

As a Microsoft Most Valuable Professional (MVP), Gold Partner, and Power BI Red Carpet Partner, I've been privileged to enjoy close relationships with the Microsoft product groups. It's great to see them working together! Special thanks to the Power BI, Analysis Services, and Reporting Services teams.

Finally, thank *you* for purchasing this book!

about the book

The book doesn't assume any prior experience with data analytics. It's designed as an easy-to-follow guide for navigating the personal-team-organizational BI continuum with Power BI and shows you how the technology can benefit the four types of users: information workers, data analysts, pros, and developers. It starts by introducing you to the Microsoft Data Platform and to Power BI. You need to know that each chapter builds upon the previous ones, to introduce new concepts and to practice them with step-by-step exercises. Therefore, I'd recommend do the exercises in the order they appear in the book.

Part 1, *Power BI for Information Works*, teaches regular users interested in basic data analytics how to analyze simple datasets without modeling and how to analyze data from popular cloud services with pre-defined dashboards and reports. Chapter 2, *The Power BI Service*, lays out the foundation of personal BI, and teaches you how to connect to your data. In Chapter 3, *Creating Reports*, information workers will learn how to create their own reports. Chapter 4, *Creating Dashboards*, shows you how to quickly assemble dashboards to convey important metrics. Chapter 5, *Power BI Mobile*, discusses the Power BI native mobile applications that allow you to view and annotate BI content on the go.

Part 2, *Power BI for Data Analysts*, educates power users how to create self-service data models with Power BI Desktop. Chapter 6, *Data Modeling Fundamentals*, lays out the ground work to understand self-service data modeling and shows you how to import data from virtually everywhere. Because source data is almost never clean, Chapter 7, *Transforming Data*, shows you how you can leverage the unique query capabilities of Power BI Desktop to transform and shape the data. Chapter 8, *Refining the Model*, shows you how to make your self-service model more intuitive and how to join data from different data sources. And, in Chapter 9, *Implementing Calculations*, you'll further extend the model with useful business calculations.

Part 3, *Power BI for Pros*, teaches IT pros how to set up a secured environment for sharing and collaboration, and it teaches BI pros how to implement Power BI-centric solutions. Chapter 10, *Enabling Team BI*, shows you how to use Power BI workspaces and organizational content packs to promote sharing and collaboration, where multiple coworkers work on the same BI artifacts, and how to centralize access to on-premises data. Written for BI pros, Chapter 11, *Organizational BI*, walks you through the steps to implement descriptive, predictive, and real-time solutions that integrate with Power BI.

Part 4, *Power BI for Developers*, shows developers how to integrate and extend Power BI. Chapter 12, *Programming Fundamentals*, introduces you to the Power BI REST APIs and teaches you how to use OAuth to authenticate custom applications with Power BI. In Chapter 13, *Embedding Reports*, you'll learn how to report-enable custom applications with embedded dashboards and reports. In Chapter 14, *Creating Custom Visuals*, you'll learn how to extend the Power BI visualization capabilities by creating custom visuals to present effectively any data.

source code

Applied Microsoft Power BI covers the entire spectrum of Power BI features for meeting the data analytics needs of information workers, data analysts, pros, and developers. This requires installing and configuring various software products and technologies. **Table 1** lists the software that you need for all the exercises in the book. Depending on your computer setup, you might need to download and install other components, as I explain throughout the book.

Table 1   The complete software requirements for practices and code samples in the book

Software	Setup	Purpose	Chapters
Power BI Desktop	Required	Implementing self-service data models	6, 7, 8, 9
Visual Studio 2015 (or higher) Community Edition	Required	Power BI programming	12, 13, 14
Power BI Mobile native apps (iOS, Android, or Windows depending on your mobile device)	Recommended	Practicing Power BI mobile capabilities	5
SQL Server Database Engine Developer, Standard, or Enterprise 2012 or later with the AdventureWorksDW database	Recommended	Importing and processing data	6
Analysis Services Tabular Developer, Business Intelligence, or Enterprise 2012 or later edition	Recommended	Live connectivity to Tabular	2, 11
Analysis Services Multidimensional Developer, Standard, Business Intelligence, or Enterprise 2012 or later edition	Optional	Live connectivity to Multidimensional	6
Reporting Services (version 2016 recommended) Developer, Standard, Business Intelligence, or Enterprise	Optional	Importing from SSRS and integrating Power BI with SSRS	4, 6

Although the list is long, don't despair! As you can see, most of the software is not required. In addition, the book provides the source data as text files and it has alternative steps to complete the exercises if you don't install some of the software, such as SQL Server or Analysis Services.

You can download the book source code from the book page at http://bit.ly/powerbibook. After downloading the zip file, extract it to any folder of your hard drive. Once this is done, you'll see a folder for each chapter that contains the source code for that chapter. The source code in each folder includes the changes you need to make in the exercises in the corresponding chapter, plus any supporting files required for the exercises. For example, the Adventure Works.pbix file in the Ch06 folder includes the changes that you'll make during the Chapter 6 practices and includes additional files for importing data. Save your files under different names or in different folders in order to avoid overwriting the files that are included in the source code.

 NOTE   The data source settings of the sample Power BI Desktop models in this book have connection strings to databases and text files. If you decide to test the provided samples and refresh the data, you have to update some data sources to reflect your specific setup. To do so, open the Power BI Desktop model, and then click the Edit Queries button in the ribbon's Home tab. Select the query that fails to refresh in the Queries pane, and then double-click the Source step in the Applied Steps list (Query Settings pane). Change the server name or file location as needed.

Installing the Adventure Works databases

Some of the code samples import data from the AdventureWorksDW database. This is a Microsoft-provided database that simulates a data warehouse. I recommend you install it on a local or shared SQL Server because importing form a relational database is a common requirement. Again, you don't have to do this (installing a SQL Server alone can be challenging) because I provide the necessary data extracts.

 NOTE   Microsoft ships Adventure Works databases with each version of SQL Server. More recent versions of the databases have incremental changes and they might have different data. Although the book exercises were tested with the Adventure-WorksDW2012 database, you can use a later version if you want. Depending on the database version you install, you might find that reports might show somewhat different data.

Follow these steps to download the AdventureWorksDW2012 database:

1. Open the Microsoft SQL Server Product Samples Database webpage on Codeplex (http://msftdbprodsamples.codeplex.com).
2. Click the SQL Server 2012 DW tile. The link URL as of the time of this writing is http://msftdbprodsamples.codeplex.com/releases/view/55330. Click the AdventureWorksDW2012 Data File link.
3. When Internet Explorer prompts you, click Run to download the file.
4. Open SQL Server Management Studio (SSMS) and connect to your SQL Server database instance. Attach the AdventureWorksDW2012_Data.mdf file. If you're not sure how to attach a database file, read the instructions at https://msdn.microsoft.com/en-us/library/ms190209.aspx.

Installing the Adventure Works Analysis Services models

In chapter 2 and 11, you connect to the Adventure Works Tabular model, and chapter 6 has an exercise for importing data from Analysis Services. If you decide to do these exercises, install the Analysis Services models as follows:

1. Open the Microsoft SQL Server Product Samples Database webpage on Codeplex (http://msftdbprodsamples.codeplex.com).
2. Click the SQL Server 2012 DW tile. The link URL as of the time of this writing is http://msftdbprodsamples.codeplex.com/releases/view/55330.
3. Click the "AdventureWorks Multidimensional Models SQL Server 2012" link to download the zip file.
4. Follow the steps in the "Readme for Analysis Services Tutorial on Multidimensional Modeling" section of the of the "SQL Server Samples Readme" document at http://bit.ly/1PwLLP2 to deploy the Adventure Works cube.
5. Back to the SQL Server 2012 DW Codeplex page, download and unzip the "AdventureWorks Tabular Model SQL Server 2012" file.
6. Follow the steps in the "Readme for Adventure Works DW Tabular SQL 2012" section of the of the "SQL Server Samples Readme" document at http://bit.ly/1PwLLP2 to deploy the Adventure Works Tabular model.
7. In SQL Server Management Studio, connect to your Analysis Services instance. (Multidimensional and Tabular must be installed on separate instances.)
8. Expand the Databases folder. You should see the SSAS database.

Reporting errors

Please submit bug reports to the book discussion list on http://bit.ly/powerbibook. Confirmed bugs and inaccuracies will be published to the book errata document. A link to the errata document is provided in the book web page. The book includes links to web resources for further study. Due to the transient nature of the Internet, some links might be no longer valid or might be broken. Searching for the document title is usually sufficient to recover the new link.

Your purchase of APPLIED MICROSOFT POWER BI includes free access to a web forum sponsored by the author, where you can make comments about the book, ask technical questions, and receive help from the author and the community. The author is not committed to a specific amount of participation or successful resolution of the question and his participation remains voluntary. You can subscribe to the forum from the author's personal website http://bit.ly/powerbibook.

Chapter 1

Introducing Power BI

Without supporting data, you are just another person with an opinion. But data is useless if you can't derive knowledge from it. And, this is where Microsoft data analytics and Power BI can help! Power BI changes the way you gain insights from data; it brings you a cloud-hosted, business intelligence and analytics platform that democratizes and opens BI to everyone. Power BI makes data analytics pervasive and accessible to all users under a simple promise "five seconds to sign up, five minutes to wow!"

This guide discusses the capabilities of Power BI, and this chapter introduces its innovative features. I'll start by explaining how Power BI fits into the Microsoft Data Platform and when to use it. You'll learn what Power BI can do for different types of users, including business users, data analysts, professionals, and developers. I'll also take you on a tour of the Power BI features and its toolset.

1.1   What is Microsoft Power BI?

Before I show you what Power BI is, I'll explain business intelligence (BI). You'll probably be surprised to learn that even BI professionals disagree about its definition. In fact, Forester Research offers two definitions (see https://en.wikipedia.org/wiki/Business_intelligence).

 DEFINITION   Broadly defined, BI is a set of methodologies, processes, architectures, and technologies that transform raw data into meaningful and useful information that's used to enable more effective strategic, tactical, and operational insights and decision-making. A narrower definition of BI might refer to just the top layers of the BI architectural stack, such as reporting, analytics, and dashboards.

Regardless of which definition you follow, Power BI can help you with your data analytics needs.

1.1.1   Understanding Business Intelligence

The definition above is a good starting point but to understand BI better, you need to understand its flavors. First, I'll categorize who's producing the BI artifacts, and then I'll show you the different types of analytical tasks that these producers perform.

Understanding BI usage scenarios
I'll classify BI by its main users and produced artifacts and divide it into self-service, team, and organizational BI.

- Self-service BI (or personal BI) – Self-service BI enables data analysts to offload effort from IT pros. For example, Maya is a business user and she wants to analyze CRM data from Salesforce. Maya can connect Power BI to Salesforce and get prepackaged dashboards and reports without building a data model. In the more advanced scenario, Power BI empowers analysts to build data models for self-service data exploration and reporting. Suppose that Martin from the sales department wants to analyze some sales data that's stored in a Microsoft Access database or in an Excel workbook. With a few clicks, Martin can import the data from various data sources into a data model (similar to the one shown in **Figure 1.1**), build reports, and gain valuable insights. In other words, Power BI makes data analytics more pervasive because it enables more employees to perform BI tasks.

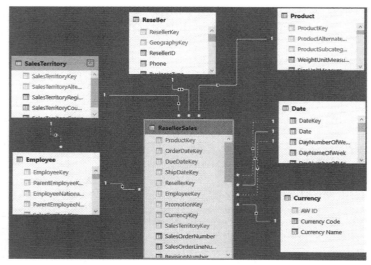

Figure 1.1 Power BI allows business users to build data models whose features are on par with professional models implemented by BI pros.

- Team BI – Business users can share the reports and dashboards they've implemented with other team members without requiring them to install modeling or reporting tools. Suppose that Martin would like to share his sales model with his coworker, Maya. Once Martin has uploaded the model to Power BI, Maya can go online and view the reports and dashboards Martin has shared with her. She can even create her own reports and dashboards that connect to Martin's model.

- Organizational BI (or corporate BI) – BI professionals who implement organizational BI solutions, such as data warehouses or semantic models, will find that Power BI allows them to implement hybrid solutions that eliminate the need to move data to Power BI. For example, as a BI pro, Elena has developed a Multidimensional or Tabular model layered on top of the company's data warehouse. Elena can install connectivity software on an on-premises computer so that Power BI can connect to her model. This allows business users to create instant reports and dashboards in Power BI by leveraging the existing investment in Analysis Services without moving data to the cloud!

 NOTE To learn more about Analysis Services, I covered implementing Analysis Services Multidimensional models in my book "Applied Microsoft Analysis Services 2005" and Tabular models in "Applied Microsoft SQL Server 2012 Analysis Services: Tabular Modeling".

Understanding types of data analytics
The main goal of BI is to get actionable insights that lead to smarter decisions and better business outcomes. There are three types of data analytics (descriptive, predictive, and prescriptive) that can help users achieve this goal.

Descriptive analytics is retrospective. It focuses on what has happened in the past to understand the company's performance. This type of analytics is the most common and well understood. Coupled with a good data exploration tool, such as Power BI or Microsoft Excel, descriptive analytics helps you discover import trends and understand the factors that led to these trends. You do descriptive analytics when you slice and dice data. For example, a business analyst can create a Power BI report to discover sale trends by year. Descriptive analytics can answer questions, such as "Who are my top 10 customers?", "What is the company's sales by year, quarter, month, and so on?", or "How does the company's profit compare against the predefined goal by business unit, product, time, and other subject areas?"

Predictive analytics is concerned with what will happen in the future. It uses data mining and machine learning algorithms to determine probable future outcomes and discover patterns that might not be easily discernible based on historical data. These hidden patterns can't be discovered with traditional data exploration since data relationships might be too complex, or because there's too much data for a human to analyze. Typical predictive tasks include forecasting, customer profiling, and basket analysis. Data mining can answer questions, such as, "What are the forecasted sales numbers for the next few months?", "What other products is a customer likely to buy along with the product he or she already chose?", and, "What type of customer (described in terms of gender, age group, income, and so on) is likely to buy a given product?" Power BI includes several predictive features. Quick Insights applies machine learning algorithms to find hidden patterns, such as that the revenue for a particular product is steadily decreasing. You can add time-series forecasting to a line chart, such to predict sales for future periods. Thanks to the huge investments that Microsoft has made in R, a data analyst can use R scripts for data cleansing, statistical analysis, data mining, and visualizing data. Power BI can integrate with Azure Machine Learning experiments. For example, an analyst can build a predictive experiment with the Azure Machine Learning service and then visualize the results in Power BI.

Finally, *prescriptive analytics* goes beyond predictive analytics to not only attempt to predict the future but also recommend the best course of action and the implications of each decision option. Typical prescriptive tasks are optimization, simulation, and goal seek. While tools for descriptive and predictive needs have matured, prescriptive analytics is a newcomer and currently is in the realm of startup companies. The good news is that you can get prepackaged advanced analytics and prescriptive solutions with Cortana Analytics Suite, such as solutions for product recommendations and customer churn. In July 2015, Microsoft unveiled Cortana Analytics Suite as "a fully managed big data and advanced analytics suite that enables you to transform your data into intelligent action". The suite includes various cloud-based services, such as Azure Machine Learning for predictive analytics, Stream Analytics for real-time BI, and Power BI for dashboards and reporting. I'll show you some of these capabilities, including the Cortana digital assistant in Chapter 4, and Azure Machine Learning and Stream Analytics in Chapter 11.

1.1.2   Introducing the Power BI Products

Now that you understand BI better, let's discuss what Power BI is. Power BI is a set of products and services that enable you to connect to your data, visualize it, and share insights with other users. At a high level, Power BI consists of four products:

- Power BI Service – A *cloud-based* business analytics service (powerbi.com) that allows you to host your data, reports, and dashboards online and share them with your coworkers. Because Power BI is hosted in the cloud and maintained by Microsoft, your organization doesn't have to purchase, install, and maintain an on-premises infrastructure. Microsoft delivers weekly updates to the Power BI Service so the pace of innovation and improvement will continue unabated. To stay up to date with the latest features, follow the Power BI blog (https://powerbi.microsoft.com/blog/).

- Power BI Mobile – A set of native applications for iOS, Android, and Windows that allow users to use mobile devices, such as tablets and smartphones, to get data insights on the go. For example, a mobile user can view and interact with reports and dashboards deployed to Power BI.

- Power BI Desktop – A freely available Windows desktop application that allows analysts to design data models and reports. For readers familiar with Power Pivot for Excel, Power BI Desktop offers similar self-service BI features in a standalone application outside Excel.

- Power BI Embedded – A cloud service, Power BI Embedded allows developers to embed interactive Power BI reports in custom applications for third party. For example, Teo has developed a web application for external customers. Teo can use Power BI Embedded to allow customers to view interactive Power BI reports.

DEFINITION Microsoft Power BI is a data analytics platform for self-service, team, and organizational BI that consists of Power BI Service, Power BI Mobile, Power BI Desktop, and Power BI Embedded products. Sometimes referred to as Power BI 2.0, it replaces Power BI for Office 365, and it doesn't require an Office 365 subscription. However, if your organization has Office 365 E5 plan, you'll find that Power BI is included in it.

As you could imagine, Power BI is a versatile platform that enables different groups of users to implement a wide range of BI solutions depending on the task at hand.

1.1.3 How Did We Get Here?

Before I delve into the Power BI capabilities, let's step back for a moment and review what events led to its existence. **Figure 1.2** shows the major milestones in the Power BI journey.

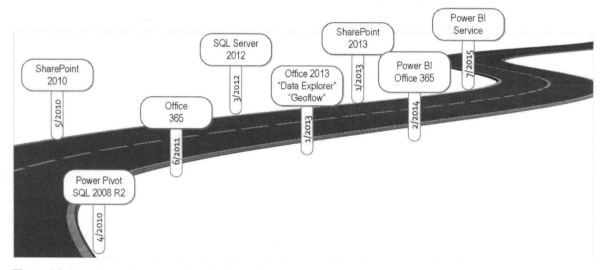

Figure 1.2 Important milestones related to Power BI.

Power Pivot
Realizing the growing importance of self-service BI, in 2010 Microsoft introduced a new technology for personal and team BI called PowerPivot (renamed to Power Pivot in 2013 as a result of Power BI rebranding). Power Pivot was initially implemented as a freely available add-in to Excel 2010 that had to be manually downloaded and installed. Office 2013 delivered deeper integration with Power Pivot, including distributing it with Excel 2013 and allowing users to import data directly into the Power Pivot data model.

NOTE I covered Excel and Power Pivot data modelling in my book "Applied Microsoft SQL Server 2012 Analysis Services: Tabular Modeling". If you prefer using Excel for self-service BI, the book should give you the necessary foundation to understand Power Pivot and learn how to use it to implement self-service data models and how to integrate them with SharePoint Server.

The Power Pivot innovative engine, called xVelocity, transcended the limitations of the Excel native pivot reports. It allows users to load multiple datasets and import more than one million rows (the maximum number of rows that can fit in an Excel spreadsheet). xVelocity compresses the data efficiently and stores it in the computer's main memory. For example, using Power Pivot, a business user can import data from a variety of data sources, relate the data, and create a data model. Then the user can create pivot reports or Power View reports to gain insights from the data model.

 DEFINITION   xVelocity is a data engine that compresses and stores data in memory. Originally introduced in Power Pivot, the xVelocity data engine has a very important role in Microsoft BI. xVelocity is now included in other Microsoft offerings, including SQL Server columnstore indexes, Tabular models in Analysis Services, Power BI Desktop, and Power BI.

SQL Server

Originally developed as a relational database management system (RDBMS), Microsoft SQL Server is now a multi-product offering. In the context of organizational BI, SQL Server includes Analysis Services, which has traditionally allowed BI professionals to implement multidimensional cubes. SQL Server 2012 introduced another path for implementing organizational models called Tabular. Think of Analysis Services Tabular as Power Pivot on steroids. Just like Power Pivot, Tabular allows you to create in-memory data models but it also adds security and performance features to allow BI pros to scale these models and implement data security that is more granular.

SQL Server includes also Reporting Services, which has been traditionally used to implement paper-oriented standard reports (also referred to as paginated reports). However, SQL Server 2012 introduced a SharePoint 2010-integrated reporting tool, named Power View, for authoring ad hoc interactive reports. Power View targets business users without requiring query knowledge and report authoring experience. Suppose that Martin has uploaded his Power Pivot model to SharePoint Server. Now Maya (or anyone else who has access to the model) can quickly build a great-looking tabular or chart report in a few minutes to visualize the data from the Power Pivot model. Or, Maya can use Power View to explore data in Multidimensional or Tabular organizational model. Microsoft used some of the Power View features to deliver the same interactive experience to Power BI reports.

In Office 2013, Microsoft integrated Power View with Excel 2013 to allow business users to create interactive reports from Power Pivot models and organizational Tabular models. And Excel 2016 extended Power View to connect to multidimensional cubes. However, Microsoft probably won't enhance Power View in Excel anymore (it's actually disabled by default in Excel 2016) to encourage users to transition to Power BI Desktop, which is now the Microsoft premium desktop tool for self-service BI.

SharePoint Server

Up to the release of Power BI, Microsoft BI has been intertwined with SharePoint. SharePoint Server is a Microsoft on-premises product for document storage, collaboration, and business intelligence. In SharePoint Server 2010, Microsoft added new services, collectively referred to as Power Pivot for SharePoint, which allowed users to deploy Power Pivot data models to SharePoint and then share reports that connect to these data models. For example, a business user can upload the Excel file containing a data model and reports to SharePoint. Authorized users can view the embedded reports and create their own reports.

SharePoint Server 2013 brought better integration with Power Pivot and support for data models and reports created in Excel 2013. When integrated with SQL Server 2012, SharePoint Server 2013 offers other compelling BI features, including deploying and managing SQL Server Reporting Services (SSRS) reports, team BI powered by Power Pivot for SharePoint, and PerformancePoint Services dashboards.

Later on, Microsoft realized that SharePoint presents adoption barriers for the fast-paced world of BI. Therefore, Microsoft deemphasized the role of SharePoint as a BI platform in SharePoint Server 2016 in favor of Power BI in the cloud and SQL Server 2016 Reporting Services on premises. SharePoint Server can still be integrated with Power Pivot and Reporting Services but it's no longer a strategic on-premises BI platform.

Microsoft Excel

While prior to Power BI, SharePoint Server was the Microsoft premium server-based platform for BI, Microsoft Excel was their premium BI tool on the desktop. Besides Power Pivot and Power View, which I already introduced, Microsoft added other BI-related add-ins to extend the Excel data analytics features. To help end users perform predictive tasks in Excel, Microsoft released a Data Mining add-in for Microsoft Excel 2007, which is also available with newer Excel versions. For example, using this add-in an analyst can perform a market basket analysis, such as to find which products customers tend to buy together.

 NOTE In 2014, Microsoft introduced a cloud-based Azure Machine Learning Service (http://azure.microsoft.com/en-us/services/machine-learning) to allow users to create predictive models in the cloud, such as a model that predicts the customer churn probability. SQL Server 2016 added integration with R. Azure Machine Learning and R supersede the Data Mining add-in for self-service predictive analytics and Analysis Services data mining for organizational predictive analytics. It's unlikely that we'll see future Microsoft investments in these two technologies.

In January 2013, Microsoft introduced a freely available Data Explorer add-in for Excel, which was later renamed to Power Query. Power Query is now included in Excel 2016. Unique in the self-service BI tools market, Power Query allows business users to transform and cleanse data before it's imported. For example, Martin can use Power Query to replace wrong values in the source data or to un-pivot a crosstab report. In Excel, Power Query is an optional path for importing data. If data doesn't require transformation, a business user can directly import the data using the Excel or Power Pivot data import capabilities. However, Power BI always uses Power Query when you import data so that its data transformation capabilities are there if you need them.

Another data analytics add-in that deserves attention is Power Map. Originally named Geoflow, Power Map is another freely available Excel add-in that's specifically designed for geospatial reporting. Using Power Map, a business user can create interactive 3D maps, such as the one shown in **Figure 1.3**. In this case, Power Map is used to analyze the correlation of power consumption and the age of the buildings in a particular geographic region. You can get some of the Power Map capabilities in Power BI when you import the GlobeMap custom visual from the Power BI visual gallery (http://visuals.powerbi.com).

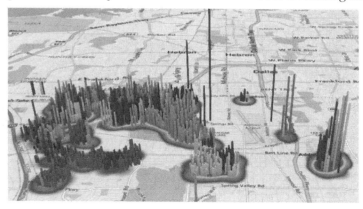

Figure 1.3 A free Excel add-in, Power Map enables you to analyze geospatial data by creating 3D visualizations with Bing maps.

Power BI for Office 365

Unless you live under a rock, you know that one of the most prominent IT trends nowadays is toward cloud computing. Chances are that your organization is already using the Microsoft Azure Services Platform - a Microsoft cloud offering for hosting and scaling applications and databases through Microsoft datacenters. Microsoft Azure gives you the ability to focus on your business and to outsource infrastructure maintenance to Microsoft.

In 2011, Microsoft unveiled its Office 365 cloud service to allow organizations to subscribe to and use a variety of Microsoft products online, including Microsoft Exchange and SharePoint. For example, at

Prologika we use Office 365 for email, a subscription-based (click-to-run) version of Microsoft Office, OneDrive for Business, Skype for Business, and other products. From a BI standpoint, Office 365 allows business users to deploy Excel workbooks and Power Pivot data models to the cloud. Then they can view the embedded reports online, create new reports, and share BI artifacts with other users.

In early 2014, Microsoft further extended SharePoint for Office 365 with additional BI features, including natural queries (Q&A), searching and discovering organizational datasets, and mobile support for Power View reports. Together with the "power" desktop add-ins (Power Pivot, Power View, Power Query, and Power Map), the service was marketed and sold under the name "Power BI for Office 365". While the desktop add-ins were freely available, Power BI for Office 365 required a subscription. Microsoft sold Power BI for Office 365 independently or as an add-on to Office 365 business plans.

Because of its dependency to SharePoint and Office, Power BI for Office 365 didn't gain wide adoption. One year after unveiling the new Power BI platform, Microsoft discontinued Power BI for Office 365. Power BI for Office 365 shouldn't be confused with the new Power BI Service, which was completely re-architected for agile and modern BI.

Power BI Service

Finally, the winding road brings us to Power BI, which is the subject of this book. In July 2015, after several months of public preview, Microsoft officially launched a standalone version of Power BI that had no dependencies on Office 365, SharePoint and Microsoft Office. What caused this change? The short answer is removing adoption barriers for both Microsoft and consumers. For Microsoft it became clear that to be competitive in today's fast-paced marketplace, its BI offerings can't depend on other product groups and release cycles. Waiting for new product releases on two and three-year cadences couldn't introduce the new features Microsoft needed to compete effectively with "pure" BI vendors (competitors who focus only on BI tools) who have entered the BI market in the past few years.

After more than a decade working with different BI technologies and many customers, I do believe that Microsoft BI is the best and most comprehensive BI platform on the market! But it's not perfect. One ongoing challenge is coordinating BI features across product groups. Take for example SharePoint, which Microsoft promoted as a platform for sharing BI artifacts. Major effort underwent to extend SharePoint with SSRS in SharePoint integration mode, PerformancePoint, Power Pivot, and so on. But these products are owned by different product groups and apparently coordination has been problematic. For example, after years of promises for mobile rendering, Power View in SharePoint Server still requires Microsoft Silverlight for rendering, thus barring access from non-Windows devices.

Seeking a stronger motivation for customers to upgrade, Excel added the "power" add-ins and was promoted as the Microsoft premium BI tool on the desktop. However, the Excel dependency turned out to be a double-edge sword. While there could be a billion Excel users worldwide, adding a new feature has to be thoroughly tested to ensure that there are no backward compatibility issues or breaking changes, and that takes a lot of time. Case in point: we had to wait almost three years until Excel 2016 to connect Power View reports to multidimensional cubes (only Tabular was supported before), although Analysis Services Multidimensional has much broader adoption than Tabular.

For consumers, rolling out a Microsoft BI solution has been problematic. Microsoft BI has been traditionally criticized for its deployment complexity and steep price tag. Although SharePoint Server offers much more than just data analytics, having a SharePoint server integrated with SQL Server has been a cost-prohibitive proposition for smaller organizations. As many of you would probably agree, SharePoint Server adds complexity and troubleshooting it isn't for the faint of heart. Power BI for Office 365 alleviated some of these concerns by shifting maintenance to become Microsoft's responsibility but many customers still find its "everything but the kitchen sink" approach too overwhelming and cost-prohibitive if all they want is the ability to deploy and share BI artifacts.

Going back to the desktop, Excel wasn't originally designed as a BI tool, leaving the end user with the impression that BI was something Microsoft bolted on top of Excel. For example, navigating add-ins and learning how to navigate the cornucopia of features has been too much to ask from novice business users.

How does the new Power BI address these challenges?

Power BI embraces the following design tenets to address the previous pain points:

- Simplicity – Power BI was designed for BI from the ground up. As you'll see, Microsoft streamlined and simplified the user interface to ensure that your experience is intuitive and you aren't distracted by other non-BI features and menus.

- No dependencies to SharePoint and Office – Because it doesn't depend on SharePoint and Excel, Power BI can evolve independently. This doesn't mean that business users are now asked to forgo Excel. To the contrary, if you like Excel and prefer to create data models in Excel, you'll find that you can still deploy them to Power BI.

- Frequent updates – Microsoft delivers weekly updates for Power BI Service and monthly updates for Power BI Desktop. This should allow Microsoft to stay at the forefront of the BI market. For example, Microsoft delivered near 200 Power BI Desktop improvements over the course of 11 releases in 2016!

- Always up to date – Because of its service-based nature, as a Power BI subscriber you're always on the latest and greatest version.

- Free – As you'll see in "Power BI Editions and Pricing" (later in this chapter), Power BI has the best business model: most of it is free! Power BI Desktop and Power BI Mobile are free. Power BI Service is free and has a Power BI Pro subscription option that you could pay for, following a freemium model. Cost was the biggest hindrance of Power BI, and it's now been turned around completely. You can't beat free!

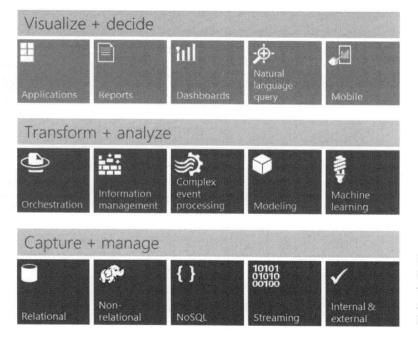

Figure 1.4 The Microsoft Data Platform provides services and tools that address various data analytics and management needs on premises and in the cloud.

1.1.4 Power BI and the Microsoft Data Platform

Power BI isn't the only BI product that Microsoft provides. It's an integral part of the Microsoft Data Platform that started in early 2004 with the powerful promise to bring "BI to the masses." Microsoft subsequently extended the message to "BI to the masses, by the masses" to emphasize its commitment to democratize. Indeed, a few years after Microsoft got into the BI space, the BI landscape changed dramatically. Once a domain of cost-prohibitive and highly specialized tools, BI is now within the reach of every user and organization!

Understanding the Microsoft Data Platform

Figure 1.4 illustrates the most prominent services of the Microsoft Data Platform (and there are new cloud services added almost every month!)

 DEFINITION The Microsoft Data Platform is a multi-service offering that addresses the data capturing, transformation, and analytics needs to create modern BI solutions. It's powered by Microsoft SQL Server on premises and Microsoft Azure in the cloud.

Table 1.1 summarizes the various services of the Microsoft Data Platform and their purposes.

Table 1.1   The Microsoft Data Platform consists of many products and services, with the most prominent described below.

Category	Service	Audience	Purpose
Capture and manage	Relational	IT	Capture relational data in SQL Server, Analytics Platform System, Azure SQL Database, Azure SQL Data Warehouse, and others.
	Non-relational	IT	Capture Big Data in Azure HDInsight Service and Microsoft HDInsight Server.
	NoSQL	IT	Capture NoSQL data in cloud structures, such as Azure Table Storage, DocumentDB, and others.
	Streaming	IT	Allow capturing of data streams from Internet of Things (IoT) with Azure Stream Insight.
	Internal and External	IT/Business	Referring to cloud on your terms, allow connecting to both internal and external data, such as connecting Power BI to online services (Google Analytics, Salesforce, Dynamics CRM, and many others).
Transform and analyze	Orchestration	IT/Business	Create data orchestration workflows with SQL Server Integration Services (SSIS), Azure Data Factory, Power Query, Power BI Desktop, and Data Quality Services (DQS).
	Information management	IT/Business	Allow IT to establish rules for information management and data governance using SharePoint, Azure Data Catalog, and Office 365, as well as manage master data using SQL Server Master Data Services.
	Complex event processing	IT	Process data streams using SQL Server StreamInsight on premise and Azure Stream Analytics Service in the cloud.
	Modelling	IT/Business	Transform data in semantic structures with Analysis Services Multidimensional, Tabular, Power Pivot, and Power BI.
	Machine learning	IT/Business	Create data mining models in SQL Server Analysis Services, Excel data mining add-in, and Azure Machine Learning Service.
Visualize and decide	Applications	IT/Business	Analyze data with desktop applications, including Excel, Power BI Desktop, SSRS Designer, Report Builder, Power View, Power Map.
	Reports	IT/Business	Create operational and ad hoc reports with Power BI, SSRS, and Excel.
	Dashboards	IT/Business	Implement and share dashboards with Power BI and SSRS.
	Mobile	IT/Business	View reports and dashboards on mobile devices with Power BI Mobile.

For more information about the Microsoft Data Platform, please visit https://www.microsoft.com/en-us/server-cloud/solutions/business-intelligence.

About *Cortana Analytics Suite*

While on the subject of the Microsoft Data Platform, you should know that it is a part of a much broader vision that Microsoft has for building intelligent applications. During the 2015 World Partner Conference, Microsoft announced Cortana Analytics Suite – a cloud-based data analytics platform (see **Figure 1.5**).

Cortana Analytics Suite was built on years of Microsoft's research in perceptual intelligence, including speech recognition, natural user interaction, and predictive analytics. The key benefit is that over time, Cortana Analytics will let you roll out prepackaged analytics solutions, reducing time to market and project costs over do-it-all-yourself approaches. For example, there will be prepackaged solutions for Sales and Marketing (customer acquisition, cross-sell, upsell, loyalty programs, and marketing mix optimization), Finance and Risk (fraud detection and credit risk management), Customer Relationships Management (lifetime customer value, personalized offers, and product recommendation), and Operations and Workspace (operational efficiency, smart buildings, predictive maintenance, and supply chain).

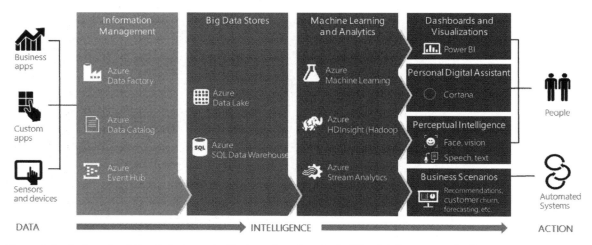

Figure 1.5 Cortana Analytics Suite is a set of tools and services for building intelligence applications.

Cortana Analytics Suite provides services to bring data in so that you can analyze it. For example, you can use Azure Data Factory (a cloud ETL service) so that you can pull data from any source (both relational and non-relational data sources), in an automated and scheduled way, while performing the necessary data transforms. As I mentioned, Event Hubs ingests data streams. The incoming data can be persisted in Big Data storage services, such as Data Lake and Azure SQL Data Warehouse.

You can then use a wide range of analytics services from Azure Machine Learning and Stream Analytics to analyze the data that is stored in Big Data storage. This means you can create analytics services and models that are specific to your business needs, such as real time-demand forecasting. The resulting analytics services and models that you create by taking these steps, can then be surfaced as interactive dashboards and visualizations powered by Power BI.

These same analytics services and models can also be integrated with various applications (web, mobile, or rich-client applications), as well as via integrations with Cortana Personal Digital Assistant (demonstrated in Chapter 4). This way, end users can naturally interact with them via speech. For example, end users can be notified proactively by Cortana if the analytics model finds a new data anomaly, or whatever deserves the attention of the business users. For more information about Cortana Analytics Suite, visit http://www.microsoft.com/en-us/server-cloud/cortana-analytics-suite/overview.aspx.

The role of Power BI in the Microsoft Data Platform

In **Table 1.1**, you can see that Power BI plays an important role in the Microsoft Data Platform by providing services for getting, transforming and visualizing your data. As far as data acquisition goes, it can connect to cloud and on-premises data sources so that you can import and relate data irrespective of its origin.

Capturing data is one thing but making dirty data suitable for analysis is quite another. However, you can use the data transformation capabilities of Power BI Desktop (or Power Query in Excel) to cleanse and enrich your data. For example, someone might give you an Excel crosstab report. If you import the data as it is, you'll quickly find that you won't be able to relate it to the other tables in your data model. However, with a few clicks, you can un-pivot your data and remove unwanted rows. Moreover, the transformation steps are recorded so that you can repeat the same transformations later if you're given an updated file.

The main purpose and strength of Power BI is visualizing data in reports and dashboards without requiring any special skills. You can explore and understand your data by having fun with it. To summarize insights from these reports, you can then compile a dashboard. Or, you can build the dashboard by asking natural questions. **Figure 1.6** shows a sample dashboard assembled from existing reports.

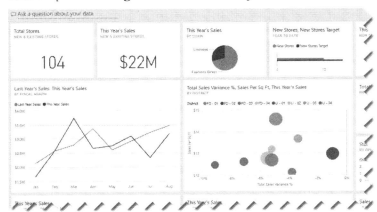

Figure 1.6   Power BI lets you assemble dashboards from existing reports or by asking natural questions.

1.1.5 Power BI Editions and Pricing

Power BI editions and pricing is simple and explained at https://powerbi.microsoft.com/pricing. This page also includes a table showing which features are supported by which edition. As it stands, Power BI is available in two editions: Power BI (Free) and Power BI Pro.

NOTE   These editions apply to Power BI Service (powerbi.com) only. Power BI Desktop and Power BI Mobile are freely available and they don't require a Power BI Service subscription. Power BI Embedded has its own consumption-based licensing model that doesn't require a per-user subscription.

Understanding the Power BI Free edition

The Power BI edition is a free offering but it has the following limitations:

■ Data capacity – If you import data, you are limited to one GB of data storage.

■ Data refresh – If you connect to online services, such as Google Analytics or Salesforce, you can't refresh data more frequently than daily.

■ Data streaming – For real-time scenarios requiring data to be streamed in Power BI datasets, streaming is capped at 10,000 rows per hour.

■ Data connectivity – You can't connect directly or refresh data from on-premises data sources. Let's say you've imported data from a corporate data warehouse into Power BI Desktop and deployed the model to Power BI. While you can analyze the imported data, this limitation prevents you from scheduling an automated refresh schedule to update the model. In addition, the free edition doesn't allow you to connect to on-premises data sources that support live connections, such as Analysis Services and SQL Server.

- Content sharing and collaboration – Only read-only dashboard sharing is supported.

Despite these limitations, the free edition is packed with features. For example, Power BI Free will be appealing to a business user who's interested in Power BI content packs to analyze online data. This edition would allow a data analyst to create and publish sophisticated data models, refresh imported data, and share dashboards with a limited number of people.

 NOTE Microsoft views Power BI Free as an experimental edition for testing Power BI features without requiring a formal approval or on-boarding process. The main missing features that will motivate you to upgrade to Power BI Pro are content sharing and live connections to on-premises data sources.

Understanding the Power BI Pro edition
This paid edition has a sticker price of $9.99 per user per month. Microsoft offers discounts so check with your Microsoft reseller. Also, if your organization uses Office 365, you'll find that Power BI Pro is included in the E5 business plan. Power BI Pro offers the following extra features:

- Data capacity – It increases the data storage quota to 10 GB per user.
- Data refresh – It supports hourly data refreshes.
- Data streaming – It supports streaming to one million rows per second in real-time dashboards.
- Data connectivity – No data connectivity limitations.
- Report subscriptions – Users can subscribe to reports and receive them via email on a set schedule.
- Content sharing and collaboration – Besides simple sharing, Power BI Pro also supports workspaces and organizational content packs.

 NOTE Not sure if the Power BI Pro edition is right for you? You can evaluate it for free for 60 days. To start the trial period, log in the Power BI portal, click the Settings menu in the top right corner, and then click "Manage Personal Storage". Then click the "Try Pro for free" link.

1.2   Understanding the Power BI Products

Now that I've introduced you to Power BI and the Microsoft Data Platform, let's take a closer look at the Power BI building blocks. Don't worry if you don't immediately understand some of these technologies or if you find this section too technical. I'll clarify them throughout the rest of this chapter and the book. As I mentioned in section 1.1, Power BI is an umbrella name that unifies four products: Power BI Service, Power BI Mobile, Power BI Desktop, and Power BI Embedded.

1.2.1   Understanding Power BI Service

At the heart of Power BI is the cloud-based business analytics service referred to as *Power BI Service* or just *Power BI*. You use the service every time you utilize any of the powerbi.com features, such as connecting to online services, deploying and refreshing data models, viewing reports and dashboards, sharing content, or using Q&A (the natural language search feature). Next, I'll introduce you to some of Power BI Service's most prominent features.

Connect to any data source

The BI journey starts with connecting to data that could be a single file or multiple data sources. Power BI allows you to connect to virtually any accessible data source, either hosted on the cloud or in your company's data center. Your self-service project can start small. If all you need is to analyze a single file, such as an Excel workbook, you might not need a data model. Instead, you can connect Power BI to your file, import its data, and start analyzing data immediately. However, if your data acquisition needs are more involved, such as when you have to relate data from multiple sources, you can use Power BI Desktop to build a data model whose capabilities can be on par with professional data models and cubes!

Some data sources, such as Analysis Services models, support live connections. Because data isn't imported, live connections allow reports and dashboards to be always up to date. In the case when you have to import data, you can specify how often the data will be refreshed to keep it synchronized with changes in the original data source. For example, Martin might have decided to import data from the corporate data warehouse and deploy the model to Power BI. To keep the published model up to date, Martin can schedule the data model to refresh daily.

Content packs for online services

Continuing on data connectivity, chances are that your organization uses popular cloud services, such as Salesforce, Marketo, Dynamics CRM, Google Analytics, Zendesk, and others. Power BI content packs for online services allow business users to connect to such services and analyze their data without technical setup and data modeling. Content packs include a curated collection of dashboards and reports that continuously update with the latest data from these services. With a few clicks, you can connect to one of the supported online services and start analyzing data using prepackaged reports and dashboards. If the provided content isn't enough, you can create your own reports and dashboards. **Figure 1.7** shows a prepackaged dashboard for analyzing website traffic. This dashboard is included in the Power BI Google Analytics content pack.

Figure 1.7 Content packs allow you to connect to online services and analyze data using prepackaged reports and dashboards.

Dashboards and reports

Collected data is meaningless without useful reports. Insightful dashboards and reports is what Power BI Service is all about. To offer more engaging experience and let users have fun with data while exploring it, Power BI reports are interactive. For example, the report in **Figure 1.8** demonstrates one of these interactive features. In this case, the user selected Linda in the Bar Chart on the right. This action filtered the Column Chart on the left so that the user can see Linda's contribution to the overall sales.

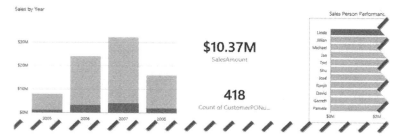

Figure 1.8 Interactive reports allow users to explore data in different ways.

Natural queries (Q&A)

Based on my experience, the feature that excites the users the most is Power BI natural queries or Q&A. End users are often overwhelmed when asked to create ad hoc reports from a data model. They don't know which fields to use and where to find them. The unfortunate "solution" by IT is to create new reports in an attempt to answer new questions. This might result in a ton of reports that are replaced by new reports and are never used again. However, Power BI allows users to ask natural questions, such as "this year's sales by district in descending order by this year's sales" (see **Figure 1.9**).

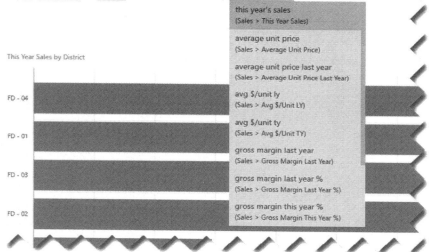

Figure 1.9 Q&A allows users to explore data by asking natural questions.

Not only can Power BI interpret natural questions, but it also chooses the best visualization! While in this case Q&A has decided to use a Bar Chart, it might have chosen a map if the question was phrased in a different way. And, you can always change the visualization manually if the Power BI selection isn't adequate.

NOTE As of the time of writing this book, Q&A is supported only when data is imported into Power BI, such as when you create a Power BI Desktop model that sources data, and then upload the model to Power BI Service. Q&A is also available when Power BI connects live to Analysis Services Tabular model but not with other data sources that support direct connections. Q&A is also currently in English only.

Sharing and collaboration

Once you've created informative reports and dashboards, you might want to share them with your coworkers. Power BI supports several sharing options. Power BI Free allows you to share dashboards as read-only with your coworkers. Or you can use Power BI Pro workspaces to allow groups of people to have access to the same workspace content. For example, if Maya works in sales, she can create a Sales Department workspace and grant her coworkers access to the workspace. Then all content added to the Sales Department workspace will be shared among the group members.

Yet a third way to share content is to create an organizational content pack. Organizational content packs allow you to share content across teams or even with everyone from your organization. Users can discover and open content packs from the Power BI AppSource (see **Figure 1.10**). In this case, the user sees that someone has published a Reseller Sales content pack. The user can connect to the pack and access its content as read-only by default. The user can also copy the content and personalize it.

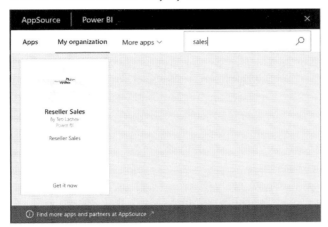

Figure 1.10 Users within your organization can use the Power BI AppSource to discover published organizational content packs.

Alerts and subscriptions
Do you want to be notified when your data changes beyond certain levels? Of course you do! You can set up as many alerts as you want in both Power BI Service and Power BI Mobile. You can set rules to be alerted when single number tiles in your dashboard exceed limits that you set. With data-driven alerts, you can gain insights and take action wherever you're located.

Would you like Power BI to email you your favorite report when its data changes? Just view the report in Power BI Service and subscribe to a report page of interest. Power BI will regularly send a screenshot of that report page directly to your mail inbox and a link to the actual report.

1.2.2 Understanding Power BI Mobile

Power BI Mobile is a set of native mobile applications for iOS, Windows and Android devices. You can access the download links from https://powerbi.microsoft.com/mobile. Why do you need these applications? After all, thanks to Power BI HTML5 rendering, you can view Power BI reports and dashboards in your favorite Internet browser. However, the native applications offer features that go beyond just rendering. Although there are some implementation differences, this section covers some of the most compelling features (chapter 4 has more details).

Optimized viewing
Mobile devices have limited display capabilities. The native apps adjust the layout of dashboards and reports so they display better on mobile devices. For example, by default viewing a dashboard in a phone in portrait mode will position each dashboard tile after another. Rotating the phone to landscape will show the dashboard as it appears in Power BI Service (**Figure 1.11**). You can further tune the mobile layout by making changes to dashboards and reports in a special Phone View layout mode.

Figure 1.11 Power BI Mobile adjusts the dashboard layout when you rotate your phone from portrait to landscape.

Favorite dashboard tiles

Suppose that, while viewing dashboard tiles on your iPad, you want to put your favorite tiles in one place. You can just tap a tile to mark it as a favorite. These tiles appear in a separate "Favorites" folder. The dashboard tiles displayed on your device are live snapshots of your data. To interact with a tile, just tap it!

Alerts

Instead of going to powerbi.com to set up an alert on a dashboard tile, you can set up alerts directly in your mobile app. For example, **Figure 1.12** shows that I've enabled an iPhone data alert to be notified when this year's sales exceed $23 million. When the condition is met, I'll get a notification and email.

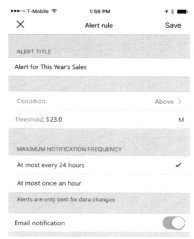

Figure 1.12 Alerts notify you about important data changes, such as when sales exceed a certain threshold.

Annotations

Annotations allow you to add comments (lines, text, and stamps) to dashboard tiles (see **Figure 1.13**). Then you can mail a screen snapshot to recipients, such as to your manager.

Sharing

Similar to Power BI simple sharing, you can use mobile device to share a dashboard by inviting coworkers to access the dashboard. Dashboards shared by mail are read-only, meaning that the people you shared with can only view the dashboard without making changes.

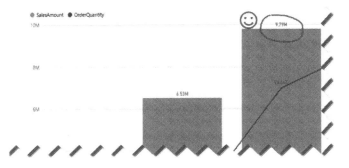

Figure 1.13 Annotations allow you to add comments to tiles and then send screenshots to your coworkers.

1.2.3 Understanding Power BI Desktop

Oftentimes, data analytics go beyond a single dataset. To meet more advanced needs, business analysts create data models, such as to relate data from multiple data sources and then implement business calculations. The Power BI premium design tool for implementing such models is Power BI Desktop.

Installing Power BI Desktop

Power BI Desktop is a freely available Windows application for implementing self-service data models and reports. You can download it for free from https://powerbi.microsoft.com/desktop or from the Downloads menu in Power BI Service. Power BI Desktop is available as 32-bit and 64-bit Windows installations. The download page determines what version of Windows you have (32-bit or 64-bit) and downloads the appropriate executable.

Nowadays, you can't buy a 32-bit computer (not easily, anyway). However, even if you have a 64-bit computer and 64-bit Windows OS, you can still install 32-bit applications. The problem is that 32-bit applications are limited to 2 GB of memory. By contrast, 64-bit computing enables applications to use more than 2 GB of memory. This is especially useful for in-memory databases that import data, such as xVelocity (remember that xVelocity is the storage engine of Power BI Service and Power BI Desktop). In general, if you have a 64-bit version of Windows, you should install the 64-bit version of any software if a 64-bit version is available. Therefore, the 64-bit version of Power BI Desktop is a better choice. However, although your model on the desktop can grow and grow until it exhausts all the memory, remember that Power BI Service won't let you upload a file that is larger than 1 GB (this limit will probably increase) so keep this in mind as well if you plan to publish the model.

 NOTE Readers familiar with Excel data modeling might remember that the Office setup installs the 32-bit version of Office by default and getting IT to install the 64-bit version has been a struggle. The Office setup favors the 32-bit version in case you use 32-bit add-ins. Because Power BI Desktop doesn't depend on Office, you can go ahead and install the 64-bit version even if you have the 32-bit version of Office installed.

Understanding Power BI Desktop features

Before Power BI, data analysts could implement data models in Excel. This option is still available, and you can upload your Excel data models to Power BI. However, to overcome the challenges associated with Excel data modeling (see section 1.1.3), Microsoft introduced Power BI Desktop.

If you are familiar with Excel self-service BI, think of Power BI Desktop as the unification of Power Pivot, Power Query, and Power View. Previously available as Excel add-ins, these tools now blend into a single flow. No more guessing which add-in to use and where to find it! At a high level, the data modelling experience in Power BI Desktop now encompasses the following steps (see **Figure 1.14**).

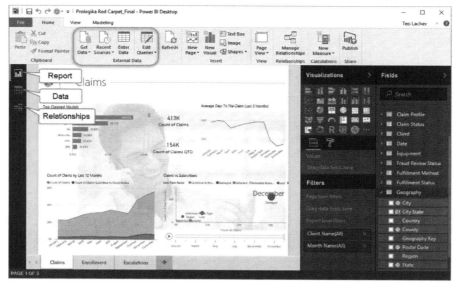

Figure 1.14 Power BI Desktop unifies the capabilities of Power Pivot, Power Query, and Power View.

1. Former Power Query – Use the Get Data button in the ribbon to connect to and transform the data. This process is similar to using Excel Power Query. When you import a dataset, Power BI Desktop creates a table and loads the data. The data is stored in a highly compressed format and loaded in memory to allow you to slice and dice the data without sacrificing performance. However, unlike Excel, Power BI Desktop allows you to connect directly to a limited number of fast databases, such as Analysis Services and Azure SQL Data Warehouse, where it doesn't make sense to import the data.

2. Former Power Pivot – View and make changes to the data model using the Data and Relationships tabs in the left navigation bar. This is the former Power Pivot part.

3. Former Power View – Create interactive reports using the Report tab on the left, as you can do using Power View in Excel (version 2013 or higher).

 NOTE Some data sources, such as Analysis Services, support live connectivity. Once you connect to a live data source, you can jump directly to step 3 above and start creating reports because there are no queries to edit and models to design. In this case, Power BI Desktop acts as a presentation layer that's directly connected to the data source.

Comparing design environments

Because there are many Power Pivot models out there, Power BI allows data analysts to deploy Excel files with embedded data models to Power BI Service and view the included pivot reports and Power View reports online. Analysts can now choose which modeling tool to use:

- Microsoft Excel – Use this option if you prefer to work with Excel and you're familiar with the data modelling features delivered by Power Pivot, Power Query, Power View and Power Map.

- Power BI Desktop – Use this free option if you prefer a simplified tool that's specifically designed for data analytics and that's updated more frequently than Excel.

Table 1.2 compares these two design options side by side to help you choose a design environment. Let's go quickly through the list. While Excel supports at least three ways to import data, many users might struggle in understanding how they compare. By contrast, Power BI Desktop has only one data import option, which is the equivalent of Power Query in Excel. Similarly, Excel has various menus in different places that relate to data modelling. By contrast, if you use Power BI Desktop to import data, your data modelling experience is much more simplified.

Table 1.2 This table compares the data modelling capabilities of Microsoft Excel and Power BI Desktop.

Feature	Excel	Power BI Desktop
Data import	Excel native import, Power Pivot, Power Query	Query Editor
Data transformation	Power Query	Query Editor
Modeling	Power Pivot	Data and Relationships tabs
Reporting	Excel pivot reports, Power View, Power Map	Power BI reports (similar to Power View reports)
Update frequency	Office releases or more often with Office 365 click-to-run	Monthly
Server deployment	SharePoint Server and Power BI	Power BI (SSRS support expected in mid-2017)
Power BI deployment	Deployed as Excel (*.xlsx) file	Deployed as Power BI Desktop (pbix) file
Convert models	Can't import Power BI Desktop models	Can import Excel data model
Upgrade to Tabular	Yes	Yes, but not officially supported
Object model for automation	Yes	No
Cost	Excel license	Free

Excel allows you to create pivot, Power View, and Power Map reports from data models. At this point, Power BI Desktop supports interactive Power BI reports (think of Power View reports on steroids) and some of the Power Map features (available as a GlobeMap custom visual), although it regularly adds more visualizations and features.

The Excel update frequency depends on how it's installed. If you install it from a setup disk (MSI installation), you need to wait for the next version to get new features. Office 365 includes subscription-based Microsoft Office (click-to-run installation) which delivers new features as they get available. If you take the Power BI Desktop path, you'll need to download and install updates as they become available. Power BI Desktop is updated monthly so you're always on the latest!

As far as deployment goes, you can deploy Excel files with data models to Power BI, just like you can deploy them to SharePoint Server or Office 365. Power BI Desktop models (files with extension *.pbix) can be deployed to Power BI only. Behind the scenes, both Excel and Power BI Desktop use the in-memory xVelocity engine to compress and store imported data.

 NOTE   At the PASS Summit in October 2016, Microsoft released a technology preview demonstrating how a future SQL Server Reporting Services edition (past SQL Server 2016) will support publishing and online rendering of Power BI Desktop files. Currently, among the Microsoft BI offerings, only Power BI Service supports online rendering of Power BI Desktop models. According to this blog (http://bit.ly/ssrs_pbi) by Microsoft, the SSRS-Power BI integration is expected in mid-2017.

As of the time of writing, Power BI Desktop supports importing Power Pivot models from Excel to allow you to migrate models from Excel to Power BI Desktop. Excel doesn't support importing Power BI Desktop models yet so you can't convert your Power BI Desktop files to Excel data models. A BI pro can migrate Excel data models to Tabular models when organizational features, such as scalability and security, are desirable. Currently, Tabular can't officially import Power BI Desktop models because Power BI adds features constantly, which could put it ahead of the Tabular box features. However, I have an unsupported workaround (see my blog "Upgrading Power BI Desktop Models to Tabular" at http://prologika.com/upgrading-power-bi-desktop-models-to-tabular).

1.2.4   Understanding Power BI Embedded

Almost every application requires some reporting capabilities. Traditionally, developers would either use third-party widgets or embed Reporting Services reports using the Microsoft ReportViewer control. The first approach requires a lot of custom code. The latter limits your users to static (canned) reports. What if you want to deliver the Power BI interactive experience to your external users? Microsoft didn't have a good answer in the past. Enter Power BI Embedded!

Introducing Power BI Embedded features
Power BI Embedded is a Microsoft Azure cloud service that allows developers and Independent Software Vendors (ISV) to add interactive Power BI reports in their custom apps for third party. As other Azure services, Power BI Embedded requires an Azure subscription (not a Power BI subscription).

Figure 1.15 Power BI Embedded allows developers to embed Power BI reports in custom applications for third party.

Suppose Teo has developed an ASP.NET MVP app for external customers. The app authenticates users any way it wants, such as by using Forms Authentication. Teo has signed up for Azure and subscribed to Power BI Embedded. Teo has created some nice reports in Power BI Desktop that connect directly to an Azure SQL Database or to data imported in Power BI Desktop (Power BI Embedded is expected to add support for more data sources, including Analysis Services on premises and on Azure).

With a few lines of code, Teo can embed these reports in his app (see **Figure 1.15**). If the app connects to a multi-tenant database (customers share the same database), the app can pass the user identity to Power BI Embedded, which in turn can pass it to Power BI Desktop. Then, row-level security (RLS) filters can limit access to data.

Power BI Embedded is extensible. Teo can use its JavaScript APIs to programmatically manipulate the client-side object model. For example, he can replace the Filters pane with a customized user interface to filter data. Or, can navigate the user programmatically to a specific report page.

Understanding Power BI Embedded licensing

To support cost-effective options for delivering reports to a large number of users, Power BI Embedded has its own licensing model. Unlike the Power BI Service per-user, per-month licensing model, Power BI Embedded introduces per-session pricing. A session associates a user with a report and it includes all interactions with that report up to an hour.

So, the first time a user requests a report, Power BI initiates a new session and starts the session clock. All user interactions with that report (filtering, sorting, page navigation) are included in the session and are not charged separately. The first 100 sessions per month are free and then a new session costs only 5 cents. You can hardly beat this pricing model!

1.3   Understanding the Power BI Service Architecture

Microsoft has put a significant effort into building Power BI Service that consists of various Azure services that handle data storage, security, load balancing, disaster recovery, logging, tracing, and so on. Although it's all implemented and managed by Microsoft (that's why we like the cloud) and it's completely transparent for you, the following sections give you a high-level overview of these services to help you understand their value and Microsoft's decision to make Power BI a cloud service.

The Power BI Service is hosted on Microsoft Azure cloud platform and it's deployed in various data centers around the world. **Figure 1.16** shows a summarized view of the overall technical architecture that consists of two clusters: a Web Front End (WFE) cluster and a Back End cluster.

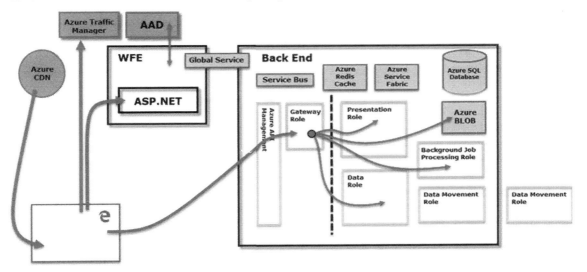

Figure 1.16 Power BI is powered by Microsoft Azure clusters.

1.3.1   The Web Front End (WFE) Cluster

The WFE cluster manages connectivity and authentication. Power BI relies on Azure Active Directory (AAD) to manage account authentication and management. Power BI uses the Azure Traffic Manager (ATM) to direct user traffic to the nearest datacenter. Which data center is used is determined by the DNS record of the client attempting to connect. The DNS Service can communicate with the Azure Traffic Manager to find the nearest datacenter with a Power BI deployment.

Power BI uses the Azure Content Delivery Network (CDN) to deliver the necessary static content and files to end users based on their geographical locale. The WFE cluster nearest to the user manages the user login and authentication, and provides an access token to the user once authentication is successful. The ASP.NET component within the WFE cluster parses the request to determine which organization the user belongs to, and then consults the Power BI Global Service.

The Global Service is implemented as a single Azure Table that is shared among all worldwide WFE and Back End clusters. This service maps users and customer organizations to the datacenter that hosts their Power BI tenant. The WFE specifies to the browser which Back End cluster houses the organization's tenant. Once a user is authenticated, subsequent client interactions occur with the Back End cluster directly and the WFE cluster is not used.

1.3.2   The Back End Cluster

The Back End cluster manages all actions the user does in Power BI Service, including visualizations, dashboards, datasets, reports, data storage, data connections, data refresh, and others. The Gateway Role acts as a gateway between user requests and the Power BI service. As you can see in the diagram, only the Gateway Role and Azure API Management (APIM) services are accessible from the public Internet.

When an authenticated user connects to the Power BI Service, the connection and any request by the client is accepted and managed by the Gateway Role, which then interacts on the user's behalf with the rest of the Power BI Service. For example, when a client attempts to view a dashboard, the Gateway Role accepts that request, and then sends a request to the Presentation Role to retrieve the data needed by the browser to render the dashboard.

Where is data stored?
As far as data storage goes, Power BI uses two primary repositories for storing and managing data. Data that is uploaded from users is typically sent to Azure BLOB storage, but all the metadata definitions (dashboards, reports, recent data sources, workspaces, organizational information, tenant information) are stored in Azure SQL Database.

The working horse of the Power BI service is Microsoft Analysis Services in Tabular mode, which has been architected to fulfill the role of a highly scalable data engine where many servers (nodes) participate in a multi-tenant, load-balanced farm. For example, when you import some data into Power BI, the actual data is stored in Azure BLOB storage but an in-memory Tabular database is created to service queries.

Analysis Services Tabular enhancements
For BI pros who are familiar with Tabular, new components have been implemented so that Tabular is up to its new role. These components enable various cloud operations including tracing, logging, service-to-service operations, reporting loads and others. For example, Tabular has been enhanced to support the following features required by Power BI:

- Custom authentication – Because the traditional Windows NTLM authentication isn't appropriate in the cloud world, certificate-based authentication and custom security were added.

- Resource governance per database – Because databases from different customers (tenants) are hosted on the same server, Tabular ensures that any one database doesn't use all the resources.

- Diskless mode – For performance reasons, the data files aren't initially extracted to disk.

- Faster commit operations – This feature is used to isolate databases from each other. When committing data, the server-level lock is now only taken for a fraction of time, although database-level commit locks are still taken and queries can still block commits and vice versa.
- Additional Dynamic Management Views (DMVs) – For better status discovery and load balancing.
- Data refresh – From the on-premises data using a gateway.
- Additional features – Such as the new features added to Analysis Services in SQL Server 2016.

1.3.3 Data on Your Terms

The increasing number of security exploits in the recent years have made many organizations cautious about protecting their data and skeptical about the cloud. You might be curious to know what is uploaded to the Power BI service and how you can reduce your risk for unauthorized access to your data. In addition, you control where your data is stored. Although Power BI is a cloud service, this doesn't necessarily mean that your data must be uploaded to Power BI.

Live connections
In a nutshell, you have two options to access your data. If the data source supports live connectivity, you can choose to leave the data where it is and only create reports and dashboards that connect live to your data. Currently, a subset of the supported data sources supports live connectivity but that number is growing! Among them are Analysis Services, SQL Server (on premises and on Azure), Oracle, Azure SQL Data Warehouse, and Hadoop Spark.

For example, if Elena has implemented an Analysis Services model and deployed to a server in her organization's data center, Maya can create reports and dashboards in Power BI Service by directly connecting to the model. In this case, the data remains on premises; only the report and dashboard definitions are hosted in Power BI. When Maya runs a report, the report generates a query and sends the query to the model. Then, the model returns the query results to Power BI. Finally, Power BI generates the report and sends the output to the user's web browser. Power BI always uses the Secure Sockets Layer (SSL) protocol to encrypt the traffic between the Internet browser and the Power BI Service so that sensitive data is protected.

NOTE   Although in this case the data remains on premises, aggregated data needed on reports and dashboards still travel from your data center to Power BI Service. This could be an issue for software vendors who have service level agreements prohibiting data movement. You can address such concerns by referring the customer to the Power BI Security document (http://bit.ly/1SkEzTP) and the accompanying Power BI Security whitepaper. Or, you can wait for the next version of Reporting Services that will support deploying Power BI Desktop models to your on-premises report server.

Importing data
The second option is to import and store the data in Power BI. For example, Martin might want to build a data model to analyze data from multiple data sources. Martin can use Power BI Desktop to import the data and analyze it locally. To share reports and allow other users to create reports, Martin decides to deploy the model to Power BI. In this case, the model and the imported data are uploaded to Power BI, where they're securely stored. To synchronize data changes, Martin can schedule a data refresh. Martin doesn't need to worry about security because data transfer between Power BI and on-premises data sources is secured through Azure Service Bus. Azure Service Bus creates a secure channel between Power BI Service and your computer. Because the secure connection happens over HTPS, there's no need to open a port in your company's firewall.

TIP If you want to avoid moving data to the cloud, one solution you can consider is implementing an Analysis Services model layered on top your data source. Not only does this approach keep the data local, but it also offers other important benefits, such as the ability to handle larger datasets (millions of rows), a single version of the truth by centralizing business calculations, row-level security, and others.

1.4   Power BI and You

Now that I've introduced you to Power BI and its building blocks, let's see what Power BI means for you. As you'll see, Power BI has plenty to offer to anyone interested in data analytics, irrespective of whether you're a content producer or consumer, as shown in **Figure 1.17**.

By the way, the book content follows the same organization so that you can quickly find the relevant information depending on what type of user you are. For example, if you're a business user, the first part of the book is for you and it has three chapters for the first three features shown in the "For business users" section in the diagram.

1.4.1   Power BI for Business Users

To clarify the term, a business user is someone in your organization who is mostly interested in consuming BI artifacts, such as reports and dashboards. This group of users typically includes executives, managers, business strategists, and regular information works. To get better and faster insights, some business users often become basic content producers, such as when they create reports to analyze simple datasets or data from online services.

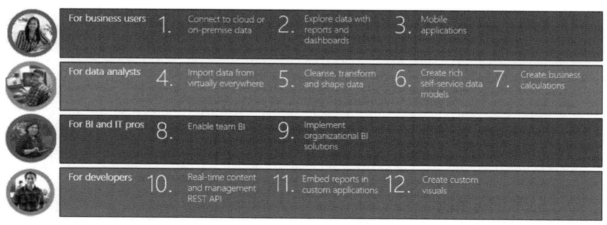

Figure 1.17   Power BI supports the BI needs of business users, analysts, pros, and developers.

For example, Maya is a manager in the Adventure Works Sales & Marketing department. She doesn't have skills to create sophisticated data models and business calculations. However, she's interested in monitoring the Adventure Works sales by using reports and dashboards produced by other users. She's also a BI content producer because she has to create reports for analyzing data in Excel spreadsheets, website traffic, and customer relationship management (CRM) data.

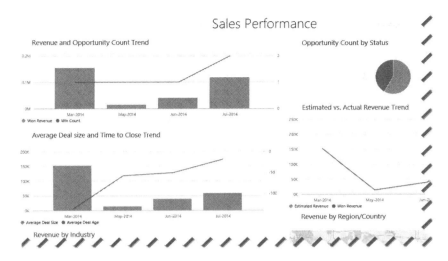

Figure 1.18 The Dynamics CRM content pack includes pre-packaged reports and dashboards.

Connect to your data without creating models

Thanks to the Power BI content packs, Maya can connect to popular cloud services, such as Google Analytics and Dynamics CRM, and get instant dashboards. She can also benefit from prepackaged datasets, reports, and dashboards, created jointly by Software as a Service (SaaS) partners and Microsoft.

For example, the Dynamics CRM connector provides an easy access to analyze data from the cloud-hosted version of Dynamics CRM. This connector uses the Dynamics CRM OData feed to auto-create a descriptive model that contains the most important entities, such as Accounts, Activities, Opportunities, Products, Leads, and others. Pre-built dashboards and reports, such as the one shown in **Figure 1.18**, provide immediate insights and can be further customized.

Similarly, if Adventure Works uses Salesforce as a CRM platform, Power BI has a connector to allow Maya to connect to Salesforce in a minute. Power BI content packs support data refresh, such as to allow Maya to refresh the CRM data daily.

Explore data

Power BI can also help Maya analyze simple datasets without data modeling. For example, if Maya receives an Excel file with some sales data, she can import the data into Power BI and create ad hoc reports and dashboards with a few mouse clicks. She can easily share dashboards with coworkers. For example, Maya can navigate to the Power BI portal, select a dashboard, and then click the Share button next to the dashboard name (see **Figure 1.19**).

Figure 1.19 Business users can easily share dashboards with coworkers using the Power BI portal or Power BI Mobile.

Mobile applications

Some business users, especially managers, executives, and sales people, would need access to BI reports on the go. This type of users would benefit from the Power BI Mobile native applications for iPad, iPhone, Android, and Windows. As I explained in section 1.2.2, Power BI Mobile allows users to not only to view Power BI reports and dashboards, but to also receive alerts about important data changes, as well to share and annotate dashboards.

For example, while Maya travels on business trips, she needs access to her reports and dashboards. Thanks to the cloud-based nature of Power BI, she can access them anywhere she has an Internet connection. Depending on what type of mobile device she uses, she can also install a Power BI native app so she can benefit from additional useful features, such as favorites, annotations, and content sharing.

1.4.2 Power BI for Data Analysts

A data analyst or BI analyst is a power user who has the skills and desire to create self-service data models. A data analyst typically prefers to work directly with the raw data, such as to relate corporate sales data coming from the corporate data warehouse with external data, such as economic data, demographics data, weather data, or any other data purchased from a third party provider.

For example, Martin is a BI analyst with Adventure Works. Martin has experience in analyzing data with Excel and Microsoft Access. To offload effort from IT, Martin wants to create his own data model by combining data from multiple data sources.

Import and mash up data from virtually everywhere

As I mentioned previously, to create data models, Martin can use Microsoft Excel and/or Power BI Desktop, which combines the best of Power Query, Power Pivot, and Power View in a single and simplified design environment. If he has prior Power Pivot experience, Martin will find Power BI Desktop easier to use and he might decide to switch to it in order to stay on top of the latest Power BI features. Irrespective of the design environment chosen, Martin can use either Excel or Power BI Desktop to connect to any accessible data source, such as a relational database, file, cloud-based services, SharePoint lists, Exchange servers, and many more.

Figure 1.20 shows the supported data sources in Power BI Desktop and Excel. Microsoft regularly adds new data sources and content packs. Once Martin deploys the model to Power BI, he can schedule a data refresh to keep the imported data up to date.

Figure 1.20 Power BI self-service data models can connect to a plethora of data sources.

Cleanse, transform, and shape data

Data is rarely cleaned. A unique feature of Power BI Desktop is cleansing and transforming data. Inheriting these features from Power Query, Power BI Desktop allows a data analyst to apply popular transformation tasks that save tremendous data cleansing effort, such as replacing values, un-pivoting data, combining datasets and columns, and many more tasks.

For example, Martin may need to import an Excel financial report that was given to him in a crosstab format where data is pivoted by months on columns. Martin realizes that if he imports the data as it is, he won't be able to relate it to a date table that he has in the model. However, with a couple of mouse clicks, Martin can use a Power BI Desktop query to un-pivot months from columns to rows. And once Martin gets a new file, the query will apply the same transformations so that Martin doesn't have to go through the steps again.

Implement self-service data models

Once the data is imported, Martin can relate the datasets to analyze the data from different angles by relating multiple datasets (see **Figure 1.1** again). No matter which source the data came from, Martin can use Power BI Desktop or Excel to relate tables and create data models whose features are on par with professional models. Power BI supports relationships natively with one-to-many and many-to-many cardinality so Martin can model complex requirements, such as analyzing financial balances of joint bank accounts.

Create business calculations

Martin can also implement sophisticated business calculations, such as time calculations, weighted averages, variances, period growth, and so on. To do so, Martin will use the Data Analysis Expression (DAX) language and Excel-like formulas, such as the formula shown in **Figure 1.21**. This formula calculates the year-to-date (YTD) sales amount. As you can see, Power BI Desktop supports IntelliSense and color coding to help you with the formula syntax. IntelliSense offers suggestions as you type.

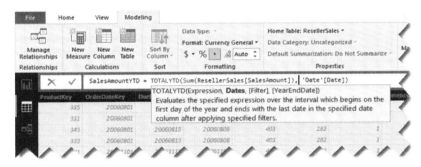

Figure 1.21 Business calculations are implemented in DAX.

Once the model is created, the analyst can visualize and explore the data with interactive reports. If you come from using Excel Power Pivot and would like to give Power BI Desktop a try, you'll find that not only does it simplify the design experience, but it also supports new visualizations, including Funnel and Combo Charts, Treemap, Filled Map, and Gauge visualizations, as shown in **Figure 1.22**.

And when the Microsoft-provided visualizations aren't enough, Martin can download a custom visual contributed by Microsoft and the Power BI community. To do this, Martin will go to the Power BI visuals gallery (http://visuals.powerbi.com) and download a visual file with the *.pbiviz file extension. Then, Martin can import the visual into Power BI Service or Power BI Desktop and start using it immediately!

Once Martin is done with the report in Power BI Desktop, he can publish the model and reports to Power BI, so that he can share insights with other users. If they have permissions, his coworkers can view reports, gain more insights with natural query (Q&A) questions, and create dashboards.

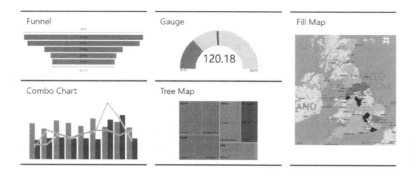

Figure 1.22 Power BI Desktop adds new visualizations.

1.4.3 Power BI for Pros

BI pros and IT pros have much to gain from Power BI. BI pros are typically tasked to create the backend infrastructure required to support organizational BI initiatives, such as data marts, data warehouses, cubes, ETL packages, operational reports, and dashboards. IT pros are also concerned with setting up and maintaining the necessary environment that facilitates self-service and organizational BI, such as providing access to data, managing security, data governance, and other services.

In a department or smaller organization, a single person typically fulfills both BI and IT pro tasks. For example, Elena has developed an Analysis Services model on top of the corporate data warehouse. She needs to ensure that business users can gain insights from the model without compromising security.

Enable team BI
Once she provided connectivity to the on-premises model, Elena must establish a trustworthy environment needed to facilitate content sharing and collaboration. To do so, she can use Power BI workspaces (a Power BI Pro feature). As a first step, Elena would set up groups and add members to these groups. Then Elena can create workspaces for the organizational units interested in analyzing the SSAS model. For example, if the Sales department needs access to the organizational model, Elena can set up a Sales Department group. Next, she can create a Sales Department workspace and grant the group access to it. Finally, she can deploy to the workspace her sales-related dashboards and reports that connect to the model.

If Elena needs to distribute BI artifacts to a wider audience, such as the entire organization, she can create an organizational content pack and publish it to the Power BI AppSource gallery. Then her coworkers can search, discover, and use the content pack. Furthermore, they can create their own copies of the original dashboard and reports so that they can make changes without affecting the original copy.

Implementing BI solutions
Based on my experience, most organizations could benefit from what I refer to as a classic BI architecture that includes a data warehouse and semantic model (Analysis Services Multidimensional or Tabular mode) layered on top of the data warehouse. I'll discuss the benefits of this architecture in Part 3 of this book. If you already have or are planning such a solution, you can use Power BI as a presentation layer. This works because Power BI can connect to the on-premises Analysis Services, as shown in **Figure 1.23**.

So that Power BI can connect to on-premises SSAS models, Elena needs to download and install a component called On-premises Data Gateway to an on-premises computer that can connect to the model. The gateway allows Elena to centralize management and access to on-premises data sources. Then Elena can implement reports and dashboards that connect live to Analysis Services and deploy them to Power BI. When users open a report, the report will generate a query and send it to the on-premises model via the gateway. Now you have a hybrid solution where data stays on premises but reports are hosted in Power BI.

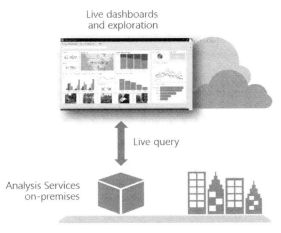

Live dashboards
and exploration

Live query

Analysis Services
on-premises

Figure 1.23 Power BI can directly connect to on-premises Analysis Services models.

If you're concerned about the performance of this architecture, you should know that Power BI only sends queries to the on-premises data source so there isn't much overhead on the trip from Power BI to the source. Typically, BI reports and dashboards summarize data. Therefore, the size of the datasets that travel back to Power BI probably won't be very large either. Of course, the speed of the connection between Power BI and the data center where the model resides will affect the duration of the round trip.

Another increasingly popular scenario that Power BI enables is real-time BI. You've probably heard about Internet of Things (IoT) which refers to an environment of many connected devices, such as barcode readers, sensors, or cell phones, that transfer data over a network without requiring human-to-human or human-to-computer interaction. If your organization is looking for a real-time platform, you should seriously consider Power BI. Its streamed datasets allow an application to stream directly to Power BI with a few lines of code. If you need to implement Complex Event Processing (CEP) solutions, Microsoft Azure Stream Analytics lets you monitor event streams in real time and push results to a Power BI dashboard.

Finally, BI pros can implement predictive data analytics solutions that integrate with Power BI. For example, Elena can use the Azure Machine Learning Service to implement a data mining model that predicts the customer probability to purchase a product. Then she can easily set up a REST API web service, which Power BI can integrate with to display results.

If all these BI pro features sound interesting, I'll walk you through these scenarios in detail in Part 3 of this book.

1.4.4 Power BI for Developers

Power BI has plenty to offer to developers as well because it's built on an open and extensible architecture. In the context of data analytics, developers are primarily interested in incorporating BI features in their applications or in providing access to data to support integration scenarios. For example, Teo is a developer with Adventure Works. Teo might be interested in embedding Power BI dashboards and reports in a web application that will be used by external customers. Power BI supports several extensibility options, including content packs, real-time reporting, custom visuals, and embedded reporting.

Real-time content and management
Power BI has a set of REST APIs to allow developers to programmatically manage certain Power BI resources, such as enumerating datasets, creating new datasets, and adding and removing rows to a dataset table. This allows developers to push data to Power BI, such as to create real-time dashboards. In fact, this is how Azure Stream Analytics integrates with Power BI. When new data is streamed, Azure Stream Analytics pushes the data to Power BI to update real-time dashboards.

The process for creating such applications is straightforward. First, you need to register your application with Microsoft Azure. Then you write OAuth2 security code to authenticate your application with Power BI. Then you'd write code to manipulate the Power BI objects using REST APIs. For example, here's a sample method invocation for adding one row to a table:

```
POST https://api.powerbi.com/beta/myorg/datasets/2C0CCF12-A369-4985-A643-0995C249D5B9/Tables/Product/Rows HTTP/1.1
Authorization: Bearer {AAD Token}
Content-Type: application/json
{     "rows":
     [
          {
                         "ProductID":1,
                         "Name":"Adjustable Race",
                         "Category":"Components",
                         "IsCompete":true,
                         "ManufacturedOn":"07/30/2014"
          }
     ]}
```

Microsoft supports a Power BI Developer Center website (https://powerbi.microsoft.com/developers) where you can read the REST API documentation and try the REST APIs.

Embed reports in custom applications

Many of you would like to embed beautiful Power BI dashboards and reports in custom applications. For example, your company might have a web portal to allow external customers to log in and access reports and dashboards. Up until Power BI, Microsoft hasn't had a good solution to support this scenario.

For internal applications where users are already using Power BI, developers can call the Power BI REST APIs to embed dashboard tiles and reports. As I mentioned, external applications can benefit from Power BI Embedded. And, because embedded reports preserve interactive features, users can enjoy the same engaging experience, including report filtering, interactive sorting and highlighting. I cover these integration scenarios in Chapter 13.

Implement custom visuals

Microsoft has published the required interfaces to allow developers to implement and publish custom visuals using any of the JavaScript-based visualization frameworks, such as D3.js, WebGL, Canvas, or SVG. Do you need visualizations that Power BI doesn't support to display data more effectively? With some coding wizardry, you can implement your own!

Moreover, to speed up development Microsoft has provided Custom Visual Developer Tools (https://github.com/Microsoft/PowerBI-visuals). You can use whatever tool you prefer to code the custom visual (visuals are coded in TypeScript), such as Microsoft Visual Code or Visual Studio. Custom Visual Developer Tools integrates with Power BI and allows you to test the visual exactly as the end user would use it on a report. When the custom visual is ready, you can publish it to the Power BI visuals gallery at https://visuals.powerbi.com where Power BI users can search for it and download it.

Implement content packs

I've already discussed how Power BI content packs can help you connect to popular online data sources, such as Dynamics CRM or Google Analytics. If you work for an independent software vendor (ISV) or System Integrator (SI), you can implement new content packs to facilitate access to data and to provide prepackaged content. You can contact Microsoft at http://solutions.powerbi.com/appsuggestion.html and sign up for the Microsoft partner program which coordinates this initiative.

As part of implementing a content pack, you'd need to create a connector using REST, OData, ODBC or other APIs to allow Power BI to connect to your data source and retrieve data. Your content pack can also include custom data models, reports, and dashboards.

1.5   Summary

This chapter has been a whirlwind tour of the innovative Power BI cloud data analytics service and its features. By now, you should view Power BI as a flexible platform that meets a variety of BI requirements. An important part of the Microsoft Data Platform, Power BI is a collective name of four products: Power BI Service, Power BI Mobile, Power BI Desktop, and Power BI Embedded. You've learned about the major reasons that led to the release of Power BI. You've also taken a close look at the Power BI architecture and its components, as well as its editions and pricing model.

Next, this chapter discussed how Power BI can help different types of users with their data analytics needs. It allows business users to connect to their data and gain quick insights. It empowers data analysts to create sophisticated data models. It enables IT and BI pros to implement hybrid solutions that span on-premises data models and reports deployed to the cloud. Finally, its extensible and open architecture lets developers enhance the Power BI data capabilities and integrate Power BI with custom applications.

Having laid the foundation of Power BI, you're ready to continue the journey. Next, you'll witness the value that Power BI can deliver to business users.

PART

Power BI for Business Users

If you're new to Power BI, welcome! This part of the book provides the essential fundamentals to help you get started with Power BI. It specifically targets business users: people who use Excel as part of their job, such as information workers, executives, financial managers, business managers, people man-agers, HR managers, and marketing managers. But it'll also benefit anyone new to Power BI. Remember from Chapter 1 that Power BI consists of Power BI Service, Power BI Mobile, and Power BI Desktop. This part of the book teaches business users how to use the first two products, Power BI Service and Power BI Mobile.

First, you'll learn how to sign up and navigate the Power BI portal. You'll also learn how to use content packs so that you connect to popular online services. Because business users often have to analyze simple datasets, this chapter will teach you how to import data from files without explicit data modelling.

Next, you'll learn how to use Power BI Service to create reports and dashboards and uncover valuable insights from your data. As you'll soon see, Power BI doesn't assume you have any query knowledge or reporting skills. With a few clicks, you'll be able to create ad hoc interactive reports! Then you'll create dashboards from existing visualizations or by asking natural questions.

If you frequently find yourself on the go, I'll show you how you can use Power BI Mobile to access your reports and dashboards on the go as long as you have Internet connectivity. Besides mobile rendering, Power BI Mobile offers interesting features to help you stay on top of your business, including data alerts, favorites, and annotations.

As with the rest of the book, step-by-step instructions will guide you through the tour. Most of the features that I'll show you in this part of the book are available in the free edition of Power BI, so you can start practicing immediately. The features that require Power BI Pro will be explicitly stated.

Chapter 2

The Power BI Service

In the previous chapter, I explained that Power BI aims to democratize data analytics and make it available to any user...BI for the masses! As a business user, you can use Power BI to get instant insights from your data irrespective if it's located on premises or in the cloud. Although no clear boundaries exist, I define a business user as someone who would be mostly interested in consuming BI artifacts, such as reports and dashboards. However, when requirements call for it, business users could also produce content, such as to visualize data stored in Excel files. Moreover, basic data analytics requirements can be met without explicit modeling.

This chapter lays out the foundation of self-service data analytics with Power BI. First, I'll help you understand when self-service BI is a good choice. Then I'll get you started with Power BI by showing you how to sign up and navigate the Power BI portal. Next, I'll show you how to use content packs to connect to a cloud service and quickly gain insights from prepackaged reports and dashboards. If you find yourself frequently analyzing data in Excel files, I'll teach you how do so using the Power BI Free edition.

2.1 Understanding Types of Business Intelligence

Remember that self-service BI enables business users (information workers, like business managers or marketing managers, and power users) to offload effort from IT pros so they have to stay in line waiting for someone to enable BI for them. And, team BI allows the same users to share their reports with other team members without requiring them to install modeling or reporting tools. Before we go deeper in personal and team BI, let's take a moment to compare it with organizational BI. This will help you view self-service BI not as a competing technology but as a completing technology to organizational BI. In other words, self-service BI and organizational BI are both necessary for most businesses, and they complement each other.

2.1.1 Understanding Organizational BI

Organizational BI defines a set of technologies and processes for implementing an end-to-end BI solution where the implementation effort is shifted to IT professionals (as opposed to information workers and people who use Power BI Desktop or Excel as part of their job).

Classic organizational BI architecture
The main objective of organizational BI is to provide accurate and trusted analysis and reporting. **Figure 2.1** shows a classic organizational BI solution.

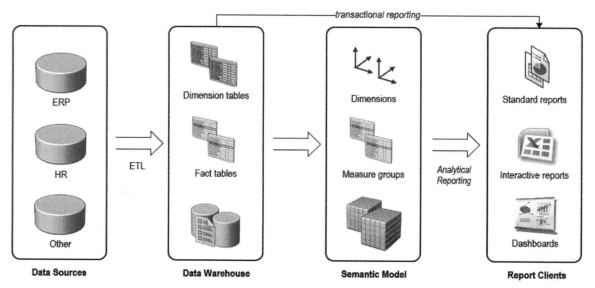

Figure 2.1 Organizational BI typically includes ETL processes, data warehousing, and a semantic layer.

In a typical corporate environment, data is scattered in a variety of data sources, and consolidating it presents a major challenge. Extraction, transformation, and loading (ETL) processes extract data from the original data sources, clean it, and then load the trusted data in a data warehouse or data mart. The data warehouse organizes data in a set of dimensions and fact tables. When designing the data warehouse, BI pros strive to reduce the number of tables in order to make the schema more intuitive and facilitate reporting processes. For example, an operational database might be highly normalized and have Product, Subcategory, and Category tables. However, when designing a data warehouse, the modeler might decide to have a single Product table that includes columns from the Subcategory and Category tables. So instead of three tables, the data warehouse now has only one table, and end users don't need to join multiple tables.

While end users could run transactional reports directly from the data warehouse, many organizations also implement a semantic model in the form of one or more Analysis Services Multidimensional cubes or Tabular models for analytical reporting. As an information worker, you can use Power BI Desktop, Excel, or another tool to connect to the semantic model and author your own reports so that you don't have to wait for IT to create them for you. And IT pros can create a set of standard operational reports and dashboards from the semantic model.

 NOTE Everyone is talking about self-service BI, and there are hundreds of vendors out there offering tools to enable business users to take BI in their own hands. However, my experience shows that the best self-service BI is empowering users to analyze data from trusted semantic models sanctioned and owned by IT. If the architecture shown in **Figure 2.1** is in place, a data analyst can focus on the primary task, which is analyzing data, without being preoccupied with the data logistics (importing data, shaping data, modeling data). This will require more upfront effort but the investment should pay for itself in time.

Understanding organizational BI challenges

Although it's well-defined and established, organizational BI might face a few challenges, including the following:

■ Upfront planning and implementation effort – Depending on the data integration effort required, implementing an organizational BI solution might not be a simple task. Business users and IT pros must work together to derive requirements. Most of the implementation effort goes into data logistics processes to clean, verify, and load data. For example, Elena from the IT department is tasked to implement an organizational BI solution. First, she needs to meet with business users to obtain the necessary business knowledge and gather requirements (business requirements might be hard to come by). Then she has to identify where the data resides and how to extract, clean, and transform the data. Next, Elena must implement ETL processes, models, and reports. Quality Assurance must test the solution. And IT pros must configure the hardware and software, as well as deploy and maintain the solution. Security and large data volumes bring additional challenges.

■ Highly specialized skillset – Organizational BI requires specialized talent, such as ETL developers, Analysis Services developers, and report developers. System engineers and developers must work together to plan the security, which sometimes might be more complicated than the actual BI solution.

■ Less flexibility – Organization BI might not be flexible enough to react quickly to new or changing business requirements. For example, Maya from the Marketing department might be tasked to analyze CRM data that isn't in the data warehouse. Maya might need to wait for a few months before the data is imported and validated.

The good news is that self-service BI can complement organizational BI quite well to address these challenges. Given the above example, while waiting for the pros to enhance the organization BI solution, Maya can use Power BI to analyze CRM data or Excel files. She already has the domain knowledge. Moreover, she doesn't need to know modeling concepts. At the beginning, she might need some guidance from IT, such as how to get access to the data and understand how the data is stored. She also needs to take *responsibility* that her analysis is correct and can be trusted. But isn't self-service BI better than waiting?

REAL WORLD Influenced by the propaganda by vendors and consultants, my experience shows that many organizations get overly excited about the perceived quick gains with self-service BI. Unfortunately, many underestimate the data complexity and integration. After pushing the tool to its limits for some time, they realize the challenges related to data quality and the extent of the transformation required before the data is ready for analysis. Although I mentioned that upfront planning and implementation is a negative for organizational BI, it's often a must and it needs to be done by a pro with a professional toolset. If your data doesn't require much transformation and it doesn't exceed a few millions rows (if you decide to import the data), then by all means go ahead with self-service BI. However, if you need to integrate data from multiple source systems, then a self-service BI would probably be a stretch. Don't say I didn't warn you!

2.1.2 Understanding Self-service BI

Self-service BI empowers business users to take analytics in their own hands with guidance from their IT department. For companies that don't have organizational BI or can't afford it, self-service BI presents an opportunity for building customized ad hoc solutions to gain data insights outside the capabilities of organizational BI solutions and line-of-business applications. On the other hand, organizations that have invested in organizational BI might find that self-service BI opens additional options for valuable data exploration and analysis.

REAL WORLD I led a self-service BI training class for a large company that has invested heavily in organizational BI. They had a data warehouse and OLAP cubes. Only a subset of data in the data warehouse was loaded in the cubes. Their business analysts were looking for a tool that would let them join and analyze data from the cubes and data warehouse. In another case, an educational institution had to analyze expense report data that wasn't stored in a data warehouse. Such scenarios can benefit greatly from self-service BI.

Self-service BI benefits
When done right, self-service BI offers important benefits. First, it makes BI pervasive and accessible to practically everyone! Anyone can gain insights if they have access to and understand the data. Users can import data from virtually any data source, ranging from flat files to cloud applications. Then they can

mash it up and gain insights. Once data is imported, the users can build their own reports. For example, Maya understands Excel but she doesn't know SQL or relational databases. Fortunately, Power BI doesn't require any technical skills. Maya could import her Excel file and build instant reports.

Besides democratizing BI, the agility of self-service BI can complement organizational BI well, such as to promote ideation and divergent thinking. For example, as a BI analyst, Martin might want to test a hypothesis that customer feedback on social media, such as Facebook and Twitter, affects the company's bottom line. Even though such data isn't collected and stored in the data warehouse, Martin can import data from social media sites, relate it to the sales data in the data warehouse and validate his idea.

Finally, analysts can use self-service BI tools, such as Power BI Desktop and Power Pivot, to create prototypes of the data models they envision. This can help BI pros to understand their requirements.

Self-service BI cautions

Self-service BI isn't new. After all, business users have been using tools like Microsoft Excel and Microsoft Access for isolated data analysis for quite a while (Excel has been around since 1985 and Access since 1992). Here are some considerations you should keep in mind about self-service BI:

- What kind of user are you? – Are you a data analyst (power user) who has the time, desire, and patience to learn a new technology? If you consider yourself a data analyst, then you should be able to accomplish a lot by creating data models with Power BI Desktop and Excel Power Pivot. If you're new to BI or you lack data analyst skills, then you can still gain a lot from Power BI, and this part of the book shows you how.

- Data access – How will you access data? What subset of data do you need? Data quality issues can quickly turn away any user, so you must work with your IT to get started. A role of IT is to ensure access to clean and trusted data. Analysts can use Power BI Desktop or Excel Power Query for simple data transformations and corrections, but these aren't meant as ETL tools.

- IT involvement – Self-service BI might be good, but managed self-service BI (self-service BI under the supervision of IT pros) is even better and sometimes a must. Therefore, the IT group must budget time and resources to help end users when needed, such as to give users access to data, to help with data integrity and more complex business calculations, and to troubleshoot issues when things go wrong. They also must monitor the utilization of the self-service rollout.

- With great power comes great responsibility – If you make wrong conclusions, damage can be easily contained. But if your entire department or even organization uses wrong reports, you have a serious problem! You must take the responsibility and time to verify that your model and calculations can be trusted.

- "Spreadmarts" – I left the most important consideration for the CIO for last. If your IT department has spent a lot of effort to avoid decentralized and isolated analysis, should you allow the corporate data to be constantly copied and duplicated?

> **TIP** Although every organization is different, I recommend an 80/20 split between organizational BI and self-service BI. This means that 80% of the effort and budget should be spent in organizational BI, such as a data warehouse, improving data quality, centralized semantic models, trusted reports, dashboards, Big Data initiatives, master data management, and so on. The remaining 20% would be focused on agile and managed self-service BI.

Now that you understand how organizational BI and self-service BI compares and completes each other, let's dive into the Power BI self-service BI capabilities which benefit business users like you.

2.2   Getting Started with Power BI Service

In Chapter 1, I introduced you to Power BI and its products. Recall that the main component of Power BI is its cloud-hosted Power BI Service (powerbi.com). Assuming that you're a novice user, this section lays out the necessary startup steps, including signing up for Power BI and understanding its web interface. As you'll soon find out, because Power BI was designed with business users and data analytics in mind, it won't take long to learn it!

2.2.1   Signing Up for Power BI

The Power BI motto is, "5 seconds to sign up, 5 minutes to wow!" Because Power BI is a cloud-based offering, there's nothing for you to install and set up. But if you haven't signed up for Power BI yet, let's put this promise to the test. But first, read the following steps.

Five seconds to sign up
Follow these steps to sign up for the Power BI Service:

1. Open your Internet browser, navigate to http://www.powerbi.com, and then click "Get started free" (see **Figure 2.2**).

Figure 2.2 This is the landing Power BI Service web page.

2. The next page asks you how you want to start with Power BI: download Power BI Desktop so that you can create a self-service data model on your desktop, or sign up for Power BI so that you can use the Power BI Service. A data analyst can use Power BI Desktop to create self-service BI models. I'll discuss Power BI Desktop in Part 2 of this book so let's ignore this option for now. Click the Sign Up button because you want to use Power BI Service.

3. In the Get Started page, enter your work email address. Notice that the email address must be your work email. At this time, you can't use a common email, such as @hotmail.com, @outlook.com, or @gmail.com. This might be an issue if you plan to use Power BI for your personal use. As a workaround, consider registering a domain, such as a domain for your family (some providers give away free domains).

4. If your organization already uses Office 365, Power BI will detect this and ask you to sign up using your Office 365 account. If you don't have an Office 365 subscription, Power BI will ask you to confirm the email you entered and then to check your inbox for a confirmation email.

5. Once you receive your email conformation with the subject "Time to complete Microsoft Power BI signup", click the "Complete Microsoft Power BI Signup" link in the email. Clicking on the link will take you to a page to create your account (see **Figure 2.3**).

Figure 2.3   Use this page to create a Power BI account.

6. You need to provide a name and a password, and then click Start.

This completes the process which Microsoft refers to as the "Information Worker (IW) Sign Up" flow. As I said, this signup flow is geared for an organization that doesn't have an Office 365 tenant. By the way, this is similar to the signup process for the Office 365 Educational plan (EDU) for Office 365.

The main page
After you complete the signup process, the next time you go to powerbi.com, click the Sign In button in the top-right corner of the main page (see **Figure 2.2** again). The main page includes the following menus:

- Products – Explains the Power BI product family and pricing. The Power BI Mobile page includes download links for the native mobile applications.

- Solutions – Explains how Power BI addresses various data analytics needs.

- Support – Includes links to the product documentation, the community forums where you can ask questions, a page to provide feedback to Microsoft, the Power BI blog, and a page to find a Microsoft partner to help you if you need training or implementation assistance.

What happens during signup?
You might be curious why you're asked to provide a password given that you sign up with your work email. Behind the scenes, Power BI stores the user credentials in Azure Active Directory (Azure AD). If your organization doesn't have an Office 365 subscription, the Information Worker flow creates a tenant for the domain you used to sign up. For example, if I sign up as teo@prologika.com and my company doesn't have an Office 365 subscription, a prologika.onmicrosoft.com tenant will be created in Azure AD and that tenant won't be managed by anyone at my company. As long as the domain in the email address matches the tenant, Power BI will add your coworkers to the same tenant when they sign up.

NOTE   What is a Power BI tenant? A tenant is a dedicated instance of the Azure Active Directory that an organization receives and owns when it signs up for a Microsoft cloud service such as Azure, Microsoft Intune, Power BI, or Office 365. A tenant houses the users in a company and the information about them - their passwords, user profile data, permissions, and so on. It also contains groups, applications, and other information pertaining to an organization and its security. For more information about tenants, see "What is an Azure AD tenant" at http://bit.ly/1FTFObb.

If your organization decides one day to have better integration with Microsoft Azure, such as to have a single sign-on (SSO), it can synchronize or federate the corporate Active Directory with Azure, but this isn't required. To unify the corporate and cloud directories, the company IT administrator can then take over the shadow tenant. I provide more details about managing the Power BI tenant in Chapter 10.

2.2.2   Understanding the Power BI Portal

I hope it took you five seconds or less to sign up with Power BI. (Or at least hopefully it feels quick.) After completing these signup steps, you'll have access to the free edition of Power BI. Let's take a moment to get familiar with the Power BI portal where you'll spend most of your time when analyzing data.

Welcome to Power BI page

Upon signup, Power BI discovers that you don't have any BI artifacts yet. This is why it navigates you to the "Welcome to Power BI" page, which is shown in **Figure 2.4**.

 NOTE   Currently, the Power BI portal isn't customizable. For example, you can't rearrange or remove menus, and you can't brand the portal. If these features are important to your organization, your IT department can consider installing an on-premises SharePoint Server or SharePoint Online and them embed Power BI dashboards and reports inside SharePoint. SharePoint supports a comprehensive set of branding and UI customization features, and you can embed Power BI content on SharePoint pages. I'll discuss Power BI content embedding in Chapter 13.

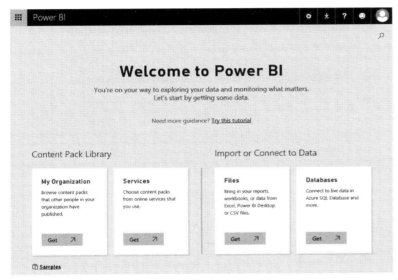

Figure 2.4   The "Welcome to Power BI" page allows you to connect to data and install samples.

Before analyzing data, you need to first connect to wherever it resides. This is why the "Welcome to Power BI" page prompts you to start your data journey by connecting to your data. The My Organization tile under the "Content Pack Library" section allows you to browse and use organizational packs (discussed in Chapter 10), assuming that someone within your organization has already published BI content as organizational packs. The Services tile allows you to use Microsoft-provided content packs to connect to popular online services, such as Google Analytics, Salesforce, Microsoft Dynamics CRM, and many more.

The Files tile under the "Import or Connect to Data" section lets you import data from Excel, Power BI Desktop, and CSV files. The Databases tile allows you to connect to data sources that support live connections, such as Azure SQL Database and SQL Server Analysis Services.

 NOTE   As you'll quickly discover, a popular option that's missing in the Databases tile is connecting to an on-premises database, such a SQL Server or Oracle. Currently, this scenario requires you create a data model using Power BI Desktop or Excel before you can import data from on-premises databases. Power BI Desktop also supports connecting directly to some data sources, such as SQL Server. Then you can upload the model to Power BI. Because it's a more advanced scenario, I'll postpone discussing Power BI Desktop until Chapter 6.

1. To get some content you can explore in Power BI, click the Samples link.

2. In the Samples page, click the Retail Analysis Sample tile. As the popup informs you, the Retail Analysis Sample is a sample dashboard provided by Microsoft to demonstrate some of the Power BI capabilities. Click the Connect button. Are you concerned that samples might clutter the portal? Don't worry; it's easy to delete the sample later. To do this, you can just delete the Retail Analysis Sample dataset which will delete the dependent reports and dashboards.

The Power BI portal

After installing the Retail Analysis Sample, Power BI navigates you to the home page, which has the following main sections (see the numbered areas in **Figure 2.5**):

1. Navigation Pane – The navigation pane organizes the content deployed to Power BI.

> **NOTE** Veteran Power BI users would notice that the Power BI navigation has been redesigned. Previously, all published content would appear in Dashboard, Reports, and Datasets sections in the navigation pane, making it difficult to find content as the number of published items grew. That's why Microsoft introduced new navigation experience in December 2016. As of this time, the new navigation experience is in preview. If it's not released by the time you read this book, in Power BI Service click the gear icon in the upper-right corner, then click Settings and turn on the "Early access to features" option in the "Preview features" tab.

Starting from the top, you can show/hide the navigation pane by toggling the "Hide the navigation pane" button. You might prefer Power BI to show a specific "featured" dashboard when you open the portal (instead of navigating you to the last dashboard you visited). If you have marked a dashboard as featured, you can click the "Featured dashboard" link to navigate quickly to that dashboard no matter where you are in the portal. While you can have one featured dashboard, you can have several favorite dashboards that you can access from the Favorites link. And the Recent link shows a list of the last 20 reports and dashboards that you've visited recently.

Figure 2.5 The Power BI home page.

Think of My Workspace as your private desk. By default, all BI content you publish to Power BI is deployed to My Workspace. Unless you share content with other users, no one else can see what's in your workspace. If you have a Power BI Pro subscription and you create other workspaces to collaborate with coworkers, you can use the "Switch workspace" button to navigate to another workspace. To see the actual published content, simply click on the workspace name. For example, to see what's inside My Workspace, click My Workspace in the navigation pane. This will open the content page, where the published content is organized in several tabs, as shown in **Figure 2.6**.

Figure 2.6 The workspace content is organized in several tabs.

The Dashboards tab includes the dashboards that you've developed or that someone shared with you. Similarly, the Reports section contains all reports that are available to you. The Workbooks session brings you to Excel files that you've connected to and let's view their content (yes, Power BI allows you to bring in existing Excel reports). The Datasets section shows all the datasets that you've created or that someone shared with you. If you have a lot of items and you still find it difficult to locate something, use the "Search content" field to search within the content in the corresponding tab. Besides simply clicking the item to open it, you can perform additional tasks from the Actions column, such as to share a dashboard, delete a dashboard, and access the dashboard settings.

Going down the navigation pane, the Get Data button at the bottom brings you to the Get Data page. Similar to the "Welcome to Power BI" page, the Get Data page allows you to connect to your cloud and on-premises data.

2. Office 365 Application Launcher – If you have an Office 365 subscription, this menu allows you to access the Office 365 applications you are licensed to use. Doesn't Microsoft encourage you to use Office 365?

3. Power BI Home – No matter which page you've navigated to, this menu takes you to the portal home page (see again **Figure 2.5**).

4. Application Toolbar – Let's explain the available menus starting from the left:

   ■ Enter Full Screen Mode menu – Shows the active content in full screen and removes the Power BI UI (also called "chrome"). Once you're in Full Screen mode, you have options to resize the content to fit to screen and to exit this mode (or press Esc). Another way to open a dashboard in a full screen mode is to append the chromeless=1 parameter to the dashboard URL, such as:

   https://app.powerbi.com/groups/me/dashboards/3065afc5-63a5-4cab-bcd3-0160b3c5f741?chromeless=1

   ■ Notifications menu – Power BI publishes important events, such as when someone shares a dashboard with you or when you get a data alert, to the Power BI Notification Center.

   ■ Settings menu – This menu expands to several submenus. Click "Manage Personal Storage" to check how much storage space you've used (recall that the Power BI Free and Power BI Pro editions have different storage limits) or to start a Power BI Pro 60-day trial. If you have Power BI Pro, the "Create content pack" submenu allows you to create an organizational content pack (discussed in Chapter 10), while "View content pack" allows you to access published content packs. If you are a Power BI administrator, you can use the Admin Portal to monitor usage and manage tenant-wide settings, such as if users can publish content to web for anonymous access. The "Manage gateways" menu allows you to view and manage gateways that are set up to let Power BI access on-premises data. Use the Settings submenu to view and change some Power BI Service settings, such as if the Q&A box is available for a given dashboard, or to view your report subscriptions. The "Manage embed codes" menu is to obtain the embedded iframe code for content you shared to the web.

> **TIP** Not sure what Power BI edition you have? Click the Settings menu, and then click "Manage Personal Storage". At the top of the next page, notice the message next to your name. If it says "Free User" you have the Power BI free edition. If it says "Pro User" then you have Power BI Pro subscription.

- Download menu – This menu allows you to download useful Power BI components, including Power BI Desktop (for analysts wanting to create self-service data models) , data gateways (to connect to on-premises data sources), Power BI for Mobile (a set of native Power BI apps for your mobile devices), Power BI publisher for Excel (an Excel add-in to connect to your Power BI data and to create and publish pivot reports), and Analyze in Excel updates (to download updates for the Power BI Analyze in Excel feature).

- Help and Support menu – Includes several links to useful resources, such as product documentation, the community site, and developer resources.

- Feedback menu – Rate your experience with Power BI on a scale from 1 to 10, submit an idea (new Power BI features are ranked based on the number of votes each idea gets), and submit an issue to community discussion lists.

5. Navigation breadcrumb – Displays the navigation path to the displayed content. In the case of dashboard, the buttons to the right of the dashboard name, let you add a tile, mark the dashboard a favorite, and share a dashboard with your coworkers. And the ellipsis menu (…) lets you perform additional tasks, such as to print the dashboard or go to the dashboard settings.

6. Natural question box (Q&A) – When you select a dashboard and the dashboard uses a dataset that supports natural queries, you can use this box to enter the natural query. For example, you can ask it how many units were shipped in February last year.

7. Content area – This is where the content of the selected item in the navigation pane is shown. For example, if a dashboard is selected, the content pane shows the dashboard tiles.

2.3   Understanding Power BI Content Items

The key to understanding how Power BI works is to understand its three main content items: datasets, reports, and dashboards. These elements are interdependent, and you must understand how they relate to each other. For example, you can't have a report or dashboard without creating one or more datasets. **Figure 2.7** should help you understand these dependencies.

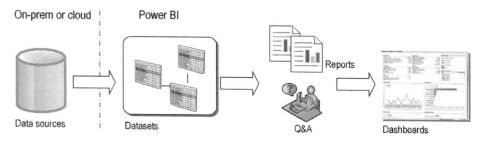

Figure 2.7 The Power BI main content items are datasets, reports, and dashboards.

2.3.1 Understanding Datasets

Think of a dataset as a blueprint or a definition of the data that you analyze. For example, if you want to analyze some data stored in an Excel spreadsheet, the corresponding dataset represents the data in the Excel spreadsheet. Or, if you import data from a database table, the dataset will represent that table. Notice in **Figure 2.7**, however, that a dataset can have more than one table. For example, if Martin uses Power BI Desktop or Excel to create a data model, the model might have multiple tables (potentially from different data sources). When Martin uploads the model to Power BI, his entire model will be shown as a single dataset, but when he explores it (he can click the Create Report icon next to the dataset under the Datasets tab to create a new report), he'll see that the Fields pane shows multiple tables. You'll encounter another case of a dataset with multiple tables when you connect to an Analysis Services model.

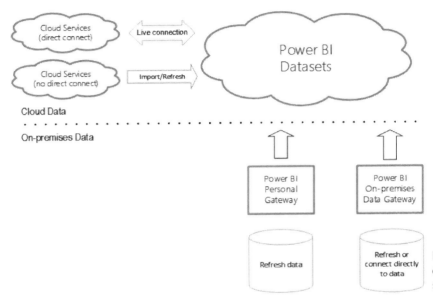

Figure 2.8 Power BI can import data or create live connections to some data sources.

Getting data

Data sources with useful data for analysis are everywhere (see **Figure 2.8**). As far as the data source location goes, we can identify two main types of data sources:

- Cloud (SaaS) services – These data sources are hosted in the cloud and available as online services. Examples of Microsoft cloud data sources that Power BI supports include OneDrive, Dynamics CRM, Azure SQL Database, Azure SQL Data Warehouse, and Spark on Azure HDInsight. Power BI can also access many popular cloud data sources from other vendors, such as Salesforce, Google Analytics, Marketo, and many others (the list is growing every month!).

- On-premises data sources – This category encompasses all other data sources that are internal to your organization, such as databases, cubes, Excel, and other files. In order for Power BI to access on-premises data sources, it needs a special connectivity software called a gateway.

Depending on the capabilities and location of the data source, data can be either a) imported in a Power BI dataset or b) left in the original data source without importing it, but it can be accessed directly via a live connection. If the data source supports it, direct connectivity is appropriate when you have fast data sources. In this case, when you generate a report, Power BI creates a query using the syntax of the data source and sends the query directly to the data source. So, the Power BI dataset has only the definition of the data but not the actual data. Not all data sources support direct connections. Examples of cloud data sources that support direct connections include Azure SQL Database, Azure SQL Data Warehouse, Spark on Azure HDInsight, and Azure Analysis Services. And on-premises data sources that support direct queries include SQL Server, Analysis Services, SAP, Oracle, and Teradata. The list of directly accessible data sources is growing in time.

Because only a limited set of data sources supports direct connectivity, in most cases you'll be *importing* data irrespective of whether you access cloud and on-premises data sources. When you import data, the Power BI dataset has the definition of the data *and* the actual data. In Chapter 1, I showed you how when you import data, Microsoft deploys the dataset to scalable and highly-performant Azure backend services. Therefore, when you create reports from imported datasets, performance is good and predictable. But the moment the data is imported, it becomes outdated because changes in the original data source aren't synchronized with the Power BI datasets. Which brings me to the subject of refreshing data.

Refreshing data

Deriving insights from outdated data is rarely useful. Fortunately, Power BI supports automatic data refresh from many data sources. Refreshing data from cloud services is easy because most vendors already have connectivity APIs that allow Power BI to get to the data. In fact, chances are that if you use a content pack to access a cloud data source, it'll enable automatic data refresh by default. For example, the Google Analytics dataset refreshes by default every hour without any manual configuration.

 TIP OneDrive and SharePoint Online are special locations for storing Excel, Power BI Desktop, and CSV files because Power BI automatically synchronizes changes to these files once every hour.

On-premises data sources are more problematic because Power BI needs to connect to your corporate network, which isn't accessible from outside. Therefore, if you import corporate data, you or IT will need to install special software, called a "gateway", to let Power BI connect to the original data source. For personal use, you can install the Personal Power BI Gateway to refresh imported data without waiting for IT help, but remember that it requires Power BI Pro. For enterprise deployments, IT can centralize data access by setting up On-premises Data Gateway (discussed in chapter 10). Besides refreshing data, the On-premises Data Gateway can be configured also for direct connections to data sources that supports this connectivity option. **Table 2.1** summarizes the refresh options for popular data sources.

Table 2.1   This table summarizes data refresh options when data is imported from cloud and on-premises data sources.

Location	Data Source	Refresh Type	Frequency
Cloud (Gateway not required)	Most cloud data sources, including Dynamics CRM, Salesforce, Marketo, Zendesk, and many others.	Automatic	Once a day
	Excel, CSV, and Power BI Desktop files uploaded to OneDrive, OneDrive for Business, or SharePoint Online	Automatic	Once every hour
On premises (via gateway)	Supported data sources (see https://powerbi.microsoft.com/en-us/documentation/powerbi-refresh-data/)	Scheduled or manual	Hourly (Power BI Pro needed)
	Excel 2013 (or later) data models with Power Query data connections or Power BI Desktop data models	Scheduled or manual	Supported except Exchange, Active Directory and ODBC
	Excel files via Get Data in Power BI Service	Not supported	

Understanding dataset actions

Once the dataset is created, it appears under the Datasets tab in the workspace content. For example, when you installed the Retail Analysis Sample, Power BI added a dataset with the same name. You can perform several actions from the Datasets tab (**Figure 2.9**).

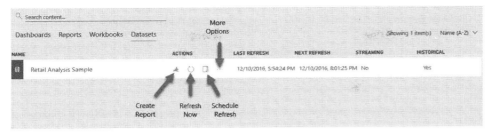

Figure 2.9 The Dataset tab allows you to perform several dataset actions.

Create Report lets you visualize the data by creating a new report (the subject of the next section). Refresh Now initiates an immediate refresh while Schedule Refresh allows you to schedule the refresh tasks (refreshing applies to datasets with imported data). Use the More Options (…) button link to access additional tasks, such as renaming, deleting, analyzing in Excel, getting insights (Quick Insights), setting up data security, and accessing dataset settings. What tasks will be available depends on the data source and how the dataset is configured. For example, Security won't be available if the dataset doesn't have row-level security (RLS) settings (you need Power BI Desktop to set up RLS).

Don't worry if you have existing reports connected to the dataset when you rename it because changing the dataset name won't break dependent reports and dashboards. If you delete a dataset, Power BI will automatically remove dependent reports and dashboard tiles that connect to that dataset. Analyze in Excel allows you to create pivot reports in Excel Desktop connected to the dataset. Quick Insights auto-generates useful reports that might help you to understand the root cause of data fluctuations. The Security menu allows you to add members to RLS roles. And the Settings menu allows you to see how the dataset is configured for refresh, to enable integration with Windows Cortana, and to enter featured Q&A questions.

There are additional properties next to the dataset. The Last Refresh and Next Refresh columns show the dates when the dataset was last refreshed and will be refreshed next respectively. Power BI supports streaming datasets to allow developers to implement real-time dashboards (discussed in Chapter 11) and such a dataset is denoted in the Streaming column. Related to streaming dataset, the Historical property shows you if the dataset retains all the data or the old data is removed as new data streams in.

2.3.2 Understanding Reports

Let's define a Power BI report as an interactive view for quick data exploration. Unlike other reporting tools that you might be familiar with and that require report authoring and database querying skills, Power BI reports are designed for business users in mind and they don't assume any technical skills. Reports are the main way to analyze data in Power BI. Reports are found under the Reports section in the left navigation pane (see **Figure 2.10**).

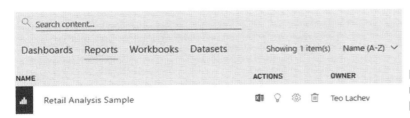

Figure 2.10 The Reports tab lists the reports in the workspace and lets you perform report-related actions.

Understanding report actions

Going through the list of available actions, the Excel icon lets you analyze the report data in Excel pivot reports by connecting Excel desktop to the report dataset. The light bulb icon is for generating and viewing quick insights from the report data. Currently, the only available option in the Settings action is to rename the report. And the Delete action removes the report from the workspace. Deleting a report removes any dashboard tiles that came from the report, but keeps the underlying report dataset.

Viewing reports

Clicking the report name in the Reports tab opens the report for viewing. For example, if you click the Retail Analysis Sample report, Power BI will open it in a reading mode (called Reading View) that supports interactive features, such as filtering, but it doesn't allow you to change the report layout. You can change the report layout by clicking the Edit Report menu on the top of the report (see **Figure 2.11**).

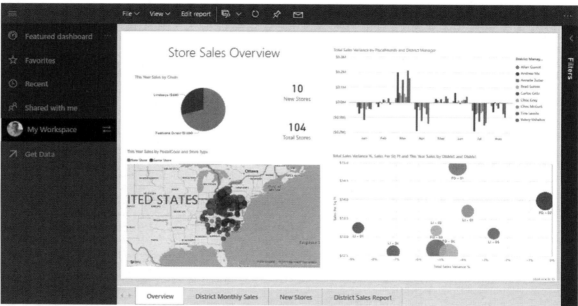

Figure 2.11 A report helps you visualize data from a single dataset.

Creating reports

Reports can be created in several ways:

■ Creating reports from scratch – Once you have a dataset, you can create a new report by exploring the dataset (the Create Report action in the dataset context menu). Then you can save the report.

■ Importing reports – If you import a Power BI Desktop file and the file includes a report, Power BI will import the report and add it to the Reports tab. If you import Excel Power Pivot data models, only Power View reports are imported (Excel pivot and chart reports aren't imported).

 NOTE Power BI Service can also connect to Excel files and show pivot table reports and chart reports contained in Excel files. The Excel workbooks you connected to will appear under the Workbooks tab. I'll postpone discussing Excel reports to the next chapter. For now, when I talk about reports I'll mean the type of reports you can create in the Power BI portal.

■ Distributing reports – If you use Power BI or organizational content packs, the reports included in the content pack are automatically distributed when you use the content pack. This is how you got the Retail Analysis Sample report when you installed the sample.

How reports relate to datasets

Currently, a Power BI report can only connect to and source data from a single dataset only. Suppose you have two datasets: Internet Sales and Reseller Sales. You can't have a report that combines data from these two datasets. Although this might sound like a limitation, you have options:

1. Create a dashboard – If all you want is to show data from multiple datasets as separate visualizations on a single page, you can just create a dashboard.

2. Implement a self-service model – Remember that a dataset can include multiple tables. So, if you need a consolidated report that combines multiple datasets, you can build a self-service data model using Power BI Desktop or Excel. This works because when published to Power BI, the model will be exposed as a single dataset with multiple tables.

3. Connect to an organizational model – To promote a single version of the truth, a BI pro can implement an organizational data model using Analysis Services. Then you can just connect to the model; there's nothing to build or import. Finally, if all you want is to show data from multiple datasets as separate visualizations on a single page, you can just create a dashboard.

For the purposes of this chapter, this is all you need to know about reports. You'll revisit them in more detail in the next chapter.

2.3.3 Understanding Dashboards

For a lack of a better definition, a dashboard is a summarized one-page view with important metrics related to the data you're analyzing. Dashboards convey important metrics so that management can get a high-level view of the business. To support root cause analysis, dashboards typically allow users to drill from summary sections (called tiles in Power BI) down to more detailed reports. A Power BI dashboard can combine data from multiple reports. This is why dashboards are available only in Power BI Service and not available in Power BI Desktop.

Understanding dashboard actions

Dashboards are listed under the Dashboards section in the workspace content page (see again **Figure 2.6**). The first icon to the right of the dashboard name is for sharing the dashboard with someone else (besides this sharing option, Power BI supports other sharing options to distribute content to a larger audience). The Settings action allows you to rename the dashboard, turn off Q&A, turn on a feature called "tile flow" to automatically align dashboard tiles to the top left corner of the canvas (instead of the default layout to freely position tiles on the dashboard), and change the dashboard classification (classifications are discussed in Chapter 10). And the Delete icon removes the dashboard from the workspace content. Deleting a dashboard doesn't affect the dependent datasets and reports.

Creating dashboards

Power BI dashboard tiles can be created in several ways:

■ From existing reports – If you have an existing report, you can pin one or more of its visualizations to a dashboard or even an entire report page! For example, the Retail Analysis Sample dashboard was created by pinning visualizations from the report with the same name. It's important to understand that you can pin visualizations from multiple reports into the same dashboard. This allows the dashboard to display a consolidated view that spans multiple reports and datasets.

■ By using Q&A – Another way to create a dashboard is to type in a question in the natural question box (see **Figure 2.5** again). This allows you to pin the resulting visualization without creating a report. For example, you can type a question like "sales by country" if you have a dataset with sales and geography entities. If Power BI understands your question, it will show you the most appropriate visualization.

- By using Quick Insights – This powerful predictive feature examines your dataset for hidden trends and produces a set of visualizations. You can pin a Quick Insights visualization to a dashboard.

- From Excel – If you connect to an Excel file, you can pin any Excel range as an image to a dashboard. Or, if you use Analyze in Excel, you can pin the pivot report.

- From Reporting Services reports – If your organization uses SQL Server Reporting Services 2016 and has enabled Power BI integration, you can pin image-producing report items (charts, gauges, maps) to dashboards.

- Distributing dashboards – Dashboard can be shared via mail or distributed with content packs.

Drilling through content

To allow users to see more details below the dashboards, users can drill into dashboard tiles. What happens when you drill through depends on how the tile was created. For example, if it was created by pinning a report visualization, you'll be navigated to the corresponding report page. Or, if it was created through Q&A, you'll be navigated to the page that has the visualization and the natural question that was asked. Or, if it was pinned from an Excel or SSRS report, you'd be navigated to the source report.

1. In the Power BI portal, click the Retail Analysis Sample dashboard in the Dashboard tab.
2. Click the "This Year Sales, Last Year Sales" surface Area Chart. Notice that Power BI navigates to the "District Monthly Sales" tab of the Retail Analysis Sample report.

That's all about dashboards for now. You'll learn much more in Chapter 4. Now let's get back to the topic of data and practice the different connectivity options.

2.4   Connecting to Data

As a first step in the data exploration journey, you need to connect to your data. Let's practice what we've learned about datasets. Because this part of the book targets business users, we'll practice three data connectivity scenarios that don't require creating data models. It might be useful to refer back to **Figure 2.4** or click the Get Data button to see these options. First, you'll see how you can use a Power BI content pack to analyze Google Analytics data. Next, I'll show you how you can import an Excel file. Finally, I'll show you how to connect live to an organizational Analysis Services model.

2.4.1   Using Content Packs

Power BI comes with pre-defined content packs that allow business users to connect to popular online services. Suppose that Maya wants to analyze the Adventure Works website traffic. Fortunately, Power BI includes a Google Analytics content pack to get her started with minimum effort. On the downside, Maya will be limited to whatever data the content pack author has decided to import which could be just a small subset of the available data.

> **TIP** If you need more data than what's included in the content pack, consider creating a data model using Excel or Power BI Desktop that connects to the online service to access all the data. For example, your organization might have added custom fields or tables Salesforce that you need for analysis. Besides data modeling knowledge, this approach requires that you understand the entities and how they relate to each other. So, I suggest you first determine if the content pack has the data you need.

To perform this exercise, you'll need a Google Analytics account and you must add a tracking code to the website you want to analyze. Google supports free Google Analytics accounts. For more information about the setup, refer to http://www.google.com/analytics. If setting up Google Analytics is too much trouble, you can use similar steps to connect to any other online service that you use in your organization, provided that it has a Power BI connector. To see the list of the available connectors, click the Get Data link in the navigation bar, and then click the Get button in the Services tile.

Connecting to Google Analytics

Assuming that Maya has already done the required Google Analytics setup, connecting to her Google Analytics account takes a few simple steps:

1. To avoid cookie issues with cached accounts, I suggest you use private browsing. If you use Internet Explorer (IE), open it and then press Ctrl-Shift-P to start a private session that ignores cookies. (Or right-click IE on the start bar and click "Start InPrivate Browsing".) If you use Google Chrome, open it and press Ctrl-Shift-N to start an incognito session. (Or right-click it on the start bar and click "New incognito window".)

2. Go to powerbi.com and sign in with your Power BI account. In the Power BI portal, click the Get Data link in the navigation pane.

3. In the Get Data page, click the Get button in the Services tile whose message reads "Choose content packs from online services that you use".

4. In the Services page, click Google Analytics. In the popup that follows, click Connect.

Figure 2.12 As a part of using the Google Analytics content pack, you need to specify the account details.

5. In the "Connect to Google Analytics" window, specify the Google Analytics details, including account, property, and view. You can get these details by logging into Google Analytics and navigating to the Administration section (Property Settings page). In my case, I'm using a fictitious company provided by Google for testing purposes (see **Figure 2.12**). Click Next.

6. When asked to choose an authentication method, the only option you should see is OAuth. Click Next.

7. In the Google confirmation page that follows, click the Allow button to let Power BI connect to Google Analytics. When asked to authenticate, enter your Google account credentials (typically your Gmail account credentials).

8. Return to the Power BI portal. If all is well, Power BI should display a popup informing you that it's importing your content.

Understanding changes

Similar to the Retail Analysis Sample, the Google Analytics content pack installs the following content in Power BI:

- A Google Analytics dataset – A dataset that connects to the Google Analytics data.
- A Google Analytics report – This report has multiple pages to let you analyze site traffic, system usage, total users, page performance, and top requested pages.
- A Google Analytics dashboard – A dashboard with pinned visualizations from the Google Analytics report.

That's it! After a few clicks and no explicit modeling you now have prepackaged reports and dashboards to analyze your website data! If the included visualizations aren't enough, you can explore the Google Analytics dataset and create your own reports. As I previously mentioned, content packs usually schedule an automatic data refresh to keep your data up to date. To verify:

1. In the navigation pane, click My Workspace and then click the Datasets tab. Notice that the Last Refresh column shows you the time when the dataset was last refreshed.

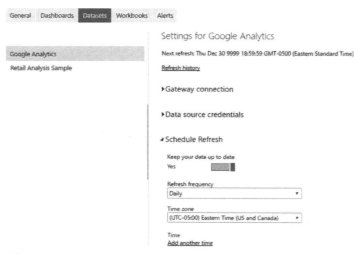

Figure 2.13 The content pack configures automatic daily refresh to synchronize the imported data with the latest changes in the data source.

2. Click the Schedule Refresh action to open the dataset settings page. Notice the content pack is scheduled for a daily refresh (see **Figure 2.13**).

 NOTE As you can imagine, thousands of unattended data refreshes scheduled by many users can be expensive in a multi-tenant environment, such as Power BI. This is why Power BI limits the Power BI Free edition to daily refreshes and you can't specify the exact refresh time. Power BI queues and distributes the refresh jobs using internal rules. However, the Power BI Pro edition allows you to configure more frequent refreshes at specific times during the day.

3. Expand the "Gateway connection" section. It shows that the content pack connects directly to Google Analytics. That's because both Power BI and Google Analytics are cloud services and no gateway is needed.

2.4.2 Importing Local Files

Another option to get data is to upload a file. Suppose that Maya wants to analyze some sales data given to her as an Excel file. Thanks to the Power BI Get Data feature, Maya can import the Excel file in Power BI and analyze it without creating a model.

 NOTE As it stands, Power BI Service limits the size of the imported file to 1 GB. This is still a lot of data but if you find this limiting there are other options. For example, IT can implement an on-premises Tabular model as I discuss in Chapter 11.

Importing Excel data

In this exercise, you will explore the sample dataset that you will analyze later in Power BI. Start by familiarizing yourself with the raw data in the Excel workbook.

1. Open the Internet Sales.xlsx workbook in Excel. You can find this file in the \Source\ch02 folder of the source code.

2. If Sheet1 isn't selected, click Sheet1 to make it active. Notice that it contains some sales data. Specifically, each row represents the product sales for a given date, as shown in **Figure 2.14**. Also, notice that the Excel data is formatted as a table so that Power BI knows where the data is located.

Date	Product	SalesAmount	OrderQuantity
7/1/2005	Mountain-100 Silver, 44	30599.91	9
7/1/2005	Mountain-100 Black, 38	10124.97	3
7/1/2005	Road-650 Black, 44	1398.1964	2
7/1/2005	Road-650 Red, 52	1398.1964	2
7/1/2005	Road-650 Black, 52	1398.1964	2
7/1/2005	Road-650 Black, 58	2097.2946	3
7/1/2005	Road-150 Red, 56	53674.05	15
7/1/2005	Mountain-100 Black, 48	10124.97	3
7/1/2005	Road-150 Red, 62	78721.94	22
7/1/2005	Mountain-100 Silver, 48	10199.97	3
7/1/2005	Mountain-100 Silver, 42	6799.98	2
7/1/2005	Road-150 Red, 44	82300.21	23
7/1/2005	Road-650 Red, 44	1398.1964	2
7/1/2005	Road-650 Red, 62	699.0982	1

Figure 2.14 The first sheet contains Internet sales data where each row represents the product sales amount and order quantity for a specific date and product.

 TIP The Excel file can have multiple sheets with data, and you can import them as separate tables. Currently, Power BI Service doesn't allow you to relate multiple tables (you need a data model to do so). In addition, Power BI requires that the Excel data is formatted as a table. You can format tabular Excel data as a table by clicking any cell with data and pressing Ctrl-T. Excel will automatically detect the tabular section. After you confirm, Excel will format the data as a table!

3. Close Excel.

4. Next, you'll import the data from the Internet Sales.xlsx file in Power BI. In Power BI, click Get Data.

5. In the Files tile, click the Get button. If you are in the workspace content page, another way to add content is to click the plus (+) sign in the upper-right corner of this page.

6. In the Files page, click "Local File" because you'll be importing from a local Excel file. Navigate to the source code \Source\ch2 folder, and then double-click the Internet Sales file.

7. In the Local File page, click the Import button to import the file (let's postpone connecting to Excel files until the next chapter).

8. Power BI imports the data from the Excel file into the Power BI Service. Once the task completes, you'll see a notification that your dataset is ready. If you click View Dataset, you'll be able to create a report from the dataset but let's not do this now.

Understanding changes

Let's see where the content went:

1. In the navigation pane, click My Workspace.

2. In the content page, click the Datasets tab. A new dataset Internet Sales has been added to the lists of datasets. The asterisk next to the database name denotes that this is a new dataset.

3. Click the Reports tab and notice that there isn't a new report. However, if the Excel had Power View reports, Power BI would import them and add them to the Reports tab.

4. Click the Dashboard tab and notice that there is a new dashboard with the same name as the Excel file (Internet Sales.xlsx). Click the dashboard to open it. Notice that it has a single tile "Internet Sales.xlsx".

5. Click the "Internet Sales.xlsx" tile.

Figure 2.15 The Create Report action lets you create a report from the dataset by dragging fields from the Fields pane.

6. Notice that this action opens an empty report (see **Figure 2.15**) to let you explore the data on your own. The Fields pane shows a single table (Internet Sales) whose fields correspond to the columns in the original Excel table. From here, you can just select which fields you want to see on the report. You can choose a visualization from the Visualizations pane to explore the data in different ways, such as a chart or a table.

TIP   As I mentioned previously, Power BI can't refresh local Excel files. Suppose that Maya receives an updated Excel file on a regular basis. Without the ability to schedule an automatic refresh, she needs to delete the old dataset (which will delete the dependent reports and dashboard tiles), reimport the data, and recreate the reports. As you can imagine, this can get tedious. A better option would be to save the Excel file to OneDrive, OneDrive for Business, or SharePoint Online. Power BI refreshes files saved to OneDrive every hour and whenever it detects that the file is updated.

2.4.3   Using Live Connections

Suppose that Adventure Works has implemented an organizational Analysis Services semantic model on top of the corporate data warehouse. In the next exercise, you'll see how easy it is for Maya to connect to the model and analyze its data.

Understanding prerequisites

As I explained in the "Understanding Datasets" section, Power BI requires special connectivity software, called Power BI On-premises Data Gateway, to be installed on an on-premises computer so that Power BI Service can connect to Analysis Services. This step needs to be performed by IT because it requires admin rights to Analysis Services. I provide step-by-step setup instructions to install and configure the gateway in Chapter 10 of this book.

Besides setting up the gateway, to perform this exercise, you'll need help from IT to install the sample Adventure Works database and Tabular model (as per the instructions in the book front matter) and to grant you access to the Adventure Works Tabular model. In addition, you'll need a Power BI Pro subscription because Power BI Free doesn't allow you to connect to live data sources. If you don't have Power BI Pro, you can start a free 60-day trial.

Connecting to on-premises Analysis Services

Once the gateway is set up, connecting to the Adventure Works Tabular model is easy.

1. In the Power BI portal, click Get Data.

2. In the Get Data page, click the Get button in the Databases pane that reads "Connect to live data in Azure SQL Database and more."

3. In the Databases & More page (see **Figure 2.16**), click the SQL Server Analysis Services tile. In the popup that follows, click Connect. If you don't have a Power BI Pro subscription, this is when you'll be prompted to start a free trial.

Get Data > **Databases & More**

Azure SQL Database   Azure SQL Data Warehouse   SQL Server Analysis Services   Spark on Azure HDInsight

Figure 2.16 Use the SQL Server Analysis Services tile to create a live connection to an on-premises SSAS model.

4. In the SQL Server Analysis Services page that follows, you should see all the Analysis Services databases that are registered with the gateway. Please check with your IT department which one you should use. Once you know the name, click it to select it.

5. Power BI verifies connectivity. If something goes wrong, you'll see an error message. Otherwise, you should see a list of the models and perspectives that you have access to. Select the "Adventure Works Tabular Model SQL 2012 – Model" item and click Connect. This action adds a new dataset to the Datasets tab of the workspace content page.

6. Click the Create Report action to explore the dataset. The Fields lists will show all the entities defined in the SSAS model. From here, you can create an interactive report by selecting specific fields from the Fields pane. This isn't much different from creating Excel reports that are connected to an organizational data model.

7. Click File ⇨ Save and save the report as *Adventure Works SSAS*.

2.5 Summary

Self-service BI broadens the reach of BI and enables business users to create their own solutions for data analysis and reporting. By now you should view self-service BI not as a competing technology but as a completing technology to organizational BI.

Power BI is a cloud service for data analytics and you interact with it using the Power BI portal. The portal allows you to create datasets that connect to your data. You can either import data or you can connect live to data sources that support live connections. Once you have a dataset, you can explore it to create new reports. And once you have reports, you can pin their visualizations to dashboards.

As a business user, you don't have to create data models to meet simple data analytics needs. This chapter walked you through a practice that demonstrated how you can perform basic data connectivity tasks, including using a content pack to connect to an online service (Google Analytics), importing an Excel file, and connecting live to an on-premises Analysis Services model. The next chapter will show you how you can analyze your data by creating insightful reports!

Chapter 3

Creating Reports

In the previous chapter, I showed you how Power BI allows business users to connect to data without explicit modeling. The next logical step is to visualize the data so that you can derive knowledge from it. Fortunately, Power BI lets you create meaningful reports with just a few mouse clicks. And Power BI dashboards summarize important metrics so that you can get a quick high-level view of how your business is doing at a glance.

I'll start this chapter by explaining the building blocks of Power BI reports. Then I'll walk you through the steps to explore Power BI datasets and to create reports with interactive visualizations. Because Excel is such an important tool, I'll show you three ways to integrate Power BI with Excel: importing data from Excel files, connecting to existing Excel workbooks, and creating your own pivot reports connected to Power BI datasets. You can also pin Reporting Services reports to dashboards but I'll postpone this integration scenario to the next chapter. Because this chapter builds on the previous one, make sure you've completed the exercises in the previous chapter to install the Retail Analysis Sample and to import the Internet Sales dataset from the Excel file.

3.1   Understanding Reports

In the previous chapter, I introduced you to Power BI reports. I defined a Power BI report as an interactive visual representation of a dataset. Power BI also supports Excel and SSRS reports. Let's revisit the three report types that you can have in Power BI Service:

- Power BI native reports – This report type delivers a highly visual and interactive report that has its roots in Power View. This is the report type I'll mean when I mention about Power BI reports. For example, the Retail Analysis Sample report is an example of a Power BI report. You can use Power BI Service, Power BI Desktop, and Excel Power View to create these reports.

- Excel reports – Power BI allows you to connect to Excel 2013 (or later) files and view the embedded pivot and Power View reports. For example, you might have invested significant effort into creating Power Pivot models and reports. You don't want to migrate them to Power BI Desktop, but you'd like users to view and interact with these reports. To get this to work, you can just connect Power BI to your Excel files. However, you still must use Excel Desktop to create or modify the reports and data model (if the Excel file has a Power Pivot model).

- Reporting Services reports – SSRS is the Microsoft's most customizable reporting tool. If your organization has SQL Server Reporting Services (SSRS) 2016 and it's configured for Power BI integration, you can pin report items to Power BI dashboards. For example, a report developer might have implemented a sophisticated map with multiple layers. Now Maya wants to add this map to her dashboard.

Maya can open the report and pin the map image as a dashboard tile. When Maya clicks the map, she's navigated to the SSRS report, but Maya needs to be on the corporate network for this to happen.

Most of this chapter will be focused on Power BI native reports but I'll also show you how Power BI integrates with Excel and SSRS reports.

3.1.1 Understanding Reading View

Power BI supports two report viewing modes. Reading View allows you to explore the report and interact with it, without worrying that you'll break something. Editing View lets you make changes to the report layout, such as to add or remove a field.

Opening a report in Reading View
Power BI defaults to Reading View when you open a report. This happens when you click the report name in the Reports tab or when you click a dashboard tile to open the underlying report.

Figure 3.1 Reading View allows you to analyze and interact with the report, without changing it.

1. In the Power BI portal, click My Workspace. In the workspace content page, click the Reports tab and then click the Retail Analysis Sample report to open it in Reading View.
2. On the bottom-left area of the report, notice that this report has four pages. A report page is conceptually similar to a slide in a PowerPoint presentation – it gives you a different view of the data story. Click the "New Stores" page to activate it. Notice that the page has five visualizations (see **Figure 3.1**).

Understanding the File menu
Expanding the File menu gives you access to the following features:

- Save as – Creates a new report with a different name in the current workspace.

- Print – Prints the current report page. Printing doesn't expand visualizations to show all the data. In other words, what you see on the screen is what you get when you print the page.

- Publish to web – If the "Publish to web" feature is enabled in the Admin Portal (it is by default), this feature allows you to publish the report for anonymous access. You'll be given a link that you can send to someone and an embed code (iframe) that you can use to embed the report on a web page, such as in a blog. To find later which reports you've published to the web, go to the Settings menu (the upper-right gear button in the portal), and then click Embed Codes. Be very careful with this feature as you might expose sensitive data to anyone on the Internet!

- Export to PowerPoint – Export the report as a Power Point presentation. Each report page becomes a slide and all visualizations are exported as static images.

- Download report (preview) – Exports the report and underlying dataset as a Power BI Desktop file. Currently, this feature works only for reports connected to datasets published from Power BI Desktop. This is why it's disabled for the Retail Analysis Sample report which you obtained from one of the Power BI samples. This menu will also be disabled for the report that you'll later create from the Internet Sales dataset because you created this dataset directly in Power BI Service. As this feature stands, its primary goal is to recover reports and data if the Power BI Desktop file ever gets lost. You can download existing, new, and changed reports, and the underlying datasets can contain imported data or connect directly to the data source.

Understanding the View menu
The View menu is for adjusting the report size. The "Fit to page" option scales the report content to best fit the page. "Fit to width" resizes the report to the width of the page. And "Actual size" displays content at full size. For now, let's skip the "Edit report" menu which switches you to Editing View to edit the report.

 TIP While I'm on the subject of sizing the report content, both Power BI Service and Power BI Desktop support predefined and custom page sizes. In Power BI Service, while editing the report, you can use the Visualizations pane (Format tab) to specify a page layout for the selected report page, such as 16:9, 4:3, Cortana Letter, or a custom size. For example, the District Sales Report page in the Retail Analysis Sample report has Cortana layout which is optimized to be rendered by Windows Cortana. Power BI Desktop supports also specifying a mobile view which optimizes the layout for viewing in a Power BI mobile app.

Understanding the Explore menu
Power BI charts allow you to drill down the data. For example, you might have a column chart that has Country and City fields added to the Axis area. The chart initially shows data by country. If you select the chart and click Explore ⇨ See Data, you can see the actual data behind the chart (as if you flip the chart to a Table visualization). Similarly, when you toggle Explore ⇨ See Records and then click a chart bar, you see the actual data behind that bar only. The rest of the exploration menus fulfill the same role as the interactive features for data exploration when you hover on the chart.

Understanding the Refresh menu
Clicking the Refresh menu refreshes the data on the report. The report always queries the underlying dataset when you view it. The report Refresh menu could be useful if the underlying dataset was refreshed or has a live connection and you want to get the latest data without closing and reopening the report.

Understanding the Pin Live Page menu
You can quickly assemble a dashboard from existing report visualizations. You can also pin entire report pages to a dashboard. This could be useful when the report page is already designed as a dashboard. You can pin the entire page instead of pinning individual visualizations. Although this might sound redundant, promoting a report to a dashboard gives you access to dashboard features, such as Q&A.

Another scenario for pinning report pages is when you want to filter dashboards tiles because dashboards don't have filtering features (the Filter pane is not available). To accomplish this, you can create a report page that has the visualizations you need, add a slicer, and then pin the entire page.

Understanding the Subscribe menu

Besides viewing a report interactively (on demand), Power BI lets you subscribe to it. The Subscribe menu is only available in Reading View. It brings you to a window where you can indicate which report pages you want to subscribe to and to manage subscriptions you've created. Once you set up a subscription, Power BI will detect data changes in the underlying report dataset and send you an email with screenshots of the subscribed pages. Subscribed report delivery is a Power BI Pro feature. If a Power BI Free user clicks the Subscribe menu, the user will be informed that this feature is not available unless the user upgrades.

Interacting with visualizations

Although the name might mislead you, Reading View allows you to interact with the report.

1. Expand the Filters pane on the right of the report. Notice that the report author has added a Store Type filter that filters only new stores. Note also that you can change the filter, such as to show all store types.

2. In the fourth visualization ("Sales Per Sq Ft by Name") on the New Stores page, click the first column "Cincinnati 2 Fashions Direct" (you can hover on the column bar and a tooltip pops up to show the full name). Notice that the other visualizations change to show data only for the selected store. This feature is called *cross filtering* (or *interactive highlighting*), and it's another way to filter data on the report. Cross filtering is automatic, and you don't need to do anything special to enable it. Click the bar again or an empty area in the same chart to show all the data.

3. Hover on the same visualization and notice that Power BI shows an ellipsis menu (More Options) in the top-right corner (see **Figure 3.2**).

Figure 3.2 You can see how the visualization is sorted and you can change or remove the sort.

4. Notice that by default the chart is sorted by the store name in an ascending order. You can sort by another field used on the chart or remove the sort. Click "Sort by Name" to sort the chart by the store name in a descending order. If you change the sort, an orange bar will appear to the left of the sorted field. Notice the pin button to the left of the ellipsis menu. It allows you to pin the visualization to a dashboard.

5. On the right of the pin button, there is another button that lets you pop out the visualization in an "in-focus" mode in case you want to examine its data in more detail. Try it out.

Exporting data

You can export the data behind a visualization in a Comma-Separated Values (CSV) or Excel format.

1. Click Export Data in the More Options menu. In the "Export data" window (see **Figure 3.3**), notice that by default Power BI will export the summarized data as it's aggregated on the chart. The "Underlying data" option is greyed out because the chart uses the "Sales by Sq Ft" calculated measure which has a custom formula. If the chart has a regular field aggregated using a built-in aggregation function, such as Sum or Count, this option will be available to let you export the underlying data.

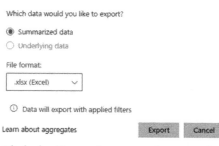

Export data   ✕

Which data would you like to export?

⦿ Summarized data
○ Underlying data

File format:

.xlsx (Excel)   ⌄

ⓘ Data will export with applied filters

Learn about aggregates   [Export]   [Cancel]

Figure 3.3 You can export the visualization data in Excel or CSV format.

2. Click the Export button and export the chart data as an Excel file. If the report has any filters applied, the exported data will be filtered accordingly.

Drilling through

If the chart had multiple fields or a hierarchy added to the Axis zone, you'll also see Explore Data indicators (shown by the red circles at the top of **Figure 3.4**) that fulfill the same role as the corresponding options in the Explore menu.

Figure 3.4 You can drill down the next level if the visualization is designed for this feature.

Because, by default, Power BI initiates cross filtering when you click a chart element, the indicators allow you to switch to a drill mode. For example, you can click the down arrow indicator (in the top-right corner) to switch to a drill mode, and then click a bar to drill through and see the underlying data. To drill up, just click the up arrow indicator in the top-left corner.

TIP Currently, Power BI caps drillthrough to 1,000 rows and exporting data to 10,000 rows. There is nothing you can do to change these limits. One workaround is to use the Analyze in Excel feature and drill through a cell in a pivot report. In this case, there is no limit on the number of rows returned.

1. If you have a chart with multiple fields in the Axis area, click the double-arrow indicator to go to the next level (the next field you have in the Axis zone). This is the same as Show Next Level in the Explore Menu. For example, if the chart had Country and City fields in the Axis area and you are initially at the Country level, clicking the double-arrow indicator would show the chart data by City as though the Country field isn't in the Axis area. By contrast, clicking the "Expand all down" button (the third one from the group on the left), would drill down all data points to the next level but it'll preserve the parent grouping, such as to show data by city grouped by country.

TIP Some visualizations, such as Column Chart allow you to add multiple fields to specific areas when you configure the chart, such as in the Axis area. So to configure a chart for drilling, you need to open the report in Editing View and just add more fields to the Axis area of the chart. These fields define the levels that you drill down to. Power BI Desktop allows the modeler to create hierarchies to define useful navigational paths. If hierarchies are defined, you can just drag the hierarchy to chart area.

2. Power BI has more interactive features. Hover on top of any column in the chart. Notice that a tooltip pops up to let you know the data series name and the exact measure amount. By default, the tooltip shows only the fields added to the chart. However, you can switch to Editing View and add more fields to the visualization's Tooltips area if you want to see these fields appear in the tooltip.

3.1.2   Understanding Editing View

If you have report editing rights, you can make changes to the report layout. You have editing rights when you're the original report author, when the report is available in a workspace you're a member of and you have rights to edit the content, or when you take ownership of the report, such as when you create a copy of a report that was distributed via an organizational content pack. You have editing rights to all content in My Workspace unless someone has shared dashboards with you because the dashboard and underlying report will be read-only. You can switch to Editing View by clicking the Edit Report menu.

Understanding menu changes
One of the first things you'll notice when you switch to Editing View is that the report menu changes (see **Figure 3.5**). Let's go quickly through the changes.

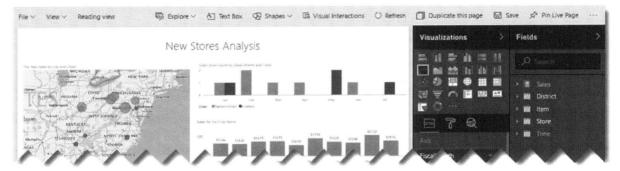

Figure 3.5   The Editing View menu adds links to create text elements and save the report.

The File menu adds a Save submenu to let you save changes to the report. The View menu adds Show Gridlines and Snap to Grid menus. When you enable "Show Gridlines", Power BI adds a grid to help you position items on the report canvas. If "Snap to Grid" is enabled, the items will snap to the grid so that you can easily align them. The "Reading view" menu brings you back to opening the report as read-only. Editing View also adds menus on the right side of the report for editing features. Use the Text Box menu to add text boxes to the report which could be useful for report or section titles, or for any text you want on the report. The Text Box menu opens a comprehensive text editor that allows you to format the text and implement hyperlinks. The Shapes menu allows you to add rectangle, oval, line, triangle, and arrow shapes to the report for decorative or illustrative purposes. Currently, you can't add images, such as a company logo. You can use Power BI Desktop to add images.

The Visual Interactions (also known as "Brushing and Linking") allows you to customize the behavior of the page's interactive features. You can select a visual that would act as the source and then set the inter-activity level for the other visualizations on the same page. For example, you can use this feature to disable interactive highlighting to selected visualizations. To see this feature in action, watch the "Power BI Desktop November 2015 Update" video at https://youtu.be/ErHvpkyQjSg.

The Duplicate Page menu creates a copy of the current report page. This could be useful if you want to add a new page to the report that has similar visualizations as an existing page but you want to show different data. The Save menu is a shortcut that does the same thing as the File ⇨ Save menu.

Understanding the Visualizations pane

The next thing you'll notice is that Editing View adds two panes on the right of the report: Visualizations and Fields. Use the Visualizations pane to configure the active visualization, such as to switch from one chart type to another.

 NOTE When you make changes to the Visualizations pane, they are applied to the currently selected (active) visualization. An active visualization has a border around it with resize handles. You need to click a visualization to activate it.

1. If it's not already active, click the "New Stores Analysis" page to select it.
2. Click the "Sales Per Sq Ft by Name" visualization to activate it. **Figure 3.6** shows the Visualizations pane. The Filters section actually occupies the bottom part of the Visualizations pane but is shown adjacent to it on the screenshot to accommodate space constraints.

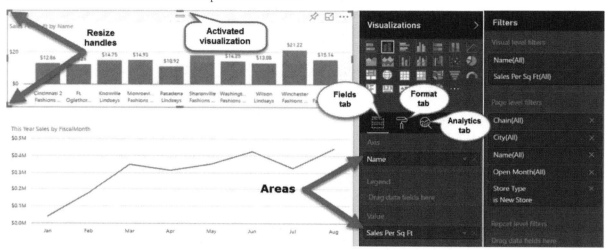

Figure 3.6 The Visualizations pane allows you to switch visualizations and to make changes to the active visualization.

The Visualizations pane consists of several sections. The first section shows the Power BI visualization types, which I'll discuss in more detail in the next section "Understanding Power BI Visualizations". The ellipsis button below the visualizations allows you to import custom visuals from the Power BI visuals gallery (http://visuals.powerbi.com) that are contributed by Microsoft and the community. So, when the Power BI-provided visualizations are not enough for your data presentation needs, check the gallery. Chances are that you'll find a custom visual that can fill in the gap!

The Fields tab consists of areas that you can use to configure the active visualization, similarly to how you would use the zones of the Excel Fields List when you configure a pivot report. For example, this visualization has the Name field of the Store table added to the Axis area and the "Sales Per Sq Ft" field from the Sales table added to the Value area.

 TIP You can find which table a field comes from by hovering on the field name. You'll see a tooltip pop up that shows the table and field names, such as 'Store'[Name]. This is the same naming convention that a data analyst would use to create custom calculations in a data model using Data Analysis Expressions (DAX).

The Filters section of the Fields tab is for filtering data on the report. Use the "Visual level filters" section to filter the data in the active visualization. By default, you can filter any field that's used in the visualization, but you can also add other fields. For example, the "Visual level filters" has the Name and "Sales per Sq Ft" fields because they are used on the chart. The (All) suffix next to the field tells you that these two fields are not filtered (the chart shows all stores irrespective of their sales). Use the "Page Level Filters" section to apply filters to all visualizations on the active page. For example, all four visualizations on this page are filtered to show data for new stores (Store Type is "New Store"). Finally, filters in the "Report Level Filters" section are applied globally to all visualizations on the report even if they are on different pages.

The Format tab of the Visualizations pane is for applying format settings to the active visualization. Different visualizations support different format settings. For example, column charts support custom colors per category (for tips and tricks for color formatting see https://powerbi.microsoft.com/en-us/documentation/powerbi-service-tips-and-tricks-for-color-formatting), data labels, title, axis labels, and other settings. As Power BI evolves, it adds more options to give you more control over customizing the visual appearance.

Finally, the Analytics tab is for adding features to the visualization to augment its analytics capabilities. For example, Maya plots revenue as a single-line chart. Now she wants to forecast revenue for future periods. She can do this by adding a Forecast line (discussed in more detail in Chapter 8). The analytics features vary among visualization types. For example, table and matrices don't currently support analytics features, a bar chart supports a constant line, while a linear charts supports constant, min, max, average, median, percentile, and forecast lines.

NOTE Do you think that Power BI visualizations are rather basic and they don't support enough customization compared to other tools, such as Excel? Remember from Chapter 1 that Microsoft committed to a weekly release cadence so features should be coming fast. But to prioritize your feature wish, I encourage you to submit your idea or vote for an existing feature at https://support.powerbi.com. If you don't want to wait, a web developer in your organization with JavaScript experience can create custom visuals. Chapter 14 shows how this can be done.

Understanding filter conditions
Revisiting the Filters section, currently Power BI supports three filter types (**Figure 3.7**):

■ Basic filtering – Presents a list of distinct values from the filtered field. The number to the right of the value tells you how many times this value appears in the dataset. You can specify which values you want to include in the filter by checking them. This creates an OR filter, such as Product is "AWC Logo Cap" or "Bike Wash – Dissolver". You can exclude items by checking "Select All" and then uncheck the values you don't need.

■ Advanced filtering – Allows you to specify more advanced filtering conditions, such as "contains", "starts with", "is not". In addition, you can chain filters using AND and OR conditions.

■ Top N filtering – Filters the top N or bottom N values of the field. You can also drag a data field to the "By value" area and specify an aggregation function. For example, you can drag SalesAmount and specify Top N 10 to return the top 10 products that sold the most.

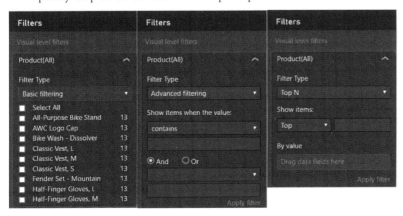

Figure 3.7 Power BI supports three filtering types: Basic, Advanced, and Top N.

Understanding the Fields pane

The Fields pane shows the tables in your dataset. When implementing the Retail Analysis Sample, the author implemented a self-service data model by importing several tables. By examining the Fields pane, you can see these tables and their fields (see **Figure 3.8**). For example, the Fields pane shows Sales, District, Item, and Store tables. The Store table is expanded and you see some of its fields, such as Average Selling Area Size, Chain, City, and so on. If you have trouble finding a field in a busy Field pane, you can search for it by entering its name (or a part of it) in the Search box.

Figure 3.8 The Fields pane shows the dataset tables and fields, and allows you to search the model metadata.

Although you can't preview the data in the Fields pane, Power BI gives you clues about the field content. For example, if the field is prefixed with a calculator icon ▦, such as the "Average Selling Area Size" field, it's a calculated field that uses a formula. Fields prefixed with a globe icon ▦ are geography-related fields, such as City, that can be visualized on a map. If the field is checked, it's used in the selected visualization. If the name of the table has an orange color, one or more of its fields are used in the selected visualization. For example, the Sales and Store tables are orange because they each have at least one field used in the selected visualization.

Each field has an ellipsis menu to the right of the field that allows you to add the field as a filter. If you have selected a visualization, the field will be added as a visual-level filter. For example, if you select a chart on the report and add the City field as a filter, you can filter the chart data by city, such as to show data for Atlanta only. If no visualization is selected, the field will be added as a page-level filter. For example, if you add the City field as a filter but you haven't selected a specific visualization, it'll get added to the "Page level filters" area and you can filter all the visualizations on the page by this field. The "Collapse All" option collapses all the fields so you can see only the table names in the Fields list. And "Expand All" expands all tables so that you can see their fields.

Working with fields

Fields are the building blocks of reports because they define what data is shown. In the process of creating a report, you add fields from the Fields pane to the report. There are several ways to do this:

- Drag a field on the report – If you drag the field to an empty area on the report canvas, you'll create a new visualization that uses that field. If you drag it to an existing visualization, Power BI will add it to one of the areas of the Visualizations pane.

 NOTE Power BI always attempts to determine the right default. For example, if you drag the City field to an empty area, it'll create a map because City is a geospatial field. If you drag a field to an existing visualization, Power BI will attempt to guess how to use it best. For example, assuming you want to aggregate a numeric field, it'll add it to the Value area.

- Check the field's checkbox – It accomplishes the same result as dragging a field.

- Drag a field to an area – Instead of relying on Power BI to infer what you want to do with the field, you can drag and drop a field into a specific area of the Fields tab in the Visualizations pane. For example, if you want a chart to create a data series using the "Sales per Sq Ft" field, you can drag this field to the Value area of the Fields tab in the Visualizations pane (see again **Figure 3.6**).

Similarly, to remove a field, you can uncheck its checkbox in the Fields pane. Or, you can drag the field away from the Visualizations pane to the Fields pane. If the field ends up in the wrong area of the Visualizations pane, you can drag it away from it and drop it in the correct area.

 TIP Besides dragging a field to an empty area, you can create a new visualization by just clicking the desired visualization type in the Visualizations pane. This adds an empty visualization to the report area. Then, you can drag and drop the required fields to bind it to data.

3.1.3   Understanding Power BI Visualizations

You use visualizations to help you analyze your data in the most intuitive way. Power BI supports various common visualizations and their number is likely to grow in time. And because Power BI supports custom visuals, you'll be hard pressed not to find a suitable way to present your data. Let's take a look at the Power BI-provided visualizations.

 TIP Need visualization best practices? I recommend the "Information Dashboard Design" book by the visualization expert Stephen Few, whose work inspired Power View and Power BI visualizations. To sum up it in one sentence: keep it simple!

Column and Bar charts
Power BI includes the most common charts, including Column Chart, Bar Chart, and other variants, such as Clustered Column Chart, Clustered Bar Chart, 100% Stacked Bar Chart, and 100% Stacked Column Chart (see **Figure 3.9**). The difference between column and bar charts is that the Bar Chart displays a series as a set of horizontal bars. In fact, the Bar Chart is the only chart type that displays data horizontally by inverting the axes, so the x-axis shows the chart values and the y-axis shows the category values.

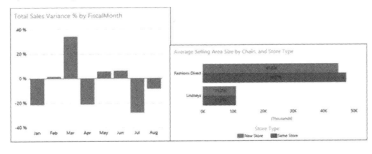

Figure 3.9   Column and bar charts display data points as bars.

Line charts
Line charts are best suited to display linear data. Power BI supports basic line charts and area charts, as shown in **Figure 3.10**. Similar to a Line Chart, an Area Chart displays a series as a set of points connected by a line with the exception that all of the area below the line is filled in. The Line Chart and Area Chart are the only chart types that display data contiguously. They're commonly used to represent data that occurs over a continuous period of time.

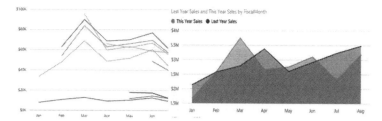

Figure 3.10 Power BI supports line charts and area charts.

Combination Chart

The Combination (combo) Chart combines a Column Chart and a Line Chart. This chart type is useful when you want to display measures on different axes, such as sales on the left Y-axis and order quantity on the right Y-axis. In such cases, displaying measures on the same axis would probably be meaningless if their units are different. Instead, you should use a Combination Chart and plot one of the measures as a Column Chart and the other as a Line Chart, as shown in **Figure 3.11**.

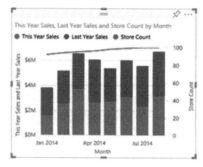

Figure 3.11 A Combo Chart allows you to plot measures on different axes. In this example, the This Year Sales and Last Year Sales measures are plotted on the left Y-axis while Store Count is plotted on the right Y-axis.

Scatter Chart

The Scatter Chart (**Figure 3.12**) is useful when you want to analyze correlation between two variables. Suppose that you want to find a correlation between units sold and revenue. You can use a scatter chart to show Units along the y-axis and Revenue along the x-axis. The resulting chart helps you understand if the two variables are related and, if so how. For example, you can determine if these two measures have a linear relationship; when units increase, revenue increases as well.

A unique feature of the scatter chart is that it can include a Play Axis. You can add any field to the Play Axis, you would typically add a date-related field, such as Month. When you "play" the chart, it animates and bubbles move!

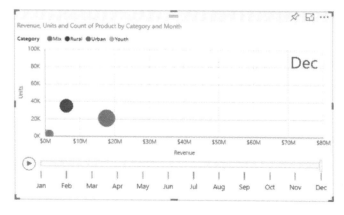

Figure 3.12 Use a Scatter Chart to analyze correlation between two variables.

Shape charts

Shape charts are commonly used to display values as percentages of a whole. Categories are represented by individual segments of the shape. The size of the segment is determined by its contribution. This makes a shape chart useful for proportional comparison between category values. Shape charts have no axes. Shape chart variations include Pie, Doughnut, and Funnel charts, as shown in **Figure 3.13**. All shape charts display each group as a slice on the chart. The Funnel Chart order categories from largest to smallest.

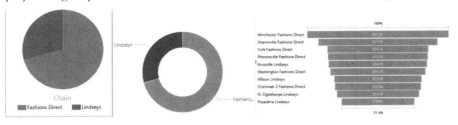

Figure 3.13 Pie, Doughnut, and Funnel charts can be used to display values as percentages of a whole.

Treemap Chart

A treemap is a hierarchical view of data. It breaks an area into rectangles representing branches of a tree. Consider the Treemap Chart when you have to display large amounts of hierarchical data that doesn't fit in column or bar charts, such as the popularity of product features. Power BI allows you to specify custom colors for the minimum and maximum values. For example, the chart shown in **Figure 3.14** uses a red color for show stores with less sales and a green color to show stores with the most sales.

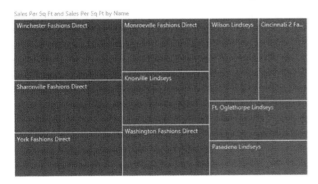

Figure 3.14 Consider Treemap to display large amounts of hierarchical data that doesn't fit in Column or Bar charts.

Table and Matrix visualizations

Use the Table and Matrix visualizations to display text data as tabular or crosstab reports. The Table visualization (left screenshot in **Figure 3.15**) displays text data in a tabular format, such as the store name and sales as separate columns.

Territory	This Year Sal...
DE	$123,446
GA	$332,246
KY	$298,656
MD	$869,726
OH	$2,616,326
Total	$4,240,401

Territory	Jan	Feb	Mar	Apr	Total
DE	$22,370	$26,705	$42,784	$31,587	$123,446
GA	$49,898	$82,267	$123,235	$76,846	$332,246
KY	$46,843	$76,086	$107,936	$67,792	$298,656
MD	$149,974	$201,722	$298,310	$219,721	$869,726
OH	$415,579	$622,028	$933,258	$645,461	$2,616,326
Total	$684,663	$1,008,808	$1,505,523	$1,041,406	$4,240,401

Figure 3.15 Use Table and Matrix visualizations for tabular and crosstab text reports.

The Matrix visualization (right screenshot in **Figure 3.15**) allows you to pivot data by one or more columns added to the Columns area of the Visualization pane, in order to create crosstab reports. Both visualizations support interactive sorting by clicking a column header, such as to sort stores in an ascending order by name.

Both visualizations support pre-defined quick styles that you can choose from in the Format tab of the Visualizations pane to beatify their appearance. For example, I chose the Alternating style to alternate the background color of the table rows. These visualizations also support basic conditional formatting as the Table demonstrates. You can access the conditional formatting settings by expanding the dropdown next to the measure in the Values area and clicking "Conditional formatting" (see **Figure 3.19**)

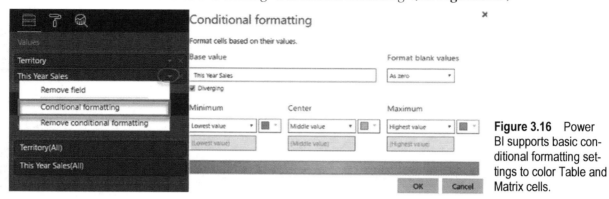

Figure 3.16 Power BI supports basic conditional formatting settings to color Table and Matrix cells.

Then you can let Power BI figure the lowest and highest value for the color range, or enter specific numbers. In **Figure 3.16**, I checked the Diverging setting to have a center zone and specified that cells with low values will be colored in Red and cells with higher values will be colored in Blue.

TIP Although to make it easier on business users, Power BI doesn't support expression-based conditional formatting (supported by Excel and Reporting Services), you can simulate it with appropriate settings. For example, to simulate this SSRS expression for changing the background color of negative numbers Iif(Fields!Sales.Value<0, "Red", "White"), enter zero for the Center Zone, and then specify Red as lowest color and White for the color of the middle and highest zones. As it stands, Power BI can change conditionally only the background cell color.

Map visualizations

Use map visualizations to illustrate geospatial data. Power BI Service includes two map visualizations (see **Figure 3.17**). Currently available as Power BI Desktop preview features, two additional maps, Shape Map and ArcGIS, will be added soon. All maps are license-free and use Microsoft Bing Maps, so you must have an Internet connection to see the maps.

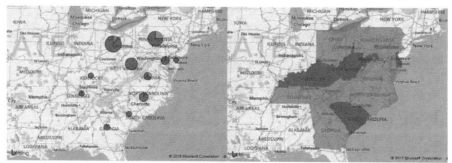

Figure 3.17 Examples of basic maps and filled maps.

You can use a Basic Map (left screenshot in **Figure 3.17**) to display categorical and quantitative information with spatial locations. Adding locations and fields places dots on the map. The larger the value, the bigger the dot. When you add a field to the Legend area of the Visualization pane, the Basic Map shows pie charts on the map, where the segments of the chart correspond to the field's values. For example, each Pie Chart in the Basic Map on the left of **Figure 3.17** breaks the sales by the store type.

As the name suggests, the Filled (choropleth) Map (right screenshot in **Figure 3.17**) fills geospatial areas, such as USA states. This visualization can use shading or patterns to display how a value differs in proportion across a geography or region. You can zoom in and out interactively, by pressing the Ctrl key and using the mouse wheel. Besides being able to plot precise locations (latitude and longitude), they can infer locations using a process called geo-coding, such as to plot addresses.

Similar to the Filled Map, the Shape Map fills geographic regions. The big difference is that the Shape Map allows you to plug in TopoJSON maps. TopoJSON is an extension of GeoJSON - an open standard format designed for representing simple geographical features based on JavaScript Object Notation (JSON).

💡 **TIP**   You can use tools, such as Map Shaper (http://mapshaper.org), to convert GeoJSON maps to TopoJSON files. David El-dersveld maintains a collection of useful TopoJSON maps that are ready to use in Power BI at github.com/deldersveld/topojson.

The latest addition to the Power BI mapping arsenal is the ArcGIS map. This map type was contributed by Esri, a leader in the geographic information systems (GIS) mapping industry. Now not only can you plot data points from Power BI, but you can also add reference layers! These layers include demographic layers provided by Esri and public web maps, or those published into Esri's Living Atlas (http://doc.arcgis.com/en/Living-Atlas). For example, the map in **Figure 3.18** plots customers in Georgia as bubbles on top of a layer showing the 2016 USA Average Household Income (the darker the state color, the higher the income). For more information about ArcGIS maps, visit http://doc.arcgis.com/en/maps-for-powerbi.

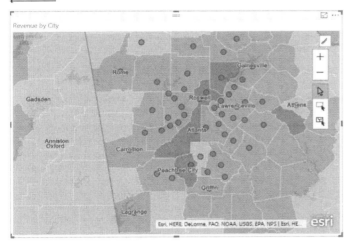

Figure 3.18 This ArcGIS map plots customers in Georgia on top of a layer showing the average household income.

Gauge visualizations
Gauges are typically used on dashboards to display key performance indicators (KPIs), such as to measure actual sales against budget sales. Power BI supports Gauge and KPI visuals for this purpose (**Figure 3.19**) but they work quite differently. To understand this, examine the data shown in the table below the visuals.

The Gauge (the left radial gauge on the left) has a circular arc and displays a single value that measures progress toward a goal. The goal, or target value, is represented by the line (pointer). Progress toward that goal is represented by the shaded scale. And the value that represents that progress is shown in bold inside the arc. The Gauge aggregates the source data and shows the totals. It's not designed to visualize the trend of the historical values over time.

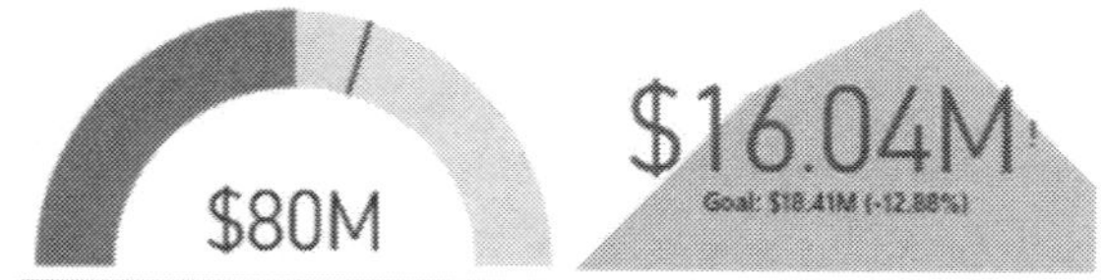

CalendarYear	SalesAmount	SalesAmountQuota
2005	$8,065,435	$9,513,000
2006	$24,144,430	$29,009,000
2007	$32,202,669	$38,782,000
2008	$16,038,063	$18,410,000
Total	**$80,450,597**	**$95,714,000**

Figure 3.19 The Gauge and KPI visuals display progress toward a goal.

By contrast, the KPI visual can be configured to show a trend, such as how the indicator value changes over years. If you add a field to the Trend axis (CalendarYear in this example), it plots an area chart for the historical values. However, the indicator value always shows the last value (in this example, 16 million for year 2008). If you add a field to the "Target goals" area, it shows the indicator value in red if it's less than the target.

Because both visuals show a single scalar value, your users can subscribe for data alerts when these visuals are added to a dashboard. For example, assuming a dashboard tile shows a Gauge visual, Maya can go to the tile properties and create an alert to be notified when the sales exceed 80 million.

Card visualizations

Power BI supports Single Card and Multi Row card visualizations, as shown in **Figure 3.20**.

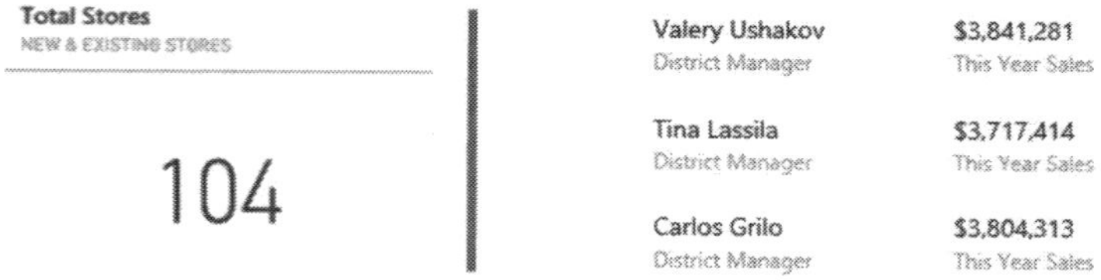

Figure 3.20 The Single Card on the left displays a single value (total stores) while the Multi Row Card displays managers and their sales.

The Single Card visualization (left screenshot in **Figure 3.20**) displays a single value to draw attention to the value. Similar to gauges, you can set up data alerts on single cards, such as to receive a notification when the number of stores exceed a given value.

If you're looking for another way to visualize tabular data than plain tables, consider the Multi Row Card visualization (right screenshot in **Figure 3.20**). It converts a table to a series of cards that display the data from each row in a card format, like an index card.

Slicer

The Slicer visualization isn't really meant to visualize data but to filter data. Unlike page-level filters, which are found in the Filter pane when the report is displayed in Reading View, the Slicer visualization is added on the report so users can see what's filtered and interact with the slicer without expanding the Filter pane. The slicer filters only visualizations on the same page.

Figure 3.21 shows three different slicer configurations. When you bind the slicer to a field of a Date data type, it becomes a slider (the upper-left configuration). You can either use the sliders to set the dates or pick the date using a calendar. The configuration on the right shows the slicer in the default vertical configuration where you can check values from a list or pick a single value from a dropdown. By default, the slicer is configured for a single selection but it also supports multi-value selection (change the Single Selection property to Off in the Format tab of the Visualizations pane). You can also configure the slicer for a horizontal layout (the bottom slicer).

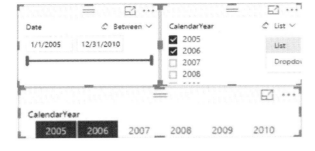

Figure 3.21 Use the Slicer visualization to create a filter that filters all visualizations on the report page.

3.1.4 Understanding Custom Visualizations

No matter how much Microsoft improves the Power BI visualizations, it might never be enough. When it comes to data presentation, beauty is in the eye of the beholder. However, the Power BI presentation framework is open and UX developers can contribute custom visuals that you can use with your reports for free!

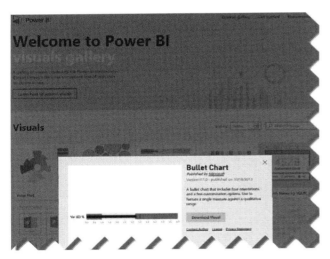

Figure 3.22 Use the Power BI visuals gallery to find and download custom visuals contributed by Microsoft and the community.

Understanding Power BI visuals gallery

To make it easier for users to find a custom visual, Microsoft hosts a Power BI visuals gallery website at http://visuals.powerbi.com (see **Figure 3.22**).

The gallery allows you to search and view custom visuals. When you find an interesting visual, click it to see more information about the visual and its author. Custom visuals are contributed by Microsoft and the Power BI community. If you decide to use the visual, click Download Visual to download the visual, and import it using the ellipsis menu (…) in the Visualizations pane. Visuals are distributed as files with the *.pbiviz extension.

Using custom visuals

Business users can use custom visuals in Power BI Service and data analysts can do the same in Power BI Desktop. As a first step, you need to import the visual. To do this, in the Visualizations pane, click the ellipsis (…) button found below the visualization icons. Read the prompt that warns you that custom visuals could contain security and privacy risks. Although the Microsoft terms of agreement requires the developer to agree that the code doesn't contain any threats, Microsoft isn't responsible for any damages the code might cause. So use custom visuals at your own risk.

 NOTE Custom visuals are written in JavaScript, which browsers run in a protected sandbox environment that restricts what the script can do. However, the script is executed on every user who renders a report with a custom visual. When it comes to security you should do your homework to verity the visual origin and safety. If you're unsure, consider involving IT to test the visual with anti-virus software and make sure that it doesn't pose any threats. For more information about how you or IT can test the visual, read the "Review custom visuals for security and privacy" document at https://support.powerbi.com/knowledgebase/articles/750219.

Finally, navigate to the location where you downloaded the custom visual file and import the visual. Power BI adds the visual to the Visualizations pane. Once you import the visual, you can use it on reports just like any other visual. **Figure 3.23** shows that I imported the Bullet Chart visual and its icon appears at the bottom of the Visualizations pane. Then I added the visual and configured it to show this year sales.

Figure 3.23 The Bullet Chart custom visual is added to the Visualizations pane and can be used on reports.

3.1.5 Understanding Subscriptions

Besides on-demand report delivery where you view a report interactively, Power BI can deliver the report to you once you set up a subscription. Subscriptions let you automate the process of generating and distributing reports. Subscribed report delivery is convenient because you don't have to go to Power BI Service to view the report online. Instead, Power BI sends the report to you. Every Power BI Pro user can create individual report subscriptions, provided that the user has rights to view the report.

Creating subscriptions
Creating a subscription takes a few clicks. Open the report in Reading View and click the Subscribe menu. In the "Subscribe to emails" window, select which report page you want to subscribe to. **Figure 3.24.** shows the available options for two reports that connect to different dataset types.

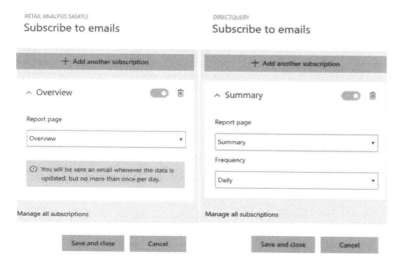

Figure 3.24 When setting up a subscription, specify which page you want to subscribe to and the subscription frequency for DirectQuery reports.

The Retail Analysis Sample report (the screenshot on the left) connects to a dataset with imported data. In this case, you can't specify the subscription frequency. Instead, you'll get an email when the dataset is refreshed, as long as you haven't gotten an email in the last 24 hours. In the other words, the subscription schedule follows the dataset refresh schedule although you get an email at most once a day. The DirectQuery report (the screenshot on the right) connects directly to the data source. In this case, you can specify the mail frequency (Daily or Weekly).

As you know by now, a report can have multiple pages. When you create a subscription, you subscribe to a particular page in a report. For example, if Maya wants to subscribe to all four pages in the "Retail Analysis Sample" report, she'll have to create four subscriptions. She can do that by clicking "Add another subscription". If the report connects directly to the data source, each subscribed page can have its own frequency for sending mails.

Once you done configuring your subscriptions, click "Save and close" to save your changes. You'll start receiving emails periodically with screenshots of each page you subscribe to. If you want to temporarily disable a subscription for a given page, turn the slider for that page off. To permanently delete a page subscription, click the trashcan icon next to the page.

Understanding subscription frequency
The subscription schedule (the frequency you receive emails) depends on how the report dataset connects to the source data. **Table 3.1** summarizes the schedule options.

Table 3.1   Schedule options for report subscriptions.

Dataset	Custom schedule interval	Can detect data changes?	Description
Imported data with scheduled refresh	None	No	Follows the dataset refresh schedule. You can't specify a different schedule. You will get an email every time the scheduled refresh happens, as long as you haven't gotten an email in the last 24 hours.
DirectQuery	Daily or Weekly	No	Power BI checks the data source every 15 minutes. You'll get an email as soon as the next check happens, provided that you haven't gotten an email in the last 24 hours (if Daily is selected), or in the last seven days (if Weekly is selected).
Live connection to Analysis Services (on premise/cloud)	None	Yes	Power BI checks the data source every 15 minutes and it's capable of detecting if the data has changed. You'll get an email only if the data has changed if you haven't gotten an email in the last 24 hours.
Connected Excel reports	None	Yes	Power BI checks the data source every hour. You'll get an email only if the data has changed if you haven't gotten an email in the last 24 hours.

Managing your subscriptions
As the number of your subscriptions grow, you might find it difficult to keep track of which reports you've subscribed to. Luckily, Power BI lets you view your subscriptions in one place - the Subscriptions tab in the Power BI Settings page (**Figure 3.25**). To get there, click the "Manage all subscriptions" link in the "Subscribe to emails" window. Alternatively, click the Power BI Settings (cog) menu in the upper-right corner of the Power BI portal and then click Settings. You can see the number of pages you subscribed to for each report. Click the Actions icon if you want to make changes to a given report subscription. This brings you to the "Subscribe to emails" window.

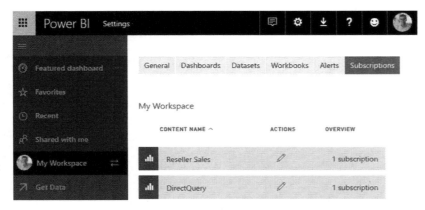

Figure 3.25 Use the Sub-
scriptions tab in the Settings
page to view and manage
your subscriptions.

Understanding subscription limitations

As of time of writing, Power BI subscriptions have these limitations:

- The only export option is screenshot. You can't receive the page exported to PowerPoint, for example.

- You can create individual subscriptions only. You can't subscribe other users as you can do with Reporting Services data-driven subscriptions.

- You can specify subscription frequency for reports that connect directly to the data source (DirectQuery connections). For other datasets, subscriptions either follow the dataset refresh schedule (for imported datasets), or Power BI determines when to send emails (for datasets connected to Analysis Services or Excel).

- The Power BI admin can't see or manage subscriptions across the tenant.

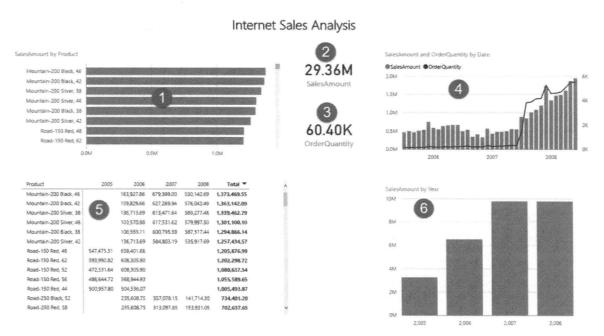

Figure 3.26 The Summary page of the Internet Sales Analysis report includes six visualizations.

3.2   Working with Power BI Reports

Now that you know about visualizations, let's use them on reports. In the first exercise that follows, you'll create a report from scratch. The report will source data from the Internet Sales dataset that you created in Chapter 2. In the second exercise, you'll modify an existing report. You'll also practice working with Excel and Reporting Services reports.

3.2.1   Creating Your First Report

In Chapter 2, you imported the Internet Sales Excel file in Power BI. As a result, Power BI created a dataset with the same name. Let's analyze the sales data by creating the report shown in **Figure 3.26**. This report consists of two pages. The Summary page has six visualizations and the Treemap page (not shown in **Figure 3.26**) uses a Treemap visualization to help you analyze sales by product at a glance. (For an example of a Treemap visualization skip ahead to **Figure 3.28**.)

Getting started with report authoring
One way to create a new report in Power BI is to explore a dataset.

1. In the Power BI portal, click My Workspace. In the workspace content page, select the Datasets tab. Click the Create Report icon () next to the Internet Sales dataset to create a new report that is connected to this dataset.

2. Power BI opens a blank report in Editing View. Click the Text Box menu to create a text box for the report title. Type *"Internet Sales Analysis"* and format as needed. Position the text box on top of the report.

3. Note the Fields pane shows only the table "Internet Sales" because the Internet Sales dataset, which you imported from an Excel file, has only one table.

4. Click the Save menu and save the report as *Internet Sales Analysis*. Remind yourself to save the report (you can press Ctrl-S) every now and then so that you don't lose changes.

 NOTE   Power BI times out your session after a certain period of inactivity to conserve resources in a shared environment. When this happens and you return to the browser, it'll ask you to refresh the page. If you have unsaved changes, you might lose them when you refresh the page so get in the habit to press Ctrl-S often.

Creating a Bar Chart
Follow these steps to create a bar chart that shows the top selling products.

1. In the Fields pane, check the SalesAmount field. Power BI defaults to a Column Chart visualization that displays the grand total of the SalesAmount field.

2. In the Fields pane, check the Product field. Power BI adds it to the Axis area of the chart.

3. In the Visualizations pane, click the Bar Chart icon to flip the Column Chart to a Bar Chart. Power BI sorts the bar chart by the product name in an ascending order.

4. Point your mouse cursor to the top-right corner of the chart. Click the ellipsis "..." menu and change the sorting order to sort by SalesAmount in a descending order. Compare your results with the "SalesAmount by Product" visualization in upper left of **Figure 3.26**.

5. (Optional) With bar chart selected, select the Format tab in the Visualizations pane. Switch "Data labels" to On to show data labels on the chart.

TIP   Clicked the wrong button or menu? Don't worry, you can undo your last step by pressing Ctrl-Z. To undo multiple steps in a reverse order, press Ctrl-Z repeatedly.

Adding Card visualizations

Let's show the total sales amount and order quantity as separate card visualizations (items 2 and 3 in **Figure 3.26**) to draw attention to them:

1. Click an empty space on the report canvas outside the Bar Chart to deactivate it.

 TIP As I explained, another way to create a new visualization is to drag a field to an empty space on the canvas. If the field is numeric, Power BI will create a Column Chart. For text fields, it'll default to a Table. And for geo fields, such as Country, it will default to a Map.

2. In the Field list, check the SalesAmount field. Change the visualization to Card. Position it as needed.

3. Repeat the last two steps to create a new card visualization using the OrderQuantity field.

4. (Optional) Experiment with the card format settings. For example, suppose you want a more descriptive title. In the Format tab of the Visualization pane, switch "Category label" to Off. Switch Title to On. Type in a descriptive title and change its font and alignment settings.

Creating a Combo Chart visualization

The fourth chart in **Figure 3.26** shows how the sales amount and order quantity change over time:

1. Drag the SalesAmount field and drop it onto an empty area next to the card visualizations to create a Column Chart.

2. Drag the Date field and drop it onto the new chart.

3. Switch the visualization to "Line and Stacked Column Chart". This adds a new Line Values area to the Visualizations pane.

4. Drag the OrderQuantity field and drop it on the Line Values area. Power BI adds a line chart to the visualization and plots its values to a secondary Y-axis. Compare your results with the "SalesAmount and OrderQuantity by Date" visualization (item 4 in **Figure 3.26**).

5. To avoid the sharp dip in the last bar of the chart caused by incomplete sales, apply a visual-level filter to exclude the last date. To do so, with the combo chart selected, expand the Date field in the "Visual level filters" area, check "Select All", scroll all the way down the list of values, and then uncheck '7/1/2008'.

Creating a Matrix visualization

The fifth visualization (from **Figure 3.26**) represents a crosstab report showing sales by product on rows and years on columns. Let's build this with the Matrix visualization:

1. Drag the SalesAmount field and drop it onto an empty space on the report canvas to create a new visualization. Change the visualization to Matrix.

2. Check the Product field to add it to the visualization on rows.

3. Drag the Year field and drop it on the Columns zone to pivot on Year on columns.

4. Resize the visualization as needed. Click any of the column headers to sort the visualization interactively in an ascending or descending order.

5. (Optional) In the Format tab of the Visualizations pane, change the matrix style to Minimal. Change the "Horiz grid" to Off.

6. (Optional) In the Fields tab of the Visualizations pane, expand the drop-down button next to the SalesAmount field in the Values area. Notice that the SalesAmount is aggregated using the Sum aggregation function but you can choose another aggregation function. In the same drop-down menu, click "Conditional formatting" and experiment with different conditional format settings, such as to color cells with lower values in Red.

Creating a Column Chart visualization

The sixth visualization listed shows sales by year:

1. Create a new visualization that uses the SalesAmount field. Power BI should default to Column Chart.

2. In the Fields pane, check the Year field to place it in the Axis area of the Column Chart.

3. Hover on one of the chart columns. Notice that a tooltip pops up to show Year and SalesAmount. Assuming you want to see the order quantity as well, drag OrderQuantity from the Fields pane and drop it to the Tooltips area of the Fields tab in the Visualizations pane.

4. (Optional) Suppose you want to change the color of the column showing the 2008 data. Switch to the Format tab in the Visualizations pane. Expand Data Colors and turn "Show all" to On. Change the color of the 2008 item.

5. (Optional) Suppose you need a trend line on the chart. Switch to the Analytics tab in the Visualizations pane. Expand the Trend Line section and then click Add. Change the format settings of the trend line as needed.

6. (Optional) Change the chart type to Line Chart. Notice that the Analytics tab adds a Forecast section. Add a forecast line to predict sales for future periods.

Filtering the report

Next, you'll implement page-level and visual-level filters. Let's start by creating a page-level Date filter that will allow you to filter all visualizations on the page by date.

1. Click an empty area on the report canvas to make sure that no visualization is activated.

2. Drag the Date field onto the Page Level Filters area. This creates a page-level filter that filters all visualizations on the activated page.

3. Practice different ways to filter. For example, switch to Advanced Filtering mode and filter out dates after June 30th, 2008, as shown on the left screenshot in **Figure 3.27**.

4. To work with visual-level filters, click the fifth (Matrix) visualization. To practice another way to create a filter besides drag and drop, hover on the Product field in the Fields pane. Then expand the ellipsis menu and click Add Filter.

Because there's an activated visualization, this action configures a visual-level filter. Notice that the Visual Level Filters (see the right screenshot in **Figure 3.27**) already includes the three fields used in the visualization so that you can filter on these fields without explicitly adding them as filters.

Figure 3.27 The Advanced Filter mode (left screenshot) allows you to specify more complex criteria and multiple conditions for filtering, such as filter dates where the Date field is after June 30th, 2008. The Visual Level Filters area (right screenshot) includes by default all the fields that are used in the visualization.

Creating a Treemap

Let's add a second page to the report that will help you analyze product sales using a Treemap visualization (see **Figure 3.28**).

1. At the bottom of the report, click the plus sign to add a new page. Rename the page in place to *Treemap*.
2. In the Fields list, check the SalesAmount and Product fields.
3. Change the visualization type to Treemap.
4. By default, Power BI uses arbitrary colors for the tree map tiles. Assuming you want to color the bestselling products in green and worst-selling products in red, drag the SalesAmount field to the Color Saturation area of the Visualizations pane.

Figure 3.28   The Treemap visualization helps you analyze product sales.

5. In the Format tab of the Visualizations pane, change the Data Colors settings, as shown in **Figure 3.28**. Turning off the Diverging option allows you to specify a color for the values that fall in the middle. You can use the Minimum, Center, and Maximum fields to fine tune the ranges.
6. Save your report.

3.2.2   Getting Quick Insights

Let's face it, slicing and dicing data to perform root cause analysis (RCA) could be time consuming and tedious. For example, a report might show you that sales are increasing or decreasing, but it won't tell you why. Retrospectively, such tasks required you to produce more detail reports, in order to explain sudden data fluctuations. And this gets even more difficult if you're analyzing a model created by someone else because you don't know which fields to use and how to use them to get answers. Enter Quick Insights!

Understanding Quick Insights

Power BI Quick Insights gives you new ways to find insights hidden in your data. With a click of button, Quick Insights run various sophisticated algorithms on your data to search for interesting fluctuations. Originating from Microsoft Research, these algorithms can discover correlations, outliers, trends, seasonality changes, change points in trends, automatically and within seconds. **Table 3.2** lists some of the insights that these algorithms can uncover.

Table 3.2 This table summarizes the available insights.

Insight	Explanation
Major factors(s)	Finds cases where a majority of a total value can be attributed to a single factor when broken down by another dimension.
Category outliers (top/bottom)	Highlights cases where, for a measure in the model, one or two members of a dimension have much larger values than other members of the dimension.
Time series outliers	For data across a time series, detects when there are specific dates or times with values significantly different than the other date/time values.
Overall trends in time series	Detects upward or downward trends in time series data.
Seasonality in time series	Finds periodic patterns in time series data, such as weekly, monthly, or yearly seasonality.
Steady Share	Highlights cases where there is a parent-child correlation between the share of a child value in relation to the overall value of the parent across a continuous variable.
Correlation	Detects cases where multiple measures show a correlation between each other when plotted against a dimension in the dataset

By default, Quick Insights queries as much of the dataset as possible in a fixed time window (about 20 seconds). As it stands, similar to Q&A, Quick Insights requires data to be imported in Power BI. Quick Insights isn't available for datasets that connect directly to data.

Working with Quick Insights

Let's find what insights we can uncover by applying Quick Insights to the Retail Analysis Sample dataset:

1. In Power BI, click My Workspace in the navigation pane. In the workspace content page, select the Datasets tab. Click the ellipsis (…) button to the right of the "Retail Analysis Sample" dataset, and the click "Get insights". Alternatively, you can select the Reports tab and click the bulb icon to the right of the "Retail Analysis Sample" report to start Quick Insights.

2. While Power BI runs the algorithms, it displays a "Searching for insights" message. Once it's done, it shows "Insights are ready" message.

3. Click the ellipsis next to the "Retail Analysis Sample" dataset again. Note that the Quick Insights link is renamed to View Insights. Click View Insights.

Quick Insights for **Retail Analysis Sample** ↻

A subset of your data was analyzed and the following insights were found. **Learn more**

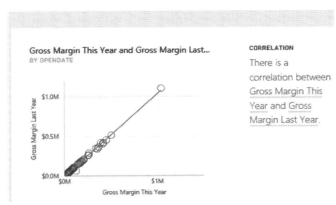

Figure 3.29 The first Quick Insight report shows a correlation between two measures.

Power BI opens a "Quick Insights for Retail Analysis Sample" page that shows four auto-generated insights. **Figure 3.29** shows the first report. The "Gross Margin This Year" report has found a correlation between the "Gross Margin This Year" and "Gross Margin Last Year" measures. This is an example of a Correlation insight. As you can see, Quick Insights can really help understand data changes. The refresh button (next to the page title) allows you to rerun the Quick Insight algorithms. Currently, Power BI deactivates them when you close your browser. However, if you find a particular insight useful, you can click the pin button in the top-right corner to pin to a dashboard. (I discuss creating dashboards in more detail in the next chapter.

3.2.3   Subscribing to Reports

In the previous chapter, I walked you through the steps to create the Adventure Works report from an Analysis Services model. Suppose that Maya would like to subscribe to a report so that she receives the report by email when the underlying data has changed.

NOTE   You might wonder why not use the Internet Sales report that you just created. Recall that this report imports data from an Excel file and you created it directly in Power BI Service (without using Power BI Desktop). As I explained in section 2.3.1, Power BI can't refresh these type of reports or the included sample reports, such as Retail Analysis Sample. Although you can subscribe to such reports, you won't get an email because there will be nothing to trigger the subscription. If you haven't created the Adventure Works report, fast forward and follow the instructions in section 10.2.3 to deploy the Adventure Works Power BI Desktop model and schedule it for refresh. Then, create and test a subscription to the Adventure Works report.

Creating a subscription
Follow these steps to create a subscription to an existing report.

1. In Power BI Service, click My Workspace to go to the workspace content page.
2. Click the Adventure Works report to open it in Reading View. Click the Subscribe menu.
3. In the "Subscribe to emails" window, leave the default settings to the subscribe to the first page of the report. Or, if the report has multiple pages and you want to subscribe to them, click the "Add another subscription" button to create more subscriptions, one page at the time.
4. Click "Save and close" to create the subscription.

Receiving reports
When the Analysis Services model is refreshed, you'll get an email with screenshots of all report pages that you subscribed to. Power BI will determine the exact time when this will happen.

TIP   If you've subscribed to a report connected to a dataset with imported data and you've scheduled the dataset for refresh, you can manually refresh the dataset to get the email faster. To do so, go to the workspace content page, click the Datasets tab, and then click the "Refresh Now" icon next to the dataset name.

1. Check your mail inbox for an email from no-reply@email.powerbi.com. **Figure 3.30** shows the content of a sample email. The email includes screenshots of all subscribed pages. In this case, I've subscribed to only one page so I get only one screenshot.
2. Suppose you want to open the report and interact with it. Click the "Go to Report" button and Power BI navigates you to the report.
3. Back to the email, click the "Manage subscription" link. This navigates you to the report and opens the "Subscribe to emails" window so that you can review and make changes to your report subscription.
4. In the "Subscribe to emails" window, click the "Manage all subscriptions" link. This navigates you to the Settings page that shows all of your subscriptions that exist in the current workspace.

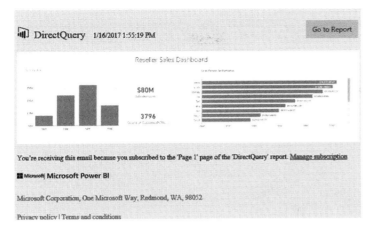

Figure 3.30 The subscription email includes page screenshots, a link to the report, and a link to change the subscription settings.

3.3 Working with Excel Reports

Ask a business user what tools they currently use for analytics and Excel comes on top. Thanks to its integration with SharePoint Online, Power BI is capable of connecting to existing Excel table or pivot reports and rendering them online (without importing the Excel file). In addition, business users can connect Excel desktop to Power BI datasets and create Excel pivot reports, just like they can connect Excel to Analysis Services models. Let's take a more detailed look at these two integration options with Excel.

3.3.1 Connecting to Excel Reports

Before you connect to your Excel reports, you need to pay attention where the Excel file is stored:

- Excel files stored locally – If the Excel file is stored on your computer, Power BI needs to upload the file before Excel Online can connect to it. Because Excel Online can't synchronize the uploaded version with the local file (even if you set up a gateway), you have to re-upload the file after you make changes if you want the connected reports to show the latest.

- Excel files stored in the cloud – If your Excel file is saved to OneDrive for Business or SharePoint Online, Power BI doesn't have to upload the file because it can connect directly to it. As long as you save changes to the same location in the cloud, Power BI will always show the latest.

OneDrive for Business is a place where business users can store, sync, and share work files. While the personal edition of OneDrive is free, OneDrive for Business requires an Office 365 plan. For example, Maya might maintain an Excel file with some calculations. Or, Martin might give her an Excel file with Power Pivot model and pivot reports. Maya can upload these files to her OneDrive for Business and then add these reports to Power BI, and even pin them to a dashboard!

NOTE   Online Excel reports have limitations which are detailed in the "Bring Excel files in Power BI" article by Microsoft at https://powerbi.microsoft.com/en-us/documentation/powerbi-service-excel-workbook-files. One popular and frequently requested scenario that Power BI still doesn't support is Excel reports connected to Analysis Services although reports connected to Power Pivot data models work just fine. That's because currently SharePoint Online doesn't support external connections, even if you have a gateway set up. This might be a serious issue if you plan to migrate your BI reports from on-premises SharePoint Server to Power BI.

Connecting to Excel

In this exercise, you'll connect an Excel file saved to OneDrive for Business and you'll view its containing reports online. As a prerequisite, your organization must have an Office 365 business plan and you must have access to OneDrive for Business. If you don't have access to OneDrive for Business, you can use a local Excel file. The Reseller Sales.xlsx file in the \Source\ch03 folder includes a Power Pivot data model with several tables. The first two sheets have Excel pivot tables and chart reports, while the third sheet has a Power View report. While all reports connect to an embedded Power Pivot data model, they don't have to. For example, your pivot reports can connect to Excel tables.

1. Copy and save the Reseller Sales.xlsx to your OneDrive for Business. To open OneDrive, click the Office 365 Application Launcher button (the yellow button in the upper-left corner in the Power BI portal) and then click OneDrive. If you don't see the OneDrive icon, your organization doesn't have an Office 365 business plan (to complete this exercise, go back to Get Data and choose the Local File option).

2. In Power BI, click Get Data. Then click the Get button in the Files tile.

3. In the next page, click the "One Drive – Business" tile. In the "OneDrive for Business" page, navigate to the folder where you saved the Reseller Sales.xlsx file, select the file, and then click Connect.

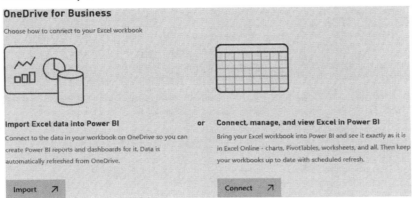

Figure 3.31 When you connect to an Excel file stored on OneDrive for Business, Power BI asks you how you want to work with the file.

Power BI prompts you how to work with the file (see **Figure 3.31**). You practiced importing from Excel in Chapter 2. If you take this path, Power BI will import only the data from the Excel file. If there are any pivot reports in the Excel workbook, they won't be added to Power BI.

 NOTE If you've selected the Local File option in Get Data, you'll see an Upload button instead of the Connect button. This is to emphasize the Power BI will upload the file to its cloud storage before it connects to it.

4. Click the Connect button to connect directly to the Excel file. Power BI processes the Excel file and notifies you that it's added to your list of workbooks.

Interacting with Excel reports

Excel Online (a component of SharePoint Online) renders the Excel reports in HTML so you don't need Excel on the desktop to view the Excel reports added to Power BI. And not only can you view the Excel reports but you can also interact with them, just you can do so in Excel Desktop.

1. In the Power BI portal, click My Workspace. In the workspace content page, click the Workbooks tab. You should see Reseller Sales listed. This represents the Excel file that is now available to Power BI.

2. Click the Reseller Sales workbook. Power BI renders the pivot reports and the Power View report online via Excel Online (see **Figure 3.32**).

Figure 3.32 Power BI supports rendering Excel reports online if the Excel file is stored in OneDrive for Business.

3. (Optional) Try some interactive features, such as changing the report filters and slicers, and notice that they work the same as they work in SharePoint Server or SharePoint Online. For example, you can change report filters and slicers, and you can add or remove fields.

 TIP You can pin a range from an Excel report as a static image to a Power BI dashboard. To do so, select the range on the report and then click the Pin button in the upper-right corner of the report (see again **Figure 3.32**). The Pin to Dashboard window allows you to preview the selected section and prompts you if you want to pin it to a new or an existing dashboard. For more information about this feature, read the "Pin a range from Excel to your dashboard!" blog at https://powerbi.microsoft.com/en-us/blog/pin-a-range-from-excel-to-your-dashboard. Q&A is not available for Excel tiles.

3.3.2 Analyzing Data in Excel

Besides consuming existing Excel reports, business users can create their own Excel pivot reports connected to Power BI datasets. This feature, called Analyze in Excel, brings you another option to explore Power BI datasets (besides creating Power BI reports). For example, Maya knows Excel pivot reports and she wants to create a pivot report that's connected to the Retailer Analysis Sample dataset. She can use the Analyze in Excel feature to connect to her data in Power BI, just like she can do so by connecting Excel to a multidimensional cube. She can then use the Power BI publisher for Excel add-in to pin her report as an image to a dashboard as she can do when connecting to Excel files.

Creating Excel reports
Follow these steps to create an Excel report connected to the Retailer Analysis Sample dataset:

1. In Power BI portal, click My Workspace. In the workspace content page, click the Datasets tab.
2. Expand the ellipsis (…) menu next to the Retailer Analysis Sample dataset and click Analyze in Excel. You'll be asked to install some updates to enable this feature. Accept to install these updates. They will install a newer version of the MSOLAP OLEDB provider that Excel needs to connect to Power BI. Then your web browser downloads a Retailer Analysis Sample.odc file which includes the connection details to connect Excel to the Power BI dataset.
3. Click the download file. Excel opens and prompts you to enable the connection. Once you confirm the prompt, Excel adds an empty pivot table report connected to the Power BI dataset.

NOTE As far as Excel is concerned, Analyze in Excel connects to Power BI using the same mechanism as it uses to connect to cubes. Excel parses the dataset metadata and it looks for measures and dimensions. Therefore, if you want to aggregate data you must define explicit measures in the datasets. In other words, the dataset must be created in Power BI Desktop and it must have explicit DAX measures. In fact, Analyze in Excel won't work if you have created the dataset directly in Power BI Service (as you did with the Internet Sales file).

Besides creating ad-hoc Excel pivot reports, another practical benefit of using Analyze in Excel is that it doesn't limit the number of rows when drilling through data (just double-click an aggregated cell in the pivot report to drill through).

Using Power BI publisher for Excel

If you like Analyze in Excel, consider installing the "Power BI publisher for Excel" add-in. The tool adds the ability to connect to Power BI datasets directly from Excel (without downloading the *.odc file from Power BI portal) and to pin Excel ranges as static images to Power BI dashboards.

1. In Power BI portal, expand the Downloads menu and then click "Power BI publisher for Excel". Run the setup to install the tool.

2. Open Excel. Notice that the add-in adds a Power BI menu to the Excel ribbon (see **Figure 3.33**).

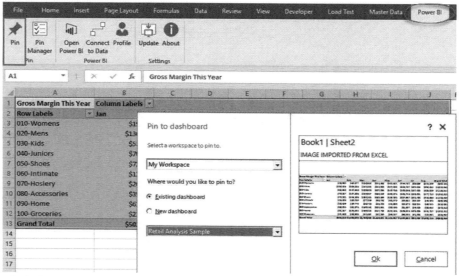

Figure 3.33 Power BI publisher for Excel lets you pin reports to dashboards.

3. Click the "Connect to Data" button. Log in to Power BI and connect to the Retailer Analysis Sample datasets in My Workspace. The publisher will create an empty PivotTable report connected to the dataset.

4. Drag some fields on the report, such as the "Gross Margin This Year" measure (Sales Table) in the Values area, Category (Item table) in the Rows area, and Fiscal Year (Time table) in the Columns area.

5. Let's pin this report to a dashboard. Select the entire report and then click Pin. In the "Pin to dashboard" window, select My Workspace and then select the "Retail Analysis Sample" dashboard.

6. In Power BI Service, open the "Retail Analysis Sample" dashboard and notice that it includes an image of the Excel pivot report. Unlike connecting to an Excel file, you can't open the report online and interact with it. That's because the report was produced on the desktop.

For more information about the Power BI publisher for Excel, read the "Power BI publisher for Excel" article at https://powerbi.microsoft.com/en-us/documentation/powerbi-publisher-for-excel.

NOTE In an attempt to have an interactive report, you might decide to try uploading the Excel workbook to OneDrive or SharePoint Online and using Get Data to connect to the Excel file. However, you'll find that although you'll be able to render the report in Excel Online, you won't be able to interact with it. That's because the report has an external connection to the Power BI dataset. This is the same limitation as with Excel reports connected to Analysis Services.

3.3.3 Comparing Excel Reporting Options

At this point, you might be confused about which option to use when working with Excel files. **Table 3.3** should help you make the right choice. To recap, Power BI offers three Excel integration options.

Table 3.3   This table compares the Power BI options to work with Excel.

Criteria	Import Excel files	Connect to Excel files	Analyze in Excel
Data acquisition	Power BI parses the Excel file, imports data, and creates a dataset.	Power BI doesn't parse and import the data. Instead, Power BI connects to the Excel file hosted on OneDrive or SharePoint Online.	Connects to existing dataset in Power BI
Data model (Power Pivot)	Power BI imports the data model and creates a dataset.	Power BI doesn't import the data model.	N/A
Pivot reports	Power BI doesn't import pivot reports.	Power BI renders pivot reports via Excel Online.	Create your pivot reports
Power View reports	Power BI imports Power View reports and adds them to Reports section in the left navigation bar.	Power BI renders Power View reports via Excel Online (requires Silverlight).	N/A
Change reports	You can change the imported Power View reports but the original reports in the Excel file remain intact.	You can't change reports. You must open the file in Excel, make report changes, and upload the file to OneDrive.	You can change reports saved in the Excel file.
Publish reports	Import or create new Power BI reports	Reports are available in the Workbooks tab; you can pin Excel ranges as static images to Power BI dashboards.	Pin Excel ranges as static images to Power BI dashboards
Data refresh	Scheduled dataset refresh (automatic refresh if saved to OneDrive or OneDrive for Business).	Dashboard tiles from Excel reports are refreshed automatically every few minutes.	N/A

Importing Excel files
Use this option when you need only the Excel data and you'll later create Power BI reports to analyze it. As a prerequisite for importing Excel files directly in Power BI Service, the data must be formatted as an Excel table (Power BI Desktop doesn't have this limitation). If the Excel file has Power View reports, Power BI will create a corresponding Power BI report but it won't import any pivot reports. Because data is imported, you'd probably need to set up a data refresh. However, a scheduled refreshed is not required if the workbook is saved in OneDrive or SharePoint Online because Power BI synchronizes changes every hour.

Connecting to Excel files
Use this option when you need to bring in existing Excel pivot reports and Power View reports to Power BI. In this case, Power BI doesn't import the data. Instead, it leaves the Excel file where it is and it just connects to it. However, you must upload the file to OneDrive for Business or SharePoint Online. All connected Excel workbooks appears under the Workbooks tab in the workspace content page.

When you open the workbook, you can see its reports online without needing Excel on the desktop. You'll be able to interact with the reports if the data is imported in the Excel workbooks. At this point, external connections are not supported. You can select a range and pin to a dashboard as an image.

Analyze in Excel

Use this option when you want to create your own PivotTable and PivotChart reports connected to datasets published to Power BI Service. If you use Power BI publisher for Excel, you can pin the pivot reports as images to dashboards, just like you can do when connecting to Excel files.

3.4   Summary

As a business user, you don't need any special skills to gain insights from data. With a few clicks, you can create interactive reports for presenting information in a variety of ways that range from basic reports to professional-looking dashboards.

You can create a new report by exploring a dataset. Power BI supports popular visualizations, including charts, maps, gauges, cards, and tables. When those visualizations just won't do the job, you can import custom visuals from the Power BI visuals gallery.

Because Excel is a very pervasive tool for self-service, BI supports several integration options with Excel. You can import data from Excel tables. To preserve your investment in Excel pivot and Power View reports, save the Excel files in OneDrive for Business and connect to these files to view the included reports in Excel Online. Finally, you can connect Excel to Power BI datasets and create ad-hoc pivot reports.

Now that you know how to create reports, let's learn more about Power BI dashboards.

Chapter 4

Creating Dashboards

In Chapter 2, I introduced you to Power BI dashboards and you learned that dashboards are one of the three main Power BI content items (the other two are datasets and reports). I defined a Power BI dashboard as a summarized view of important metrics that typically fit on a single page. You need a dashboard when you want to combine data from multiple reports (datasets), or when you need dashboards-specific features, such as Q&A.

This chapter takes a deep dive into Power BI dashboards. I'll start by discussing the anatomy of a Power BI dashboard. I'll walk you through different ways to create a dashboard, including pinning visualizations, using natural queries by typing them in the Q&A box, using the Cortana digital assistant, from quick insights, and from SSRS reports. You'll also learn how to share dashboards with your co-workers.

4.1   Understanding Dashboards

Similar to an automobile's dashboard, a digital dashboard enables users to get a "bird's eye view" of the company's health and performance. A dashboard page typically hosts several sections that display data visually in charts, graphs, or gauges, so that data is easier to understand and analyze. You can use Power BI to quickly assemble dashboards from existing or new visualizations.

 NOTE   Power BI isn't the only Microsoft-provided tool for creating dashboards. For example, if you need an entirely on-premises dashboard solution, dashboards can be implemented with Excel (requires SharePoint Server) and Reporting Services (requires SQL Server). While Power BI dashboards might not be as customizable as SSRS reports, they are by far the easiest to implement. They also gain in interactive features, the ability to use natural queries, and even to get real-time updates (when data is streamed to Power BI)!

4.1.1   Understanding Dashboard Tiles

A Power BI dashboard has one or more tiles. Each tile shows data from one source, such as from one report. For example, the Total Stores tile in the Retail Analysis Sample dashboard (see **Figure 4.1**) shows the total number of stores. The Card visualization came from the Retail Analysis Sample report. Although you can add as many tiles as you want, as a rule of thumb try to limit the number of tiles so that they can fit into a single page and so the user doesn't have to scroll horizontally or vertically.

A tile has a resize handle that allows you to change the tile size to one of the predefined tile sizes (from 1x1 tile units up to 5x5). Because tiles can't overlap, when you enlarge a tile it pushes the rest of the content out of the way. If the tile flow setting is enabled, when you make the tile smaller, adjacent tiles "snap in" to occupy the empty space.

Figure 4.1 When you hover on a tile, the ellipsis menu (...) allows you to access the tile settings.

If the tile flow setting is not enabled, Power BI won't reclaim the empty space. To turn on tile flow, open the dashboard, click the ellipsis menu in the upper-right corner of the dashboard (next to the Share button), click Settings, and then slide the "Dashboard tile flow" slider to On. You can move a tile by just dragging it to a new location. You don't need to explicitly save the layout changes you've made to a dashboard when you resize or move its tiles.

Understanding tile settings

Power BI supports a limited customization of dashboard tiles. When you hover on a tile, an ellipsis menu (…) shows up in the top-right corner of the tile. When you click the ellipsis menu, the tile changes (see the right snapshot in **Figure 4.1**) and it has the following buttons (numbers corresponds to the numbers in the figure):

1. In-focus mode – Similar to popping out visualizations on a report, this button pops out the tile so that you can examine it in more detail. Another way to pop out a tile is to hover on the tile and click the "Focus mode" icon in the tile upper-right corner.
2. Related insights – Similar to Quick Insights but targets the specific tile for discovering insights. Power BI will search the tile and its related data for correlations, outliers, trends, seasonality, change points in trends, and major factors automatically, within seconds.
3. Pin visual – Pins a tile to another dashboard. Why would you pin a tile from a dashboard instead of from the report? Pinning it from a dashboard allows you to apply the same customizations, such as the title, subtitle, and custom link, to the other dashboard, even though they're not shared (once you pin the tile to another dashboard, both titles have independent customizations).
4. Manage alerts – A tile pinned from a visualization showing a scalar value (Single Card, Gauge, KPI) can have one or more data alerts, such as to notify you when the number of stores reaches 105.
5. Tile details – Allows you to change the tile settings, such as the tile title and subtitle.
6. Delete tile – Removes the tile from the dashboard.
7. Go to report – By default, when you click a tile, Power BI "drills through" it and navigates you to the underlying source. For example, if the tile is pinned from a report, you'll be taken to the underlying report. Another way to navigate to the report is to click the arrow button next to the report name in the tile.

Let's explain some of these features in more detail.

Understanding the in-focus mode

When you click the "In-focus mode" button, Power BI opens another page and zooms out the visualization (see **Figure 4.2**). Tooltips allow you to get precise values. If you pop out a line chart, you can also drag a vertical line to see the precise value of a measure at the intersection of the vertical bar and the line. The Filter pane is available so that you can filter the displayed data by specifying visual-level filters.

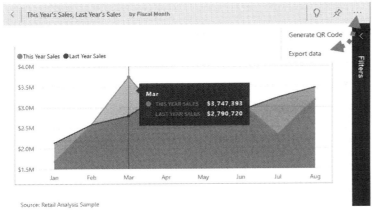

Figure 4.2 The in-focus mode page allows you to examine the tile in more details, generate a QR code, and export the tile data.

The in-focus page has an ellipsis menu (…) in the top-right corner. When you click it, a "Generate QR Code" menu appears. A QR Code (abbreviated from Quick Response Code) is a barcode that contains information about the item to which it is attached. In the case of a Power BI tile, it contains the URL of the tile. How's this useful, you might wonder? You can download the code, print it, and display it somewhere or post the image online. When other people scan the code (there are many QR Code reader mobile apps, including the one included in the Power BI iPhone app), they'll get the tile URL. Now they can quickly navigate to the dashboard tile. So QR codes give users convenient and instant access to dashboard tiles.

For example, suppose you're visiting a potential customer and they give you a pamphlet. It starts gushing about all these stats about how great their performance has been. You have a hard time believing what you hear or even understanding the numbers. You see the QR Code. You scan it with your phone. It pops up Power BI Mobile on your phone, and rather than just reading the pamphlet, now you're sliding the controls around in Power BI and exploring the data. You go back and forth between reading the pamphlet and then exploring the associated data on your phone.

Or, suppose you're in a meeting. The presenter is showing some data, but wants you to explore it independently. He includes a QR Code on their deck. He also might pass around a paper with the QR Code on it. You scan the code and navigate to Power BI to examine the data in more details. As you can imagine, QR codes open new opportunities for getting access to relevant information that's available in Power BI. For more information about the QR code feature, read the blog "Bridge the gap between your physical world and your BI using QR codes" at http://bit.ly/1lsVGJ5.

Understanding Related Insights
In the previous chapter, you saw how Quick Insights makes it easy to apply brute-force predictive analytics to a dataset in order to discover hidden trends. Instead of examining the entire dataset, you can scope Quick Insights to a specific tile. You can do so by clicking the Related Insights button found in the tile's properties and in the upper-right corner of the tile while it's in focus.

Power BI will scan the data related to the tile and display a list of visualizations you may want to explore further. **Figure 4.3** shows two of the Related Insights visuals for the Total Stores card of the Retail Analysis Sample dashboard. To get even more specifics insights, you can click a data point in the visual, and Related Insights will focus on that data point when searching for insights. If you find a particular insight useful, you can hover on the visual and click the pin button to pin it to a dashboard.

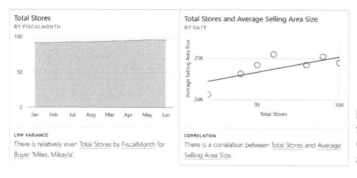

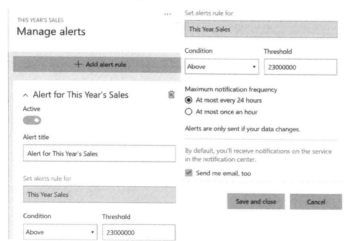

Figure 4.3 Related Insights applies the same predictive algorithms as Quick Insights but limits their scope to a specific tile.

Understanding data alerts

Wouldn't it be nice to be notified for important data changes, such as when this year's revenue reaches a specific goal? Now you can be with Power BI data alerts! You can create alerts on Single Card, Gauge, and KPI tiles. A tile can have multiple alerts, such as to notify you when the value is both above and below certain thresholds. You can create a data alert in Power BI Service (click the bell icon in the tile properties) or in Power BI Mobile native applications for mobile devices. This brings you to the "Manage alerts" window (see **Figure 4.4**) where you can create one or more alerts.

Figure 4.4 When you create an alert, you specify a condition and notification frequency.

Currently, Power BI supports only two conditions (Above and Below) and two notification intervals (daily and hourly). By default, you'll get an email when the condition is met in addition to a notification in the Power BI Notification Center. If you have Power BI Mobile installed on your mobile device, you'll also get an in-app notification.

 TIP To view all of your data alerts defined for dashboards in My Workspace, in Power BI Portal expand the Settings menu, click Settings, and then select the Alerts tab. There you can deactivate the alert, edit it, or delete it. Currently, there isn't a way for the tenant admin to see alerts by all users.

Understanding tile details

Additional tile configuration options are available when you click the Tile Details button (button 5 in **Figure 4.1**). It brings you to the Tile Details window (see **Figure 4.5**). Since report visualizations might have Power BI-generated titles that might not be very descriptive, the Tile Details window allows you to specify a custom title and subtitle for the tile.

Figure 4.5 The Tile Details window lets you change the tile's title, subtitle, and specify a custom link.

As you know by now, clicking a tile brings you to the report where the tile was pinned from. However, if you want the user to be navigated to another web resource, you can overwrite this behavior by checking the "Set custom link" checkbox and entering the link URL. You can also specify if the link will open in a new browser tab.

 TIP A custom link could navigate the user to any URL-based resource, such as to an on-premises SSRS report. This could be useful if you want to link the tile to a more detailed report.

Understanding dashboard actions

Additional dashboard-related actions are available to you from the menu in the upper-right corner of the dashboard, as shown in **Figure 4.6**. The "Add tile" menu is yet another way to add a tile to a dashboard. It allows you to add media, such as web content, image, video, and custom streaming data (streamed datasets are covered in Chapter 11).

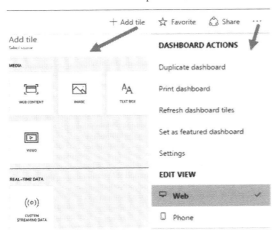

Figure 4.6 Additional actions are available from the menus in the upper-right corner of the open dashboard.

Clicking the Favorite button adds the dashboard to the Favorites section of the Power BI navigation bar. Let's skip the Share button for now. Clicking the ellipsis menu (...) opens a list of dashboard-related actions. Going quickly through the list, "Duplicate dashboard" clones the dashboard with a new name. Duplicating a dashboard could be useful if you want to retain the existing dashboard customization settings, but make layout changes, such as to add or remove tiles. "Print dashboard" prints the dashboard content exactly as it appears on the screen.

By default, Power BI updates the cache for dashboard tiles every fifteen minutes to synchronize them with data changes. You can force a tile refresh by clicking "Refresh dashboard tiles". "Set as featured dashboard" marks the dashboard as featured so that you see this dashboard when you log in to Power BI. If you don't have a dashboard, you'll be navigated to the last dashboard you visited.

Power BI supports two dashboard views. The default Web view is for large screens. However, when you view dashboards in the Power BI Mobile app on a phone, you'll notice the dashboard tiles are laid out one after another, and they're all the same size. You can switch to Phone view to create a customized view that targets the limited display capabilities of phones. When you're in Phone view, you can unpin, resize, and rearrange tiles to fit the display. Changes in Phone view don't affect the web version of the dashboard.

Understanding dashboard settings

The Settings menu brings you to the dashboard settings window (see **Figure 4.7**), which is also accessible from the Dashboard tab in the workspace content page. You can rename the dashboard, disable Q&A, and turn on tile flow. If your tenant administrator has enabled data classification (discussed in Chapter 10), you can assign a data classification category to a dashboard. For example, Maya's dashboard might show some sensitive information. Maya goes to the dashboard settings and tags the dashboard as Confidential Data. When Maya shares the dashboard with co-workers, they can see this classification next to the dashboard name.

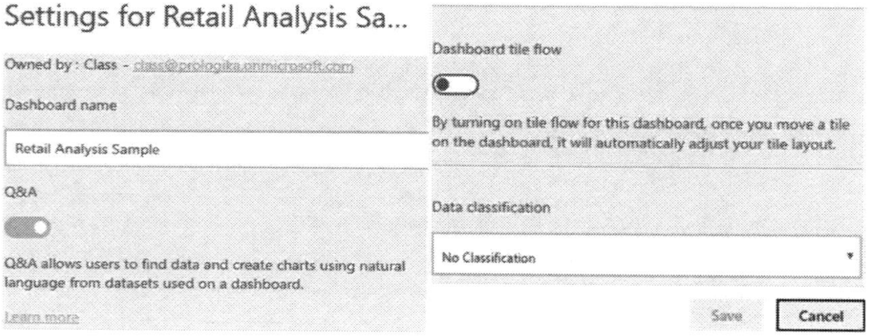

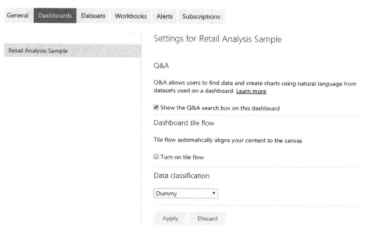

Figure 4.7 Use the dashboard Settings window to make dashboard-wide configuration changes.

You can also find the same dashboard settings in the Power BI Service Settings page (click the Settings menu in the Power BI Application Toolbar on the upper-right side of the portal and then click Settings), as shown in **Figure 4.8**.

Figure 4.8 Dashboard settings are also available in the Power BI Service Settings page.

4.1.2 Sharing Dashboards

Power BI allows you to share dashboards easily with your coworkers. This type of sharing allows other people to see the dashboards you've created, and it's only sharing option in Power BI Free. However, if the dashboard uses any Power BI Pro features, such as connecting to on-premises data sources, all recipients must have a Power BI Pro subscription. Shared dashboards and associated reports are ready-only to people you invite, and recipients can't personalize them.

> **NOTE** Besides simple dashboard sharing, Power BI Pro supports two other sharing options: workspaces and organizational content packs. Workspaces allow groups of users to contribute to shared content and organizational packs are for broader content sharing with the ability to copy and personalized the shared content. Because these options require more planning, I discuss them in Chapter 10.

Understanding sharing access

Consider using simple dashboard sharing when you need a quick and easy way to share your content with a limited number of people. It works only with dashboards; you can't use simple sharing to directly share reports and datasets. When sharing a dashboard with your coworkers, they can still click the dashboard tiles and interact with the underlying reports in Reading View (the Edit Report menu will be disabled). They can't create new reports or make changes to existing reports. When the dashboard author makes changes, the recipients can immediately see the changes. They can access all shared dashboards in the "Shared with me" section of the Power BI navigation pane (see **Figure 4.9**). They can further filter the list of shared dashboards for a specific author by clicking that person's name.

Figure 4.9 Recipients can find shared dashboards win the "Shared with me" section.

Sharing a dashboard

To share a dashboard, click the Share link in the upper-right corner of an open dashboard (see **Figure 4.6** again). This brings you to the "Share dashboard" window, as shown in **Figure 4.10**.

Figure 4.10 Use the "Share dashboard" window to enter a list of recipient emails, separated with a comma or semi-colon.

Enter the email addresses of the recipients separated by comma (,) or semi-colon (;). You can even use both. Power BI will validate the emails and inform you if they are incorrect.

> **TIP** Want to share with many users, such as with everyone in your department, but don't have Power BI Pro? If your organization uses Office 365 for email, you can share with members of a distribution group by entering in the email address associated with the distribution group. If you have Power BI Pro, consider asking IT to create a workspace instead of simple sharing. I discuss workspaces in Part 3 of this book.

Next, enter an optional message. To allow your coworkers to re-share your dashboard with others, check "Allow recipients to share your dashboard". If you change your mind later on and you want to stop sharing, click the Access tab. This tab allows you to stop sharing and/or disable re-shares for each coworker you shared the dashboard with.

By default, the "Send email notification to recipients" checkbox is checked. When you click the Share button, Power BI will send an e-mail notification with a link to your dashboard. When the recipient clicks the dashboard link and signs in to Power BI, the shared dashboard will be added to the navigation bar. You might not always want the person you share a dashboard with to go through the effort of checking their email and clicking a link just for your dashboard to show up in their workspace. If you uncheck the "Send email notification to recipients" checkbox, you can share dashboards directly to a user's My Workspace without them having to do anything. Now when you click Share, the dashboard will just show up in the other users' My Workspace with no additional steps required on their end.

Sharing with external users

You can share dashboards with people within your organization and with external organizations. For example, if Maya's email is maya@adventureworks.com, she can share with martin@adventureworks.com. If Maya wants to share with Mathew who works for Contoso (an external organization), she can do so by just typing in Mathew's business email address. Mathew will receive a notification with a link to the dashboard. When he clicks the link, he'll be asked to sign in to Power BI (or create a Power BI account if he doesn't have one).

Once Mathew has signed in, he'll see the shared dashboard in the web browser without the Power BI left navigation pane. Similar to internal sharing, Mathew can drill through tiles and access the underlying reports. All interactive features work but the reports are real-only. Maya can see all the external users who have access to this dashboard and revoke their permission from the Access tab in the "Share dashboard" window. All the external users who have access to this dashboard are marked as "Guest".

> **NOTE** Currently external sharing doesn't work with Power BI Desktop models that have Row-Level Security (RLS) and with dynamic data security in Analysis Services models. Recipients won't see any data when they access shared dashboards that have these security features.

4.2   Adding Dashboard Content

You can create as many dashboards as you want. One way to get started is to create an empty dashboard by clicking the plus sign (+) in the upper-right corner of the workspace content page and then giving the new dashboard a name. Then you can add content to the dashboard. Or, instead of creating an empty dashboard, you can tell Power BI to create a new dashboard when pinning content. You can add content to a dashboard in several ways:

- Pin content from existing Power BI reports or other dashboards
- Pin ranges from Excel Online reports or from Power BI publisher for Excel
- Pin content from Q&A reports
- Pin content from Quick Insights or Related Insights

- Pin content from Reporting Services reports
- Add tiles from media and streamed datasets

I showed in Chapter 3 how to add content from Excel ranges. I mentioned about adding tiles from media in the "Understanding Dashboard Tiles" section. I'll cover streamed datasets in Chapter 11. Next, I'll explain the rest of the options for adding content to dashboards.

4.2.1 Adding Content from Power BI Reports

The most common way to add dashboard content is to pin visualizations from existing reports or dashboards. This allows you to implement a consolidated summary view that spans multiple reports and datasets. Users can drill through the dashboard tiles to the underlying reports.

Pinning visualizations

To pin a visualization to a dashboard from an existing report or dashboard, you hover on the visualization and click the pushpin button (📌). This opens the Pin to Dashboard window, as shown in **Figure 4.11**. This window shows a preview of the selected visualization and asks if you want to add the visualization to an existing dashboard or to create a new dashboard. If you choose the "Existing dashboard", you can select the target dashboard from a drop-down list. Power BI defaults to the last dashboard that you open. If you choose a new dashboard, you need to type in the dashboard name and then Power BI will create it for you.

Figure 4.11 Use the Pin to Dashboard window to select which dashboard you want the visualization to be added to.

Think of pinning a visualization like adding a shortcut to the visualization on the dashboard. You can't make layout changes to the visualization on the dashboard once it's pinned as a dashboard tile. You must make such changes to the underlying report where the visualization is pinned from. Interactive features, such as automatic highlighting and filtering, also aren't available in dashboards. You'll need to click the visualization to drill through the underlying report in order to make changes or use interactive features.

 TIP When pinning a visualization to a dashboard, you might want to show a subset of its data. You can do this by applying a filter (or a slicer) to the report prior to pinning the visualization. If the visualization is filtered, the filter will propagate to the dashboard.

Pinning report pages

As you've seen, pinning specific visualizations allows you to quickly assemble a dashboard from various reports in a single summary view. However, the pinned visualizations "lose" their interactive features, including interactive highlighting, sorting, and tooltips. The only way to restore these features is to drill the dashboard tile through the underlying report. However, besides pinning specific report visualizations, you can pin entire report pages. This has the following advantages:

- Preserve report interactive features – When you pin a report page, the tile preserves the report layout and interactivity. You can fully interact with all the visualizations in the report tile, just as you would with the actual report.

- Reuse existing reports for dashboard content – You might have already designed your report as a dashboard. Instead of pinning individual report visualizations one by one, you can simple pin the whole report page.

- Synchronize changes – A report tile is always synchronized with the report layout. So if you need to change a visualization on the report, such as from a Table to a Chart, the dashboard tile is updated automatically. No need to delete the old tile and re-pin it.

Follow these steps to pin a report page to a dashboard:

1. Open the report in Reading View or Editing View.
2. Click "Pin Live Page" in the top menu.
3. In the "Pin to Dashboard" window, select a new or existing dashboard to pin the report page to, as you do when pinning single visualizations. Now you have the entire report page pinned and interactivity works! For example, **Figure 4.12** shows the "New Stores Analysis" page from the "Retail Analysis Sample" report that is now pinned to a dashboard.

Figure 4.12 You can pin report pages to your dashboards to preserve interactive features, reuse reports as dashboards, and synchronize layout changes.

4.2.2 Adding Content from Q&A

Another way to add dashboard content is to use natural questions (Q&A). Natural queries let data speak for itself by responding to questions entered in natural language, similar to how you search the Internet. The Q&A box appears on top of every dashboard that connects to datasets with imported data.

 NOTE As of the time of writing, natural queries are available only with datasets created by importing data and datasets with direct connections to Analysis Services Tabular models. Also, Q&A currently supports English only (as each language is so different).

Understanding natural questions

When you click the Q&A box, it suggests questions you could ask about the dashboard data (see **Figure 4.13**). If the dashboard uses content from multiple datasets, there will be suggested questions from all datasets.

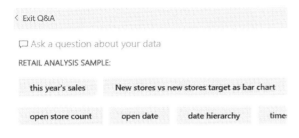

Figure 4.13 The Q&A box has predefined questions which are derived from the dataset metadata.

Of course, these suggestions are just a starting point. Power BI inferred them from the table and column names in the underlying dataset. You can add more predefined questions by following these steps:

1. In Power BI portal, click the Settings (cog) menu in the upper-right corner, and then click Settings.
2. Click the Datasets tab (see **Figure 4.8** again) and then select the desired dataset.
3. In the dataset settings, expand the "Featured Q&A Questions" section.
4. Click "Add a question" and then type a statement that uses dataset fields, such as "sales by country".

Users aren't limited to predefined questions. They can ask for something else, such as "what were this year sales", as shown in **Figure 4.14**.

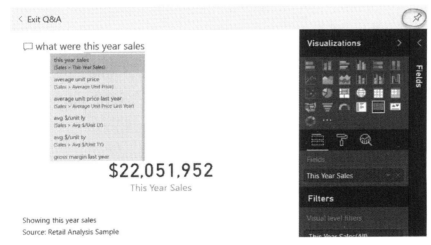

Figure 4.14 The Q&A box interprets the natural question and defaults to the best visualization.

As you type a question, Power BI shows suggestions from a drop-down list. These suggestions correspond to fields in the dataset tables. The drop-down list also shows which table and field correspond to the suggestion. Q&A shows you how it interpreted the question below the visualization. By doing so, Power BI searches the datasets used in the dashboard. So that you can understand which dataset answers your question, Power BI displays the source dataset below the visualization. **Figure 4.14** shows "Source: Retail Analysis Sample" because this question was answered from the Retail Analysis Sample dataset.

Understanding Q&A reports

Power BI attempts to use the best visualization, depending on the question and supporting data. In this case, Power BI has interpreted the question as "Showing this year sales" and decided to use a card visualization. If you continue typing so the question becomes "what were this year sales by product", it would probably switch over to a Bar Chart. However, if you don't have much luck visualizing the data the way you want, you can always use the Visualizations and Fields panes to customize the visualization, as you can do with reports.

In other words, think of Q&A as a way to jump start your data exploration by creating a report that you can customize further, such as changing the color of the lines, adding labels to the axes, or even choose another visualization type! Once you're done with the visualization, you can click the pushpin button to add the visualization to the dashboard. Once the tile is added, you can click it to drill through into the dataset. Power BI brings you the visualization you created and shows the natural question that was used.

So how smart is Q&A? Can it answer any question you might have? Q&A searches metadata, including table, column, and field names. It also has built-in smarts on how to filter, sort, aggregate, group, and display data. For example, the Internet Sales dataset you imported from Excel has columns titled "Product", "Month", "SalesAmount", and "OrderQuantity". You could ask questions about any of those entities. You could ask it to show SalesAmount by Product or by Month, and others. You should also note that Q&A is smart enough to interpret that SalesAmount is actually "sales amount", and you can use both interchangeably.

 NOTE   Data analysts creating Power BI Desktop and Excel Power Pivot data models can fine tune the model metadata for Q&A. For example, Martin can create a synonym (discussed in Chapter 8) to tell Power BI that State and Province mean the same thing.

4.2.3   Adding Content from Predictive Insights

Recall from the previous chapter that Power BI includes an interesting predictive feature called Quick Insights. When you apply Quick Insights at a dataset level it runs predictive algorithms on the entire dataset to find hidden patterns that might not be easily discernable, such as outliers and correlations. A similar feature, called Related Insights, can be applied to a dashboard tile to limit the data to whatever is shown in the tile. In both cases, Quick Insights results are available within the current session. Once you close Power BI, they are removed but you can regenerate them quickly when you need them (they only take 20 or so seconds to create).

Adding Quick Insights

To generate Quick Insights at the dataset level, go to the workspace content page, click the Datasets tab, expand the ellipsis menu (…) next to the dataset name, and then click Get Insights. Once Quick Insights are ready, the menu changes to View Insights. You can add one or more of the resulting reports you like to a dashboard by pinning the visualization (hover on the visualization and click the pin button).

Once the visualization is added to the dashboard it becomes a regular dashboard tile. However, when you click it, Power BI opens the visualization in the in-focus mode so that you can examine it in more detail and apply visual-level filters.

Adding Related Insights

To generate Related Insights for a specific dashboard tile, hover on the tile and click the ellipsis menu (…) in the upper-right corner of the tile to go to the tile properties. Then click the Related Insights (bulb) icon. This pops up the tile and shows the related insights in the Insights pane on the right. You can add one or more of the resulting visualizations you like to a dashboard by pinning the visualization (hover on the visualization in the Insights pane and click the pushpin button).

Similar to Quick Insights tiles, once a Related Insights visualization is added to the dashboard it becomes a regular dashboard tile. When you click it, Power BI opens the visualization in focus so that you can examine it in more detail and apply visual-level filters.

4.2.4 Adding Content from Reporting Services

The chances are that your organization uses SQL Server Reporting Services for distributing paginated reports. If you use Reporting Services 2016 in native mode (outside SharePoint) and your SSRS administrator has configured it for Power BI integration, you can add report items to Power BI dashboards. I'll provide general guidance to the administrator about this integration scenario and explain its limitations in Chapter 11. In this section, I'll show you how you can add content from SSRS reports to dashboards.

Pinning report items
Follow these steps to pin a report item:

1. Open the Reporting Services 2016 portal. Open a report you want to pin content from. The report's data source(s) must use stored credentials to connect to data (verify this with your report administrator).

2. Click the "Pin to Power BI Dashboard" toolbar button (see **Figure 4.15**). If you don't see this button, SSRS is not configured for Power BI integration. If you see it and click it but you get a message that the report is not configured for stored credentials, you need to change the report data sources(s) to used stored credentials instead of other authentication options. Ask your SSRS administrator for help.

Figure 4.15 If SSRS 2016 is configured for Power BI integration, you can click the "Pin to Power BI Dashboard" toolbar button to pin report items.

3. If you are not already signed in to Power BI, you'll be prompted to do so.

4. The report page background changes to black and the report items you can pin are highlighted while the items that you cannot pin, will be shaded dark. Currently, you can pin only image-generating report items, including charts, gauges, maps, and images. You can't pin tables and lists. Continuing on the list of limitations, the items must be in the report body.

5. Click the report item you want to add to your Power BI dashboard.

6. In the "Pin to Power BI Dashboard" window (see **Figure 4.16**), choose a workspace, dashboard, and update frequency (Hourly, Daily, or Weekly). The frequency interval specifies how often the dashboard tile will check for changes in the report data.

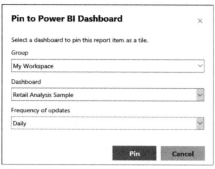

Figure 4.16 When you pin an SSRS item, you can specify the frequency of updates.

7. Click Pin. You should see a Pin Successful dialog. Click the provided link to open the Power BI dashboard.

NOTE Behind the scenes to synchronize changes, SSRS creates an individual subscription with the same frequency. You can see the subscription in the SSRS portal (expand the Settings menu and then click My Subscriptions). It's important to know that SSRS doesn't remove the subscription when you remove the tile from the dashboard. To avoid performance degradation to the report server, you must manually remove your unused subscriptions.

Understanding tile changes

Once the report item is pinned to a dashboard, its tile looks like just any other tile except that it's subtitle shows the date and time the tile was pinned or when the report was last refreshed. If you open the tile properties (click the ellipsis menu (...) in the upper-right corner of the tile), you'll see that SSRS tiles don't have all the features of regular tiles (see **Figure 4.17**). For example, Related Insights and In-Focus Mode are not available. Continuing on the list of limitations, Q&A is not available for Reporting Services tiles.

Figure 4.17 The dashboard tile with a pinned report item has a link to the original report.

If you click Tile Details, you can see that the custom link includes the report URL. Consequently, when you click the tile, you'll be navigated to the report in the SSRS portal. However, you must be on your corporate network for this to work. Otherwise, the report server won't be reachable and you'll get an error in your web browser.

4.3   Working with Dashboards

Next, you'll go through an exercise to create the Internet Sales dashboard shown in **Figure 4.18**. You'll create the first three tiles by pinning visualizations from an existing report. Then you'll use Q&A to create the fourth tile that will show a Line Chart. Finally, you'll see how you can ask natural questions from the dashboard data in Windows without navigating to Power BI by using the Cortana Digital Assistant.

Figure 4.18 The Internet Sales dashboard was created by pinning visualizations and then using a natural query.

4.3.1 Creating and Modifying Tiles

Let's start implementing the dashboard by adding content from a report. Then you'll customize the tiles and practice drilling through the content.

Pinning visualizations

Follow these steps to pin visualizations from the Internet Sales Analysis report that you created in the previous chapter:

1. In the navigation bar, click the Internet Sales Analysis report to open it in Reading View or Editing View.
2. Hover on the SalesAmount card and click the pushpin button.
3. In the Pin to Dashboard window, select the "New dashboard" option, enter *Internet Sales*, and click Pin.

   This creates a new dashboard named Internet Sales. You can find the dashboard in the workspace content page (Dashboards tab). Power BI shows a message that the visualization has been pinned to the Internet Sales dashboard.

4. In the Internet Sales Analysis report, pin also the OrderQuantity Card and the "SalesAmount and Order-Quantity by Date" Combo Chart, but this time pin them to the Internet Sales existing dashboard.
5. In the workspace content page (Dashboards tab), click the Internet Sales dashboard. Hover on the SalesAmount Card, and click the ellipsis menu (…). Click the pencil button. In the Tile Details window, enter *Sales* as a tile title.
6. Change the title for the second Card to *Orders*. Configure the Combo Chart tile to have *Sales vs Orders* as a title and *BY DATE* as a subtitle.
7. Rearrange the tiles to recreate the layout shown back in **Figure 4.18**.

Drilling through the content

You can drill through the dashboard tiles to the underlying reports to see more details and to use the interactive features.

1. Click any of the three tiles, such as the Sales card tile. This action navigates to the Internet Sales Analysis report which opens in Reading View.
2. To go back to the dashboard, click its name in the Dashboards section of the navigation bar or click your Internet browser's Back button.

3. (Optional) Pin visualizations from other reports or dashboards, such as from the Retail Analysis Sample report or dashboard.

4. (Optional) To remove a dashboard tile, click its ellipsis (…) button, and then click the X button.

4.3.2 Using Natural Queries

Another way to create dashboard content is to use natural queries. Use this option when you don't have an existing report or dashboard to start from, or when you want to add new visualizations without creating reports first.

Using Q&A to create a chart

Next, you'll use Q&A to add a Line Chart to the dashboard.

1. In the Q&A box, enter "sales amount by date". Note that Power BI interprets the question as "Showing sales amount sorted by date" and it defaults to a Line Chart, as shown in **Figure 4.19**.

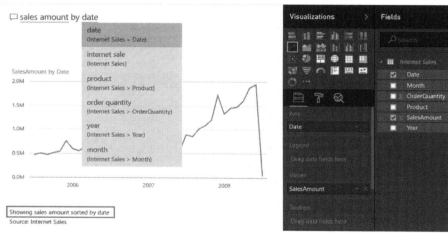

Figure 4.19 Create a Line Chart by typing a natural question.

2. You should also notice that you can use the Visualizations pane to change the visualization. Another way to use a specific visualization is to specify the visualization type in the question. Change the question to "sales amount by date as column chart". Power BI changes the visualization to a Column Chart.

3. (Optional) Practice your reporting skills to customize the visualization using the Visualizations and Fields pane. For example, use the Format tab of the Visualizations pane to turn on data labels.

4. Click the pushpin button to pin the visualization as a new dashboard tile in the Internet Sales dashboard.

Drilling through content

Similar to tiles bound to report visualizations, Power BI supports drilling through tiles that are created by Q&A:

1. Back in the dashboard, click the new tile that you created with Q&A. Power BI brings you back to the visualization as you left it (see **Figure 4.19**). In addition, Power BI shows the natural question you asked in the Q&A box.

2. (Optional) Use a different question or make some other changes, and then click the pushpin button again. This will bring you to the Pin to Dashboard window. If you choose to pin the visualization to the same dashboard, Power BI will add a new tile to the dashboard.

4.3.3 Integrating with Cortana Digital Assistant

You've seen how Q&A can help you gain insights from your data using natural queries. Wouldn't be nice to bring this experience directly to your Windows laptop without having to even open Power BI? If you use Windows 10, you're in luck because Cortana can use the same Q&A capabilities to provide data-driven answers to your questions.

Configuring Cortana for Power BI Q&A

Cortana is an intelligent personal assistant that Microsoft included in Windows phones, Xbox One, and Windows 10. Cortana can help you update your schedule and answer questions using information from Bing, such as current weather and traffic conditions, sports scores, and biographies. For more information about Cortana's features, read "What is Cortana?" at http://windows.microsoft.com/en-us/windows-10/getstarted-what-is-cortana. Follow these steps to integrate Cortana with Power BI:

1. Ensure that you have Windows 10 with Windows 10 November Update (version 1511) or higher. To check, in Windows press the hotkey Win+R to open the Run dialog, type *winver*, and then press Enter.

2. To find if Cortana is activated, type *Cortana* in the Windows search box (located in the taskbar on the left).

3. In the Search results window, click "Cortana & Search settings". In the Settings window, make sure that the first setting "Cortana can give you suggestions…" is on. If you want Cortana to respond to your voice when you say "Hey Cortana", turn on the "Hey Cortana" setting as well.

4. So that Cortana can reach out to Power BI and access your datasets, you must first add your work or school account to Windows. Click the Windows button to the left of the search box in the Windows taskbar, and then click Settings. In the Settings page, click Accounts. Scroll to the bottom of the page.

5. In the "Accounts used by other apps", check if the account you use to sign in to Power BI is listed (see **Figure 4.20**). If the account is not listed, click the "Add a Microsoft account" link, and then add the account.

Accounts used by other apps

Figure 4.20 Add your work or school account so that Cortana can integrate with Power BI.

6. By default, Power BI datasets are not enabled for Cortana. You must turn on the Cortana integration for each dataset that you want Cortana to access. Open your web browser and log in to the Power BI portal. In the Application Toolbar at the top-right corner, expand the Settings (gear) menu, and then click Settings.

7. In the Settings page, click the Datasets tab (**Figure 4.21**).

8. To enable Cortana for the "Retail Analysis Sample" dataset, click that dataset, and then check the "Enable Cortana to access this dataset" checkbox. Click Apply.

Now Cortana can access this dataset, but give it some time to discover it and learn about its data.

Getting data insights with Cortana

Once you've integrated Cortana with Power BI, getting insights is easy. As you've seen, by utilizing Power BI's Q&A data visualization capabilities, answers can range from simple numerical values ("sales for the last quarter"), charts ("gross margin by store"), maps ("this year sales by state"), and even entire reports that are specifically optimized for Cortana! Potential answers are either determined by Cortana on the fly directly from the data, or by using reports that are already created in Power BI that help answer a question.

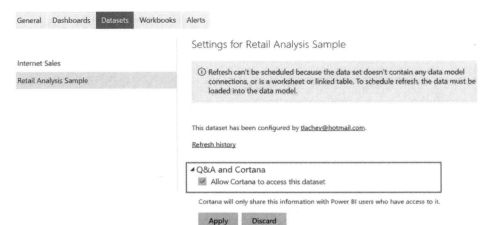

Settings for Retail Analysis Sample

ⓘ Refresh can't be scheduled because the data set doesn't contain any data model connections, or is a worksheet or linked table. To schedule refresh, the data must be loaded into the data model.

This dataset has been configured by tlachev@hotmail.com.

Refresh history

▲ Q&A and Cortana
☑ Allow Cortana to access this dataset

Cortana will only share this information with Power BI users who have access to it.

[Apply]   [Discard]

Figure 4.21 Use the Settings page to enable Cortana to access datasets.

1. In the Windows search box, enter "gross margin by store". Cortana should show some matches under the Power BI category. Alternatively, you can say "Hey Cortana" to activate Cortana and dictate your question.

2. Click the "gross margin by store – in Retail Analysis Sample" match. Cortana shows a Power BI visualization with the results (see **Figure 4.22**). Note that you can hover on a data value and get a tooltip.

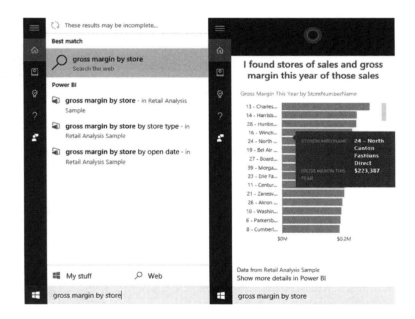

Figure 4.22 Cortana finds Power BI matches to your questions and visualizes your data.

3. (Optional) To further explore an answer, click the "Show more details in Power BI" link under the visualization. This opens your Web browser and navigates you to the Power BI Q&A page that is prepopulated with the same question.

 TIP Data analysts creating self-service models in Power BI Desktop can customize the Cortana answers by adding pages to a report that are optimized for Cortana. For more information about this feature, read the "Use Power BI Desktop to create a custom Answer Page for Cortana" topic at https://powerbi.microsoft.com/documentation/powerbi-service-cortana-desktop-entity-cards.

As you can see, Cortana opens new opportunities to enable your business, and your customers' businesses, to get things done in more helpful, proactive, and natural ways.

4.4   Summary

Consider dashboards for displaying important metrics at a glance. You can easily create dashboards by pinning existing visualizations from reports or from other dashboards. Or, you can use natural queries to let the data speak for itself by responding to questions, such as "show me sales for last year". You can drill through to the underlying reports to explore the data in more detail.

You can add content to your dashboards from predictive reports generated by Quick Insights or Related Insights. If your organization has invested in SQL Server 2016 Reporting Services, you can pin report items from your reports to Power BI dashboards. You can also pin ranges from Excel Online reports and from pivot reports created in Power BI publisher for Excel.

Besides using the Power BI portal, you can access reports and dashboards on mobile devices, as you'll learn in the next chapter.

Chapter 5

Power BI Mobile

To reach its full potential, data analytics must not only be insightful but also pervasive. Pervasive analytics is achieved by enabling information workers to access actionable data from anywhere. Mobile computing is everywhere and most organizations have empowered their employees with mobile devices, such as tablets and smartphones. Preserving this investment, Power BI Mobile enriches the user's mobile data analytics experience. Not only does it allow viewing reports and dashboards on mobile devices, but it also enables additional features that your users would appreciate. It does so by providing native mobile applications for iOS, Android, and Windows devices.

This chapter will help you understand the Power BI Mobile capabilities. Although native applications differ somewhat due to differences in device capabilities and roadmap priorities, there's a common set of features shared across all the applications. To keep things simple, I'll demonstrate most of these features with the Windows native application, except for annotations, which are not included in the Windows app but are available with Windows Ink Sketch Tool for touch-enabled devices.

5.1   Introducing Native Applications

Power BI is designed to render reports and dashboards in HTML5. As a result, you can view and edit Power BI content from most modern Internet browsers. Currently, Power BI officially supports Microsoft Edge, Microsoft Explorer 10 and 11, the Chrome desktop version, the latest version of Safari for Mac, and the latest Firefox desktop version.

To provide additional features that enrich the user's mobile experience outside the web browser, Power BI currently offers three native applications that target the most popular devices: iOS (iPad and iPhone), Android, and Windows devices. These native applications are collectively known as Power BI Mobile (https://powerbi.microsoft.com/en-us/mobile). These apps are for viewing dashboard and reports; you can't use them to make changes. That's understandable considering the limited display capabilities of mobile devices. Next, I'll introduce you briefly to each of these applications.

 TIP Your organization can use Microsoft Intune to manage devices and applications, including the Power BI Mobile apps. Microsoft Intune provides mobile device management, mobile application management, and PC management capabilities from the Microsoft Azure cloud. For example, your organization can use Microsoft Intune to configure mobile apps to require an access pin, control how data is handled by the application, and encrypt application data when the app isn't in use. For more information about Microsoft Intune, go to https://www.microsoft.com/en-us/cloud-platform/microsoft-intune.

5.1.1 Introducing the iOS Application

Microsoft released the iOS application on December 18th, 2014, and it was the first native app for Power BI. Initially, the application targeted iPad devices but was later enhanced to support iPhone, Apple Watch, and iPod Touch. Users with these devices can download the Power BI iOS application from the Apple App Store. Realizing the market realities for mobile computing, the iOS app receives the most attention and it's prioritized to be the first to get any new features.

Viewing content
The iOS application supports an intuitive, touch optimized experience for monitoring business data on iPad or iPhone. You can view your dashboards, interact with charts and tiles, explore additional data by browsing reports, and share dashboard images with your colleagues by email. **Figure 5.1** shows the Retail Sales Analysis dashboard in landscape mode on iPhone.

Figure 5.1 The iOS application targets iPad and iPhone devices.

In portrait mode, the app shows dashboard tiles positioned one after another. Remember that if this is not desired, you can go to Power BI Service and open the dashboard in Phone edit view (click the ellipsis button in the upper-right corner of the dashboard and then click Phone in the Edit View section). Then, you can optimize the dashboard layout for portrait mode. Landscape mode lets you view and navigate your dashboards in the same way as you do in the Power BI portal. To view your dashboard in landscape, open it and simply rotate your phone. The dashboard layout changes from a vertical list of tiles to a "Bird's eye" landscape view. Now you can see all of your dashboard's tiles as they are in the Power BI portal.

Understanding tile actions
While we are on the subject of viewing a dashboard with the iPhone app, let's see what happens when you click a tile. Clicking a tile opens it in in-focus mode (see **Figure 5.2**) as opposed to going to the underlying report in Power BI Service. This behavior applies to all mobile apps. The buttons at the bottom are for the three most common tile actions: create data alerts (remember that alerts are available for Single Card, Gauge, and KPI visuals only), go to the report, and annotate. The same commands are available from the ellipsis menu in the bottom-right corner.

Figure 5.2 The iOS app supports data alerts, drilling through the underlying report, and annotations.

5.1.2 Introducing the Android Application

Microsoft released the Power BI Mobile Android application in July 2015 (see **Figure 5.3**). This application is designed for Android smartphones and Android tablets (Android 5.0 operating system or later) and it's available for download from Google Play Store.

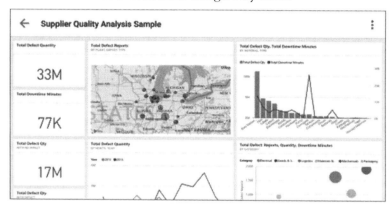

Figure 5.3 The Android application targets Android phones and tablets.

Android users can use this app to explore dashboards, invite colleagues to view data, add annotations, and share insights over email.

5.1.3 Introducing the Windows Application

In May 2015, Power BI Mobile added a native application for Windows 8.1 and Windows 10 devices, such as Surface tablets (see **Figure 5.4**). Microsoft has enhanced the app for Windows 10 phones. You can download the app from Windows Store (search for *Microsoft Power BI*). Your Windows device needs to be running Windows 10 and Microsoft recommends at least 2 GB RAM.

For the most part, the Windows app has identical features as the other Power BI Mobile apps. One feature that was originally included but Microsoft later removed was annotations. However, the Windows Ink Sketch Tool (only available in touch-enabled devices) has similar features, including taking a snapshot, annotating and sharing. For more information about how to use the Sketch Tool, refer to "Windows Ink: How to use Screen Sketch" article at http://windowscentral.com/windows-ink-how-use-screen-sketch.

Figure 5.4 The Windows application targets Windows 10 devices and phones.

5.2 Viewing Content

Power BI Mobile provides simple and intuitive interface for viewing reports and dashboards. As it stands, Power BI Mobile doesn't allow users to edit the published content. This shouldn't be viewed as a limitation because mobile display capabilities are limited, and mobile users would be primarily interested in viewing content. Next, you'll practice viewing the BI content you created in the previous two chapters using the Windows native app. As a prerequisite, install the Windows native app either on your Windows laptop or on a Windows device, such as a Windows Surface or Windows 10 phone. For the best experience, I recommend you use a touch-enabled device, such as Microsoft Surface.

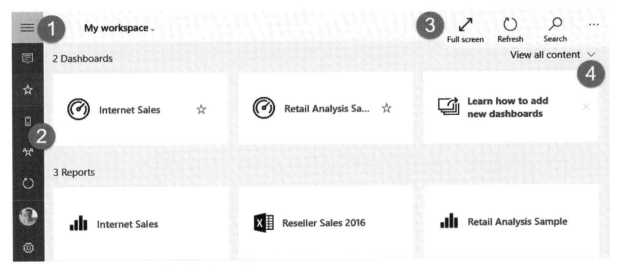

Figure 5.5 The home page of the Windows native app.

5.2.1 Getting Started with Power BI Mobile

When you open the Windows native app and sign in to Power BI, you'll be presented with the home page shown in **Figure 5.5**. Let's take a moment to get familiar with the home page.

Understanding menus

The global navigation button (1) is in the top-left corner. When you click it, it drops a menu. Think of the drop-down menu as an expanded version of the navigation bar (2) that shows the name for each link. Let's go quickly through the links in the navigation bar starting from the top:

- Notifications – Shows the notifications from the Power BI Service Notification Center.

- Favorites – Shows dashboards that you marked as favorites.

- Reporting Services – If your organization has integrated Reporting Services with Power BI, this link allows you to navigate the report catalog, and to view mobile reports and KPIs

- Workspaces – Shows the workspaces you are a member of so that you can select a workspace to work with. My Workspace is the default workspace.

- Sync – Synchronizes (refreshes) the app content with Power BI Service. Suppose Maya wants to add a new dashboard. Because she can't do that in the mobile app (it's limited to viewing content only), she needs to create the dashboard in Power BI Service. If the app is open on her iPhone, she clicks the Sync button for her new dashboard to appear so she doesn't have to close and reopen the app or log out and log in.

- Settings -- Gives you access to certain settings, such as to see the version of the Windows app, to send usage data to Microsoft, to view and change your Power BI and Reporting Services account settings, to check what's new in Power BI Mobile, and to send feedback to Microsoft.

> **TIP** Looking for an easy way to demonstrate Power BI content in mobile apps? Try the samples. In the Settings page, go to the Accounts tab, right-click on your Power BI account, and then click "View samples". Currently, there are six dashboards available for VP Sales, Director of Operations, Customer Care, Director of Marketing, CFO, and HR Manager. And, if you connect your mobile app to your SQL Server 2016 Reporting Services, you can get Reporting Services samples as well.

- Scanner – This link shows only on mobile phones. It allows you to scan a Power BI QR code so that you can navigate to the report tagged with that code.

Application toolbar

The application toolbar (3) includes buttons for common tasks. Click the "Full screen" button to open the app in full screen without the navigation bar. The Refresh button fulfills the same role as the Sync link in the navigation bar. Use the Search button to view most recent content you've visited and to search for content, such as type "sales" to see all sales-related reports and dashboards. Matches are organized in dashboards, reports, and groups (workspaces) sections.

Additional buttons are added to the menu depending on what content is shown. For example, if a dashboard is shown, Favorite and Pushpin buttons are added to let you favorite or pin the dashboard to the Windows Start menu as a live tile (so you can quickly navigate to the dashboard).

The "View all content" menu

This drop-down menu allows you to filter the workspace content. It has two options: Dashboards and Reports. If you wonder why there is no option for datasets, recall that the mobile app is for viewing content only. Because you can't create new reports, it doesn't give you access to datasets.

5.2.2 Viewing Dashboards

Mobile users will primarily use Power BI Mobile to view dashboards that they've created or that are shared with them. Let's see what options are available for viewing dashboards.

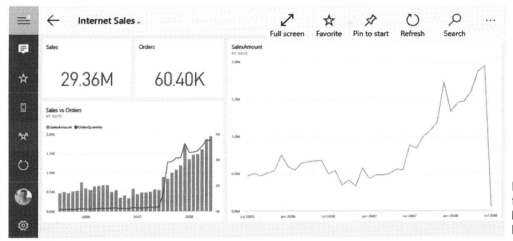

Figure 5.6 The Internet Sales dashboard open in Power BI Mobile.

Viewing dashboard tiles

This exercise uses the Internet Sales dashboard that you created in the previous chapter.

1. On your Windows device, open the Microsoft Power BI application.
2. In the Home page, click the Internet Sales dashboard to open it (see **Figure 5.6**). Power BI Mobile renders the dashboard content as it appears in the Power BI portal. However, the Q&A box is missing because Power BI Mobile doesn't currently support natural queries.
3. Click the Sales tile. As you would recall, clicking a tile in Power BI Portal drills the tile through the underlying visualization (which could originate from several sources, including pinning a visual from a report or created via Q&A). However, instead of drilling through, Power BI Mobile pops the tile out so that you can examine the tile data (see **Figure 5.7**).

Figure 5.7 Clicking a tile opens the tile in focus mode.

Microsoft refers to this as "in-focus" mode. Because the display of mobile devices is limited, the in-focus mode makes it easier to view and explore the tile data. That's why this is the default action when you click a tile.

Understanding tile actions

When a tile is in focus, users can take several actions from the top menu. The "Sales" drop-down menu in the top-left corner tells you that this is the Sales tile. The back arrow button lets you navigate backward to the content. For example, if you click it, the mobile app will navigate you to the Internet Sales dashboard. If you click again, you'll be in My Workspace if the Internet Sales dashboard is located in this workspace.

I've already discussed the purpose of the "Full screen" and "Pin to Start" menus. The "Manage alerts" icon allows you to create and manage alerts for Single Card, Gauge, and KPIs tiles. It has the identical settings as in Power BI Service to allow mobile users to create alerts while they are on the go. The "Open Report" icon navigates you to the underlying report (if the tile was pinned from a Power BI report). And the Share icon is for sending a screenshot of the tile to someone else.

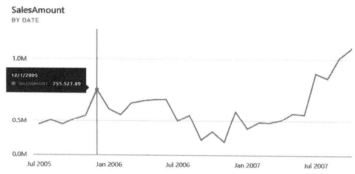

Figure 5.8 You can drag the vertical bar to see the precise chart value.

Examining the data

It might be challenging to understand the precise values of a busy chart on a mobile device. However, Power BI Mobile has a useful feature that you might find helpful.

1. Navigate back to the Internet Sales dashboard.
2. In the line chart, drag the vertical bar to intersect the chart line for Jan 2006, as shown in **Figure 5.8**.

Notice that Power BI Mobile shows the precise value of the sales amount at the intersection. If you have a Scatter Chart (the Retail Analysis Sample dashboard has a Scatter Chart), you can pop out a chart and select a bubble by positioning the intersection of a vertical line and a horizontal line. This allows you to see the values of the fields placed in the X Axis, Y Axis, and Size areas of the Scatter visualization. And for a Pie Chart, you can spin the chart to position the slices so that you can get the exact values.

5.2.3   Viewing Reports

As you've seen, Power BI Mobile makes it easy for business users to view dashboards on the go. You can also view reports. As I mentioned, Power BI Mobile doesn't allow you to edit reports; you can only open and interact with them in Reading View.

Viewing Power BI reports

Let's open the Internet Sales Analysis report in Power BI Mobile:

1. Navigate to the Home page. You can do this by clicking the Back button in the top-left area of the screen or by clicking the Home menu in the top app command bar.
2. Under the Reports section, click the Internet Sales Analysis report to open it. Power BI Mobile opens the report in Reading View, as shown in **Figure 5.9**.

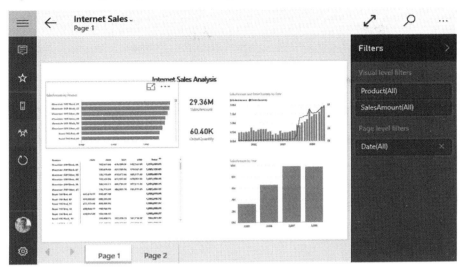

Figure 5.9 Power BI Mobile opens reports in Reading View but supports interactive features.

Notice that you can't switch to Editing View to change the report. You shouldn't view this as a limitation because the small display size of mobile devices would probably make reporting editing difficult anyway. Although you can't change the report layout, you can interact with the report:

3. Hover over the Bar Chart and note that an ellipsis "..." menu appears in the top-right corner. Recall that this menu allows you to sort and export the chart data.
4. Click any bar in the Bar Chart or a column in the Column Chart. Notice that automatic highlighting works and you can see the contribution of the selected value to the data shown in the other visualizations.
5. Click a column header in the Matrix visualization and note that every click toggles the column sort order.
6. The Filters pane let you change or remove existing report filters. However, you can't add new filters and the Fields pane is missing. To add filters or make any other report changes, you need to go to Power BI Service, make changes, and save the report.

Viewing Excel reports
Remember that Power BI allows you connect existing Excel reports. Let's see what happens when you open an Excel report.

1. Click the Workspaces icon in the navigation bar and then click My Workspace.
2. In the Reports section of the workspace content page, click the "Reseller Sales 2016" report.

Notice that the report won't open inside the app. Instead, the app asks you to sign in to Power BI Service. That's because Excel reports are rendered in Excel Online, which is a cloud service and it's not available in the mobile app. Once you sign in, you'll be navigated to Power BI portal and the Excel report will open.

Viewing Reporting Services reports
If your organization uses SQL Server 2016 Reporting Services, you can view content from a report server running in native mode. Currently, you can view two types of content:

- KPIs – Starting with SQL Server 2016 Reporting Services, you can define key performance indicators (KPIs) directly in a SSRS folder (without creating a report). These KPIs will show up in the Power BI mobile apps.

- Mobile reports – A new report type in SQL Server 2016 Reporting Services, mobile reports are optimized for mobile devices. When you navigate to a report folder that has mobile reports, you'll see thumbnail images of the reports. Clicking a report opens it inside the mobile app.

NOTE Currently, traditional (paginated) Reporting Services reports won't show up in the mobile apps. You can navigate the report catalog but you can't see them. Only mobile reports and KPIs are supported by Power BI Mobile.

Before you can access SSRS content, you need to register your report server:

1. In the navigation bar, click Settings. On the Accounts tab click "Connect to server".
2. Fill in the server address, such as http://<servernname/reports.
3. (Optional) Under "Advanced options", give the server a user-friendly name, such as Reporting Services. This is the name you'll see when you click the global navigation button (the yellow home button in the top-left corner).
4. Click Connect.

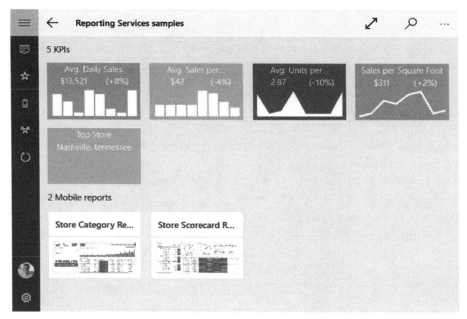

Figure 5.10 Access SSRS KPIs and mobile reports in your mobile app.

Once you are connected, you can view the KPIs and mobile reports that you're authorized to access.

5. In the navigation bar, tap your report server.
6. Navigate to the folder provided to you by your administrator. If the folder has KPIs or mobile reports, they'll show up (see **Figure 5.10**).
7. Tap a KPI to pop it up in focus mode so you can examine it in more detail. Tap a mobile report to open it and interact with it.

TIP If you mark KPIs and mobile reports as favorites on your Reporting Services portal, they'll appear in the Power BI Favorites folder and you can access them by clicking Favorites in the navigation bar.

5.3 Sharing and Collaboration

Power BI Mobile goes beyond just content viewing. It lets mobile workers share BI content and collaborate while on the go. Specifically, they can share dashboards with other users and annotate dashboard tiles and reports. Let's examine these two features in more detail.

5.3.1 Sharing Dashboards

Remember from the previous chapter that Power BI Service allows you to share dashboards with your colleagues by sending email invitations. You can do the same with Power BI Mobile. Both options are interchangeable. For example, if you initiate dashboard sharing in Power BI Service, you can see the sharing settings in Power BI Mobile, and vice versa. Let's share a dashboard:

1. Back to the Home page, click the Internet Sales dashboard to open it.

2. Click the Invite button 🕭 in the top-right corner.

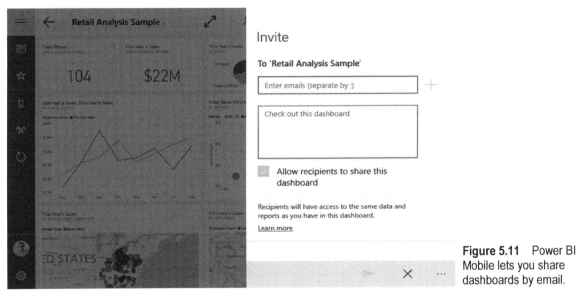

Figure 5.11 Power BI Mobile lets you share dashboards by email.

This action opens the Invite flyout window (see **Figure 5.11**). You need to enter the recipient email addresses, type in an optional message, and decide if you want them to be able to re-share the dashboards.

5.3.2 Annotating Tiles and Reports

While you're viewing the dashboard content, you might want to comment on some data and then share the comment with your coworkers. For example, after sharing her dashboard with a manager, Maya might ask the manager to formally approve that the data is correct. Her manager can open the dashboard on his mobile device, sign the dashboard, and then send a screenshot to Maya. Annotations allow you to enter text, simple graphics, or a smiley, and then share a screenshot of the annotated content. Annotations aren't saved in the Power BI content. Once you exit the annotation mode, all annotations are lost.

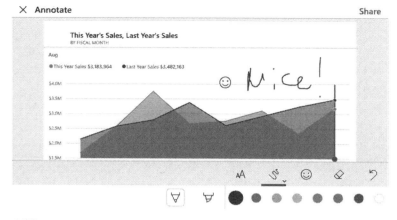

Figure 5.12   You can annotate a tile by typing text, drawing lines, or paste stamps.

Adding annotations

As I mentioned, the Windows app doesn't currently support annotations so I'll demonstrate them with the iPhone app. You can annotate dashboard tiles, entire reports, or specific report visualizations. Let's annotate a dashboard tile:

1. With the Retail Analysis Sample dashboard open, click the "This Year's Sales, Last Year's Sales" surface chart to open it in focus mode.
2. Click the Annotate (pencil) button in the bottom-right corner. This switches the tile to annotation mode.
3. Click the Smiley button and then click the first smiley icon to add a smiley to the tile. Position the smiley as shown in **Figure 5.12**.
4. Click the curve icon to the right of the smiley icon, and type some text on the tile. If you make a mistake, you can click the Undo button in the bottom-right corner. The eraser button discards all your annotations.

Figure 5.13   You can share screenshots of your annotations with your coworkers by email.

Sharing screenshots

You can send screenshots to your colleagues by a text message or email. Let's send a screenshot of your annotations:

1. In annotation mode, click the Share link in the top right corner of the screen.
2. A flyout window asks you if you want to choose a delivery mechanism. Click Mail or whatever application you use as email client.

3. Power BI Mobile captures a screenshot of the annotated item (tile, report, or specific report visualization), and attaches it to the email (see **Figure 5.13**). It also includes a link to the item. Enter the recipient addresses separated by a semi-colon (;) and click the Send button.

If the recipients have rights to view the annotated item, such as when you've already shared the dashboard with them or you share the same workspace, they can click the link to go straight to the item.

5.4 Summary

Power BI Mobile is a collective name of three native applications for iOS, Android, and Windows devices. Power BI Mobile enriches the data analysis experience of mobile workers. Besides dashboard and report viewing, it allows you to share dashboards and annotate dashboard tiles. You can also create data alerts to get a notification when data exceeds specific thresholds values that you specify.

This chapter concludes our Power BI tour for business users. Power BI has much more to offer than what you've seen so far, but it requires more knowledge. In the next part of the book, you'll see how data analysts (also referred to as power users) can create sophisticated data models to address more complicated data analytics needs.

PART

Power BI for Data Analysts

I f you consider yourself a data analyst or power user, welcome! This part of the book teaches you how to implement self-service models with Power BI Desktop. If you're new to self-service data analytics, I recommend you review the "Introducing Self-service Business Intelligence" section in chapter 2 beforehand.

As you've seen in the first part of the book, Power BI lets business users perform rudimentary data analysis without requiring data models. However, once the self-service BI path goes beyond content packs and single datasets, you'll need a data model. Although you can still implement models with Excel, Power BI Desktop is the Power BI premium modeling tool for self-service BI. Packed with features, Power BI Desktop is a free tool that you can download and start using immediately to gain insights from your data.

If you have experience with Excel data modeling, you'll find that Power BI Desktop combines the best of Power Pivot, Power Query, and Power View in a simplified and standalone desktop tool. In this part of the book, I'll introduce you to Power BI Desktop and fundamental data modeling concepts. Next, you'll learn how to connect to data from a variety of data sources, ranging from relational databases, text files, Excel files, and cloud services.

Data quality is a big issue with many organizations and chances are that your data is no exception. Fortunately, Power BI Desktop has features that allow you to cleanse and transform dirty data before it enters your model. so you won't have to rely on someone else to clean the data for you. A self-service data model is rarely complete without important business metrics. Thanks to its Data Analysis Expressions (DAX) language, Power BI Desktop lets you implement sophisticated calculations using Excel-like formulas. Then you can explore your data by creating interactive reports as you can do with Power BI Service.

If you're already a Power Pivot user, you'll undoubtedly breeze through the content of this part of the book (this will be a review with some important new changes). As you'll find out, you can almost seamlessly transfer your Excel data modeling knowledge to Power BI Desktop. Again, that's because the underlying technology is the same. However, with Power BI Desktop, you'll always have the latest Power BI features because Microsoft updates it every month.

Also, know that Power BI Desktop and Analysis Services Tabular share the same foundation – the in-memory xVelocity data engine. Therefore, a nice bonus awaits you ahead. While you're learning Power BI Desktop, you're also learning Analysis Services Tabular. So, if one day you decide to upgrade your self-service model from Power BI Desktop to a scalable organizational model powered by Analysis Services Tabular, you'll find that you already have most of the knowledge. You're now a BI pro!

To practice what you'll learn, the book includes plenty of exercises that will walk you through the steps for implementing a self-service model for analyzing sales data.

Chapter 6

Data Modeling Fundamentals

As a first step to building a data model, you need to acquire the data that you'll analyze and report on. Power BI Desktop makes it easy to access data from a variety of data sources, ranging from relational databases, such as a SQL Server database, to text files, such as a comma-delimited file extracted from a mainframe system. The most common way of bringing data into Power BI Desktop is by importing it from relational databases. When the data isn't in a database, Power BI Desktop supports other data acquisition methods, including text files, cubes, data feeds, and much more. And for some fast databases, Power BI Desktop allows you to connect directly to the data source without importing the data.

In this chapter, you'll learn the fundamentals of self-service data modeling with Power BI Desktop. To put your knowledge in practice, you'll implement a raw data model for analyzing the Adventure Works reseller sales. You'll exercise a variety of basic data import options to load data from the Adventure Works data warehouse, a cube, an Excel workbook, a comma-delimited file, and even from a Reporting Services report. You'll find the resulting Adventure Works model in the \Source\ch06 folder.

6.1   Understanding Data Models

When you work with Power BI Desktop, you create a self-service data model with the data you need to analyze. As a first step, you need to obtain the data. The primary data acquisition option with Power BI Desktop is importing it. This option allows you to load and mash up data from different data sources into a consolidated data model. For example, Martin could import some CRM data from Salesforce, finance data from Excel reports, and sales data from the corporate data warehouse. Once Martin relates all of this data into a single model, he can then create a report that combines all of these three business areas. As you might realize, Power BI Desktop gives you tremendous power and flexibility for creating self-service data models!

Power BI Desktop allows you to import data from a variety of data sources with a few mouse clicks. While getting data is easy, relating data in your model requires some planning on your side in order to avoid inconsistent or even incorrect results. For example, you might have imported a Customer table and a Sales table, but if there isn't a way to relate the data in these tables, you'll get the same sales amount repeated for each customer. Therefore, before you click the Get Data button, you should have some basic understanding about the Power BI data modeling requirements and limitations. So let's start by learning some important fundamentals of data modeling. Among other things, they will help you understand why having a single monolithic dataset is not always the best approach and why you should always have a date table.

6.1.1 Understanding Schemas

I previously wrote that Power BI Desktop imports data in tables, similar to how Excel allows you to organize data into Excel tables. Each table consists of columns, also referred to as *fields* or *attributes*. If all the data is provided to you as just one table, then you could congratulate yourself and skip this section altogether. In fact, as you've seen in Part 1 of this book, you can skip Power BI Desktop and modeling because you can analyze a single dataset directly with Power BI Service. Chances are, however, that you might need to import multiple tables from the same or different data sources. This requires learning some basic database and schema concepts. The term "schema" here is used to describe the table definitions and how tables relate to each other. I'll keep the discussion light on purpose to get you started with data modeling as fast as possible. I'll revisit table relationships in the next chapter.

NOTE Importing all data as a single table might not require modeling but it isn't a best practice. Suppose you initially wanted to analyze reseller sales and you've imported a single dataset with columns such as Reseller, Sales Territory, and so on. Then you decide to extend the model with direct sales to consumers to consolidate reporting that spans now two business areas. Now you have a problem. Because you merged business dimensions into the reseller sales dataset, you won't be able to slice and dice the two datasets by the same lookup tables (Reseller, Sales Territory, Date, and others). In addition, a large table might strain your computer resources as it'll require more time to import and more memory to store the data. At the same time, a fully normalized schema, such as modeling a product entity with Product, Subcategory, and Category tables, is also not desirable because you'll end up with many tables and the model might become difficult to understand and navigate. When modeling your data, it's important to find a good balance between business requirements and normalization, and that balance is the star schema.

Understanding star schemas

For a lack of better terms, I'll use the dimensional modeling terminology to illustrate the star schema (for more information about star schemas, see 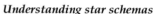http://en.wikipedia.org/wiki/Star_schema). **Figure 6.1** shows two schema types. The left diagram illustrates a star schema, where the ResellerSales table is in the center. This table stores the history of the Adventure Works reseller sales, and each row represents the most atomic information about the sale transaction. This could be a line item in the sales order that includes the order quantity, sales amount, tax amount, discount, and other numeric fields.

Dimensional modeling refers to these tables as *fact tables*. As you can imagine, the ResellerSales table can be very long if it keeps several years of sales data. Don't be alarmed about the dataset size though. Thanks to the state-of-the art underlying storage technology, your data model can still import and store millions of rows!

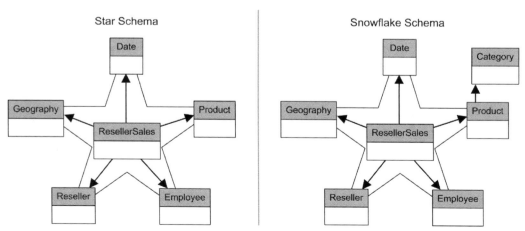

Figure 6.1   Power BI models support both star and snowflake schema types.

The ResellerSales table is related to other tables, called *lookup* or *dimension* tables. These tables provide contextual information to each row stored in the ResellerSales table. For example, the Date table might include date-related fields, such as Date, Quarter, and Year columns, to allow you to aggregate data at day, quarter, and year levels, respectively. The Product table might include ProductName, Color, and Size fields, and so on.

The reason why your data model should have these fields in separate lookup tables, is that, for the most part, their content doesn't need a historical record. For example, if the product name changes, this probably would be an in-place change. By contrast, if you were to continue adding columns to the ResellerSales table, you might end up with performance and maintenance issues. If you need to make a change, you might have to update millions of rows of data as opposed to updating a single row. Similarly, if you were to add a new column to the Date table, such as FiscalYear, you'll have to update all the rows in the ResellerSales table.

Are you limited to only one fact table with Power BI? Absolutely not! For example, you can add an InternetSales fact table that stores direct sales to individuals. In the case of multiple fact tables, you should model the fact tables to share some common lookup tables so that you could match and consolidate data for cross-reporting purposes, such as to show reseller and Internet sales side by side and grouped by year and product. This is another reason to avoid a single monolithic dataset and to have logically related fields in separate tables (if you have this option). Don't worry if this isn't immediately clear. Designing a model that accurately represents business requirements is difficult even for BI pros but it gets easier with practice.

NOTE Another common issue that I witness with novice users is creating a separate dataset for each report, e.g. one dataset for a report showing reseller sales and another dataset for a report showing direct sales. Similar to the "single dataset" issue I discussed above, this design will lead to data duplication and inability to produce consolidated reports that span multiple areas. Even worse would be to embed calculations in the dataset, such as calculating Profit or Year-to-Date in a SQL view that is used to source the data. Similar to the issue with defining calculations in a report, this approach will surely lead to redundant calculations or calculations that produce different results from one report to another.

Understanding snowflake schemas

A *snowflake* schema is where some lookup tables relate to other lookup tables, but not directly to the fact table. Going back to **Figure 6.1**, you can see that for whatever reason, the product categories are kept in a Category table that relates to the Product table and not directly to the ResellerSales table. One strong motivation for snowflaking is that you might have another fact table, such as SalesQuota, that stores data not at a product level but at a category level. If you keep categories in their own Category table, this design would allow you to join the Category lookup table to the SalesQuota table, and you'll still be able to have a report that shows aggregated sales and quota values grouped by category.

Power BI supports snowflake schemas just fine. However, if you have a choice, you should minimize snowflaking when it's not needed. This is because snowflaking increases the number of tables in the model, making it more difficult for other users to understand your model. If you import data from a database with a normalized schema, you can minimize snowflaking by merging snowflaked tables. For example, you can use a SQL query that joins the Product and Category tables. However, if you import text files, you won't have that option because you can't use SQL. However, when you use Power BI Desktop, you can still handle denormalization tasks in the Query Editor, or by adding calculated columns that use DAX expressions to accomplish the same goal, such as by adding a column to the Product table to look up the product category from the Category table. Then you can hide the Category table.

To recap this schema discussion, you can view the star schema as the opposite of its snowflake counterpart. While the snowflake schema embraces normalization as the preferred designed technique to reduce data duplication, the star schema favors denormalization or data entities and reducing the overall number of tables, although this process results in data duplication (a category is repeated for each product that has the same category). Demormalization (star schemas) and BI go hand in hand. That's because star schemas reduce the number of tables and required joins. This makes your model faster and more intuitive.

Understanding date tables

Even if the data is given to you as a single dataset, you should strongly consider having a separate date table. A date table stores a range of dates that you need for data analysis. A date table typically includes additional columns for flexible time exploration, such as Quarter, Year, Fiscal Quarter, Fiscal Year, Holiday Flag, and so on. In addition, DAX time calculations, such as TOTALYTD, TOTALQTD, and so on, require a separate date table. A date table must meet several requirements:

- It must have a column of a Date data type.
- It must also have a day granularity, where each row in the table represents a calendar day.
- It must contain a consecutive range of dates you need for analysis, such as starting from the first day with data to a few years in the future. More importantly, a date table can't have gaps (it can't skip days). If it has gaps, DAX time calculations will produce wrong results.

There are many ways to create a date table. You can import it from your corporate data warehouse, if you have one. You can maintain it in an Excel file and import it from there. You can import it from the DateStream feed, as I'll show you in section 6.2.7. You can even generate it in the Query Editor using custom code written in the query language (referred to as "M"), as I'll show you in the next chapter. And you can have more than one date table in your model. This could be useful if you want to aggregate the same fact table by multiple dates, such as order date, ship date, and due date.

6.1.2 Introducing Relationships

Once you import multiple tables, you need a way to relate them. If two tables aren't related, your model won't aggregate data correctly when you use both tables on a report. To understand how to relate tables, you need to learn about Power BI relationships.

Understanding relationships

In order to relate two tables, there must be schema and data commonalities between the two tables. This isn't much different than joins in relational databases, such as Microsoft Access or SQL Server. For example, you won't be able to analyze sales by product if there isn't a common column between the ResellerSales and Date tables that ties a date to a sale (see **Figure 6.2**).

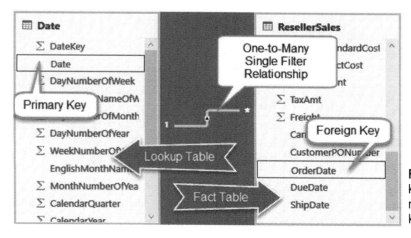

Figure 6.2 The Date column (primary key) in the Date table is related to the matching OrderDate column (foreign key) in the ResellerSales table.

If the underlying data source has relationships (referential integrity constraints) defined, Power BI Desktop will detect and carry them to the model (this is controlled by the "Import relationships from data sources" setting in File ⇨ Options and setting ⇨ Options ⇨ Data Load under the Current File session). If not,

Power BI is capable of auto-detecting relationships using internal rules (this is controlled by the "Autodetect new relationships after data is loaded" setting in the same section). Of course, you can also create relationships manually. It's important to understand that your data model is layered on top of the original data. No model changes affect the original data source and its design. You only need rights to read from the data source so that you can import the data you need.

Understanding keys

Common columns in each pair of tables are called *keys*. A *primary key* is a column that uniquely identifies each row in a table. A primary key column can't have duplicate values. For example, the Date column uniquely identifies each row in the Date table and no other row has the same value. An employee identifier or an e-mail address can be used as a primary key in an Employee table. To join Date to ResellerSales, in the ResellerSales table, you must have a matching column, which is called a *foreign key*. For example, the OrderDate column in the ResellerSales table is a foreign key.

A matching column means a column in the fact table that has matching values in the lookup table. The column names of the primary key and foreign key don't have to be the same (values are important). For example, if the ResellerSales table has a sale recorded on 1/1/2015, there should be a row in the Date table with date in the Date column of 1/1/2016. If there isn't, the data model won't show an error, but all the sales that don't have matching dates in the Data table would appear under an unknown (blank) value in a report that groups ResellerSales data by some column in the Date table.

Typically, a fact table has several foreign keys, so it can be related to different lookup tables. For performance reasons, you should use shorter data types, such as integers or dates. For example, the Date column could be a column of a Date data type. Or if you're importing from a data warehouse database, it might have an Integer data type, with values such as 20110101 for January 1st, 2011, and 20110102 for January 2nd, 2011, and so on.

 NOTE Relationships from fact tables to the same lookup table don't have to use the same column. For example, ResellerSales can join Date on the Date column but InternetSales might join it on the DateKey column, for example in the case where there isn't a column of a Date data type in InternetSales. As long as a column uniquely identifies each row, the lookup table can have different "primary key" columns.

About relationship cardinality

Note back in in **Figure 6.2**, the number 1 is shown on the left side of the relationship towards the Date table and an asterisk (*) is shown next to the Reseller Sales table. This denotes a one-to-many cardinality. To understand this better, consider that one row (one date) in the Date table can have zero, one, or many recorded sales in ResellerSales, and one product in the Product table corresponds to one or many sales in ResellerSales, and so on. The important word here is "many".

Although not a common cardinality, Power BI also supports a one-to-one relationship type. For example, you might have Employee and SalesPerson tables in a snowflake schema, where a sales person is a type of an employee and each sales person relates to a single employee. By specifying a one-to-one relationship between Employee and SalesPerson, you're telling Power BI to check the data cardinality and show an error if the one-to-many relationship is detected on data refresh. A one-to-one relationship also brings additional simplifications when working with DAX calculations, such as to let you interchangeably use the DAX RELATED and RELATEDTABLE functions.

About relationship cross filter direction

Note also that in **Figure 6.2**, there's an arrow indicator pointing toward the ResellerSales table. This indicates that this relationship has a single cross filtering direction between the Date and Reseller tables. In other words, the ResellerSales table can be analyzed using the Date table, but not the other way around. For example, you can have a report that groups sales by any of the fields of the Date table. However, you can't group dates by a field in the ResellerSales table, which is probably meaningless anyway.

Now suppose you want to know how many times a product is sold by date. You might be able to find the answer by counting on a ProductKey field in the ResellerSales table without involving the Product table at all. However, what if you need to find how many times a particular product model (the ModelName column in the Product table) was sold on a given date? To avoid adding this column to the ResellerSales table, you'd want to count on the ModelName field in the Product table. However, this will cause the relationship direction to reverse. First, you need to follow the Date ⇨ ResellerSales relationship, which is one-to-many (no problems here), but then to get to the Product table, we need to traverse the many-to-one ResellerSales ⇨ Product relationship. Although Power BI Desktop won't show any error, the report will return meaningless results.

This is where a cross filtering direction set to Both can help. This cross filtering type is commonly referred to as a many-to-many relationship (many products can be sold on a single day and a single product can be sold on many days). It has a double arrow indicator (see **Figure 6.3**).

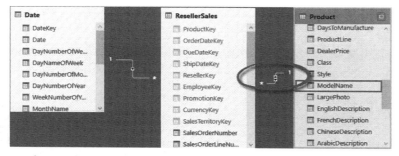

Figure 6.3 The relationship between the ResellerSales and Product table has a cross filtering direction set to Both.

Readers with prior experience in Power Pivot for Excel and Analysis Services Tabular (prior to SQL Server 2016) might recall that these tools didn't support declarative many-to-many relationships. This scenario required custom calculations so that aggregations are computed properly. Interestingly, the many-to-many relationship type (cross filtering set to both) is the default cross filtering type for new relationships in Power BI Desktop.

NOTE At this point, you might be concerned about the performance overhead associated with bidirectional cross filtering. Rest assured that there isn't any additional performance overhead, so I welcome the decision to set relationship cross filtering to Both by default. There are scenarios, such as relationships to a Date table and closed-looped relationships, which require Single cross filtering, as you'll see in Chapter 7. To learn more about bidirectional cross filtering, read the related whitepaper by Kasper De Jonge at http://bit.ly/2eZUQ2Z.

That's all you need to know about data modeling for now. Next, let's see what options you have for connecting to your data.

6.1.3 Understanding Data Connectivity

In Chapter 2, I mentioned that Power BI supports two options for accessing data: data import and live connections, but this was a simplified statement. Technically, Power BI Service and Power BI Desktop support three options to connect to your data. Let me explain them to you now, because it's important to understand how they differ and when to use each one (if you have a choice). **Figure 6.4** should help you understand their differences.

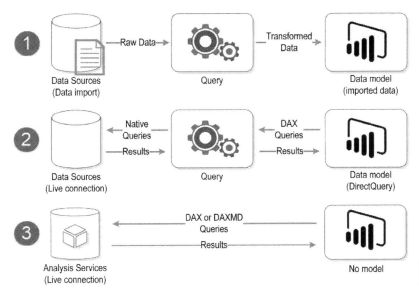

Figure 6.4 Power BI supports three connectivity options.

Importing data

Unless you connect to a single data source that supports direct connectivity, you'll need to import data. This is option 1 in the **Figure 6.4** diagram. What if you need to relate data from a data source that supports direct connections to some other data coming from a data source that doesn't support direct access? You'd still need to import the data and you need to do so from *both* data sources. As it stands, Power BI only supports a live connection to a single data source, and you can't mix "live" and imported data.

When Power BI imports the data, it stores the data in the xVelocity in-memory data engine. The in-memory engine is hosted in an out-of-process Analysis Services instance that is distributed with Power BI Desktop. So that you can pack millions of rows, data is stored in a highly compressed format and loaded in memory when you analyze the data. When you import data, you can transform and clean it before it's loaded into the model. Power BI Desktop always connects to raw data that you import via a connectivity component called a "query". Think of a query as a layer between the raw data and your data model. Yes, the Power BI Desktop query is a successor of Excel Power Query, which you might be familiar with. However, unlike Excel, queries aren't optional when you import data in Power BI Desktop.

NOTE   Data analysts experienced with Excel data modelling might know that Excel has at least three ways to import data into a data model – Excel native import, Power Pivot Table Import Wizard, and Power Query. There hasn't been a way in Excel to switch easily from one import option to another without recreating your table, such as from Table Import Wizard to Power Query, in order to use the Power Query transformation features. To simplify this, in Power BI Desktop, all the data import roads go through queries, which are the equivalent of Power Query in Excel. On the downside, even if you don't transform the data, queries add some performance overhead when extracting the data from the data source.

Unless you use advanced query features, such as query functions to automate importing data from multiple files, each imported table has a corresponding query. So if you import three tables from a database and then import two files, you'll end up with five queries. A query is your insurance against current and future data quality issues. Even if the data is clean, such as when you load it from a data warehouse, it might still require some shaping later on, and the query is the best place to perform these transformations.

Once the data is imported, the data is cached inside the Power BI Desktop file. Data exploration queries are handled internally by Power BI Desktop (or Power BI Service when the model is deployed). In other words, once the data is imported, Power BI Desktop doesn't open connections and query the original data source unless you refresh the data.

Connecting live via DirectQuery

You might decide to connect Power BI Desktop to fast data sources that support direct (live) connectivity and then create reports that send native queries directly to these data sources (no data is cached in the model). This is option 2 in the **Figure 6.4** diagram. Only a subset of the data sources supports direct connectivity. The list includes Analysis Services, SQL Server, Oracle, Azure SQL Database, Azure SQL Data Warehouse, Teradata, Amazon Redshit, Spark on Azure HDInsight, Impala, or SAP Hana, but the list is growing as Power BI evolves. One of the DirectQuery limtiations is that you can connect live to a *single* data source only. For example, if you connect to a SQL Server database, that's the only data source you can use in your model. As I explained, you can't connect to other data sources live or to import some other data. You can't even connect live to another database in the same server. When you connect live to any of the supported data sources (other than SSAS), Power BI Desktop configures xVelocity in a special DirectQuery mode.

With DirectQuery, Power BI Desktop doesn't import any data, and xVelocity doesn't store any data. Instead, xVelocity generates DAX queries that the query layer translates to native queries. For example, if you connect Power BI Desktop to SQL Server with DirectQuery, the model will send T-SQL queries to SQL Server. Note that because Power BI uses the query layer in between, you can still perform basic data transformation tasks, such as column renaming. You can also create DAX calculations with some limitations. For example, DAX time calculations, such as TOTALYTD, are currently not supported with DirectQuery.

When you connect to a data source that supports DirectQuery and before you load a table, Power BI Desktop will ask you how you want to get data: by importing data or by using DirectQuery (see **Figure 6.5**).

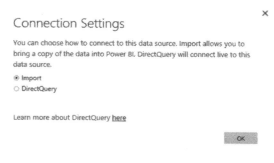

Figure 6.5 When connecting to a data source that supports DirectQuery, you need to decide how to access the data.

In this case, I'm connecting to SQL Server and Power BI Desktop asks me if I want to import the data or use DirectQuery. If I select DirectQuery, Power BI Desktop will auto-generate native queries as a result of my data exploration actions and will show me the results it gets from SQL Server. DirectQuery supports limited modeling capabilities using the Data View and the Fields pane. You can create and manage relationships, rename the metadata (table and column names), and perform basic data transformations.

As I previously said, DirectQuery is currently limited to a single data source. If you attempt to import data from another data source (even if it supports DirectQuery), Power BI Desktop will disallow this. You'll be given a choice to cancel the import process or to switch to a data import mode and import all the data.

If you publish a DirectQuery model to Power BI Service, the dataset needs the Power BI on-premises data gateway to be installed on premises in order to connect live to the original data source. If the gateway is not configured, the dataset will be published but it will be disabled (it will show grayed out in the Power BI navigation bar) and you won't be able to use it.

Connecting live to Analysis Services

Finally, a special live connectivity option exists when you connect live to Analysis Services Multidimensional or Tabular (see option 3 in the **Figure 6.4** diagram). In this case, the xVelocity engine isn't used at all. Instead, Power BI connects directly to SSAS. Power BI generates DAX queries when connected to Analysis Services (Multidimensional handles DAX queries through a special DAXMD interop mechanism). There is no additional query layer in between Power BI Desktop and SSAS.

In other words, Power BI becomes a presentation layer that is connected directly to SSAS, and the Fields pane shows the metadata from the SSAS model. This is conceptually very similar to connecting Excel to Analysis Services. When Power BI discovers that you connect to SSAS, it opens the window shown in **Figure 6.6**. The Explore Live option connects you directly to SSAS.

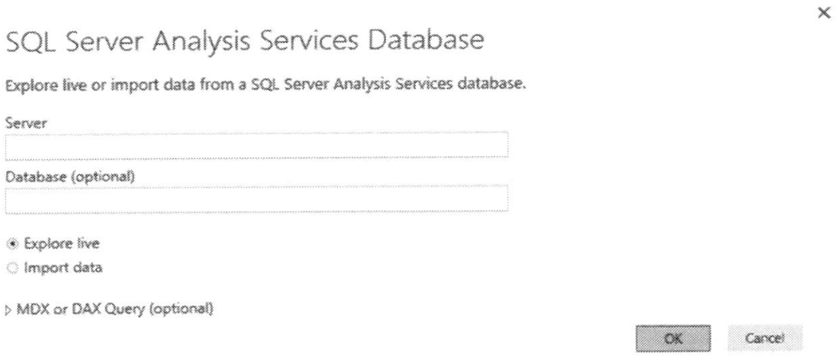

×

SQL Server Analysis Services Database

Explore live or import data from a SQL Server Analysis Services database.

Server

Database (optional)

◉ Explore live
○ Import data

▷ MDX or DAX Query (optional)

OK   Cancel

Figure 6.6 When connecting to SSAS, Power BI allows you to connect live or import the data.

Similar to DirectQuery, if you publish a model that connects live to SSAS, the dataset needs the Power BI on-premises data gateway to be installed on premises in order to connect to Analysis Services. If the connector is not configured, the dataset will be published, but it will be disabled (it will be grayed out in the Power BI navigation bar) and you won't be able to use it.

NOTE At the SQL PASS SUMMIT 2016 in October, Microsoft announced a technical preview of Azure Analysis Services Tabular. Similar to Azure SQL Database, this PaaS service allows you to host Tabular models on Azure. If Power BI Desktop connects to Azure Analysis Services, it doesn't need a gateway. However, you will still need a gateway to process (refresh) your model from an on-premises data source if this is where the model is configured to get data from.

Table 6.1 summarizes the key points about the three data connectivity options. Because most real-life needs would require importing data, this chapter focuses on this option exclusively. If you plan to connect to live data sources, your experience would be very similar to how you would do this in Power BI Service (refer to the section "Using Live Connections" in Chapter 2).

Table 6.1 This table compares the three connectivity options.

Feature	Data import	Connecting Live (DirectQuery)	Connecting Live (SSAS)
Data sources	Any data source	SQL Server (on premises), Azure SQL Database, Azure SQL Data Warehouse, Spark on Azure HDInsight, Azure SQL Data Warehouse, Oracle, Teradata, Amazon Redshift, Impala, SAP Hana	Analysis Services (Tabular and Multidimensional)
Usage scenario	When you need data from multiple data sources or a data source that doesn't support DirectQuery	When you connect to a single fast and/or large database that supports DirectQuery and you don't want to import data	When you connect to a single Analysis Services model
Queries for data cleansing and transformation	Available	Available (basic transformations only)	Not available
Connect to multiple data sources	Yes	No	No
Data storage	Data imported in xVelocity	Data is left at the data source	Data is left at the SSAS model
Connect to on-premises data from published models	Personal or on-premises gateway is required to refresh data	On-premises gateway is required to connect to data	On-premises gateway is required to connect to SSAS models
Data modeling	Available	Available with limitations	Not available
Relationships	Available	Available with limitations	Not available
Business calculations in a data model	All DAX calculations	DAX calculations with limitations	No DAX calculations (usually defined in SSAS)
Data exploration	Handled internally by Power BI Desktop or Power BI Service when the model is deployed without making connections to the original data sources	Power BI Desktop/Power BI Service (published models) autogenerates native queries, sends them to the data source, and shows the results	Power BI Desktop/Power BI Service (published models) autogenerates DAX/DAXMD queries, sends them to SSAS, and shows the results

6.2   Understanding Power BI Desktop

As I mentioned in Chapter 1, data analysts have two tool options for creating self-service data models. If you prefer Excel, you can continue using the Excel data modeling capabilities and deploy Excel workbooks to Power BI Service (or SharePoint). Be aware though that Excel has its own roadmap, so its BI features lag behind Power BI. By contrast, if you prefer to stay always on the latest BI features, consider Power BI Desktop, which combines the best of Excel Power Pivot, Power Query, and Power View in a standalone, freely available tool that Microsoft updates every month. However, as it stands, Power BI Desktop can publish only to Power BI Service.

 NOTE At the PASS Summit in October 2015, Microsoft revealed a long-term reporting roadmap (see "Microsoft Business Intelligence – our reporting roadmap" at http://bit.ly/2dUf6SM). At the PASS Summit in October 2016, Microsoft released a public preview for publishing Power BI Desktop models to on-premises SQL Server Reporting Services in native mode, and promised to deliver this feature by mid-2017. For more information, read the blog post "Power BI reports in SQL Server Reporting Services" at http://bit.ly/ssrs_pbi. When this feature becomes generally available, you'd be able to publish and share Power BI Desktop models and reports to a third destination: on-premises SQL Server Reporting Services!

6.2.1 Understanding Design Environment

Let's get familiar with the Power BI Desktop design environment. **Figure 6.7** shows its main elements numbered in the typical order of steps you'd take to create and refine self-service data models.

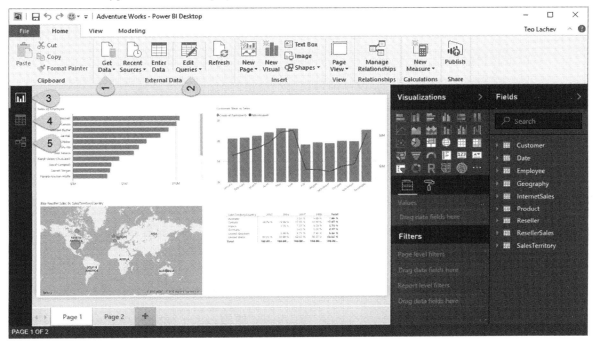

Figure 6.7 Power BI Desktop has five commonly used areas that correspond to the main modeling steps.

Understanding data modeling steps
A typical self-service data modeling workflow consists of the following five main steps (each step refers back to the numbers in **Figure 6.7**):

1. Get data – The process starts with connecting to your data by clicking the Get Data button. Remember that when you import the data or use DirectQuery, Power BI Desktop creates a query for each table you import (except when you connect to Analysis Services, in which case there is no query).

2. Transform data – If the data requires cleansing or transformations, click the Edit Queries button to modify the existing queries and perform data transformation tasks, such as replacing column values.

3. Explore and refine data – Switch to the Data View to explore and refine the imported data, such as to change column data types and create business calculations. The Data View isn't available when you connect to DirectQuery sources or to Analysis Services.

4. Create relationships – As a part of refining the data model, if you import multiple tables you need to relate them either using the Relationships View or the Manage Relationships button in the ribbon's Home tab. Relationships aren't available when connecting live to Analysis Services.

5. Visualize data – Finally, you build reports to visualize your data by switching to the Report View, which is available with all the data connectivity options.

Visualizations and Fields panes
The Visualizations and Fields panes should be familiar to you by now, as you've already worked with them in the first part of the book. The Fields pane shows the model metadata consisting of tables and fields. A

field can be a table column or a calculation, such as Sales YTD. You can also use the Fields pane to create DAX calculations. The Fields pane is available when you're in the Report and Data views.

The Visualizations pane (on the right) is only available when the Report View is active. It includes Microsoft-provided and custom visualizations. You can click the ellipsis menu (…) below the visualization icons to import custom visualizations that you downloaded from the Power BI visuals gallery or created by yourself. You can use the Visualizations pane to configure the visual data options and formatting.

6.2.2 Understanding Navigation

Power BI Desktop has a simplified navigation experience using a ribbon interface that should be familiar to you from other Microsoft products, such as Excel. But if you come from Excel data modeling, you'll undoubtedly appreciate the change toward simplicity. There is no more confusion about which ribbon to use and which button to click! By the way, if you need more space, you can minimize the ribbon by clicking the chevron button in the top-right corner or by pressing Ctrl-F1.

Understanding the ribbon's Home tab
The ribbon's Home tab (see **Figure 6.7** again) is your one-stop navigation for common tasks. The Clipboard group allows you to copy and paste text, such as a DAX calculation formula. It doesn't allow you to create tables by pasting data as you can with Excel Power Pivot. However, you can use the Enter Data button in the External Data group to create tables by pasting or entering data. Similar to other Microsoft Office applications, you can use the Format Painter to copy and apply limited format settings from one selection to another. Let's say you've changed the format settings, such as colors and fonts, of a chart and you want to apply the same settings to another chart. Click the first chart to select it, click the Format Painter button to copy the settings, and then click the other chart to apply the settings.

The External Data group allows you to connect to data (the Get Data button). The Edit Queries button opens a separate Query Editor window so that you can edit queries, if you want to cleanse or transform data. The Recent Sources button lets you bypass the first Get Data steps, such as when you want to import additional tables from the same database. The Refresh button deletes the data in all tables and re-imports the data. As I mentioned, the Enter Data button allows you to create your own tables by either pasting tabular data or typing in the data manually. The latter could be useful to enter some reference data, such as KPI goals.

The next two groups (Insert and View) are available when the Report View is active. The Insert group allows you to insert new visuals to a report (alternatively, you can click the visual icon in the Visualizations pane). You can also insert graphical elements, such as text boxes, images, and shapes. The Page View button zooms the report. It has three options: Fit to Page, Fit to Width, and Actual Size.

The Manage Relationships button allows you to relate tables in your model. The Calculations group is for creating DAX calculations (measures and calculated columns). And the Publish button lets you publish your model to Power BI.

Understanding the ribbon's View tab
The ribbon's View tab includes the same Page View button. More importantly, it allows you to optimize the page layout for phone devices. Power BI reports typically have a lot of visualizations and this is fine if users view them on laptops or tablets. But phones have much smaller displays. To avoid excessive scrolling, you can use the Change Layout button to define a layout optimized for phones. In **Figure 6.8**, I clicked the Change Layout button to switch to a phone layout. Then, I dragged an existing visualization from the Visualizations pane, dropped it to the phone layout, and resized it accordingly. Now when users view this page on their phones, the Power BI native app will detect that a phone layout exists and it will apply it. If there isn't a phone-optimized view, the report will open in the non-optimized, landscape view.

Note that when you define a phone layout, you can't make changes to the visualizations; you can only resize them. Clicking the Change Layout button one more time toggles to the master layout, as you defined it in the Report View.

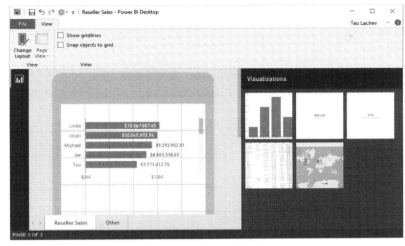

Figure 6.8 Use the Change Layout button to toggle between master and phone layouts.

When checked, the "Show gridlines" shows a grid in the Report View to help you arrange elements on the report canvas. If you want to snap items to the grid to align them precisely, check "Snap objects to grid".

Understanding the ribbon's Modeling tab
The ribbon's Modeling tab (**Figure 6.9**) allows you to extend and refine your data model. It's available only when the Data View is active.

Figure 6.9 The ribbon's Modeling tab is for performing data modeling tasks, such as creating calculations and defining data security.

The Manage Relationships button is available here as well. The Calculations group gives you access to DAX features to create calculated columns, measures, tables, and to define custom sorting. The Formatting group lets you change the data type and formatting of a table column, such as to format a sales amount with two decimal places. The Properties group is for changing the purpose of specific columns, such as to tell Power BI Desktop that a Country column has a Country category so that a map knows how to plot it.

The Security group allows you to define data security, also known as Row-Level Security (RLS). Suppose that while Martin can see all the data in the model, Elena can see United States sales. You can define a role that grants Elena rights only to United States in the Sales Territory table. Then, when Elena views the published model, she can see only the data related to the United States as though the other countries don't exist in the model. Finally, the Groups group allow you to define new custom groups, such as to group all European countries in an "European Countries" group so they can be shown as one bar on a chart (groups are discussed in more detail in Chapter 8).

Understanding the ribbon's Format tab

Two additional tabs become available when you select a visualization in the Report View: Format and Drill tabs (**Figure 6.10**). The Format tab allows you to control the placement of the selected visualization. For example, you might decide to add a background image to a report page that appears behind all visualizations. To do so, you can select the image, expand the Send Backwards button and then click Send to Back. Or, if you want to align specific visualizations, you can hold the Ctrl key to select them one by one, and then use the Align button to align them.

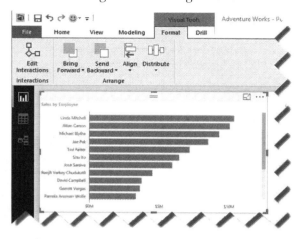

Figure 6.10 The ribbon's Format tab is for controlling placement and interaction behavior of selected visualization.

Similar to the Power BI Service Visualizations menu (also known as "Brushing and Linking"), the Edit Interactions button controls how visualizations on a report page interact with each other, such as in the case when you want to disable the default cross-highlighting to other charts on the page when you select a category in a chart.

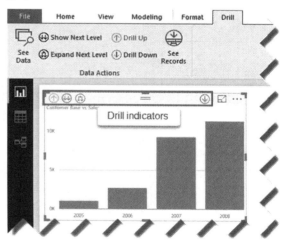

Figure 6.11 The ribbon's Drill tab is to see the levels of detail behind a visualization, such as to drill down.

Understanding the ribbon's Drill tab

Some visualizations, such as charts and maps, allow users to interactively drill down data. For example, if you add Year and Month fields to the chart's Axis area, you can drill down from year to month. However, because by default clicking a chart column invokes the highlighting feature, you can use the buttons in the ribbon's Drill tab (or the indicators in the chart) to tell Power BI Desktop that you want to drill down or up instead (see **Figure 6.11**).

The See Data button opens a table below the visualization that shows the data behind the visualization at the current aggregation level. By contrast, See Records allows you to drill through to the lowest of level of detail behind a given chart. To do so, click the See Records button, and either click a chart element or right-click it and then click See Records. Power BI desktop opens a new table that shows the first 1,000 rows that contributed to the aggregated value from the underlying table.

Understanding the File menu

The File menu gives you access to additional tasks. To save space, **Figure 6.12** shows the bottom half of the menu side by side.

Figure 6.12 Use the Power BI Desktop File menu to work with files and change application settings.

Use the New menu to create a new Power BI Desktop (*.pbix) file and the Open menu to open an existing file. The Save menu saves changes to the current file, and the Save As menu saves the file as another file. If you're transitioning to Power BI Desktop from Excel, the Import menu allows you to import the Excel data model into Power BI Desktop. You can also use the Import menu as another way to import custom visuals into the open Power BI Desktop file. Finally, you can use the Import menu to import an existing Power BI template file.

DEFINITION A Power BI template (.pbit) file includes all the main elements of an existing Power BI Desktop file (report, data model and queries), but not the actual data. This could be useful if you want to send your existing model to someone without giving them access to the data, such as in the case where the user might have restricted access to a subset of the data based on the user's Windows credentials. The user can instantiate the template (create a Power BI Desktop file from it) either by double-clicking on the template file or by using the Import menu.

The Export menu allows you to export your existing model to a Power BI template. The Publish menu is for publishing the data model to Power BI Service (same as the Publish button in the ribbon's Home tab). Remember that although Power BI Desktop can load as much data as it can fit in your computer memory, Power BI Service caps the file size (currently to one gigabyte), so be aware of this limitation. If you plan to target larger data volumes, you should consider Analysis Services. When you have an Analysis Services model, your data remains on the server, while you publish only the definitions of your reports and dashboards to Power BI Service, so the dataset size is not an issue. Chapter 11 provides more details when an Analysis Services semantic model could be a better choice than Power BI Desktop. The "Options and settings" menu lets you configure certain program and data source features, as I'll discuss in the next section.

The Help menu includes several useful resources. The Get Help submenu brings you to the Power BI support page where you can access guided learning, samples, documentation, discussion lists, report an issue, and submit an idea about improving Power BI. Use the About submenu to see the version and monthly release (recall that Power BI Desktop is updated every month!) of the installed Power BI Desktop. The "Power BI for Developers" submenu brings you to the Power BI Developer Center, which contains useful resources for developers interested in implementing Power BI-centric solutions. The "Submit an idea" submenu is a shortcut for submitting a suggestion for improving Power BI. The "Rate your experience" submenu lets you rate your Power BI Desktop experience with Microsoft (you can send feedback and any issues directly to Microsoft).

The "Getting started" menu opens the Power BI Desktop startup screen, which has shortcuts (Get Data, Recent Sources, and recent files), video tutorials, and links to useful resources. If you haven't signed in to Power BI, you can do this right from the startup screen. Signing in to Power BI Desktop helps later on when you are publishing to Power BI Service. Continuing on the menu list, the "What's new" menu brings you to the Power BI blog to read about the new features in the installed release of Power BI Desktop. The Sign Out menu signs you out of Power BI Service in case you want to sign under another account when you publish the model to Power BI. And the Exit menu closes Power BI Desktop.

Understanding Options and Settings menu

Currently, the "Options and settings" menu has two submenus: Options and Data Source Settings. The Data Source Settings menu lets you change certain security settings of the data sources in the current model (you initially specified these settings when you used Get Data). For example, you can use the Data Source Settings menu to switch from SQL Server Windows authentication to standard authentication (requires a login and password). For data sources that support encrypted connections, such as SQL Server, it also allows you to change the connection encryption settings.

The Options menu brings you to the Options window (see **Figure 6.13**) that allows you to change various program features and settings. I'll cover most of them in appropriate places in this and subsequent chapters but I'd like to explain some now.

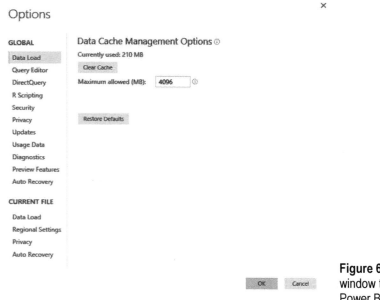

Figure 6.13 Use the Options window to configure various Power BI Desktop features.

The Updates tab allows you to configure Power BI Desktop to receive a notification when there's a Power BI Desktop update (enabled by default). If you experience issues with Power BI Desktop, you can enable tracing from the Diagnostics tab and send the trace to Microsoft. An interesting setting is Preview Features. It allows you to test "beta" features that Microsoft makes available for testing. The goal is to get your feedback to help Microsoft improve these features before enabling them by default. Similar to automatic recovery in other Microsoft Office applications, Auto Recovery has settings that allow you to recover your model in the case of an application or operating system crash.

Now that I've introduced you to Power BI Desktop and data modeling, let's start the process of creating a self-service data model by getting the data!

6.3 Importing Data

Now let's go back to Martin, who's a data analyst with Adventure Works. Martin realizes that to perform comprehensive sales analysis, he needs data from different data sources. He'll implement a self-service data model and he'll import data from multiple data sources, including data residing in the data warehouse, an Analysis Services cube, flat files, and so on.

6.3.1 Understanding Data Import Steps

Power BI Desktop makes it easy to import data. For those of you who are familiar with Excel data modeling, the process is very similar to using Power Query in Excel. Importing data involves the following high-level steps (you'll repeat for each new data source you use in your model):

1. Choose a data source
2. Connect to the data
3. (Optional) Transform the raw data if needed
4. Load the data into the data model

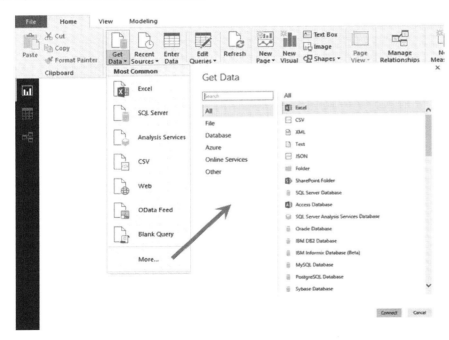

Figure 6.14 Power BI Desktop can connect to a variety of data sources without requiring any scripting or programming.

Choosing a data source

Power BI Desktop can import data from a plethora of data sources with a few clicks and without requiring any scripting or programming skills. You can start the process by clicking the Get Data button in the Power BI Desktop ribbon. The most common data sources are shown in the drop-down menu (see **Figure 6.14**), but many more are available when you click the "More…" menu. To make it easier to find the appropriate data source, the Get Data window organizes them in File, Database, Azure, Online Services, and Other categories. Table 6.2 summarizes the currently supported data sources, but expect the list to grow because Microsoft adds new data sources on a regular basis.

Table 6.2   This table summarizes the data sources supported by Power BI Desktop.

Data Source Type	Data Sources
File	Excel, CSV, XML, other delimited and fixed-width text files, JSON, a list of files in a Windows or SharePoint folder
Database	SQL Server, Microsoft Access, Analysis Services (Multidimensional, Tabular, PowerPivot workbooks deployed to SharePoint), Oracle, IBM DB2, IBM Informix, MySQL, PostgreSQL, Sybase, Teradata, SAP HANA, SAP Business Warehouse, and other ODBC-compilant databases
Azure	SQL Database, SQL Data Warehouse, Azure Marketplace, HDInsight, Blob Storage, Table Storage, HDInsight Spark, DocumentDB, Data Lake Store
Online Services	SharePoint Online list, Microsoft Exchange Online, Dynamics CRM Online, Facebook, Google Analytics, Salesforce, appFigures, Azure Enterprise, comScore, GitHub, MailChimp, Marketo, Planview, Projectplace, Quickbooks Online, SparkPost, Smartsheet, SQL Sentry, Stripe, SweetIQ, Troax, Twillio, tyGraph, Webtrends, Zendesk
Other	Web, SharePoint list, OData feed, Hadoop File from HDFS, Active Directory, Micosoft Exchange, ODBC, RScript, Spark

It's important to note that every data source requires installing appropriate connectivity software (also called provider or driver). Chances are that if you use Microsoft Office or other Microsoft applications, you already have drivers to connect to SQL Server, Excel files, and text files. If you have to connect to the data sources from other vendors, you need to research what connector (also called driver or provider) is needed and how to install it on your computer. For example, connecting to Oracle requires Oracle client software v8.1.7 or greater on your computer.

 TIP   Because Power BI Desktop borrowed the Power Query features from Excel, you can find more information about the prerequisites related to connectivity in the "Import data from external data sources (Power Query)" document by Microsoft at http://bit.ly/1FQrjF3.

What if you don't find your data source on the list? If the data source comes with an ODBC connector, try connecting to it using the ODBC option. Although the data source might not be officially supported by Microsoft, chances are that you will be able to connect via ODBC. Or, if it comes with an OLE DB driver, try the ODBC for OLE DB Microsoft driver, which is one of the ODBC drivers that come preinstalled with Windows.

Connecting to data

Once you select your data source you want to connect to, the next step depends on the type of the data source. For example, if you connect to a database, such as SQL Server, you'll see a window that looks like the one in **Figure 6.15**. The only required field is the database server name that will be given to you by your database administrator. You can also specify the database name but it's not required because you can do this in the next step.

If the Power BI Desktop supports direct connectivity to the data source, you'll be able to specify how you want to access the data: import it in the Power BI Desktop file or connect to it directly using Direct-

Query. However, if you have already imported data from the same server or another data source, the DirectQuery option will be disabled. Again, that's because currently DirectQuery supports a single data source only.

Moving to the advanced options, you can specify a command timeout in minutes to tell Power BI Desktop how long to wait before it times out the query. Instead of selecting a table or view in the next step, you can enter a custom SQL statement (also called a native database query). For example, if you need to execute a SQL Server stored procedure, you can enter the following statement:

exec <StoredProcedureName> parameter1, parameter 2, ...

One caveat about custom SQL statements is that currently, DirectQuery doesn't support them, so you must import tables (or SQL views) if you want to connect live to your data.

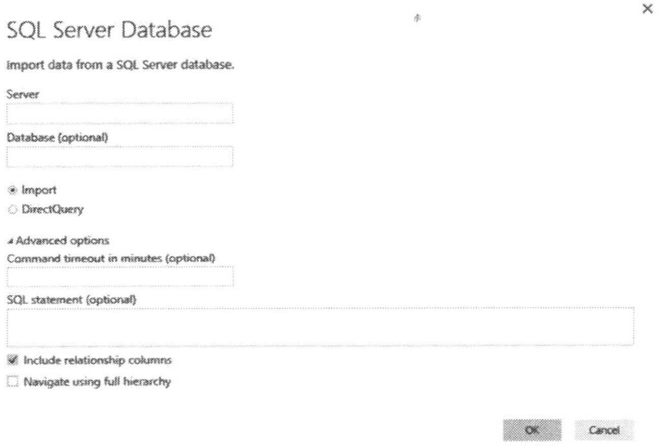

Figure 6.15 Connecting to a database requires a server name but additional options are available.

If the data source supports referential integrity and you leave "Include relationship column" checked, in the next step (Navigator window) you can let Power BI Desktop preselect the related tables. If you check the "Navigate using full hierarchy", the Navigator window will organize tables in roles and schemas defined in the database (for data sources that support these features). For example, the Adventure-Works2012 database has all sales-related tables in the Sales schema. If this checkbox is checked, the Navigator window will show the database schemas. It'll also show the tables within the Sales schema when you expand it.

Specifying credentials
If you connect to a database for the first time, the next step asks you to enter your credentials as instructed by your database administrator. For example, when connecting to SQL Server, you can use Windows credentials (behind the scenes it uses your Windows login) or standard authentication (user name and password).

Power BI Desktop shows the "Access a SQL Server Database" window (see **Figure 6.16**) to let you specify how you want to authenticate. Note the Windows tab allows you specify alternative Windows credentials. This could be useful if the database administrator has given you the credentials of a trusted Windows account. The Database tab lets you use standard authentication.

> **TIP** Once you've connected to a data source, you don't need to use Get Data to import additional tables. Instead, use the Recent Sources button in the Power BI ribbon. If you need to change the data source credentials or encryption options, use the File ⇨ Options and Settings ⇨ Data Source Settings menu.

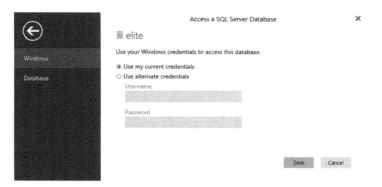

Figure 6.16 SQL Server supports Windows and standard authentication.

If you connect to a data source that is configured for encrypted connections, such as SQL Server, you'll be asked if you want to encrypt the connection while data is imported. If the data source doesn't support encrypted connections, Power BI Desktop will warn you about it.

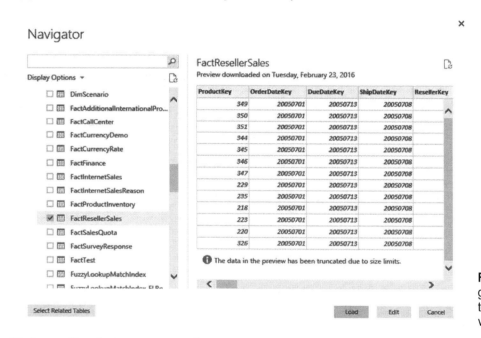

Figure 6.17 The Navigator window allows you to select tables and preview data.

Understanding the Navigator window

If the data source has multiple entities, such as a relational database that has multiple tables, or an Excel file with multiple sheets, Power BI Desktop will open the Navigator window (see **Figure 6.17**). Use this window to navigate the data source objects, such as databases and tables, and select one or more tables to import. If the database has many objects, you can search the database metadata to find objects by name. To select a table or a SQL view to import, check its checkbox. The Navigator window shows a preview of the data in the right pane.

If the database has table relationships (the AdventureWorks databases have relationships), the "Select Related Tables" button allows you to include related tables (if the "Include relationship column" setting was left checked in the previous step) so that you can import multiple tables in one step. There are two refresh buttons. The refresh button in the Navigator left pane, refreshes the metadata. This could be useful if someone makes a definition change, such as adding a column, and you don't want to close the Navigator window to start over. The refresh button on top of the preview pane refreshes the data preview so you can see the latest data changes or the effect of making column changes to the table whose data you're previewing, such as removing, adding, or renaming columns. Again, queries (and everything you do in Power BI Desktop) never make changes to the original data source, so don't worry about breaking something.

The Edit button launches the Query Editor, and this unlocks a whole new world to shape and transform data, such as if you want to replace values, merge data, unpivot columns, and so on. (I'll cover the Query Editor in detail in Chapter 7.) The Load button in the Navigator window adds a new table to the data model and loads it with the data from the selected table. If you click the Edit button to open the Query Editor, you can load the data from the Query Editor window once you're done transforming it.

 NOTE Readers familiar with Excel data modeling might know that the Power Pivot Table Import Wizard allows you to filter the data before it's imported. The Navigator window doesn't support filtering. However, you can click the Edit button to edit the query. Among many transformation options, you can apply necessary filtering in the Query Editor, such as removing columns and filtering rows for a given date range.

Next, let's go through a series of exercises to practice importing data from the most common data sources (the ones listed when you drop down the Get Data button), including databases, Excel files, text files, Web, and OData feeds. Because of the growing popularity of R, I'll also show you how you can import data using R scripts.

6.3.2 Importing from Databases

Nowadays, most corporate data resides in databases, such as SQL Server and Oracle. In this exercise, you'll import two tables from the Adventure Works data warehouse database. The first table, FactResellerSales, represents a fact table and it keeps a historical record of numeric values (facts), such as Sales Amount and Order Quantity. You'll also import the DimDate table from the same database so that you can aggregate data by date periods, such as month, quarter, year, and so on. As a prerequisite, you need to install the Power BI Desktop (read Chapter 1 for installation considerations), and you need to have the Adventure-Works2012 (or later) database installed locally or on a remote SQL Server instance.

 NOTE Installing the AdventureWorks databases too complicated? If you don't have a SQL Server to install the AdventureWorks databases, you can import the FactResellerSales.txt and DimDate.txt files from the \Source\ch06 folder to complete this practice.

Connecting to the database
Follow these steps to import data from the FactResellerSales table:

1. Open Power BI Desktop. Close the splash screen. Click File ⇨ Save (or press Ctrl-S) and then save the empty model as *Adventure Works* in a folder on your local hard drive.

2. Expand the Get Data button in the ribbon and then click SQL Server. This opens the SQL Server Database window.

3. In the Server field, enter the name of the SQL Server instance, such as *ELITE*, if SQL Server is installed on a server called ELITE, or *ELITE\2012* if the SQL Server is running on a named instance 2012 on a server called ELITE. Confirm with your database administrator (DBA) what the correct instance name is. Leave the "Import" option selected. Because you're importing data from multiple sources, you can't use Direct-Query anyway. Click OK.

 TIP If the AdventureWorksDW database is installed on your local computer, you can enter localhost, (local), or dot (.) instead of the machine name. However, I recommend that you always enter the machine name. This will avoid connectivity issues that will require you to change the connection string if you decide to move the workbook to another computer and then try to refresh the data.

4. If this is the first time you connect to that server, Power BI Desktop opens the "Access a SQL Server Database" window to ask you for your credentials. Assuming that you have access to the server via Windows security, leave the default "Use my current credentials" option selected. Or if the database administrator (DBA) has created a login for you, select the "Use alternate credentials" option, and then enter the login credentials. Click Connect, and then click OK to confirm that you want to use unencrypted connections.

Loading tables

If you connect successfully, Power BI Desktop opens the Navigator window. Let's load some tables:

1. Expand the AdventureWorksDW2012 database. It's fine if you have an older or later version of the database, such as AdventureWorksDW2014.

2. Scroll down the table list and check the FactResellerSales table. The data preview pane shows the first few rows in the table (see **Figure 6.17** again). Although the Navigator doesn't show row counts, this table is relatively small (about 60,000 rows), so you can go ahead and click the Load button to import it.

If the source table is large and you don't want to import all the data, you might want to filter the data before it's imported (as I'll show you how in the next step) so that you don't have to wait for all the data to load and end up with a huge data model.

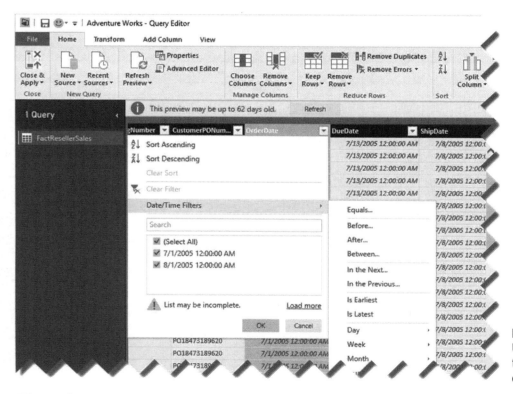

Figure 6.18
Use Query Editor to filter rows and columns.

Filtering data

As a best practice, don't import data you don't immediately need for analysis to avoid a large memory footprint and spending an unnecessary long time to load and refresh the data. The Query Editor makes it easy to filter the data before it's imported. While the Query Editor deserves much more attention (Chapter 7 has the details), let me quickly show you how to filter rows and columns:

1. While you are still in the Navigator window, click the Edit button to open Query Editor in a new window.

2. In the data preview pane, scroll horizontally to the right until you find the OrderDate column.

3. Assuming you want to filter rows by date, expand the drop-down in the OrderDate column header, as shown in **Figure 6.18**. Notice that you can filter by checking or unchecking specific dates. For more advanced filtering options, click the "Date/Time Filters" context menu and notice that you can specify date-related filters, such as After (to filter after a given date) and Between (to filter rows between two dates).

4. You can also remove columns that you don't need. This also helps keep your model more compact, especially with columns that have many unique values because they can't compress well. Right-click a column. Note that the context menu includes a Remove option, which you can use to delete a column. Don't worry if you need this column later; you can always bring back removed columns by undoing the Remove Column step.

> **TIP** A more intuitive option for removing and bringing columns back is Choose Columns. (The Choose Columns button is in the Home ribbon of Query Editor.) It allows you to search columns by name, which is very useful for wide tables. And you can bring columns back by just checking the column name.

5. If you've decided to open the Query Editor, click the "Close & Apply" button in the Query Editor ribbon to import FactResellerSales.

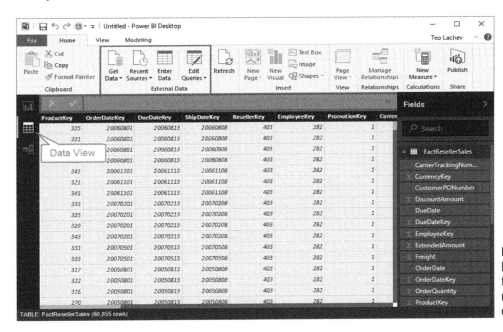

Figure 6.19 The Data View shows the tables in the model and preview of the data.

Understanding changes

Irrespective of which path you took (loading the table from the Navigator or from the Query Editor), Power BI Desktop does the following behind the scenes:

1. It creates a query that connects to the database.

2. It adds a FactResellerSales table to the model.

3. It runs the query to extract the data from the FactResellerSales table in the AdventureWorksDW database.

4. It compresses the data and loads it into the FactResellerSales table inside the model.

5. Power BI Desktop switches to the Data View to show you the new table and read-only view of the loaded data (**Figure 6.19**). The Fields pane shows you the table fields.

Don't confuse the Data View, which represents your data model, with the Query Editor, which represents the query used to load a table in the model. While both show a read-only view of the same data, it comes from different places. The Query Editor opens in another window to show you the source data after all transformations you applied but *before* it's loaded to the data model. The Data View shows the data *after* it's loaded into the data model. In other words, the Query Editor shows what will happen to the data after you transform it, while the Data View shows what actually happened after the query was applied and data is loaded.

The External Data ribbon group is your entry point for data-related tasks. You already know about the Get Data button. You can use the Recent Sources menu if you need to import another table from the data source that you've already used and if you want to jump directly to the Navigator. The Edit Queries button opens the Query Editor. And the Refresh button reloads all the data so you can get the latest data changes.

 NOTE When you work with Power BI Desktop, the only way to synchronize the imported data with the data source changes is to manually refresh the data. You can do so by clicking the Refresh button to refresh all the tables. Or, you can right-click a table in the Field List and click "Refresh data" to reload only the selected table. Recall that once you publish the model to Power BI, you have the option to schedule an automatic data refresh, such as on a daily basis.

Importing another table

As I explained at the beginning of this chapter, most models would benefit from a date table. Let's import the DimDate table from the same database:

1. In the External Data ribbon group, expand the Recent Sources button. Click the name of the database server that you specified when you connected to SQL Server. This opens the Navigator window.

2. Expand the AdventureWorksDW2012 node and check the DimDate table. Click the Load button. Power BI adds a table with the same name to the model and to the Fields pane.

As I pointed out, you should exclude columns you don't need for analysis. You can right-click a column in Data View (or the Field List) and click Delete. Alternatively, you can delete the column in the Data View. In both cases, the Query Editor will add a "Removed Columns" transformation step to the Applied Steps list. However, I prefer to use the Choose Columns transformation so I can see which columns are available and which ones are excluded.

3. Click the Edit Queries button. In the Query Editor, select DimDate in the Queries pane, and then click the Choose Columns button in the Query Editor ribbon's Home tab.

4. Uncheck all columns whose names start with "Spanish" and "French", and then click OK.

5. Click the "Close & Apply" button to apply the query changes and to reload the data. Note that these columns are removed from the DimDate table in the model.

6. Press Ctrl-S to save your data model or click File ⇨ Save. Unless you trust the auto recovery feature, get in a habit to save regularly so you don't lose changes if something unexpected happens and Power BI Desktop shuts down.

6.3.3   Importing Excel Files

Like it or not, much of corporate data ends up in Excel, so importing data from Excel files is a common requirement. If you have a choice, ask for an Excel file that has only the data in an Excel list with no formatting. If you have to import an Excel report, things might get more complicated because you'll have to use the Query Editor to strip unnecessary rows and clean the data. In this exercise, I'll show you the simple case for importing an Excel list. In Chapter 7, I'll show you a more complicated case that requires parsing and cleansing an Excel report.

Understanding source data

Suppose that you're given a list of resellers as an Excel file. You want to import this list in the model.

1. Open the Resellers file from \Source\ch06 in Excel (see **Figure 6.20**).

ResellerKey	GeographyKey	ResellerAlternateKey	Phone	BusinessType	ResellerName
1	637	AW00000001	245-555-0173	Value Added Reseller	A Bike Store
2	635	AW00000002	170-555-0127	Specialty Bike Shop	Progressive S
3	584	AW00000003	279-555-0130	Warehouse	Advanced Bik
4	572	AW00000004	710-555-0173	Value Added Reseller	Modular Cycle S
5	322	AW00000005	828-555-0186	Specialty Bike Shop	Metropolita
6	303	AW00000006	244-555-0112	Warehouse	Aerobic Exercis
7	599	AW00000007	192-555-0173	Value Added Reseller	Associated Bik
8	409	AW00000008	872-555-0171	Specialty Bike Shop	Exemplary C
9	568	AW00000009	488-555-0130	Warehouse	Tandem Bicycle
10	44	AW00000010	150-555-0127	Value Added Reseller	Rural Cycle En
11	96	AW00000011	926-555-0159	Specialty Bike Shop	Sharp Bikes
12	96	AW00000012	112-555-0191	Warehouse	Bikes and Moto

Figure 6.20 The Resellers file represents a list of resellers and it only has the data, without formatting.

2. Notice that the Excel file includes only data on the first sheet. This Excel list includes all the resellers that Adventure Works does business with. Close Excel.

Importing from Excel

Follow these steps to import from an Excel file:

1. With the Adventure Works model open in Power BI Desktop, expand Get Data, and then select Excel.
2. Navigate to the \Source\ch06 folder and double-click the Resellers file.
3. In the Navigator window, check Sheet1. The Navigator parses the Excel data and shows a preview of the data in Sheet1 (see **Figure 6.21**).

   As you've seen, importing Excel files isn't much different than importing from a database. If the Excel file has multiple sheets with data, you can select and import them in one step. Power BI Desktop will create a query and a corresponding table for each sheet.

    TIP Don't like "Sheet1" as a table name in your data model? While you can rename the table in the Data View, you can also rename the query before the data is loaded. Power BI Desktop uses the name of the query as a default table name. While you're still in the Navigator, click the Edit button to open the Query Editor, and then change the query name in the Query Settings pane.

4. Click the Edit button. In the Query Settings pane of the Query Editor, change the query name from Sheet1 to *Resellers*. Click the "Close & Apply" button. Power BI Desktop adds a third table (Resellers) to the data model.

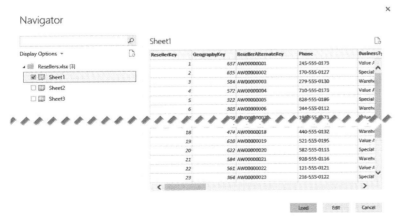

Figure 6.21 The Navigator parses the Excel data and shows a preview.

6.3.4 Importing Text Files

Importing from text files (delimited and fixed-length) is another common requirement. Security and operational requirements might prevent you from connecting directly to a database. In such cases, data could be provided to you as text files. For example, your database administrator might give you a data extract as a file as opposed to granting you direct access to a production database.

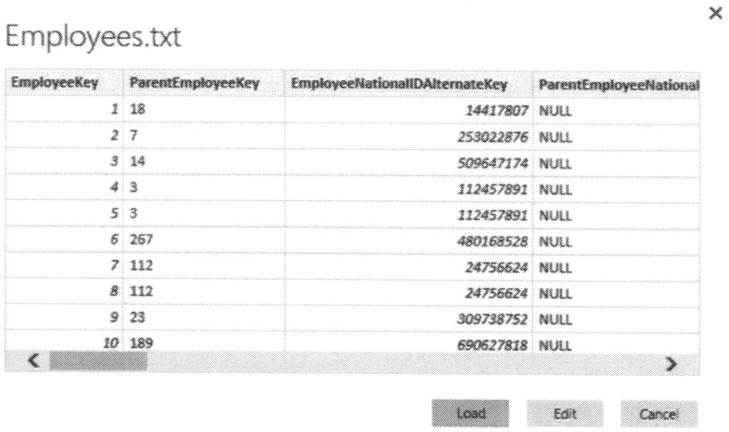

×

Employees.txt

EmployeeKey	ParentEmployeeKey	EmployeeNationalIDAlternateKey	ParentEmployeeNational
1	18	14417807	NULL
2	7	253022876	NULL
3	14	509647174	NULL
4	3	112457891	NULL
5	3	112457891	NULL
6	267	480168528	NULL
7	112	24756624	NULL
8	112	24756624	NULL
9	23	309738752	NULL
10	189	690627818	NULL

< ⟩

Load   Edit   Cancel

Figure 6.22 When importing from files, Power BI Desktop shows a data preview without opening the Navigator pane.

Importing from CSV files
Suppose that Adventure Works keeps the employee information in an HR mainframe database. Instead of having direct access to the database, you're given an extract as a comma-separated values (CSV) file. Follow these steps to import this file:

1. Expand the Get Data button and click CSV.
2. Navigate to the \Source\ch06 folder and double-click the Employees file.
3. Because a text file only has a single dataset, Power BI doesn't open the Navigator window. Instead, it just shows you a preview of the data, as shown in **Figure 6.22**. As you can see, it parses the file content and separates it in columns. Click Load to create a new Employees table and to load the data. At this point, the Adventure Works model should have four tables: DimDate, Employees, FactResellerSales, and Resellers.

Importing other formats
You might be given a file format other than CSV. For example, the file might use a pipe character (|) as a column separator. Or you might be a given a fixed-length file format, such as the one I demonstrate with the Employees2.txt file in the \Source\ch06 folder (see **Figure 6.23**).

```
EmployeeID  FirstName  LastName    Title
14417807    Guy        Gilbert     Production Technician - WC60
253022876   Kevin      Brown       Marketing Assistant
509647174   Roberto    Tamburello  Engineering Manager
112457891   Rob        Walters     Senior Tool Designer
```

Figure 6.23 The Employees2 file has a fixed-length format where each column starts at a specific position.

You can use either CSV or Text import options to parse such formats. To make it easier on you, Power BI Desktop will use its smarts to detect the file format. If it's successful, it will detect the delimiters automatically and return a multi-column table. If not, it'll return a single-column table that you can subsequently split into columns using Split Columns and other column tasks in the Query Editor.

NOTE Readers familiar with Power might know that Power Pivot was capable of parsing more complicated file formats using a schema.ini file if it's found in the same folder as the source file. The Power BI Desktop queries don't support schema.ini files.

6.3.5 Importing from Analysis Services

If your organization has invested in SQL Server Analysis Services (SSAS), you have two ways to access Multidimensional or Tabular models:

- Connect live – Choose this option when you want to create interactive reports connected to an SSAS model without importing the data, just like you would do it in Excel. For this to work, your Power BI Desktop file must not have any other connections or imported data. If you decide to connect live to SSAS, the Data and Relationships views, and the Query Editor are not available. This makes sense because you wouldn't want to have a model on top of another model.

- Import data – Choose this options if you want to mash up data from multiple data sources, including SSAS databases or Power Pivot models deployed to SharePoint. This is especially useful when your model needs the results from business calculations or from KPIs defined in a multidimensional cube or a Tabular model.

Next, you'll import the Sales Territory dimension data and a key performance indicator (KPI) from the Adventure Works cube. (The book front matter includes steps for installing the Adventure Works cube.)

 NOTE If you don't have an Analysis Services instance with the Adventure Works cube, you can import the DimSalesTerritory CSV file found in the \Source\ch06 folder. Importing DimSalesTerritory won't import the Revenue KPI because it's only defined in the cube. When going through subsequent exercises, ignore steps that reference the Revenue KPI.

Connecting to an SSAS database
Start by connecting to the Adventure Works cube as follows:

1. Expand the Get Data button and click Analysis Services to open the "SQL Server Analysis Services Database" window (see **Figure 6.24**). Remember that Analysis Services supports live connectivity, but it must be the only data source in your Power BI Desktop model. If you combine data from multiple sources, you must import all the data. This is why the "Explore live" option is disabled.

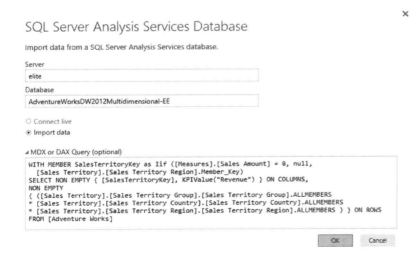

Figure 6.24 Power BI Desktop allows you to import data from SSAS.

If you don't specify a custom query (or leave the Database field empty) and click OK, the Navigator window will pop up, allowing you to select the dimensions and measures. Once you are done, the Navigator window will auto-generate the MDX query for you. However, unlike the MDX Designer included in Excel, the Navigator doesn't let you specify calculated members (business calculations in cubes). In this case, we need a simple calculation member that returns the key property of the "Sales Territory Region" dimension attribute so that we can subsequently relate the SalesTerritory table to FactResellerSales. This is why we need a custom MDX query that includes a SalesTerritoryKey calculated member.

2. In the "SQL Server Analysis Services Database" window, enter the name of your SSAS database, such as *AdventureWorksDW2012Multidimensional-EE*.

3. In the "MDX or DAX Query" field, enter the MDX query, which you can copy from the \Source\ch06\Queries file. Click OK. Power BI Desktop shows a data preview window (see **Figure 6.25**).

elite: AdventureWorksDW2012Multidimensional-EE

[Sales Territory Region].[Sales Territory	[Measures].[SalesTerritoryKey]	[Measures].[Sales Amount]
	7	7251555.649
	8	4878300.376
	10	7670721.038
	6	16355770.46
	3	7909009.007
	2	6939374.483
	1	16084942.55
	5	7879655.075
	4	24184609.6
	9	10655335.96

Load   Edit   Cancel

Figure 6.25   The SalesTerritoryKey column returns the key value of the Sales Territory Region attribute which you'll subsequently use as a primary key for creating a relationship.

Renaming metadata

If you click the Load button, you'll end up with "Query1" as a table name and system-generated column names. You can fix this later, but let's refine the metadata before the data is loaded.

1. Click the Edit button.

2. In the Query Settings pane, rename the query from "Query1" to *SalesTerritories*.

3. To rename the columns, double-click the column header of each column, and rename the columns to *SalesTerritoryGroup*, *SalesTerritoryCountry*, *SalesTerritoryRegion*, *SalesTerritoryKey*, and *SalesAmount*.

4. Click the "Close & Apply" button to create and load a new SalesTerritories table.

6.3.6   Importing from the Web

A wealth of information is available on the Web. Power BI Desktop can import tabular data that's accessible by URL. One popular Web-enabled data source is SQL Server Reporting Services (SSRS). Once a report is deployed to a report server, it's accessible by URL, which is exactly what the Web import option requires. Next, I'll show you how to import an SSRS report.

 NOTE   Readers familiar with the Power Pivot import capabilities might recall that Power Pivot supports importing SSRS reports as data feeds. Unfortunately, as it stands, the Power BI Desktop (and Power Query) OData import option doesn't support the ATOM data feed format that SSRS generates. However, the report URL can export the report as CSV, and the output then can be loaded using the Power BI Web import option.

Deploying the report

You can find a sample report named Product Catalog in the \Source\ch06 folder. This report must be deployed to a Reporting Services server that is version 2008 R2 or higher.

 NOTE If configuring Reporting Services isn't an option, you can import the required data from the \Source\ch06\DimProduct.txt file or from the AdventureWorksDW database using the custom SQL query I provided in the DimProduct.sql file. The query doesn't return the exact results as the Product Catalog report, and that's okay.

1. Upload the Product Catalog.rdl file from the \Source\ch06 folder to your report server, such as to a folder called Power BI in the SSRS catalog. Please note that the report data source uses the AdventureWorks2012 database (see the book front matter for setup instructions), and you probably need to change the connection string in the report data source to reflect your specific setup.
2. To test that the report is functional, open the Report Manager by navigating to its URL in your Web browser (assuming SSRS is running in native mode).
3. Navigate to the PowerBI folder. Click the Product Catalog report to run the report. The report should run with no errors.

Importing the report

Follow these steps to import the Product Catalog report in the Adventure Works data model:

1. In Power BI Desktop, expand the Get Data button and click Web.
2. In the "From Web" window that pops up, enter the following URL, but change it to reflect your SSRS server URL (tip: if you test the URL in your Web browser, it should execute fine and it should prompt you to download Product Catalog.csv file):

http://localhost/ReportServer?/PowerBI/Product Catalog&rs:Command=Render&rs:Format=CSV

This URL requests the Product Catalog report that's located in the PowerBI folder of my local report server. The Render command is an optimization step that tells SSRS that the requested resource is a report. The Format command instructs the server to export the report in CSV.

3. Click OK. Power BI Desktop shows a preview of the report data.
4. Click the Edit button. In the Query Editor, rename the query to *Products*.
5. Use the Choose Columns feature to remove all the columns whose names start with "Textbox". Click the "Close & Apply" button to load the Products table.

6.3.7 Importing OData Feeds

Power BI Desktop supports importing data from data feeds that use the OData protocol. Initiated by Microsoft in 2007, Open Data Protocol (OData) is a standard Web protocol for querying and updating data. The protocol allows a client application (consumer), such as Power BI Desktop or Excel, to query a service (provider) over the HTTP protocol and then get the result back in popular data formats, such as Atom Syndication Format (ATOM), JavaScript Object Notation (JSON), or Plain Old XML (POX) formats. Power BI can integrate with any OData-compliant provider, including Azure Marketplace, SharePoint, and cloud applications. This makes it possible to acquire data from virtually any application and platform where developers have implemented an OData API. For more information about OData, see http://odata.org.

To demonstrate importing OData feeds, I'll show you another approach to generate a Date table that uses the DateStream feed available on Microsoft Azure Marketplace. The Microsoft Azure Marketplace is an online market for buying and selling datasets exposed as OData feeds. Some of the datasets, such as DateStream, are freely available. Note that this is an optional exercise as it's meant to show you how the OData import works. You won't need the actual data because the data model already has a date table.

Understanding the DateStream feed

Previously, you imported the Date table from the Adventure Works data warehouse. But where do you get a Date table from if you don't have a data warehouse? While a future release of Power BI Desktop might support auto-generating date tables natively, currently this isn't supported. One option is to maintain a date table in Excel and import it from there. Another option is to obtain it from the DateStream feed (http://datamarket.azure.com/dataset/boyanpenev/datestream) available at Microsoft Azure Marketplace.

The DateStream feed is documented at http://datestream.codeplex.com. Developed by Boyan Penev, it was initially designed to be consumed by Power Pivot. However, because it's implemented as an OData feed, it can be integrated with any OData client. DateStream supports localized date calendars, including US and English calendars. If you need to analyze data by time, it also supports time tables at a minute and second grain.

Importing the DateStream feed

Because Microsoft Azure Marketplace requires authentication, you can't use the OData Feed import option. Instead, you need to import using the Microsoft Azure Marketplace option. As a prerequisite, you need to create a marketplace account so that you can authenticate to Microsoft Azure Marketplace. Once you register with Azure Marketplace, you need to go to https://datamarket.azure.com/dataset/boyanpenev/datestream and sign up to use the DateStream service (it's free!). Let's import the DateStream feed:

1. In Power BI Desktop, click the Get Data button.
2. In the Get Data window, select the Azure tab. Select Microsoft Azure Marketplace and click Connect.
3. If this is the first time you're connecting to Azure Marketplace, you need to authenticate either using a Microsoft account or an account key.
4. In the Navigator window, expand the DateStream node, and then check the appropriate calendar, depending on your localization requirements. In **Figure 6.26**, I selected BasicCalendarUS. Note that the data preview shows dates formatted as "MM/dd/yyyy".

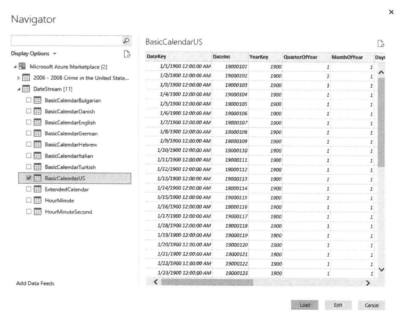

Figure 6.26 The DateStream feed includes localized calendars and time tables.

The feed starts with the year 1900 and goes all the way to 2100. If needed, you can use the Query Editor to filter a smaller range. Just click the Edit button and then apply column filtering to filter the date feed, such as on the YearKey column. And if you need additional columns, such as for fiscal years and quarters, add custom columns in the Query Editor, or add DAX calculated columns in the Data View.

5. Because you won't need this data for the purposes of the Adventure Works data model, click Cancel.

This completes the import process of the initial set of tables that you'll need in order to analyze the Adventure Works sales. At this point, the Fields list should have six tables: FactResellerSales, DimDate, SalesTerritories, Resellers, Employees, and Products.

6.3.8   Importing from R

With all the buzz surrounding R, data analysts might want to preserve their investment in R scripts and reuse them to import, transform, and analyze data with Power BI. Fortunately, Power BI supports R as a data source. The R integration brings the following benefits:

- Cleanse your data – If you prefer to do so, you can use R (instead of or in addition to the Query Editor) to cleanse your data, such as to ensure that all the data points are in place, correct outliers, and normalize to uniform scales. To learn about data shaping with R, check the "Data Cleansing with R in Power BI" blog by Sharon Laivand at http://bit.ly/2eZ6f4R.

- Visualize your R data – Once your R script's data is imported in Power BI, you can use a Power BI visualization to present the data. That's possible because the R data source is not different than any other data source.

- Share the results – You can leverage the Power BI sharing and collaboration capabilities to disseminate the results computed in R with everyone in your organization.

- Operationalize your R script – Once the data is uploaded to Power BI Service, you can configure the dataset for a scheduled refresh, so that the reports are always up to date.

- Reuse your R visualizations – You might use the R ggplot2 package to plot beautiful statistical graphs. Now you can bring these R Visuals into Power BI by using the R script visual in the Visualizations pane. You can also share your R visuals (or use the ones published by the community) at the R Script Showcase (http://community.powerbi.com/t5/R-Script-Showcase/bd-p/RVisuals). This opens up a whole world of new data visualizations! To learn more about how to create R Visuals, read the "Create Power BI visuals using R" blog by David Iseminger at http://bit.ly/2eQ5dHu.

In this exercise, I'll show you how to use R to forecast time series and visualize it (see **Figure 6.27**). The first segment in the line chart shows the actual sales, while the second segment shows the forecasted sales that are calculated in R. Because we won't need the forecasted data in the Adventure Works data model, you'll find the finished example in a separate "R Demo.pbix" file located in the \Source\ch06 folder.

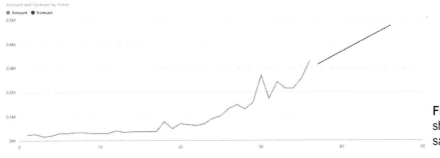

Figure 6.27 This visualization shows actual and forecasted sales.

Getting started with R

R is an open source programming language for statistical computing and data analysis. Over the years the community has contributed and extended the R capabilities through packages that provide various specialized analytical techniques and utilities. Besides supporting R in Power BI, Microsoft invested in R by acquiring Revolution Analytics, whose flagship product (Revolution R) is integrated with SQL Server 2016.

Before you can use the Power BI Desktop R integration, you must install R. R can be downloaded from various location, including the Revolution Open download page or CRAN repository.

1. Open your web browser and navigate to one of the R distribution location, such as https://mran.revolutionanalytics.com/download, and then download and install R for Windows.

2. I also recommend that you install RStudio (an open source R development environment) from http://www.rstudio.com. RStudio will allow you to prepare and test your R script before you import it in Power BI Desktop.

3. Use the Windows ODBC Data Sources (64-bit) tool (or 32-bit if you use the 32-bit version of Power BI Desktop) to set up a new ODBC system data source AdventureWorksDW that points to the AdventureWorksDW2012 (or a later version) database.

Using R for time series forecasting

Next, you'll create a basic R script for time series forecasting using RStudio. The RStudio user interface has four areas (see **Figure 6.28**). The first area (shown as 1 in the screenshot) contains the script that you're working on. The second area is the RStudio Console that allows you to test the script. For example, if you position the mouse cursor on a given script line and press Ctrl-Enter, RStudio will execute the current script line and it will show the output in the console.

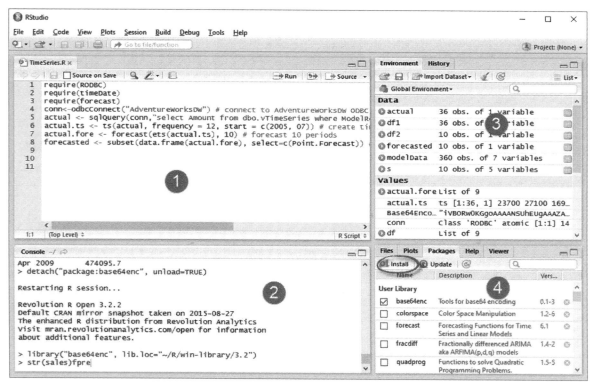

Figure 6.28   Use RStudio to develop and test R scripts.

The Global Environment area (shown as 3 in **Figure 6.28**) shows some helpful information about your script variables, such as the number of observations in a time series object. Area 4 has a tabbed interface that shows some additional information about the RStudio environment. For example, the Packages tab shows you what packages are loaded, while the Plots tab allows you to see the output when you use the R plotting capabilities. Let's start by importing the packages that our script needs:

1. Click File ⇨ New File ⇨ R Script File (or press Ctlr+Shft+N) to create a new R Script. Or, if you don't want to type the R code, click File ⇨ Open File, then open my TimeSeries.R script from the \Source\ch06 folder.

2. In the area 4, select the Packages tab, and then click Install.

3. In the Install Packages window, enter *RODBC* (IntelliSense helps you enter the correct name), and then click Install. This installs the RODBC package which allows you to connect to ODBD data sources.

4. Repeat the last two steps to install the "timeDate" and "forecast" packages.

Going through the code, lines 1-3 list the required packages. Line 4 connects to the AdventureWorksDW ODBC data source. Line 5 retrieves the Amount field from the vTimeSeries SQL view, which is one of the sample views included in the AdventureWorksDW database. The resulting dataset represents the actual sales that are saved in the "actual" data frame. Similar to a Power BI dataset, a R data frame stores data tables. Line 6 creates a time series object with a frequency of 12 because the actual sales are stored by month. Line 7 uses the R forecast package to create forecasted sales for 10 periods. Line 8 stores the Point.Forecast column from the forecasted dataset in a data frame.

 NOTE As of the time of writing, the Power BI R Source only imports data frames, so make sure the data you want to load from a R script is stored in a data frame. Going down the list of limitations, columns that are typed as Complex and Vector are not imported, and are replaced with error values in the created table. Values that are N/A are translated to NULL values in Power BI Desktop. Also, any R script that runs longer than 30 minutes will time out. Interactive calls in the R script, such as waiting for user input, halts the script's execution.

Using the R Script source
Once the R script is tested, you can import the results in Power BI Desktop.

1. Open Power BI Desktop. Click Get Data ⇨ More ⇨ R Script, and then click Connect.

2. In the "Execute R Script" window (see **Figure 6.29**), paste the R script. Expand the "R Installation Settings" section and make sure that the R installation location matches your R setup. Click OK.

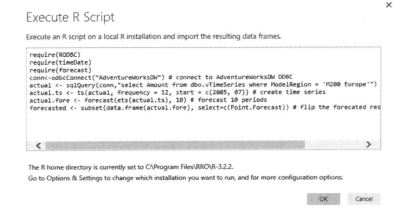

Figure 6.29 Enter the script in "Execute R Script" window and check your R installation settings.

3. In the Navigator window, notice that the script imports two tables (actual and forecasted) that correspond to the two data frames you defined in the R script. Click the Edit button to open Query Editor.

4. Click the "actuals" table.

5. With the "actuals" query selected in the Queries pane, click the Append Queries button in ribbon's Home tab.

6. In the Append window, select the "forecasted" table, and then click OK. This appends the forecasted table to the actual table so that all the data (actual and forecasted) is in a single table.

7. Rename the "actual" table to *ActualAndForecast*. Rename the Point.Forecast column to *Forecast*.

8. (Optional) If you need actual and forecasted values in a single column, in the ribbon's Add Column tab, click "Add Custom Column". Name the custom column "Result" and enter the following expression:

   ```
   if [Amount]=null then [Forecast] else [Amount]
   ```

   This formula adds a new Result column that combines Amount and Forecast values into a single column.

9. In the ribbon's Add Column tab, click "Add Index Column" to add an auto-incremented column that starts with 1.

10. In the Home ribbon, click Close & Apply to execute the script and import the data.

11. To visualize the data, create a Line Chart visualization that has the Index field added to the Axis area, and Amount and Forecast fields added to the Values area.

12. (Optional) Deploy the Power BI Desktop file to Power BI Service and schedule the dataset for refresh.

6.4   Summary

A Power BI model is a relational-like model and represents data as tables and columns. This chapter started by laying out fundamental data modeling concepts (such as table schemas, relationships, and keys) that you need to understand before you import data. It also explained data connectivity options supported by Power BI Desktop and introduced you to the Power BI premium tool for self-service data modeling.

Next, the chapter explained the data import capabilities of Power BI Desktop. As you've seen, you can acquire data from a wide variety of data sources, including relational and multidimensional databases, Excel files, text files, Web, and data feeds. If you use R to import, transform, and analyze data, you can preserve your investment and import your R scripts. Once the data is imported in the model, every dataset is an equal citizen and it doesn't matter where the data came from!

Source data is seldom clean. Next, you'll learn how to use queries to shape and transform raw data when needed.

Chapter 7

Transforming Data

As you've seen, it doesn't take much effort to import data from wherever it might reside. Importing data is one thing, but transforming arbitrary or dirty data is quite another. Fortunately, Power BI Desktop has a query layer that allows you to clean and transform data before it's loaded in the model. Remember that this layer is available when you import data or when you connect live to data sources using the Direct-Query connectivity mechanism. The query layer isn't available when you connect live to SSAS.

This chapter explores the capabilities of the Query Editor component of Power BI Desktop. It starts by introducing you to the Query Editor design environment. Next, it walks you through an exercise to practice its basic transformation steps. It also teaches you about its more advanced transformation features that require custom code. Since you won't need the results from these exercises in the Adventure Works model, you'll practice with a new Power BI Desktop file. You can find the finished query examples that you'll do in this chapter in the Query Examples.pbix file located in the \Source\ch07 folder.

7.1   Understanding the Query Editor

The Query Editor is packed with features that let you share and transform data before it enters the data model. The term "transformation" here includes any modification you apply on the raw data. All transformations are repeatable, meaning that if you have to import another data extract that has the same structure, Power BI Desktop will apply the same transformation steps.

NOTE   You might have heard of BI pros implementing Extraction, Transformation, and Loading (ETL) processes to clean data in an automated way. Think of the Query Editor (or Excel Power Query) relationship to self-service BI as what ETL is to organizational BI. Although not as flexible and powerful as professional ETL tools, the Query Editor should be able to help when issues with source data require basic cleansing and shaping. If your data requires more complex integration and transformation steps, such as when integrating data from multiple systems, consider the organization BI architecture that I discussed in chapter 2 and plan for dedicated ETL.

7.1.1   Understanding the Query Editor Environment

Before I dive into the Query Editor's plethora of features, let's take a moment to explore its environment. As I mentioned, you launch the Query Editor when you click the Edit Queries button in the Power BI Desktop ribbon's Home tab. The Query Editor opens in a new window, side by side with the Power BI Desktop main window. **Figure 7.1** shows the main elements of Query Editor when you open it in the Adventure Works model that you implemented in the previous chapter.

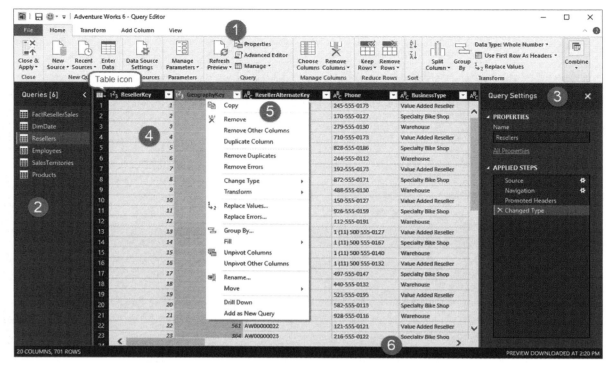

Figure 7.1 The Query Editor opens in a new window to give you access to the queries defined in the model.

Understanding the ribbon's Home tab

The Home tab in the ribbon (see item 1 in **Figure 7.1**) includes buttons for common tasks and some frequently used columns and table-level transformations. Starting from the left, you're already familiar with the Close & Apply button. When expanded, this button has three values, giving you options to close the Query Editor without applying the query changes to the data model (Close menu), to apply the changes without closing the editor (Apply), and both (Close & Apply). If you choose to close the editor without applying the changes, Power BI Desktop will display a warning that pending query changes aren't applied.

 NOTE Some structural changes, such as adding a new column, will reload the data in the corresponding table in the data model. Other changes, such as renaming columns, are handled internally without data refresh. Power BI Desktop (more accurately the xVelocity engine) always tries to apply the minimum steps for a consistent model without unnecessary data refreshes.

The New Query ribbon group is another starting point for creating new queries if you prefer to do so while you're in the Query Editor as opposed to Power BI Desktop. The New Source button is equivalent to the Get Data button in Power BI Desktop. The Recent Sources and Enter Data buttons are the Editor Query counterparts of the same buttons in the Power BI Desktop ribbon's Home tab.

The "Data Source Settings" button in the Data Sources ribbon's group brings the "Data Source Settings" window (you can also open it from the Power BI Desktop File ⇨ "Options and settings" ⇨ "Data source settings" menu) allows you to see what data sources are used in the current Power BI Desktop file, as well as change their authentication, encryption, and privacy settings (all these settings that you specified when you connected to the data source the first time). For example, you can go to the properties of a data source to change the authentication properties, such as to switch from Windows to standard authentication that requires a username and password to connect to a database.

NOTE The data source privacy level determines its level of isolation from other data sources. Suppose you import a list of customers that has some sensitive information, such as contact details. To prevent inadvertently sending this information to another data source, such as a data feed, set the data source privacy level to Private. For more information about privacy levels, read the "Power BI Desktop privacy levels" blog at http://bit.ly/2fkm2P7.

The Managed Parameters button is to define query parameters to customize conveniently certain elements of the data models, such as a query filter, a data source reference, a measure definition, and others. For example, a parameter can change the data source connection information so that you refresh data from Production or Testing environments based on the selected parameter value. I'll postpone discussing the Manage Parameters button to the "Using Advanced Feature" section in this chapter.

The ribbon's Query group is to perform query-related tasks. Specifically, the Refresh Preview button refreshes the preview of the query results, such to see a new column that you just added to an underlying table in the database. The Properties button opens a Query Properties window (**Figure 7.2**) that allows you to change the query name (another way to change the query name is to use the Query Settings pane).

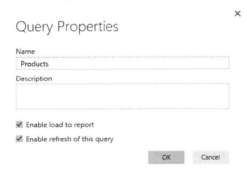

Figure 7.2 Use the Query Properties pane to change the query name, to enable data load to report, and to enable data refresh.

Sometimes, you might not want to load the query data in the data model, such as when you plan to append the query results to another query. If you don't want the query to generate a table in the data model, uncheck the "Unable load to report" checkbox. And, if you don't want to refresh the query results when the user initiates Power BI Desktop table refresh, uncheck "Enable refresh of this query". Continuing on the list of Home tab's buttons, the Advanced Editor button gives you access to the query source. Finally, you can use Manage drop-down button to delete, duplicate, and reference a query. These tasks are also available when you right-click a query in the Queries navigation pane.

NOTE Queries are described in a formula language (informally known as "M"). Every time you apply a new transformation, the Query Editor creates a formula and adds a line to the query source. For more information about the query formula language, read "Microsoft Power Query for Excel Formula Language Specification" at http://go.microsoft.com/fwlink/p/?linkid=320633.

The rest of the buttons on the Home tab let you perform common transformations, including removing columns, reducing rows, grouping by and replacing values, and combining queries. We'll practice many of these in the lab exercise that follows.

Understanding the ribbon's Transform tab
The Transform tab (see **Figure 7.3**) includes additional table and column transformations. Many of the column-level transformations from the context menu (see item 5 in **Figure 7.1**) are available when you right-click a column in the data preview pane. And, many of the table-level transformations are available when you expand or right-click the Table icon (▦) in the top-left corner of the data preview pane.

Figure 7.3 The Transform ribbon (split in the screenshot to reduce space) includes many table and column transformations.

Some transformations apply to columns that have specific data types (see the second row in **Figure** 7.3). For example, the Split Column transformation applies only to text columns, while the Rounding transformation applies only to number columns. If you have experience in R and you prefer to use R for data cleansing and shaping, the "Run R Script" is for inserting the R code. To learn about data shaping with R, check the "Data Cleansing with R in Power BI" blog by Sharon Laivand at http://bit.ly/2eZ6f4R.

Understanding the ribbon's Add Column tab
The Add Column tab (see **Figure 7.4**) lets you create custom columns. For example, I'll show you later how you can create a custom column that returns the last day of the month from a date.

Figure 7.4 Use the Add Column tab in the ribbon to create custom columns.

 NOTE Don't confuse query custom columns with data model calculated columns. Added to the query, query custom columns are created using the Power Query formula language called "M" and they can't reference fields in the data model. On the other hand, calculated columns in the data model are described in DAX and they can reference other fields in the model.

Another interesting variant of a custom column is a conditional column that lets you define different values depending on a condition. For example, similar to a SWITCH CASE statement in programming languages, you can create a conditional column that examines the product cost and assigns each row in the Product table to a cost band which values Low, Medium, or High (see **Figure 6.5**).

Add Conditional Column

Add a conditional column that is computed from the other columns or values.

New column name

CostBand

	Column Name	Operator	Value ⓘ	Output ⓘ	
If	StandardCost	is less than	10	Then Low	...
Else If	StandardCost	is less than	20	Then Medium	
Else If	StandardCost	is greater than or...	20	Then High	

Add Rule

Otherwise ⓘ
Undefined

OK   Cancel

Figure 7.5 The CostBand conditional column evaluates the ProductCost column and assigns each row to a band.

Understanding the ribbon's View tab
Figure 7.6 shows the ribbon's View tab. The Query Settings button in the Layout group toggles the visibility of the Query Settings pane (item 3 in **Figure 7.1**). The Formula Bar checkbox toggles the visibility of the formula bar that shows you the "M" formula behind the selected transformation step. Checking the Monospace checkbox in the Data Preview tab changes the text font in the Data Preview window (the window that shows the query results) to Monospace. When checked, the "Show whitespace" checkbox shows whitespace and newline characters in the Data Preview window.

Checking the "Always allow" checkbox turns on the "Parameter selection" control, so that users can interact with this widget without having to create a parameter beforehand. The Advanced Editor button does the same thing as the button with the same name (also called Advanced Editor) in the Home tab. It shows the source code of the query and allows you to change it. Finally, clicking the Query Dependencies button shows a diagram that can help visualize the dependencies between data sources and queries.

Figure 7.6 The View tab gives you access to the query source.

So what does this "M" query language do for you anyway? It allows you to implement more advanced data manipulation. For example, Martin needs to load multiple Excel files from a given folder. Looping through files isn't an out-of-box feature. However, once Martin applies the necessary transformations to a single file, he can use the Advanced Editor to modify the query source to define a query function. Now Martin can automate the process by invoking the query function for each file, passing the file path. I'll show you some of these capabilities later in this chapter.

7.1.2 Understanding Queries

I mentioned in the previous chapter that there's a query behind every table you import or access live via DirectQuery (except when you connect live to SSAS). The whole purpose of the Query Editor is to give you access to these queries so that you can add additional transformation steps if needed.

💡 **TIP** A quick way to navigate to the underlying query for a table is to right-click the table in the Fields list and then click Edit Query. This will open the Query Editor and select the query in the Queries pane.

Understanding the Queries pane
The Queries pane (see item 5 in **Figure 7.1**) shows you all the queries that exist in the Power BI Desktop file. In the Adventure Works model, there are six queries because you've loaded six tables. In general, the number of queries correspond to the number of tables you use in the model, unless you've created queries for other more advanced tasks, such as to merge a query with results from other queries.

You can right-click a query to open a context menu with additional tasks, such as to delete, duplicate, reference (reuse a base query so you can apply additional steps), enable load (same as "enable load to report" in the Query Properties window), move the query up or down, and organize queries in groups.

Understanding the Query Settings pane
As you've seen, the Query Settings pane allows you to change the query name. Renaming the query changes the name of the table in the data model and vice versa. The more significant role of Query Settings is to list all the steps you've applied to load and shape the data (see **Figure 7.7**). The query shown in the screenshot is named Products and it has four applied steps. The Source step represents the connection to the data source. Customizable steps have a cog icon () to the right.

For example, when you click this icon for the Source step, a Comma Separated-Values window opens to let you view and change the source settings, such as the name of the file and what delimiter will be used to parse the columns. If the Get Data flow used the Navigator window, such as to let you select a database table or an Excel sheet, the second step would be Navigation so that you can view or change the source table if needed. However, you imported the Products table from an SSRS report, and you didn't use the Navigator window.

Although you didn't specifically do this, Power BI Desktop applied the Promoted Headers step to promote the first row as column headers. Power BI Desktop applies the Change Type step when it discovers that it needs to overwrite the column data types. Finally, you applied the "Removed Other Columns" step when you removed some of the source columns when you imported the Product Catalog report.

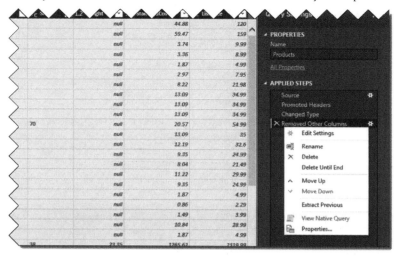

Figure 7.7 The Applied Steps section of Query Setting show all the steps applied to load and shape the data.

You can click a step to select it. If the formula bar is enabled (you can check the Formula checkbox in the ribbon's View tab to enable it), you'll see the query language formula behind the step. In addition, selecting a step updates the data preview to show you how the step affected the source data. When you select a step in the Applied Steps list, the Data Preview pane shows the transformed data after that step is applied. So you can always go back in the step history to check the effect of every step!

If the step is not needed, click the (X) button that appears to the left of the step name when you hover on it, or press the Delete key to remove a step. The Query Editor will ask you to confirm deleting intermediate steps because there might be dependent downstream steps and removing a prior step might result in breaking changes. You can also right-click a step to get additional options, such as to rename a step to make its name more descriptive, to delete it, to delete the current steps and all subsequent steps, to move the step up or down in the Applied Steps list, and to extract previous steps in a separate query.

7.1.3   Understanding Data Preview

The data preview pane (see item 4 back in **Figure 7.1**) shows a read-only view of the source schema and the data as of the time the query was created or the data preview was last refreshed. Each column has a drop-down menu that lets you sort and filter the data before it's imported. Icons in the column headers indicate the column data type, such as a calendar icon for Date/Time columns.

Understanding data filtering
Filtering allows you to exclude rows so you don't end up with more data than you need. The filtering options differ, based on the data type of the column. **Figure 7.8** shows the filtering options available for date/time columns.

NOTE   Power BI queries have smarts to push as much processing as possible to the data source. This is called query folding. For example, if you filter a table column, the query would append a WHERE clause that the query will pass on to the data source. This is much more efficient than filtering the results after all the data is loaded. Filters, joins, groupings, type conversions, and column removal are examples of work that gets folded to the source. What gets folded depends on the capabilities of the source, internal logic, and the data source privacy level. If a transformation step results in query folding, you can right-click the step in the Applied Steps pane, and then click "View Native Query" to see what query is generated. You can't change the query.

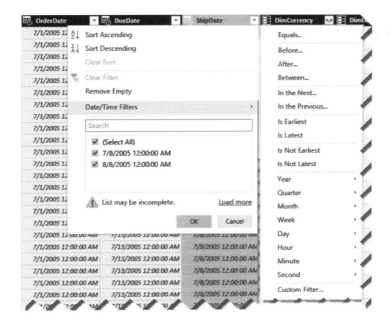

Figure 7.8 The column drop-down allows you to sort and filter the source data before it's loaded in the model

It's important to understand that unlike sorting in the Data View in Power BI Desktop, sorting and filtering in the Query Editor affects how the data is loaded in the data model. For example, if I filter the ShipDate column in FactResellerSales for the last year, this will create a new transformation step that will load only the data for last year based on the system date.

Understanding preview caching

The Query Editor status bar (see item 6 in the figure) informs you when the data preview of the selected query was last refreshed. A cached copy of the query preview results is stored on your local hard disk for faster viewing later. You can control the size of the data cache from File ⇨ Options and Settings ⇨ Options (Data Load tab). Because the preview results are cached, the data preview might get out of sync with schema and data changes in the data source. Click the Refresh Preview button to update the data preview.

If the data preview hasn't been refreshed for more than two days, a warning will be displayed above the preview pane. Don't confuse data preview refresh with table refresh in the data model (the Refresh button in the Power BI Desktop ribbon). The data model refresh executes the queries and reloads the data.

 TIP Do you want to export the data shown in the preview pane? While waiting for Microsoft to implement the "Export to Excel" feature, you can expand the Table icon in the top-left corner of the preview pane and click "Copy Entire Table". Then you can paste the data in Excel.

Auto-discovering relationships

When you import data from a database that has relationships defined between tables, the query discovers these relationships and adds corresponding columns to let you bring columns from the related tables. For example, if you select FactResellerSales and scroll the data preview pane all the way to the right, you'll see "split" columns for DimCurrency, DimDate (three columns for each relationship), DimEmployee, and all the other tables that FactResellerSales has relationships with in the AdventureWorksDW database. If you click the split button (⬌) in the column header, Query Editor opens a list that allows you to add columns from these tables. This handy feature saves you steps to create custom queries to join tables and to look up values in related tables.

NOTE The relationships in the database and in the Query Editor are different than the relationships among the tables in the model (discussed in detail in the next chapter). However, when you import tables, Power BI Desktop checks the query for database relationships during the auto-discovery process and it might add corresponding relationships in the data model.

As you've seen, you can also rename columns in the Query Editor and in the Data View interchangeably. No matter which view you use to rename the column, the new name is automatically applied to the other view. However, I encourage you to check and fix the column data types (use the Transform group in the ribbon's Home tab) in the Query Editor so you can address data type issues before your data is loaded.

For example, you might expect a sales amount field to be a numeric column. However, when Query Editor parsed the column, it changed its data type to Text because of some invalid entries, such as "N/A" or "NULL". It would be much easier to fix these data type errors in the Query Editor, such as by using the Remove Errors, Replace Errors, and Replace Values column-level transformations, than to use DAX formulas in the data model.

7.2   Shaping and Cleansing Data

Suppose that the Adventure Works Finance department gives Martin periodically (let's say every month or year) an Excel file that details accessories and parts that Adventure Works purchases from its vendors. Martin needs to analyze spending by vendor. The problem is that the source data is formatted in Excel tables that the Finance department prepared for its own analysis. This makes it very difficult for Martin to load the data and relate it to other tables that he might have in the model. Fortunately, the Query Editor component of Power BI Desktop allows Martin to transform and extract the data he needs. For the purposes of this exercise, you'll use the Vendor Parts.xlsx file that's located in the \Source\ch07 folder.

7.2.1   Applying Basic Transformations

Figure 7.9 shows the first two report sections in the Vendor Parts file. This format is not suitable for analysis and requires some preprocessing before data can be analyzed. Specifically, the data is divided in sections and each section is designed as an Excel table. However, you need just the data as a single Excel table, similar to the Resellers Excel file that you imported in the previous chapter. Another issue is that the data is presented as crosstab reports, making it impossible to join the vendor data to a Date table in the data model.

Figure 7.9 The Vendor Parts Excel file includes crosstab reports, which present a challenge for relating this data to other tables in the model.

Exploring source data
Let's follow familiar steps to connect to the Excel file. However, this time you'll launch the Query Editor before you import the data.

1. If the Vendor Parts file is open in Excel, close it so that Excel doesn't lock the file and prevent importing.

2. Open a new instance of Power BI Desktop. Save the file as *Query Examples*.

3. Expand the Get Data menu, and click Excel because you'll import an Excel file.

4. Navigate to the \Source\Ch07 folder and select the Vendor Parts.xlsx file. Then click Open.

5. In the Navigator window, check Sheet1 to select it and preview its data. The preview shows how the data would be imported if you don't apply any transformations. As you see, there are many issues with the data, including mixed column content, pivoted data by month, and null values.

6. Click the Edit button to open the Query Editor.

Removing rows

First, let's remove the unnecessary rows:

1. Right-click the first cell in the Column1 column, and then click Text Filters ⇨ "Does Not Equal" to filter only rows where the text in the first column doesn't equal "Vendor Parts – 2008". The net effect after applying this step is that the "Filtered Rows" step will exclude the first row.

2. Locate the *null* value in the first cell of Column3, and apply the same filter (Text Filters ⇨ "Does Not Equal") to exclude all the rows that have *null* in Column3.

3. Promote the first row as headers so that each column has a descriptive column name. To do so, in the ribbon's Transform tab, click the "Use First Row as Headers" button. Alternatively, you can expand the table icon (in the top-left corner of the preview window), and then click "User First Row as Headers". Compare your results with **Figure 7.10**.

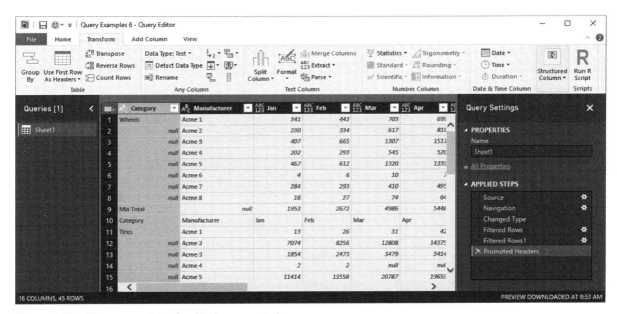

Figure 7.10 The source data after filtering unwanted rows.

4. Note that the first column (Category) has many null values. These empty values will present an issue when relating the table to other tables, such as Product. Click the first cell in the Category column (that says Wheels), and then click the ribbon's Transform tab. Click the Fill ⇨ Down button. This fills the null values with the actual categories.

5. Let's remove rows that represent report subtotals. To do so, right-click a cell in the Category column that contains the word "Category" (should be the first cell in the tenth row). Click Text Filters ⇨ "Does Not Equal" to remove all the rows that have "Category" in the first column.

6. Next, you will need to filter all the rows that contain the word "Total". Expand the column drop-down in the column header of the Category column. Click Text Filters ⇨ "Does Not Contain". In the Filter Rows dialog box, type "Total", and then click OK.

7. Hold the Ctrl key and select the last two columns, Column15 and 2014 Total. Right-click the selection, and then click Remove Columns.

Un-pivoting columns

Now that you've cleansed most of the data, there's one remaining task. Note how the months appear on columns. This makes it impossible to join the table to a Date table because you can't join on multiple columns. To make things worse, as new periods are added, the number of columns might increase. To solve this problem, you need to un-pivot the months from columns to rows. Fortunately, this is very easy to do with the Query Editor!

1. Hold the Shift key and select all the month columns, from Jan to Dec.

2. Right-click the selection, and then click Unpivot Columns. The Query Editor un-pivots the data by creating new columns called Attribute and Value, as shown in **Figure 7.11**.

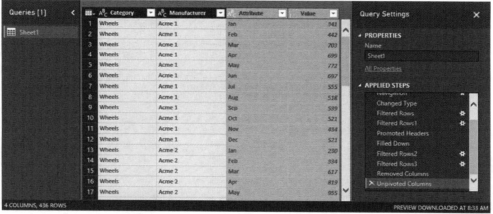

Figure 7.11 The un-pivoted dataset includes Attribute and Value columns.

8. Double-click the column header of the Attribute column, and rename it to *Month*. Rename the Value column to *Units*.

Adding custom columns

If you have a Date table in the model, you might want to join this data to it. As I mentioned, a Data table is at a day granularity. So that you can join to it, you need to convert the Month column to a date. Click the ribbon's Add Column tab, and then click "Custom Column".

1. In the "Add Custom Column" dialog box, enter *FirstDayOfMonth* as the column name. Then enter the following formula (be careful because the "M" query language is case sensitive):

```
=Date.FromText([Month] & " 1, 2008")
```

2. Compare your results with **Figure 7.12**.

Add Custom Column

New column name

FirstDayOfMonth

Custom column formula:

`=Date.FromText([Month] & " 1, 2008")`

Available columns:

Category
Manufacturer
Month
Units

<< Insert

Learn about Power BI Desktop formulas

✓ No syntax errors have been detected.

OK   Cancel

Figure 7.12 Create a custom column that converts a month to a date.

This formula converts the month value to the first day of the month in year 2008. For example, if the Month value is Jan, the resulting value will be 1/1/2008. The formula hardcodes the year to 2008 because the source data doesn't have the actual year. If you need to default to the current year, you can use the formula Date.Year(DateTime.LocalNow()). Or, had the year been present in a column, you could simply reference that column in the expression.

NOTE Unfortunately, as it stands the "Add Custom Column" window doesn't have IntelliSense or show you the formula syntax, making it difficult to work with formulas and forcing a "trial and error" approach. If you've made a mistake, the custom column will display "Error" in every row. You can click the Error link to get more information about the error. Then in the Applied Steps pane, click the Settings next to the step to get back to the formula, and try again.

3. Assuming you need the month end date instead of the first date of the month, select the FirstDayOfMonth column. In the ribbon's Transform tab, expand the Date drop-down button, and then select Month ⇨ "End of Month".

4. Rename the new column to *Date*.

That's it! With a few clicks you added a dozen steps that will transform and cleanse the source data into a format that is suitable for reporting. But the data is not loaded yet. What you just did was defining the steps that will be executed in the order that are listed in the "Applied Steps" pane once you load or refresh the data.

7.2.2 Loading Transformed Data

As I explained before, you have used the "Close & Apply" button to load the data. Recall that the first option "Close & Apply" closes the Query Editor and applies the changes to the model. You can close the Query Editor without applying the changes, but the model and queries aren't synchronized. Finally, you can choose to apply the changes without closing the Query Editor so that you can continue working on the queries.

Renaming steps and queries

Before loading the data, consider renaming the query to apply the same name to the new table. You can also rename transformation steps to make them more descriptive. Let's rename the query and a step:

1. In the Query Settings pane, rename the query to *VendorParts*. This will become the name of the table in the model.

2. In the Applied Steps pane, right-click the last step and click Rename. Change the step name to *"Renamed Column to Date"*, and click Enter.

3. (Optional) Right-click any of the steps in the Applied Steps pane, and click Properties. Notice that you can enter a description. Then when you hover on the step, the description will show in a tooltip. This is a great way to explain what a step does in more detail.

Loading transformed data
Let's load the transformed data into a new table:

1. Click the Close & Apply button in the ribbon's Home tab. Power BI Desktop imports the data, applies all the steps as the data streams into the model, closes the Query Editor, and adds the VendorParts table to the Fields pane.

2. In the ribbon's Home tab, click the Edit Queries button. This brings you to the Query Editor in case you want to apply additional transformation steps.

3. (Optional) You can disable loading query results. This could be useful if another query uses the results from the VendorParts query and it doesn't make sense to create unnecessary tables in the model. To demonstrate this, open Query Editor, right-click the VendorParts query in the Queries pane, and then uncheck "Enable Load". Accept the warning that follows that disabling the query load will delete the table from the model and break existing reports. Click Close & Apply and notice that the VendorParts table is removed from the Fields list.

7.3   Using Advanced Features

The Query Editor has much more to offer than just basic column transformations. In this section, I'll walk you through more advanced scenarios that you might encounter so that you handle them yourself instead of asking for help. First, you'll see how you can join and merge datasets. Then I'll show you how query functions can help you automate mundane data processing tasks. You'll find how to use the "M" query language to auto-generate date tables and how to parameterize connections to data sources.

7.3.1   Combining Datasets

As I mentioned previously, if relationships exist in the database, the query will discover these relationships. This allows you to expand a table and reference columns from other tables. For example, if you open the Adventure Works model (Adventure Works.pbix) and examine the data preview pane of the FactResellerSales query, you'll see columns that correspond to all the tables that are related to the FactResellerSales table in the AdventureWorksDW database. All of these columns show the text "Value" for each row in FactResellerSales and have an expansion button (➪) in the column header (see **Figure 7.13**).

When you click the expansion button, the Query Editor opens a window that lists all the columns from the related table so that you can include the columns you want in the query. This is a useful feature, but what if there are no relationships in the data source? As it turns out, as long as you have matching columns, you can merge (join) queries.

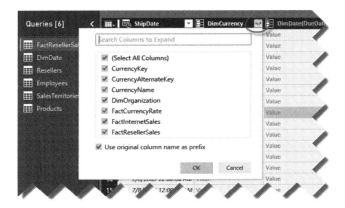

Figure 7.13 Create a custom column that converts a month to a date.

Figure 7.13 Create a custom column that converts a month to a date.

Merging queries

We're back to the Query Examples.pbix file. Suppose you have another query that returns a list of vendors that Adventure Works does business with. Let's import this list.

1. If the Query Editor is closed, click the Edit Queries button in the Power BI Desktop's ribbon to open it. In the Query Editor's Home ribbon, expand Get Data and then click Excel.

2. Navigate to the \Source\ch07 folder and select the Vendor Parts file.

3. In the Navigator window, check the Vendors sheet and then click Load. This creates a Vendors query that load the data from the Vendors sheet in the Excel file.

4. In the Queries pane, make sure the Vendors query is selected. Select the Transform ribbon tab and then click "Use First Row as Headers" button to promote the first row as column headers.

5. Compare your results with **Figure 7.14**.

Figure 7.14 The Vendors query returns a list of vendors imported from the Vendors sheet in the Vendor Parts Excel file.

Now I'd like to join the VendorParts query to the Vendors query so that I can look up some columns from the Vendor query and add them to the VendorParts query. If two queries have a matching column(s) you can join (merge) them just like you can join two tables in SQL.

6. In the Queries pane, select the VendorParts query because this will be our base query.

7. In the ribbon's Home tab, click Merge Queries (in the Combine group).

8. Configure the Merge window as shown in **Figure 7.15**. This setup joins the Manufacturer column from the VendorParts query to the Name column of the Vendors query.

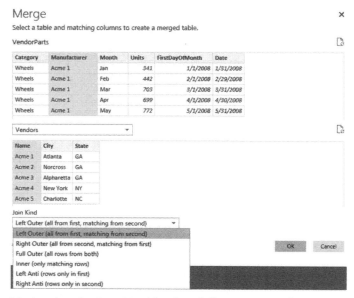

Figure 7.15 You can merge queries by one or more matching columns.

Notice that the Join Kind list has different types of joins. For example, a Left Outer Join will keep all the rows from the first query and only return the matching values from the second query, or null if no match is found. By contrast, the Inner Join will only return matching rows.

9. Click OK. The Query Editor adds a NewColumn column to the end of the VendorParts query.

10. Click the expansion button in the column header of the new column. Notice that now you can add columns from the Vendors query (**Figure 8.16**). You can also aggregate these columns, such as by using the Sum or Count aggregation functions.

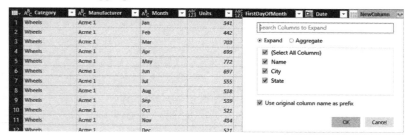

Figure 7.16 Once you merge queries, you can add columns to the source query from the merged query.

Appending queries

Suppose that some time has passed and Martin gets another Vendors Parts report, for the year 2009. Instead of overwriting the existing data for 2008 in the data model, which will happen if Martin refreshes the data, Martin wants to append the second dataset to the VendorParts table so he can analyze data across several years. If Martin is given a new file once in a while, such as in a month or year, he can use the "Append Queries" feature to append datasets manually. This will work as long as the dataset format (schema) is the same. To simulate a second dataset, you'll clone the existing VendorParts query.

1. In the Queries pane, right-click the VendorParts query, and then click Duplicate. The Query Editor adds a VendorParts (2) query.

2. In the Queries pane, select the VendorParts (2) query. Click the cog icon (✿) to the right of "Added Custom" step, and then change the formula to use year 2009. You do this to simulate that this dataset has data for the year 2009.

=Date.FromText([Month] & " 1, 2009")

3. In the Query Settings pane, rename the VendorsParts (2) query to *VendorParts 2009*.

4. Right-click *VendorParts 2009* and turn off Enable Load because you'll append this query and you don't want it to create a new table when you click Close & Apply.

5. In the Queries pane, select the VendorParts query.

6. In the ribbon's Home tab, click Append Queries (in the Combine group).

7. In the Append window, expand "Table to append" and select the VendorParts 2009 query. Click OK.

The Query Editor appends VendorParts 2009 to VendorParts. As a result, the VendorParts query returns a combined dataset for years 2008 and 2009. As long as two queries have the same columns, you can append them.

 TIP   If you need more complicated logic to look up values from another table you might find my blog "Implementing Lookups in Power Query" at http://prologika.com/implementing-lookups-in-power-query/ useful. It demonstrates a query function that uses a range filter for the lookup.

7.3.2 Using Functions

Appending datasets manually can get tedious quickly as the number of files increase. What if Martin is given Excel reports every month and he needs to combine 100 files? Well, when the going gets tough, you write some automation code, right? If you have a programming background, your first thought might be to write code that loops through files, to check if the file is an Excel file, to load it, and so on. However, the "M" language that Power BI queries are written in is a functional language, and it doesn't support loops and conditional logic. What it does support is functions and they can be incredibly useful for automation.

Creating query functions

Think of a query function as a query that can be called repeatedly from another query. Similar to functions in programming languages, such as C# and Visual Basic, a function can take parameters to make it generic. Let's create a query function that will load an Excel file given a folder path and file name.

1. The easiest way to create a function is to start with an existing query that already produces the results you need. We're back to the Query Editor. In the Queries pane, right-click the VendorParts query and then click Duplicate.

2. In the Applied Steps pane, delete the last two steps (Merged Queries and Appended Query) to avoid the error *"Query <query> references other queries or steps, so it may not directly access a data source. Please rebuild this data combination"* when you convert this query to a function. If you need these steps, you can add them after the query is converted to a function.

3. In the Queries pane, right-click the VendorParts (2) query, and then click Advanced Editor. Another way to open the Advanced Editor is to click Advanced Editor in the ribbon's Home tab or View tab. The Advanced Editor shows the M code behind the query. Each line represents a transformation step you applied.

4. Insert a new line at the beginning of the query and type in the following M code (see **Figure 7.17**):

() =>

The empty parenthesis signifies that the function has no parameters. And the "goes-to" => operator precedes the function code.

5. Click Done. Dismiss the prompt that asks you if you want to invoke the function. In the Applied Steps list of the Query Settings pane, you should see a single step called *Vendor Parts (2)*. In the Queries pane, you

should see *fx* in front of *Vendor Parts* (2) to denote that this query has been converted to a query function. The Preview pane has an Invoke button.

Figure 7.17 Use the Advanced Editor to work with the query code and create a function.

6. Rename the query function to *fnProcessFiles*. A function can be called anything but it's good to have a consistent naming convention.

Working with function parameters
The next step will be to make the function generic by taking the file path to a file to load as an argument.

1. In the Queries pane, right-click the *fnProcessFiles* query, and then click Advanced Editor. Notice that the Query Editor has changed the function code somewhat when you invoked the function.

2. Change the first let statement as follows (see **Figure 8.18**) to define two parameters:

```
let
    fnProcessFiles = (FolderPath, FileName) =>
```

Figure 7.18 The fnProcessFiles function takes two parameters.

3. Now that the function allows you to specify the file location, instead of hardcoding the path to the Excel file, change the "Source =" line as follows:

```
Source = Excel.Workbook(File.Contents(FolderPath & FileName), null, true),
```

This code uses the ampersand (&) operator to concatenate the folder path and file name parameters. The reason why I don't pass the full path as a single parameter will become obvious in a moment.

4. At the end of the function, add this code to close the first let statement:

```
in
    fnProcessFiles
```

5. Click Done to close the Advanced Editor.

6. (Optional) If you now click the *fnProcessFiles* function in the Queries pane to select it, the Query Preview pane should show the two parameters. Enter a folder path and name of an existing Excel file, such as to Vendor Parts.xlsx to test the function.

Invoking functions

Now that the function is ready, you need another query to invoke it. In our case, the outer query will loop through all files in a given folder and call the *fnProcessFiles* function to load the data from each file.

1. In the Query Editor, expand the New Source button (in the ribbon's Home tab), and then click More.

2. In the Get Data window, click the File tab and select Folder. The Folder data source returns a list of files in a specific folder. Click Connect.

3. In the Folder window, specify the folder path where the Excel source files are located. For your convenience, I saved two Excel files in the \Source\ch07\Files folder. Click OK.

4. A window opens up that shows a list of files in that folder. Click OK to create the query.

5. In the Queries pane, rename the new query to *ProcessExcelFiles*.

> 💡 **TIP** If the folder contains different types of files and you want to process files with a specific file extension(s), you can filter the Extension column in the data preview pane of the Query Editor. For example, to only process Excel 2007 or later files, filter the Extension column to include only the "*.xlsx" file extension.

6. Each row in the ProcessExcelFiles query represents a file. You need to add a custom column that invokes the *fnProcessFile* function for each file.

7. In the Queries pane, select the ProcessExcelFiles query. In the ribbon's Add Column tab, click "Custom Column". Configure the custom column as shown in **Figure 7.19**, and then click OK. As a result of these changes, the custom column will invoke the *fnProcessFunction* for each row in the ProcessExcelFiles query and pass the Folder Path and Name columns as arguments to the fnProcessFiles function.

Figure 7.19 Add a custom column to the outer query to invoke the fnProcessFiles query function.

8. The Query Editor adds the custom column to the ProcessExcelFiles query. Because the Query Editor understands that the function returns a table, it allows you to expand the custom column. In the data preview pane, expand the Custom column by clicking the double-arrow button in the column header.

9. In the Expand Custom window, leave all the columns selected. Assuming you don't want each column to be prefixed, uncheck the "Use original column name as prefix" checkbox. Click OK.

For each file in the folder, the ProcessExcelFiles query calls fnProcessFiles. Each time the function is invoked, it loads the file passed as argument and appends the results.

 NOTE If you expand the drop-down of the Date column, you'll only see dates for year 2008, which might let you believe that you have data from one file only. This is actually not the case, but it's a logical bug because year 2008 is hardcoded in the query. If the year is specified in the file name, you can add another custom column that extracts the year, passes it to a third parameter in the fnProcessFiles function, and uses that parameter instead of hardcoded references to "2008".

7.3.3 Generating Date Tables

Now that you know about query functions, I'm sure you'll think of many real-life scenarios where you can use them to automate routine data crunching tasks. Let's revisit a familiar scenario. As I mentioned in Chapter 6, even if you import a single dataset, you should strongly consider a separate date table. I also mentioned that there are different ways to import a date table, and one of them was to generate it in the Query Editor. The following code is based on an example by Matt Masson, as described in his "Creating a Date Dimension with a Power Query Script" blog post (http://www.mattmasson.com/2014/02/creating-a-date-dimension-with-a-power-query-script).

Generating dates
The Query Editor has useful functions for manipulating dates, such as for extracting date parts (day, month, quarter), and so on. The code uses many of these functions.

1. Start by creating a new blank query. To do so, in the Query Editor, expand the New Source button (the ribbon's Home tab) and click Blank Query. Rename the blank query to *GenerateDateTable*.
2. In the Queries pane, right-click the GenerateDateTable query and click Advanced Editor.
3. In the Advanced Editor, paste the following code which you can copy from the GenerateDateTable.txt file in the \Source\ch07 folder:

```
let GenerateDateTable = (StartDate as date, EndDate as date, optional Culture as nullable text) as table =>
  let
    DayCount = Duration.Days(Duration.From(EndDate - StartDate)),
    Source = List.Dates(StartDate,DayCount,#duration(1,0,0,0)),
    TableFromList = Table.FromList(Source, Splitter.SplitByNothing()),
    ChangedType = Table.TransformColumnTypes(TableFromList,{{"Column1", type date}}),
    RenamedColumns = Table.RenameColumns(ChangedType,{{"Column1", "Date"}}),
    InsertYear = Table.AddColumn(RenamedColumns, "Year", each Date.Year([Date])),
    InsertQuarter = Table.AddColumn(InsertYear, "QuarterOfYear", each Date.QuarterOfYear([Date])),
    InsertMonth = Table.AddColumn(InsertQuarter, "MonthOfYear", each Date.Month([Date])),
    InsertDay = Table.AddColumn(InsertMonth, "DayOfMonth", each Date.Day([Date])),
    InsertDayInt = Table.AddColumn(InsertDay, "DateInt", each [Year] * 10000 + [MonthOfYear] * 100 + [DayOfMonth]),
    InsertMonthName = Table.AddColumn(InsertDayInt, "MonthName", each Date.ToText([Date], "MMMM", Culture), type text),
    InsertCalendarMonth = Table.AddColumn(InsertMonthName, "MonthInCalendar", each (try(Text.Range([MonthName],0,3))
      otherwise [MonthName]) & " " & Number.ToText([Year])),
    InsertCalendarQtr = Table.AddColumn(InsertCalendarMonth, "QuarterInCalendar", each "Q" & Number.ToText([QuarterOfYear]) & " "
& Number.ToText([Year])),
    InsertDayWeek = Table.AddColumn(InsertCalendarQtr, "DayInWeek", each Date.DayOfWeek([Date])),
    InsertDayName = Table.AddColumn(InsertDayWeek, "DayOfWeekName", each Date.ToText([Date], "dddd", Culture), type text),
    InsertWeekEnding = Table.AddColumn(InsertDayName, "WeekEnding", each Date.EndOfWeek([Date]), type date)
  in
    InsertWeekEnding
in
  GenerateDateTable
```

This code creates a GenerateDateTable function that takes three parameters: start date, end date, and optional language culture, such as "en-US", to localize the date formats and correctly interpret the date parameters. The workhorse of the function is the List.Dates method, which returns a list of date values starting at the start date and adding a day to every value. Then the function applies various transformations and adds custom columns to generate date variants, such as Year, QuarterOfYear, and so on.

Invoking the function
You don't need an outer query to generate the GenerateDateTable function because you don't have to execute it repeatedly. In this case, you simply want to invoke the function for a range of dates.

1. In the Queries pane, select the GenerateDateTable query, and then click the Invoke button in the preview pane.
2. In the Enter Parameters window (see **Figure 7.20**), enter StartDate and EndDate parameters. Click OK to invoke the function.

Figure 7.20 Invoke the Generate-DateTable function and pass the required parameters.

3. Watch how the Query Editor produces a date table in a second and creates an Invoked Function query with the results. If you want to regenerate the table with a different range of values, simply delete the "Invoked Function" query in the Queries pane, and then invoke the function again with different parameters.

7.3.4 Working with Query Parameters

As you've seen, query functions can go a long way to help you create reusable queries. However, sometimes you might need a quick and easy way to customize the query behavior. Suppose you want to change the data source connection to point to a different server, such as when you want to switch from your development server to a production server. This is where query parameters can help.

A query parameter externalizes certain query settings, such as a data source reference, a column replacement value, a query filter, and others, so that you can customize the query behavior without having to change the query itself. How do you know what query settings can be parameterized? If a step in the Applied Steps pane has a cog icon next to it (has a window that let you change its settings), click it and look for settings that are prefixed with a drop-down $^{A^B_C}$ ▾. If you see it, then that setting can be parameterized.

Creating query parameters
Suppose you're given access to a development SQL Server and you have created a model with many tables. Now, you want to load data from another server, such as your production server. This isn't as bad as it sounds because you can click the "Data Source Settings" button found in the Query Editor's Home ribbon group and change the server name. But suppose you want to switch back and forth between development and production environments and you don't want to remember (and type in) the server names (they can get rather cryptic sometimes). Instead, you'll create a query parameter that will let you change the data source with a couple of mouse clicks.

1. To have a test query, in the Query Editor (Home ribbon), expand Get Data and import a table, such as DimProduct, from the AdventureWorksDW database. You can import any table you want. If you don't have access to SQL Server, you can import the \Source\ch07\DimProduct file and then follow similar steps to parameterize the query connection string.

2. In the Home ribbon's tab, click the Manage Parameters button.

3. In the Parameters window, click the New link and create a new parameter (see **Figure 7.21**).

   I've created a required parameter named *Server*. The parameter data type is Text. I've decided to choose the parameter value from a pre-defined list that includes two servers (ELITE and MILLENNIA). You can also type in the parameter value or load it from an existing query. The parameter will default to ELITE and the parameter current value is ELITE. Consequently, I'll be referencing the ELITE server in my queries.

4. Click OK to create the parameter.

Using query parameters

Now that we have the Server parameter defined, let's use it to change the data source in all queries. The following steps assume that you want to change the server name in all queries that reference the SQL Server. If you want to change only specific queries, instead of using Data Source Settings, change the Source step in the Applied Steps pane for these queries.

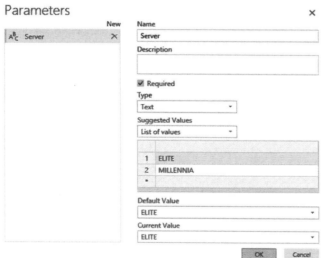

Figure 7.21 When setting up a parameter, specify its name, type, and suggested values.

1. In the Home ribbon, click the Data Source Settings button.

2. In the Data Source Settings window, select the data source that references your server, and then click the Change Source button. If the data source is SQL Server, the familiar "SQL Server Database" window opens.

3. Expand the drop-down to the left of the server name and choose Parameter. Then expand the drop-down to the right and select the Server parameter (see **Figure 7.22**). Click OK.

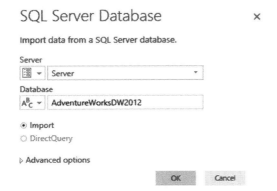

SQL Server Database   ×

Import data from a SQL Server database.

Server

[▦ ▾] | Server   ▾ |

Database

[Aᴮᴄ ▾] | AdventureWorksDW2012 |

◉ Import
○ DirectQuery

▷ Advanced options

| OK | Cancel |

Figure 7.22 You can parameterize every query setting that has a drop-down.

4. In the Query Editor, observe that a new query named Server is added to the query list. By default, the query results won't be loaded in a table, but you can right-click the query and click Enable Load.

> **TIP**   What makes query parameters even more useful is that you can reference the selected parameter value in DAX formulas, such as to show on the report which server is being used to load the data from. Assuming that you've enabled the loading of the Server query and have a Server table added to the model, you can use this DAX measure to show the server name:
> ServerName = "The current server is " & FIRSTNONBLANK('Server'[Server], TRUE)

5. Besides settings the parameter value in the Query Editor, you can do so directly in Power BI Desktop without having to open Query Editor. In the Power BI Desktop window (Home ribbon's tab), expand the Edit Queries tab and then click Edit Parameters. Notice that you can change the Server parameter.

7.4   Summary

Behind the scenes, when you import data, Power BI Desktop creates a query and there's a query for every table you import. Not only does the query give you access to the source data, but it also allows you to shape and transform data using various table and column-level transformations. To practice this, you applied a series of steps to shape and clean a crosstab Excel report so that its results can be used in a self-service data model.

You also practiced more advanced query features. You learned how to join, merge, and append datasets. Every step you apply to the query generates a line of code described in the M query language. You can view and customize the code to meet more advanced scenarios and automate repetitive tasks. You learned how to use query functions to automate importing files. And you saw how you can use custom query code to generate date tables if you can't import them from other places. You can also define query parameters to customize the query behavior.

Next, you'll learn how to extend and refine the model to make it more feature-rich and intuitive to end users!

Chapter 8

Refining the Model

In the previous two chapters, you learned how to import and transform data. The next step is to explore and refine your data model before you start gaining insights from it. Typical tasks in this phase include making table and field names more intuitive, exploring data, and changing the column type and formatting options. When your model has multiple tables, you must also set up relationships to relate tables.

In this chapter, you'll practice common tasks to enhance the Adventure Works model. First, you'll learn how to explore the loaded data and how to refine the metadata. Next, I'll show you how to manage schema and data changes, including managing connections and tables, and refreshing the model data to synchronize it with changes in the data sources. Finally, I'll walk you through the steps needed to set up table relationships so that you can perform analysis across multiple tables.

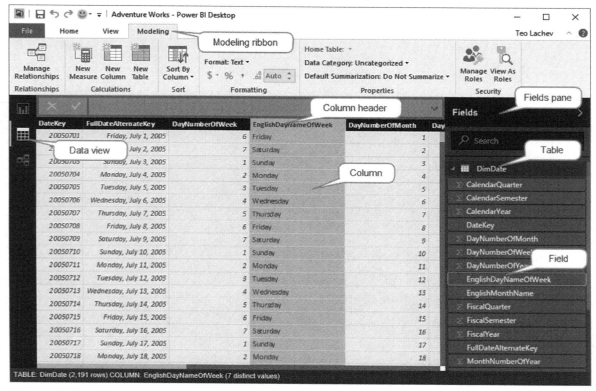

Figure 8.1 In the Data View, you can browse the model schema and data.

8.1 Understanding Tables and Columns

Recall from Chapter 7 that Power BI Desktop supports two data options: you can either import or connect directly to your data. If you decide to import, Power BI stores imported data in tables. Although the data might originate from heterogeneous data sources, once it enters the model, it's treated the same regardless of its origin. Similar to a relational database, a table consists of columns and rows. You can use the Data View to explore a table and its data, as shown in **Figure 8.1**.

8.1.1 Understanding the Data View

The Power BI Desktop navigation bar (the vertical bar on the left) has three view icons: Report, Data, and Relationships. As its name suggests, the Data View allows you to browse the model data. In contrast, the Relationships View only shows a graphical representation of the model schema. And the Report View is for creating visualizations that help you analyze the data. In Chapter 6, I covered how the Data View shows the imported data from the tables in the model. This is different from the Query Editor data preview, which shows the source data and how it's affected by the transformations you've applied.

Understanding tables

The Fields pane shows you the model metadata that you interact with when creating reports. When you select a table in the Fields pane, the Data View shows you the first rows in the table. As it stands, the Adventure Works model has six tables. The Data View and the Fields pane shows the metadata (table names and column names) sorted alphabetically. You can also use the Search box in the Fields pane to find fields quickly, such as type in *sales* to filter all fields whose name include "sales".

 NOTE What's the difference between a column and a field anyway? A field in the Fields pane can be a table column or a calculated measure, such as SalesYTD. However, a calculated measure doesn't map to a table column. So, fields include both physical table columns and calculations.

The table name is significant because it's included in the model metadata, and it's shown to the end user. In addition, when you create calculated columns and measures, the Data Analysis Expressions (DAX) formulas reference the table and field names. Therefore, spend some time to choose suitable names and to rename tables and fields accordingly.

 TIP When it comes to naming conventions, I like to keep table and column names as short as possible so that they don't occupy too much space in report labels. I prefer camel casing where the first letter of each word is capitalized. I also prefer to use a plural case for fact tables, such as ResellerSales, and a singular case for lookup (dimension) tables, such as Reseller. You don't have to follow this convention, but it's important to have a consistent naming convention and to stick to it. While I'm on this subject, Power BI supports identical column names across tables, such as SalesAmount in the ResellerSales table and SalesAmount in the InternetSales table. However, some reporting tools, such as Power BI reports, don't support renaming fields on the report, and you won't be able to tell the two fields apart if a report has both fields. Therefore, consider renaming the columns and adding a prefix to have unique column names across tables, such as ResellerSalesAmount and InternetSalesAmount. Or you can create DAX calculations with unique names and then hide the original columns.

The status bar at the bottom of the Data View shows the number of rows in the selected table. When you select a field, the status bar also shows the number of its distinct values. For example, the English-DayNameOfWeek field has seven distinct values. This is useful to know because that's how many values the users will see when they add this field to the report.

Understanding columns

The vertical bands in a table open in the Data View represent the table columns. You can click any cell to select the entire column and to highlight the column header. The Formatting group in the ribbon's Modeling tab shows the data type of the selected column. Similar to the Query Editor data preview, Data View is read-only. You can't change the data – not even a single cell. Therefore, if you need to change a value, such as when you find a data error that requires a correction, you must make the changes either in the data source or in the query. As I mentioned before, I encourage you to make data changes in the query.

Another way to select a column is to click it in the Fields pane. The Fields pane prefixes some fields with icons. For example, the sigma (Σ) icon signifies that the field is numeric and can be aggregated using any of the supported aggregate functions, such as Sum or Average. If the field is a calculated measure, it'll be prefixed with a calculator icon (▦). Even though some fields are numeric, they can't be meaningfully aggregated, such as CalendarYear. The Properties group in the ribbon's Modeling tab allows you to change the default aggregation behavior, such as to change the CalendarYear default aggregation to "Do not aggregate". This is just a default; you and other users can still overwrite the aggregation on reports.

The Data Category property in the Properties group (ribbon's Modeling tab) allows you to change the column category. For example, to help Power BI understand that this is a geospatial field, you can change the data category of the SalesTerritoryCountry column to Country/Region. This will prefix the field with a globe icon. More importantly, this helps Power BI to choose the best visualization when you add the field on an empty report, such as to use a map visualization when you add a geospatial field. Or, if a column includes hyperlinks and you would like the user to be able to navigate by clicking the link, set the column's data category to Web URL.

8.1.2 Exploring Data

If there were data modeling commandments, the first one would be "Know thy data". Realizing the common need to explore the raw data, the Power BI team has added features to both the Query Editor and Data View to help you become familiar with the source data.

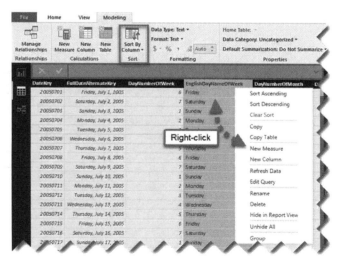

Figure 8.2 You can sort the field content in ascending or descending order.

Sorting data

Power BI doesn't sort data by default. As a result, Data View shows the imported data as it's loaded from the source. You can right-click a column and use the sort options (see **Figure 8.2**) to sort the data. You can sort the content of a table column in an ascending or descending order. This type of sorting is for your benefit, because it allows you to get familiar with the imported data, such as to find what's the minimum or maximum value. Power BI doesn't apply the sorting changes to the way the data is saved in the model, nor does it propagate the column sort to reports. For example, you might sort the EnglishDayNameOf-Week column in a descending order. However, when you create a report that uses this field, the visualization would ignore the Data View sorting changes and it will sort days in an ascending order (or whatever sort order the reporting tool prefers).

When a column is sorted in the Data View, you'll see an up or down arrow in the column header, which indicates the sort order. You can sort the table data by only one column at a time. To clear sorting and to revert to the data source sort order, right-click a column, and then click Clear Sort.

> **NOTE** Power BI Desktop automatically inherits the data collation based on the language selection in your Windows regional settings, which you can overwrite in the Options and Settings ⇨ Option ⇨ Data Load (Current File section). The default collations are case-insensitive. Consequently, if you have a source column with the values "John" and "JOHn", then Power BI Desktop imports both values as "John" and treats them the same. While this behavior helps the xVelocity storage engine compress data efficiently, sometimes a case-sensitive collation might be preferable, such as when you need a unique key to set up a relationship, and you get an error that the column contains duplicate values. However, currently there isn't an easy way to change the collation and configure a given field or a table to be case-sensitive. So you'll need to try to keep the column names distinct.

Custom sorting

Certain columns must be sorted in a specific order on reports. For example, calendar months should be sorted in their ordinal position (Jan, Feb, and so on) as opposed to alphabetically. To accomplish this, Power BI supports custom sorting. Custom sorting allows you to sort a column by another column, assuming the column to sort on has one-to-one or one-to-many cardinality with the sorted column.

Let's say you have a column MonthName with values Jan, Feb, Mar, and so on, and you have another column MonthNumberOfYear that stores the ordinal number of the month in the range from 1 to 12. Because every value in the MonthName column has only one corresponding value in MonthNumberOfYear column, you can sort MonthName by MonthNumberOfYear. However, you can't sort MonthName by a Date column because there are multiple dates for each month.

Compared to field sorting for data expiration, custom sorting has a reverse effect on data. Custom sorting doesn't change the way the data is displayed in the Data View, but it affects how the data is presented in reports. **Figure 8.3** shows how changing custom sorting will affect the sort order of the month name column on a report.

Figure 8.3 The left table shows the month with the default alphabetical sort order while the right table shows it after custom sorting was applied by MonthNumberOfYear.

Copying data

Sometimes you might want to copy the content of a column (or even an entire table) and paste it in Excel or send it to someone. You can use the Copy and Copy Table options from the context menu (see **Figure 8.2** again) to copy the content to Windows Clipboard and paste it in another application. You can't paste the copied data into the data model. Again, that's because the data model is read-only.

The Copy Table option is also available when you right-click a table in the Fields pane. Copying a table preserves the tabular format, so pasting it in Excel produces a list with columns instead of a single column.

8.1.3 Understanding the Column Data Types

A table column has a data type associated with it. In Chapter 6, I mentioned that a query column already has a data type. When a query connects to the data source, it attempts to infer the column data type from the data provider and then maps it to one of the data types it supports. Although it seems redundant to have data types in two places (query and storage), it gives you more flexibility. For example, you can keep the inferred data type in the query but change it in the table.

Currently, there isn't an exact one-to-one mapping between query and storage data types. Instead, Power BI Desktop maps the query column types to the ones that the xVelocity storage engine supports. **Table 8.1** shows these mappings. Queries support a couple of more data types (Date/Time/Timezone and Duration) than table columns.

Table 8.1   This table shows how query data types map to column data types.

Query Data Type	Storage Data Type	Description
Text	String	A Unicode character string with a max length of 268,435,456 characters
Decimal Number	Decimal Number	A 64 bit (eight-bytes) real number with decimal places
Fixed Decimal Number	Fixed Decimal Number	A decimal number with four decimal places of fixed precision useful for storing currencies.
Whole Number	Whole number	A 64 bit (eight-bytes) integer with no decimal places
Percentage	Fixed Decimal Number	A 2-digit precision decimal number
Date/Time	Date/Time	Dates and times after March 1st, 1900
Date	Date	Just the date portion of a date
Time	Time	Just the time portion of a date
Date/Time/Timezone	Date	Universal date and time
Duration	Text	Time duration, such as 5:30 for five minutes and 30 seconds
TRUE/FALSE	Boolean	True or False value
Binary	Binary data type	An image or blob

How data types get assigned
The storage data type has preference over the source data type. For example, the query might infer a column date type as Decimal Number from the data provider, and this type might get carried over to storage. However, you can overwrite the column data type in the Data View to Whole Number. Unless you change the data type in the query and apply the changes, the column data type remains Whole Number.

The storage engine tries to use the most compact data type, depending on the column values. For example, the query might have assigned a Fixed Decimal Number data type to a column that has only whole numbers. Don't be surprised if the Data View shows the column data type as Whole Number after you import the data. Power BI might also perform a widening data conversion on import if it doesn't support certain numeric data types. For example, if the underlying SQL Server data type is tinyint (one byte), Power BI will map it to Whole Number because that's the only data type that it supports for whole numbers.

Power BI won't import data types it doesn't recognize and won't import the corresponding columns. For example, Power BI won't import a SQL Server column of a geography data type that stores geodetic spatial data. The Binary data type can be used to import images. Importing images is useful for creating banded reports, such as to allow you to click a product image and filter data for that product.

If the data source doesn't provide schema information, Power BI imports data as text and uses the Text data type for all the columns. In such cases, you should overwrite the data types after import when it makes sense.

Changing the column data type

As I mentioned, the Formatting group in ribbon's Modeling tab and the Transform group in the Query Editor indicate the data type of the selected column. You should review and change the column type when needed, for the following reasons:

- Data aggregation – You can sum or average only numeric columns.
- Data validation – Suppose you're given a text file with a SalesAmount column that's supposed to store decimal data. What happens if an 'NA' value sneaks into one or more cells? The query will detect it and might change the column type to Text. You can examine the data type after import and detect such issues. As I mentioned in the previous chapter, I recommend you address such issues in the Query Editor because it has the capabilities to remove errors or replace values. Of course, it's best to fix such issues at the data source, but probably you won't have write access to the source data.

> **NOTE** What happens if all is well with the initial import, but a data type violation occurs the next month when you are given a new extract? What really happens in the case of a data type mismatch depends on the underlying data provider. The text data provider (Microsoft ACE OLE DB provider) replaces the mismatched data values with blank values, and the blank values will be imported in the model. On the query side of things, if data mismatch occurs, you'll see "Error" in the corresponding cell to notify you about dirty data, but no error will be triggered on refresh.

- Better performance – Smaller data types have more efficient storage and query performance. For example, a whole number is more efficient than text because it occupies only eight bytes irrespective of the number of digits.

Sometimes, you might want to overwrite the column data type in the Data View. You can do so by expanding the Data Type drop-down list in the Formatting ribbon group and then select another type. Power BI Desktop only shows the list of the data types that are applicable for conversion. For example, if the original data type is Currency, you can convert the data type to Text, Decimal Number, and Whole Number. If the column is of a Text data type, the Data Type drop-down list would show all the data types. However, you'll get a type mismatch error if the conversion fails, such as when trying to convert a non-numeric text value to a number.

Understanding column formatting

Each column in the Data View has a default format based on its data type and Windows regional settings. For example, my default format for Date columns is MM/dd/yyyy hh:mm:ss tt because my computer is configured for English US regional settings (such as 12/24/2011 13:55:20 PM). This might present an issue for international users. However, they can overwrite the language from the Power BI Desktop File ⇨ "Options and settings" ⇨ Options ⇨ Regional Settings (Current File section) menu to see the data formatted in their culture.

Use the Formatting group in the ribbon's Modeling tab to overwrite the default column format settings, as shown in **Figure 8.4**.

> **TIP** Unlike changing the column data type, which changes the underlying data storage, changing column formatting has no effect on how data is stored because the column format is for visualization purposes only. As a best practice, format numeric and date columns that will be used on reports using the Formatting group in the ribbon's Modeling tab. If you do this, all reports will inherit these formats and you won't have to apply format changes to reports.

You can use the format buttons in the Formatting ribbon group to apply changes interactively, such as to add a thousand separator or to increase the number of decimal places. Formatting changes apply automatically to reports the next time you switch to the Report View. If the column width is too narrow to show the formatted values in Data View, you can increase the column width by dragging the right column border. Changing the column width in Data View has no effect on reports.

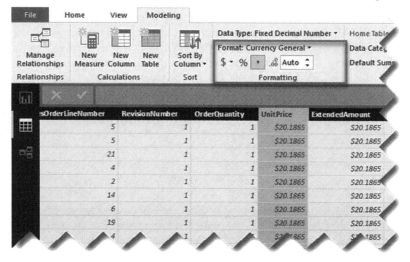

Figure 8.4 Use the Formatting ribbon group to change the column format.

8.1.4 Understanding Column Operations

You can perform various column-related tasks to explore data and improve the metadata visual appearance, including renaming columns, removing columns, and hiding columns.

Renaming columns

Table columns inherit their names from the underlying query that inherits them in turn from the data source. These names might be somewhat cryptic, such as TRANS_AMT. The column name becomes a part of the model metadata that you and the end users interact with. You can make the column name more descriptive and intuitive by renaming the column. You can rename a column interchangeably in three places: Data View, Query Editor, and Fields pane. For example, if you rename a column in the Data View and then switch to the Query Editor, you'll see that Power BI Desktop has automatically appended a Rename Column transformation step to apply the change to the query.

 NOTE No matter where you rename the column, the Power BI "smart rename" applies throughout all the column references, including calculations and reports to avoid broken references. You can see the original name of the column in the data source by inspecting the Rename Column step in the Query Editor formula bar or by looking at the query source.

To rename a column in the Data View, double-click the column header to enter edit mode, and then type in the new name. Or, right-click the column, and then click Rename Column (see **Figure 8.2** again). To rename a column in the Fields pane (in the Data and Report Views), right-click the column and click Rename (or double-click the column).

Removing and hiding columns

In Chapter 6, I advised you to not import a column that you don't need in the model. However, if this ever happens, you can always remove a column in the Data View, Query Editor, and Fields pane. I also recommended you use the Choose Columns transformation in Query Editor as a more intuitive way to remove and add columns. If the column participates in a relationship with another table in the data model, removing the column removes the associated relationship(s).

Suppose you need the column in the model, but you don't want to show it to end users. For example, you might need a primary key column or foreign key column to set up a relationship. Since such columns usually contain system values, you might want to exclude them from showing up in the Fields pane by simply hiding them. The difference between removing and hiding a column is that hiding a column allows you to use the column in the model, such as in hierarchies or custom sorting, and in DAX formulas.

To hide a column in Data View, right-click any column cell and then click "Hide in Report View". A hidden column appears grayed out in Data View. You can also hide a column in the Fields pane by right-clicking the column and clicking Hide. If you change your mind later on, you can unhide the column by toggling "Hide in Report View" (see **Figure 8.5**). Or, you can click Unhide All to unhide all the hidden columns in the selected table. Unfortunately, Power BI Desktop doesn't currently support selecting multiple columns, so you have to apply column tasks, such as renaming or hiding, to one column at the time.

Figure 8.5 Toggle the "Hide in Report View" menu to hide or unhide a column.

The Copy operation allows you to copy the content of the selected columns and paste it in another application, such as in Microsoft Excel. You can't paste the column content inside the Data View because the model is read-only. If you want to copy the entire table in the Windows Clipboard, use the Copy Table option. The Group menu (also available when you right-click a field in the Fields pane) is for creating groups (also called bins or buckets) from the values in the selected column, such as to split the SalesAmount field into 10 equally sized groups. I'll discuss groups in the "Implementing Analytical Features" section later this chapter.

8.1.5 Working with Tables and Columns

Now that you're familiar with tables and columns, let's turn our attention again to the Adventure Works model and spend some time exploring and refining it. The following steps will help you get familiar with the common tasks you'll use when working with tables and columns.

NOTE   I recommend you keep on working and enhancing your version of the Adventure Works model. However, if you haven't completed the Chapter 6 exercises, you can use the Adventure Works file from the \Source\Ch06 folder. However, remember that my samples import data from several local data sources, including the Adventure Works cube and the Product Catalog report. If you decide to refresh the data, you need to update all the data sources to reflect your specific setup. To do so, open the Query Editor, and then click the Data Source Settings button in the ribbon's Home tab and click the Change Source button for each data source. Or, double-click the Source step in the Applied Steps section (Query Settings pane) for each data source that fails to refresh. Then, change the server name and database name as needed.

Sorting data

You can gain insights into your imported data by sorting and filtering it. Suppose that you want to find which employees have been with the company the longest:

1. In Power BI Desktop, open the Adventure Works.pbix file that you worked on in Chapter 6.
2. Click Data View in the navigation bar. Click the Employees tab in the Fields pane.
3. Right-click the HireDate column, and then click Sort Ascending. Note that Guy Gilbert is the first person on the list, and he was hired on 7/31/1998.
4. Right-click the HireDate column again, and then click the Clear Sort menu to remove the sort and to revert to the original order in which data was imported from the data source.

Implementing a custom sort

Next, you'll sort the EnglishMonthName column by the MonthNumberOfYear column so that months are sorted in their ordinal position on reports.

1. In the Fields pane, click the DimDate table to select it.
2. Click a cell in the EnglishMonthName column to select this column.
3. In the ribbon's Modeling tab, click the "Sort by Column" button, and then select MonthNumberOfYear.
4. (Optional) Switch to the Report View. In the Fields pane, check the EnglishMonthName column. This creates a Table visualization that shows months. The months should be sorted in their ordinal position.

Renaming tables

The name of the table is included in the metadata that you'll see when you create reports. Therefore, it's important to have a naming convention for tables. In this case, I'll use a plural naming convention for fact tables (tables that keep a historical record of business transactions, such as ResellerSales), and a singular naming convention for lookup tables.

1. Double-click the DimDate table in the Fields pane (or right-click the DimDate table and then click Rename) and rename it to *Date*. You can rename tables and fields in any of the three views (Report, Data, and Relationships).
2. To practice another way for renaming a table, click the Edit Queries button to open the Query Editor. In the Queries pane, select the Employees query. In the Query Settings pane, rename the query to *Employee*. Click the "Apply & Close" button to return to the Data View.
3. Rename the rest of the tables using the Fields pane. Rename FactResellerSales to *ResellerSales*, Products to *Product*, Resellers to *Reseller*, and SalesTerritories to *SalesTerritory*.

Working with columns

Next, let's revisit each table and make column changes as necessary.

1. In the Fields pane (in the Data View), select the Date table. Double-click the column header of the FullDateAlternateKey column, and then rename it to *Date*. In the data preview pane, increase the Date column width by dragging the column's right border so it's wide enough to accommodate the content in the column. Rename the EnglishDayNameOfWeek column to *DayNameOfWeek* and EnglishMonthName to *MonthName*. Right-click the DateKey column and click "Hide in Report View" to hide this column.
2. You can also rename and hide columns in the Fields pane. In the Fields pane, expand the Employee table. Right-click the EmployeeKey column and then click "Hide in Report View". Also hide the ParentEmployeeKey and SalesTerritoryKey columns. Using the Data View or Fields pane, delete the columns EmployeeNationalIDAlternateKey and ParentEmployeeNationalIDAlternateKey because they're sensitive columns that probably shouldn't be available for end-user analysis.
3. Click the Product table. If you've imported the Product table from the Product Catalog report, rename the ProdCat2 column to *ProductCategory*. Increase the column width to accommodate the content. Rename

ProdSubCat column to *ProductSubcategory*, ProdModel to *ProductModel*, and ProdName to *ProductName*. Hide the ProductKey column. Using the ribbon's Modeling tab (Data View), reformat the StandardCost and ListPrice columns as Currency. To do so, expand the Format drop-down and select Currency ⇨ $ English (United States). Hide the ProductKey column.

4. Select the Reseller table. Hide the ResellerKey and GeographyKey columns. Rename the ResellerAlternate-Key column to *ResellerID*.

5. Select the ResellerSales table. The first nine foreign key columns (with the "Key" suffix) are useful for data relationships but not for data analysis. Hide them.

6. To practice formatting columns again, change the format of the SalesAmount column to two decimal places. To do so, select the column in the Data View (or in the Fields pane), and then enter 2 in the Decimal Places field in the Formatting group on the ribbon's Modeling tab. Press Enter.

7. Select the SalesTerritory table in the Fields pane. Hide the SalesTerritoryKey column. If you have imported the SalesTerritory table from the cube, rename the SalesAmount column to Revenue and format the Revenue column as Currency ⇨$ English (United States).

8. Press Ctrl-S (or click File ⇨ Save) to save the Adventure Works data model.

8.2   Managing Schema and Data Changes

To review, once Power BI Desktop imports data, it saves a copy of the data in a local file with a *.pbix file extension. The model schema and data is *not* automatically synchronized with changes in the data sources. Typically, after the initial load, you'll need to refresh the model data on a regular basis, such as when you receive a new source file or when the data in the source database is updated. Power BI Desktop provides features to keep your model up to date.

8.2.1   Managing Data Sources

It's not uncommon for a model to have several tables connected to different data sources so that you can integrate data from multiple places. As a modeler, you need to understand how to manage connections and tables.

Managing data source settings
Suppose you need to import additional tables from a data source that you've already set up a connection to. One option is to use Get Data again. If, you connect to the same server and database, Power BI Desktop will reuse the same data source definition. To see and manage all data sources defined in the current file, expand the Edit Queries button in the ribbon's Home table and then click "Data Source Settings". For example, if the server or security credentials change, you can use the "Data Source Settings" window (see **Figure 8.6**) to update the connection. Recall that you can also open the Data Source Settings window from File ⇨ "Options and settings" ⇨ "Data source settings".

For local data sources, you can select a data source and click the Change Source button to change the server, database, and advanced options, such as a custom SQL statement (the SQL Statement is disabled if you didn't specify a custom query in the Get Data steps). As you can see in **Figure 8.6**, there are drop-downs in front of the server and database fields. Recall from Chapter 7, that you can further simplify data source maintenance by using query parameters instead of typing names.

Data Source Settings

×

Manage settings for data sources that you have connected to using Power BI Desktop.

● Data Sources in Current File   ○ Global Permissions

Search Data Source Settings	SQL Server Database	×
☐ d:\users\teo\books\powerbi\source\ch05\emp	Import data from a SQL Server database.	
☐ d:\users\teo\books\powerbi\source\ch05\rese	Server	
🗄 elite;AdventureWorksDW2012	*A* ▾ elite	
⊚ elite;AdventureWorksDW2012Multidimension:	Database	
⊕ http://localhost/ReportServer	*A* ▾ AdventureWorksDW2012	
	⦿ Import	
	○ DirectQuery	
	▸ Advanced options	
	OK Cancel	

Change Source...   Edit Permissions...   Clear Permissions ▾

Close

Figure 8.6 Use the "Data Source Settings" window to view and manage data sources used in the current Power BI Desktop file.

Managing sensitive information

Power BI Desktop encrypts the connection credentials and stores them in the local AppData folder on your computer. Use the Edit Permissions button to change credentials (see **Figure 8.7**), such as to switch from Windows to standard security (username and password) or encryption options if the data source supports encryptions.

Figure 8.7 Use the "Edit Permissions" window to change the data source credentials and privacy options.

For security reasons, Power BI Desktop allows you to delete cached credentials by using the Clear Permissions button which supports two options. The first (Clear Permissions) option deletes the cached credentials of the selected data source. For local data sources, this option removes the credentials and privacy settings. For non-local data sources, this option does the same but also removes the data source from the Global Permissions list. The second option (Clear All Permissions) deletes the cached credentials for all data sources in the current file (if the Data Sources in Current File option is selected), or all data sources used by Power BI Desktop (if the Global Permissions option is selected).

Although deleting credentials might sound dangerous, nothing really gets broken and models are not affected. However, the next time you refresh the data, you'll be asked to specify credentials and encryption options as you did the first time you used Get Data to connect to that data source.

Finally, if you used custom SQL Statements (native database queries) to import data, another security feature allows you to revoke their approval. This could be useful if you have imported some data using a custom statement, such as a stored procedure, but you want to prevent other people from executing the query if you intend to share the file with someone else.

Using recent data sources

If you need more tables from the same database, instead of going through the Get Data steps and typing in the server name and database, there is a shortcut: use the Recent Sources button in the ribbon's Home tab (see **Figure 8.8**).

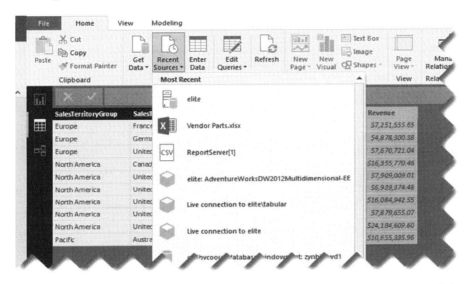

Figure 8.8 Use the Recent Data Sources window to manage the data source credentials and encryption options in one place.

If you connect to a data source that has multiple entities, such as a relational database, when you click the data source in Recent Sources, Power BI Desktop will bring you straight to the Navigator window so that you can select and import another table.

Importing additional tables

Besides wholesale data, the Adventure Works data warehouse stores retail data for direct sales to individual customers. Suppose that you want to extend the Adventure Works model to analyze direct sales to customers who placed orders on the Internet.

 NOTE Other self-service tools on the market restrict you to analyzing single datasets only. If that's all you need, feel free to skip this exercise as the model has enough tables and complexity already. However, chances are that you might need to analyze data from different subject areas side by side. This requires you to import multiple fact tables and join them to common dimensions. And this is where Power BI excels because it allows you to implement self-service models whose features are on a par with professional models. I encourage you to stay with me as the complexity cranks up and learn these features so you never say "I can't meet this requirement".

Follow these steps to import three additional tables:

1. In the ribbon's Home tab, expand the Recent Sources button, and then click the SQL Server instance that hosts the AdventureWorksDW database. Or, use Get Data to connect to it.

 NOTE If you don't have a SQL Server with AdventureWorksDW, I provide the data in the DimCustomer.csv, DimGeography.csv and FactInternetSales.csv files in the \Source\ch08 folder. Import them using the CSV or TEXT option in Get Data.

2. In the Navigator window, expand the AdventureWorksDW database, and then check the DimCustomer, DimGeorgraphy, and FactInternetSales tables. In the AdventureWorksDW database, the DimGeography

table isn't related directly to the FactInternetSales table. Instead, DimGeography joins DimCustomer, which joins FactInternetSales. This is an example of a snowflake schema, which I covered in Chapter 6.

3. Click the Edit button. In the Queries pane of the Query Editor, select DimCustomer and change the query name to *Customer*.

4. In the Queries pane, select DimGeography and change the query name to *Geography*.

5. Select the FactInternetSales query and change its name to InternetSales. Use the Choose Columns transformation to exclude the RevisionNumber, CarrierTrackingNumber, and CustomerPONumber columns.

6. Click "Close & Apply" to add the three tables to the Adventure Works model and to import the new data.

7. In the Data View, select the Customer table. Hide the CustomerKey and GeographyKey columns. Rename the CustomerAlternateKey column to *CustomerID*.

8. Select the Geography table, and hide the GeographyKey and SalesTerritoryKey columns.

9. Select the InternetSales table, and hide the first eight columns (the ones with "Key" suffix).

8.2.2 Managing Data Refresh

When you import data, Power BI Desktop caches it in the model to give you the best performance when you visualize the data. The only option to synchronize data changes on the desktop is to refresh the data manually.

NOTE Unlike Excel, Power BI Desktop doesn't support automation and macros. At the same time, there are many scenarios that might benefit from automating data refresh on the desktop. While there is an officially supported way to do so, my blog "Automating Power BI Desktop Refresh" (http://prologika.com/automating-power-bi-desktop-refresh/) lists a few options if you have such a requirement.

Refreshing data

As it stands, Power BI Desktop refresh is simple. You just need to click the Refresh button in the Report View or in the Data View. This executes all the table queries, discards the existing data, and imports all the tables from scratch. If you need to refresh a specific table, right-click the table in the Fields pane (Report View or Data View) and click "Refresh data". Currently, there isn't an option to process only a portion of a table or to refresh data incrementally, such as to process rows where LastUpdateDate is within the last 30 days.

NOTE Analysis Services Tabular, which also uses xVelocity as a storage engine, supports more processing options, including processing specific partitions of a large table. Consider Tabular when you need a centralized and scalable semantic model that can handle much larger data volumes than Power BI Desktop.

Suppose that you've been notified about changes in one or more of the tables, and now you need to refresh the data model.

1. In Power BI Desktop, click the Data View icon (or the Report View icon) in the navigation bar.

2. In the ribbon's Home tab, click the Refresh button to refresh all tables.

3. Press Ctrl-S to save the Adventure Works data model.

When you initiate the refresh operation, Power BI Desktop opens the Refresh window to show you the progress, as shown in **Figure 8.9**.

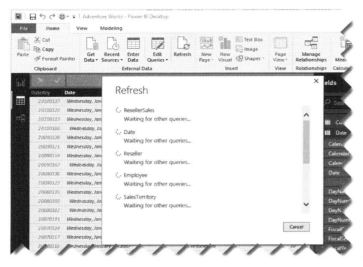

Figure 8.9 Power BI Desktop refreshes tables sequentially and cancels the entire operation if a table fails to refresh.

Power BI Desktop refreshes tables sequentially, one table at the time. The Refresh window shows the number of rows imported. You can't cancel the refresh once it has started.

NOTE Based on usability feedback, Microsoft decided on the sequential data refresh in Power Pivot and Power BI Desktop for easier failure analysis. If a table fails to refresh, the entire refresh operation stops so that the user can more easily identify which table failed.

The xVelocity storage engine is capable of importing more than 100,000 rows per second. The actual data refresh speed depends on many factors, including how fast the data source returns rows, the number and data type of columns in the table, the network speed, your machine hardware configuration, and so on.

REAL LIFE I was called a few times to troubleshoot slow processing issues with Analysis Services and Power Pivot. In all the cases, I've found that the external factors impacted the processing speed. In one case, it turned out that the IT department had decided to throttle the network speed on all non-production network segments in case a computer virus takes over.

Troubleshooting data refresh

If a table fails to refresh, such as when there's no connectivity to the data source, the Refresh window shows an error indicator and displays an error message, as shown in **Figure 8.10**. When a table fails to refresh, the entire operation is aborted because it runs in a transaction, and no data is refreshed. At this point, you need to troubleshoot the error.

Figure 8.10 If the refresh operation fails, the Refresh window shows which table failed to refresh and shows the error description.

8.3 Relating Tables

One of the most prominent Power BI strengths is that it can help an analyst analyze data across multiple tables. Back in Chapter 6, I covered that as a prerequisite for aggregating data in one table by columns in another table, you must set up a relationship between the two tables. When you import tables from a relational database that supports referential integrity and has table relationships defined, Power BI Desktop detects these relationships and applies them to the model. However, when no table joins are defined in the data source, or when you import data from different sources, Power BI Desktop might be unable to detect relationships upon import. Because of this, you must revisit the model and create appropriate relationships before you analyze the data.

8.3.1 Relationship Rules and Limitations

A relationship is a join between two tables. When you define a table relationship with one-to-many cardinality, you're telling Power BI that there's a logical one-to-many relationship between a row in the lookup (dimension) table and the corresponding rows in the fact table. For example, the relationship between the Reseller and ResellerSales tables in **Figure 8.11** means that each reseller in the Reseller table can have many corresponding rows in the ResellerSales table. Indeed, Progressive Sports (ResellerKey=1) recorded a sale on August 1st, 2006 for $100 and another sale on July 4th 2007 for $120. In this case, the ResellerKey column in the Reseller table is the primary key in the lookup (dimension) table. The ResellerKey column in the ResellerSales table fulfills the role of a foreign key in the fact table.

Figure 8.11 There's a logical one-to-many relationship between the Reseller table and the ResellerSales table because each reseller can have multiple sales recorded.

Understanding relationship rules
A relationship can be created under the following circumstances:

- The two tables have matching columns, such as a ResellerKey column in the Reseller lookup table and a ResellerKey column in the ResellerSales table. The column names don't have to be the same but the columns must have matching values. For example, you can't relate the two tables if the ResellerKey column in the ResellerSales table has reseller codes, such as PRO for Progressive Sports.

- The key column in the lookup (dimension) table must have unique values, similar to a primary key in a relational database. The key column can't have (empty) null values. In the case of the Reseller table, the ResellerKey column fulfills this requirement because its values are unique across all the rows in the table. However, this doesn't mean that all fact tables must join the lookup table on the same primary key. As long as the column is unique, it can serve as a primary key. And some fact tables can use one column while others can use another column. If you attempt to establish a join to a column that doesn't contain unique values in a lookup table, you'll get the following error:

The relationship cannot be created because each column contains duplicate values. Select at least one column that contains only unique values.

Interestingly, Power BI doesn't require the two columns to have matching data types. For example, the ResellerKey column in the Reseller table can be of a Text data type while its counterpart in the fact table could be defined as the Whole Number data type. Behind the scenes, Power BI resolves the join by converting the values in the latter column to the Text data type. However, to improve performance and to reduce storage space, use numeric data types whenever possible.

Understanding relationship limitations

Relationships have several limitations. To start, only one column can be used on each side of the relationship. If you need a combination of two or more columns (so the key column can have unique values), you can add a custom column in the query or a calculated column that uses a DAX expression to concatenate the values, such as =[ResellerKey] & "|" & [SourceID]. I use the pipe delimiter here to avoid combinations that might result in the same concatenated values. For example, combinations of ResellerKey of 1 with SourceID of 10 and ResellerKey of 11 and SourceID of 0 result in "110". To make the combinations unique, you can use a delimiter, such as the pipe character. Once you construct a primary key column, you can use this column for the relationship.

Moving down the list, you can't create relationships forming a closed loop (also called a diamond shape). For example, given the relationships Table1 ⇨ Table2 and Table2 ⇨ Table3, you can't set an active relationship Table1 ⇨ Table3. Such a relationship probably isn't needed anyway, because you'll be able to analyze the data in Table3 by Table1 with only the first two relationships in place. Power BI will actually let you create the Table1 ⇨ Table3 relationship, but it will mark it as inactive. This brings to the subject of role-playing relationships and inactive relationships.

As it stands, Power BI doesn't support role-playing relationships. A role-playing lookup table is a table that joins the same fact table multiple times, and thus plays multiple roles. For example, the InternetSales table has the OrderDateKey, ShipDateKey, and DueDateKey columns because a sales order has an order date, ship date, and due date. Suppose you want to analyze sales by these three dates. One approach is to import the Date table three times with different names and to create relationships to each date table. This approach gives you more control because you now have three separate Date tables and their data doesn't have to match. For example, you might want the ShipDate table to include different columns than the OrderDate table. On the downside, you increase your maintenance effort because now you have to maintain three tables.

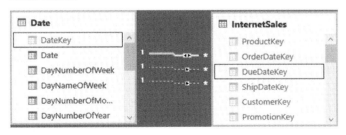

Figure 8.12 Power BI supports only one active relationship between two tables and marks the other relationships as inactive.

REAL WORLD On the subject of date tables, AdventureWorksDW uses a "smart" integer primary key for the Date table in the format YYYYMMDD. This is a common practice for data warehousing, but you should use a date field (Date data type). Not only is it more compact (3 bytes vs. 4 bytes for Integer) but it's also easier to work with. For example, if a business user imports ResellerSales, he can filter easier on a Date data type, such as to import data for the current year, than to parse integer fields. And DAX time calculations work if a date column is used as a primary key. That's why in the practice exercises that follow, you'll recreate the relationships to the date table.

Understanding active and inactive relationships

Another approach is to join the three date columns in InternetSales to the Date table. This approach allows you to reuse the same date table three times. However, Power BI supports only one active role-playing relationship. An active relationship is a relationship that Power BI follows to automatically aggregate the data between two tables. A solid line in the Relationships View indicates an active relationship while a dotted line is for inactive relationships (see **Figure 8.12**). You can also open the Manage Relationships window (click the Manage Relationships button in ribbon's Home or Modeling tabs) and inspect the Active flag.

When Power BI Desktop imports the relationships from the database, it defaults the first one to active and marks the rest as inactive. In our case, the InternetSales[DueDateKey] ⇨ DimDate[DateKey] relationship is active because this happens to be the first of the three relationships between the DimDate and FactInternetSales tables that you imported. Consequently, when you create a report that slices Internet dates by Date, Power BI automatically aggregates the sales by the due date.

NOTE   I'll use the TableName[ColumnName] notation as a shortcut when I refer to a table column. For example, InternetSales[DueDateKey] means the DueDateKey column in the InternetSales table. This notation will help you later on with DAX formulas because DAX follows the same syntax. When referencing relationships, I'll use a right arrow (⇨) to denote a relationship from a fact table to a lookup table. For example, InternetSales[OrderDateKey] ⇨ DimDate[DateKey] means a relationship between the OrderDateKey column in the InternetSales table to the DateKey column in the DimDate table.

If you want the default aggregation to happen by the order date, you must set InternetSales[OrderDateKey] ⇨ DimDate[DateKey] as an active relationship. To do so, first select the InternetSales[ShipDateKey] ⇨ DimDate[DateKey] relationship, and then click Edit. In the Edit Relationship dialog box, uncheck the Active checkbox, and then click OK. Finally, edit the InternetSales[OrderDateKey] ⇨ DimDate[DateKey] relationship, and then check the Active checkbox.

What if you want to be able to aggregate data by other dates without importing the Date table multiple times? You can create DAX calculated measures, such as ShippedSalesAmount and DueSalesAmount, that force Power BI to use a given inactive relationship by using the DAX USERELATIONSHIP function. For example, the following formula calculates ShippedSalesAmount using the ResellerSales[ShipDateKey] ⇨ DimDate[DateKey] relationship:

```
ShippedSalesAmount=CALCULATE(SUM(InternetSales[SalesAmount]),
USERELATIONSHIP(InternetSales[ShipDateKey],'Date'[DateKey])
```

Cross filtering limitations

In Chapter 6, I mentioned that a relationship can be set to cross-filter in both directions. This is a great out-of-box feature that allows you to address more advanced scenarios that previously required custom calculations with Power Pivot, such as many-to-many relationships. However, bi-directional filtering doesn't make sense and should be avoided in the following cases:

- When you have two fact tables sharing some common dimension tables – In fact, to avoid ambiguous join paths, Power BI Desktop won't let you turn on bi-directional filtering from multiple fact tables to the same lookup table. Therefore, if you start from a single fact table but anticipate additional fact tables down the road, you may also consider a uni-directional model (Cross Filtering set to Single) to keep a consistent experience to users, and then turn on bi-directional filtering only if you need it.

NOTE   To understand this limitation better, let's say you have a Product lookup table that has bi-directional relations to ResellerSales and InternetSales tables. If you define a DAX measure on the Product table, such as Count of Products, but have a filter on a Date table, Power BI won't know how to resolve the join: count of products through ResellerSales on that date, or count of products through InternetSales on that date.

- Relationships toward the date table – Relationships to date tables should be one-directional so that DAX time calculations continue to work.

- Closed-loop relationships – As I just mentioned, Power BI Desktop will automatically inactivate one of the relationships when it detects a closed loop, although you can still use DAX calculations to navigate inactive relationships. In this case, bi-directional relationships would produce meaningless results.

 NOTE As a best practice, even though Power BI might default to cross-filtering for new relationships, start with a unidirectional model (Cross Filtering Direction = Both) and then turn on cross filtering when needed, such as when you need a many-to-many relationship between tables.

8.3.2 Auto-detecting Relationships

When you create a report that uses unrelated tables, Power BI Desktop can auto-detect and create missing relationships. This behavior is enabled by default, but you can disable it by turning it off from the File ⇨ Options and Settings ⇨ Options menu, which brings you to the Options window (see **Figure 8.13**).

Figure 8.13 You can use the Relationships options in the Data Load section to control how Power BI Desktop discovers relationships.

Configuring relationships detection

There are three options that control how Power BI desktop detects relationships. The "Import relationships from data sources" option (enabled by default) instructs Power BI Desktop to detect relationships from the data source *before* the data is loaded. When this option is enabled, Power BI Desktop will examine the database schema and probe for existing relationships.

The "Update relationships when refreshing queries" option will attempt to discover missing relationships when refreshing the imported data. Because this might result in dropping existing relationships that you've created manually, this option is off by default. Finally, "Autodetect new relationships after data is loaded" will attempt to auto-detect missing relationships *after* the data is loaded. Because this option is on by default, Power BI Desktop was able to detect relationships between the InternetSales and Date tables, as well as between other tables. The auto-detection mechanism uses an internal algorithm that considers column data types and cardinality.

Understanding missing relationships

What happens when you don't have a relationship between two tables and attempt to analyze the data in a report? You'll get repeating values. In this case, I attempted to aggregate the SalesAmount column from the

ResellerSales table by the ProductName column in the Product table, but there's no relationship defined between these two tables. If reseller sales should aggregate by product, you must define a relationship to resolve this issue.

Figure 8.14 Reports show repeating values in the case of missing relationships.

Autodetecting relationships
The lazy approach to handle missing relationships is to let Power BI Desktop create them by clicking the Autodetect button in the Manage Relationship window. If the internal algorithm detects a suitable relationship candidate, it creates the relationship and informs you, as shown in **Figure 8.15**.

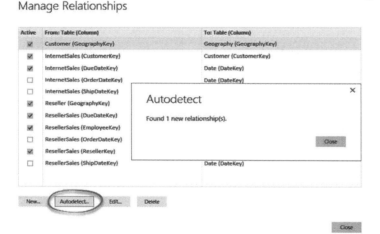

Figure 8.15 The Autodetect feature of the Manage Relationship window shows that it has detected and created a relationship successfully.

In the case of an unsuccessful detection process, the Relationship dialog box will show "Found no new relationships". If this happens and you're still missing relationships, you need to create them manually.

8.3.3 Creating Relationships Manually

Since table relationships are very important, I'd recommend that you configure them manually. You can do this by using the Manage Relationships window or by using the Relationships View. Because relationships are very important, you can find the Manage Relationships button in the ribbon in all views (Report, Data, and Relationships).

Steps to create a relationship
Follows these steps to set up a relationship:
1. Identify a foreign key column in the table on the Many side of the relationship.
2. Identify a primary key column that uniquely identifies each row in the lookup (dimension) table.

3. In the Manage Relationship window, click the New button to open the Create Relationship window. Then create a new relationship with the correct cardinality. Or you can use the Relationships View to drag the foreign key from the fact table onto the primary key of the lookup table.

Understanding the Create Relationship window
You might prefer the Create Relationship window when the number of tables in your model has grown and using the drag-and-drop technique in the Relationships View becomes impractical. **Figure 8.16** shows the Create Relationship dialog box when setting up a relationship between the ResellerSales and Product tables. Note that if you have imported the Product table from the SSRS Product Catalog report, it will have an empty row with a null value in the ProductKey column. As a mentioned before, a key column can't have a null value. To fix this issue, open Query Editor, expand the drop-down in the ProductKey column header of the Product table, and uncheck the null value.

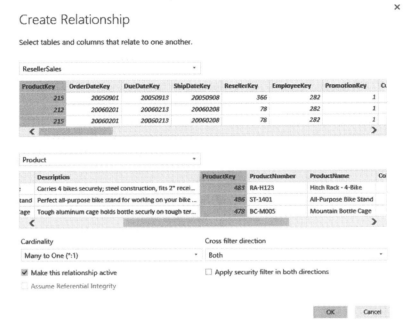

Figure 8.16   Use the Create Relationship window to specify the columns used for the relationship, cardinality and cross filter direction.

When defining a relationship, you need to select two tables and matching columns. The Create Relationships window will detect the cardinality for you. For example, if you start with the table on the many side of the relationship (ResellerSales), it'll choose the Many to One cardinality; otherwise it selects One to Many. If you attempt to set up a relationship with the wrong cardinality, you'll get an error message ("The Cardinality you selected isn't valid for this relationship"), and you won't be able to create the relationship. And if you choose a column that doesn't uniquely identify each row in the lookup table, you'll get the error message "You can't create a relationship between these two columns because one of the columns must have unique values".

Because there isn't another relationship between the two tables, Power BI Desktop defaults the "Make this relationship active" to checked. This checkbox corresponds to the Active flag in the Manage Relationship window. It also defaults the "Cross filter direction" to Both. The "Assume Referential Integrity" checkbox is disabled because it applies only to DirectQuery. When checked, it auto-generates queries that use INNER JOIN as opposed to OUTER JOIN when joining the two tables. Don't worry for now about "Apply security filter in both direction". I'll explain it when I discuss row-level security (RLS) in the next chapter.

NOTE When data is imported, all Power BI joins are treated as outer joins. For example, if ResellerSales had a transaction for a reseller that doesn't exist in the Reseller table, Power BI won't eliminate this row, as I explain in more detail in the next section.

Understanding unknown members

Consider the model shown in **Figure 8.17**, which has a Reseller lookup table and a Sales fact table. This diagram uses an Excel pivot report to demonstrate unknown members, but a Power BI Desktop report will behave the same. The Reseller table has only two resellers. However, the Sales table has data for two additional resellers with keys of 3 and 4. This is a common data integrity issue when the source data originates from heterogeneous data sources and when there isn't an ETL process to validate and clean the data.

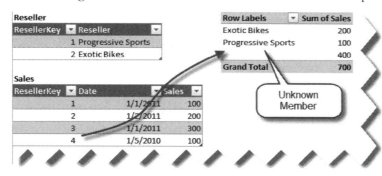

Figure 8.17   Power BI enables an unknown member to the lookup table when it encounters missing rows.

Power BI has a simple solution for this predicament. When creating a relationship, Power BI checks for missing rows in the lookup table. If it finds any, it automatically configures the lookup table to include a special unknown (Blank) member. That's why all unrelated rows appear grouped under a blank row in the report. This row represents the unknown member in the Reseller table.

 NOTE If you have imported the Product table from the SSRS Product Catalog report in Chapter 6, you'll find that it has a subset of the Adventure Works products. This is why when you create a report that shows sales by product, a large chunk of sales will be associated with a (Blank) product.

Managing relationships

You can view and manage all the relationships defined in your model by using the Manage Relationships window (see **Figure 8.15** again). In this case, the Manage Relationships window shows that there are 11 relationships defined in the Adventure Works model from which four are inactive, plus one relationship that was just discovered using the Autodiscover feature.

The Edit button opens the Edit Relationship window, which is the same as the Create Relationship window, but with all the fields pre-populated. Finally, the Delete button removes the selected relationship. Don't worry if your results differ from mine. You'll verify the relationships in the lab exercise that follows and will create the missing ones.

8.3.4   Understanding the Relationships View

Another way to view and manage relationships is to use the Relationships View. You can use the Relationships View to:

■ Visualize the model schema

■ Create and manage relationships

■ Make other limited schema changes, such as renaming, hiding, deleting objects

Recall that the Relationships view is available in models with imported data or in models that connect live to data sources, except when connecting live to Analysis Services. One of the strengths of the Relationships View is that you can quickly visualize and understand the model schema and relationships. **Figure 8.18** shows a subset of the Adventure Works model schema open in the Relationships View. Glancing at the model, you can immediately see what relationships exist in the model! If you have a lot of tables, you might find the Reset Layout useful to auto-arrange the tables in a more compact layout.

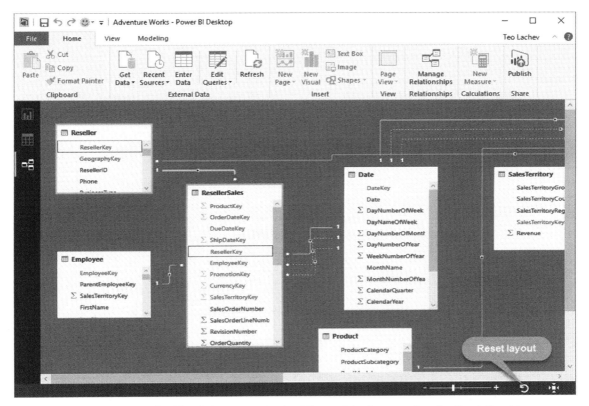

Figure 8.18   The Relationships View helps you understand the model schema and work with relationships.

Making schema changes

You can make limited schema changes in the Relationships View. When you right-click an object, a context menu opens up to show the supported operations, as shown in **Table 8.2**.

Table 8.2   This table shows the schema operations by object type.

Object Type	Supported Operations	Object Type	Supported Operations
Table	Delete, Hide, Rename, Maximize, Synonyms	Measure	Delete, Hide, Rename
Column	Delete, Hide, Rename		
Relationship	Delete		

Managing relationships

Since I'm on the subject of relationships, let's take a closer look at how the Relationships View represents relationships. A relationship is visualized as a connector between two tables. Symbols at the end of the connector help you understand the relationship cardinality. The number one (1) denotes the table on the One side of the relationship, while the asterisk (*) is shown next to the table on the Many side of the relationship. For example, after examining **Figure 8.18**, you can see that there's a relationship between the Reseller table and ResellerSales table and that the relationship cardinality is One to Many with the Reseller table on the One side of the relationship and the ResellerSales table on the many.

When you click a relationship to select it, the Relationships View highlights it in an orange color. When you hover your mouse over a relationship, the Relationships View highlights columns in the joined tables to indicate visually which columns are used in the relationship. For example, pointing the mouse to the highlighted relationship between the ResellerSales and Reseller tables reveals that the relationship is created between the ResellerSales[ResellerKey] column and the Reseller[ResellerKey] column (see **Figure 8.18** again).

As I mentioned, Power BI has a limited support of role-playing relationships where a lookup table joins multiple times to a fact table. The caveat is that only one role-playing relationship can be active. The Relationships View shows the inactive relationships with dotted lines. To make another role-playing relationship active, first you need to deactivate the currently active relationship. To do so, double-click the active relationship, and then in the Edit Relationship window uncheck the "Make this relationship active" checkbox. Next, you double-click the other role-playing relationship and then check its "Make this relationship active" checkbox.

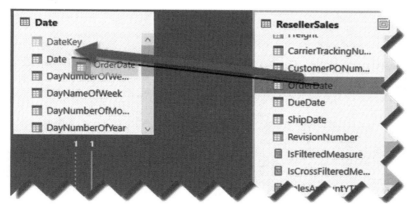

Figure 8.19 The Relationships View lets you create a relationship by dragging a foreign key column onto a primary key column.

A great feature of Relationships View is creating relationships by dragging a foreign key column and dropping it onto the primary key column in the lookup table. For example, to create a relationship between the ResellerSales and Date tables, drag the OrderDate column in the ResellerSales table and drop it onto the Date column in the Date table. The Relationships View won't allow you to create a relationship in the reverse direction. To delete a relationship, simply click the relationship to select it, and then press the Delete key. Or right-click the relationship line, and then click Delete.

Understanding synonyms

Remember the fantastic Q&A feature in Power BI that let business users gain insights in dashboards by asking natural queries? The Relationships View allows you to fine tune Q&A by defining synonyms. A synonym is an alternative name for a field. Suppose you want to allow natural queries to use "revenue" and "sales amount" interchangeably. The following steps shows how to define a synonym.

1. In the Relationships View, select the ResellerSales table.

2. In the ribbon's Modeling tab, click the Synonyms button. A Synonyms pane opens (see **Figure 8.20**). Notice that Power BI Desktop has already defined a synonym "sales amount" for the SalesAmount field.

3. Next to "sales amount", type in *revenue*. That's all it takes to define a synonym. Once you deploy your model to Power BI Service, users will be able to use the synonym in any dashboard that uses data from the Adventure Works model, such by using a natural question "revenue by product".

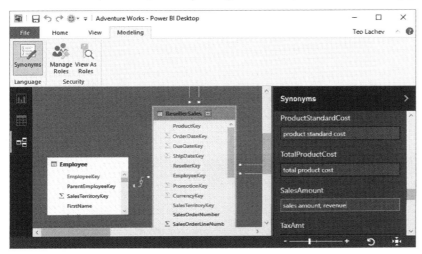

Figure 8.20 The "sales amount" and "revenue" are synonyms for the SalesAmount field.

8.3.5 Working with Relationships

As it stands, the Adventure Works model has nine tables and 11 relationships. Power BI has done a great job auto-detecting relationships. Next, you'll practice different techniques to change and create relationships.

Auto-detecting relationships

Let's see how far you can get by letting Power BI Desktop auto-detect relationships:

1. In the Data View (or Report View), click the Manage Relationships button in the ribbon's Home tab to open the Manage Relationships window.

2. Click the Autodetect button. If there's no relationship between the Customer and Geography tables, the auto-detection finds one new relationship. Click OK. Notice that a relationship Reseller[GeographyKey] ⇨ Geography[GeographyKey] is added. This relationship reflects the underlying snowflake schema consisting of the ResellerSales, Reseller, and Geography tables. The new relationship allows us to analyze reseller sales by geography using a cascading relationship spanning three tables (ResellerSales ⇨ Reseller ⇨ Geography).

 NOTE Usually a byproduct of a snowflake schema, a cascading relationship joins a fact table to a lookup table via another referenced lookup table. Power BI supports cascading relationships that can traverse multiple lookup tables.

Now let's clean up some existing relationships. As it stands, the InternetSales table has three relationships to the Date table (one active and two inactive) which Power BI Desktop auto-discovered from the underlying database. All these relationships join the Date table on the DateKey column. As I mentioned before, I suggest you use a column of a Date data type in the Date table. Luckily, both the Reseller Sales and InternetSales tables have OrderDate, ShipDate, and DueDate date columns. And the Date table has a Date column which is of a Date data type.

3. While still in the Manage Relationships window, delete the two inactive relationships (the ones with an unchecked Active flag) from the InternetSales table to the Date table. You can press and hold the Ctrl key to select multiple relationships and delete them in one step.

4. Delete also the three relationships from ResellerSales to Date: ResellerSales[DueDateKey] ⇨ Date[Date-Key], ResellerSales[ShipDateKey] ⇨ Date[DateKey] and ResellerSales[OrderDateKey] ⇨ Date[DateKey].

Using the Manage Relationships window
The Adventure Works model has two fact tables (ResellerSales and InternetSales) and seven lookup tables. Let's start creating the missing relationships using the Manage Relationships window:

> **TIP** When you have multiple fact tables, join them to common dimension tables. This allows you to create consolidated reports that include multiple subject areas, such as a report that shows Internet sales and reseller sales side by side grouped by date and sales territory.

1. First, let's rebind the InternetSales[OrderDateKey] ⇨ Date[DateKey] relationship to use another set of columns. In the Manage Relationship window, double-click the InternetSales[OrderDateKey] ⇨ Date[Date-Key] relationship (or select it and click Edit). If this relationship doesn't exist in your model, click the New button to create it. In the Edit Relationship window, select the OrderDate column (scroll all the way to the right) in the InternetSales table. Then select the Date column in the Date table and click OK.

> **NOTE** When joining fact tables to a date table on a date column, make sure that the foreign key values contain only the date portion of the date and not the time portion. Otherwise, the join will never find matching values in the date table. If you don't need it, the easiest way to discard the time portion is to change the column data type from Date/time to Date. You can also apply query transformations to strip the time portion or to create custom columns that have only the date portion.

2. Back in the Manage Relationship window, click New. Create a relationship ResellerSales[OrderDate] ⇨ Date[Date]. Leave the "Cross filter direction" drop-down to Single, and click OK.

3. Create ResellerSales[SalesTerritoryKey] ⇨ SalesTerritory[SalesTerritoryKey] and ResellerSales[ProductKey] ⇨ Product[ProductKey] relationships. However, change the "Cross filtering direction" option to *Single* to avoid errors related to ambiguous relationships later on.

4. Click the Close button to close the Manage Relationship window.

Creating relationships using the Relationships View
Next, you'll use the Relationships View to create relationships for the InternetSales table.

1. Click the Relationships View icon in the navigation bar.

2. If this relationship doesn't exist, drag the InternetSales[ProductKey] column and drop it onto the Product[ProductKey] column.

3. Drag the InternetSales[SalesTerritoryKey] column and drop it onto the SalesTerritory[SalesTerritoryKey] column.

4. Click the Manage Relationships button. Compare your results with **Figure 8.21**. As it stands, the Adventure Works model has 11 relationships. For now, let's not create inactive relationships. I'll revisit them in the next chapter when I cover DAX.

5. If there are differences between your relationships and **Figure 8.21**, make the necessary changes. Don't be afraid to delete wrong relationships if you have to recreate them to use different columns.

6. Once your setup matches **Figure 8.21**, click Close to close the Manage Relationships window. Save the Adventure Works file.

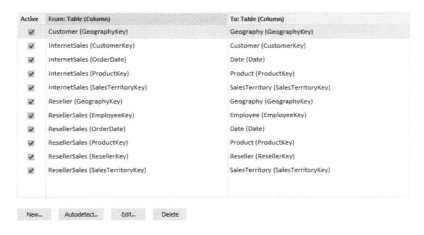

Manage Relationships

Active	From: Table (Column)	To: Table (Column)
☑	Customer (GeographyKey)	Geography (GeographyKey)
☑	InternetSales (CustomerKey)	Customer (CustomerKey)
☑	InternetSales (OrderDate)	Date (Date)
☑	InternetSales (ProductKey)	Product (ProductKey)
☑	InternetSales (SalesTerritoryKey)	SalesTerritory (SalesTerritoryKey)
☑	Reseller (GeographyKey)	Geography (GeographyKey)
☑	ResellerSales (EmployeeKey)	Employee (EmployeeKey)
☑	ResellerSales (OrderDate)	Date (Date)
☑	ResellerSales (ProductKey)	Product (ProductKey)
☑	ResellerSales (ResellerKey)	Reseller (ResellerKey)
☑	ResellerSales (SalesTerritoryKey)	SalesTerritory (SalesTerritoryKey)

New...   Autodetect...   Edit...   Delete

Close

Figure 8.21 The Manage Relationships dialog box shows 11 relationships defined in the Adventure Works model.

8.4   Implementing Analytical Features

Power BI Desktop has additional modeling capabilities for you to implement end-user features that further enrich the model. This section discusses features that don't require the Data Analysis Expressions DAX experience and are not available in Power BI Service, including hierarchies, data categories, quick calculations, time series forecasting, and grouping.

8.4.1   Working with Hierarchies

A hierarchy is a combination of fields that defines a navigational drilldown path in the model. As you've seen, Power BI allows you to use any column for slicing and dicing data in related tables. However, some fields form logical navigational paths for data exploration and drilling down. You can define hierarchies to group such fields.

Understanding hierarchies
A hierarchy defines a drill-down path using fields from a table. When you add the hierarchy to the report, you can drill down data by expanding its levels. A hierarchy can include fields from a single table only. If you want to drill down from different tables, just add the fields (don't define a hierarchy). A hierarchy offers two important benefits:

- Usability – You can add all fields for drilling down data in one click by adding the hierarchy instead of individual fields.
- Performance – Suppose you add a high-cardinality column, such as CustomerName, to a report. You might end up with a huge report. This might cause unnecessary performance degradation. Instead, you can hide the Customer field and you can define a hierarchy with levels, such as State, City, and Customer levels, to force end users to use this navigational path when browsing data by customers.

Typically, a hierarchy combines columns with logical one-to-many relationships. For example, one year can have multiple quarters and one quarter can have multiple months. This doesn't have to be the case though. For example, you can create a reporting hierarchy with ProductModel, Size, and Product columns, if you wish to analyze products that way.

Once you have a hierarchy in place, you might want to hide high-cardinality columns in order to prevent the user from adding them directly to the report and to avoid performance issues. For example, you might not want to expose the CustomerName column in the Customer table, in order to prevent users from adding it to a report outside the hierarchies it participates in.

Understanding in-line date hierarchies

The most common example of hierarchy is the date hierarchy, consisting of Year, Quarter, Month, and Date levels. In Chapter 6, I encouraged you to have a separate Date table so that you can define whatever date-related columns you need and implement DAX time calculations, such as YTD, QTD, and so on. But what if you didn't follow my advice and you want a quick and easy date hierarchy? Fortunately, Power BI Desktop is capable of generating an in-line date hierarchy. All you need to do is add a column of a Date data type to the report. For example, **Figure 8.22** shows that I've added a Date field to the Values area of a Table report. Power BI has automatically generated a hierarchy with levels Year, Quarter, Month, and Day.

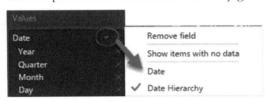

Figure 8.22 Power BI Desktop creates an inline hierarchy when you add a date field to the report.

If you don't want any of the levels, you can delete them by clicking the X button next to the level. And if you want to see just the date and not the hierarchy on the report, simply click the drop-down next to the Date hierarchy and then check the Date field.

NOTE One existing limitation of the automatic in-line date hierarchy feature is that it doesn't generate time levels, such as Hour, Minute, and so on. If you need to perform time analysis, you need to create a Time table with the required levels and join it to the table with the data. Also, keep in mind that in-line hierarchies might increase your model size (see the blog "Power BI Model Size Bloat and Auto Date/Time Tables" by Chris Webb at bit.ly2iKRbZe for more information). To remove them, go to File ⇨ Options and Settings ⇨ Options and uncheck the "Auto Date/Time" setting on the Data Load tab.

Implementing hierarchies

Follow these steps to implement a Calendar Hierarchy consisting of CalendarYear, CalendarQuarter, Month, and Date levels:

1. In the Fields pane (Report View or Data View), click the ellipsis button next to the CalendarYear field in the Date table, and then click New Hierarchy. This adds a CalendarYear Hierarchy to the Date table.
2. Click the ellipsis button next to the CalendarYear Hierarchy and then click rename. Rename the hierarchy to *Calendar Hierarchy*.
3. Click the ellipsis button next to the CalendarQuarter field and then click Add to Hierarchy ⇨ Calendar Hierarchy.
4. Repeat the last step to add MonthName and Date fields to the hierarchy. If you didn't add the fields in the correct order, you can simply drag a level in the hierarchy and move it to the correct place.
5. The name of the hierarchy level doesn't need to match the name of the underlying field. Click the ellipsis button next to the MonthName level of the Calendar Hierarchy (not to the MonthName field in the table) and rename it to *Month*. Compare you results with **Figure 8.23**.

Figure 8.23 The Calendar Year hierarchy includes CalendarYear, CalendarQuarter, Month and Date levels.

6. (Optional) Create a chart report to add the Calendar Hierarchy to the Axis area of the chart. Enable drill-down behavior of the chart and test your new hierarchy.

 TIP A quick way to create a hierarchy is simply to drag a field and drop onto another within the same table. The resulting hierarchy will have two levels with the lower level corresponding to the field that you dragged.

8.4.2 Assigning Data Categories

When Power BI Desktop imports data, not only does it get the actual data, it also gets additional metadata such as the table and column names, data types, and column cardinality. This information also helps Power BI Desktop to visualize the field when you add it to a report. A data category is additional metadata that you assign to a field to inform Power BI Desktop about the field content so that it can be visualized even better. You assign a data category to a field by using the Data Category drop-down in the ribbon's Modeling tab.

Assigning geo categories

When you expand the Data Category drop-down, you'll find that most of the data categories are geo-related, such as Address, City, Continent, and so on. Actually, when you use a geo-related field on a report, Power BI Desktop tries its best to infer the field content and geocode the field. For example, you add the AddressLine1 field from the Customer table to an empty Map visualization, Power BI Desktop will correctly interpret it as an address and plot it on the map. So, in most cases, specifying a data category is not necessary.

In some cases, however, Power BI might need extra help. Suppose you have a field with abbreviated values such as AZ, AL, and so on. Do values represent states or countries? This is where you'd need to specify a data category. For more information about Power BI geocoding and geo data categories, read my blog "Geocoding with Power View Maps" at prologika.com/geocoding-with-power-view-maps.

 TIP Maps show cities in wrong locations? Cities with the same name can exist in different states and countries. If cities end up in the wrong place on the map, consider adding Country, State and City fields (or create a hierarchy with these levels) to the map's Location area and enabling drilling down. When you do this, Power BI will attempt to plot the location within the parent territory. Of course, another solution to avoid ambiguity is to use latitude and longitude coordinates instead of location names.

Configuring navigation links

Sometimes, you might want to show a clickable navigation link (URL) to allow the user to navigate to a web page or another report. For example, the Table visual in **Figure 8.24** shows a list of reseller names and their websites (I fabricated a Website field from the Reseller Name with empty spaces removed). The user can click the website URL to navigate to it in the browser. Assuming you have a field with the links, you can simply assign it to the Web URL data category.

Figure 8.24 Assign the Web URL data category to implement clickable links.

And if you have a field that stores links to images, you can assign the Image URL category to it so that the images show in a Table or Card visuals.

8.4.3 Adding Quick Calculations

In the chapter, you'll discover that Power BI includes a very powerful programming language called Data Analysis Expressions (DAX), which is the same language that powers Analysis Services Tabular (used by BI pros). The only issue is that there is a learning curve involved. At the same time, there are frequently used calculations that shouldn't require knowing DAX. This is where quick calculations could help with the caveat that, as of this time, Power BI Desktop supports just one.

Understanding quick calculations
A quick calculation is a Power BI measure that has a predefined formula. Currently, Power BI supports only a "Percent of grand total" quick calculation, but expect the list to grow. Consider the report shown in **Figure 8.25**, where the "%GT SalesAmount" measure was created using the "Percent of grand total" quick calculation to show each country's sales as a percent of the grand total. If there wasn't a quick calculation, you had to create a DAX measure (I'll walk you through it in the next chapter)

Figure 8.25 The %GT SalesAmount field uses a quick calculation to show each value as a percent of the grand total.

Creating quick calculations
Creating a quick calculation takes a few mouse clicks.

1. Create a new Table visualization that has SalesTerritoryCountry (SalesTerritory table) and SalesAmount (ResellerSales table) fields in the Values area. Add the SalesAmount field one more time to the Values area.
2. In the Visualizations pane, expand the drop-down next to the SalesAmount field and click Quick Calc.
3. In the Quick Calc window, specify how the field will be aggregated and what quick calculation. For example, choose the Sum function to sum SalesAmount and "Percent of grant total" to calculate the percent of each line to the grand total.

Power BI Desktop implements quick calculations internally so don't try to find the DAX formula behind the quick calculation.

8.4.4 Forecasting Data

Recall from the first part of this book that Power BI Service has a nice Quick Insights feature that uses machine learning algorithms to analyze datasets and auto-generate reports with predictive insights. Another common predictive task is forecasting, such as to show revenue over future periods. Power BI Desktop supports basic forecasting capabilities to address such requirements.

 TIP If you need more sophisticated forecasting capabilities, consider R. You can extend Power BI Desktop with R to implement a wide variety of predictive and data transformation scenarios. For example, Chapter 6 showed how to use R for time series forecasting.

Understanding time series forecasting

Time series forecasting produces forecasts over data points indexed in time order. Power BI Desktop uses a built-in predictive algorithm to automatically detect the interval, such as monthly, weekly, or annually. It's also capable of detecting seasonality changes. Currently, forecasting is supported for single series line charts with a continuous (quantitative) axis. You can use the Analytics tab of the Visualization pane (see **Figure 8.26**) to add a forecast line.

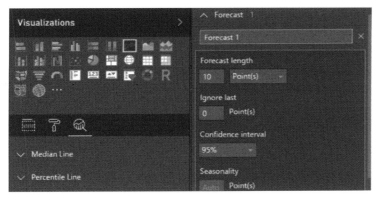

Figure 8.26 Time series forecasting uses a built-in model that supports limited customization.

You can customize certain aspects of the forecasting model. Change the "Forecast length" setting to specify the number of future intervals to forecast. Change the "Ignore last" setting to exclude a specified number of last points, such as when you know that the last period of data is incomplete. This is especially useful if you know the last month of data is still incomplete. "Confidence interval" lets you control the upper and lower boundaries of the forecasted results.

The Seasonality setting lets you override the automatically detected seasonality trend, such as 3 points if the seasonal cycle rises and falls every 3 months, assuming you're forecasting at the month level. When you hover over the line chart, you can see the exact values of the forecasted value, as well as the upper and lower bands (the shaded area width is controlled by the "Confidence interval" setting).

Implementing forecasting

Follow these steps to implement time series forecasting:

1. Add the "Line Chart" visualization to the report.

2. Add the Date field from the Date table to the Axis area of the Visualizations pane.

3. Add the SalesAmount field from the ResellerSales table to the Values area.

4. In the Format tab of the Visualizations pane, change the Type setting of the X-Axis section to Continuous. You can only do this if the data type of the field added to the Axis area is Date or Numeric.

5. In the Analytics tab of the Visualizations tab, expand the Forecast section and click the Add link.

6. (Optional) Experiment with the settings to see how they affect the forecasted area in the chart.

8.4.5 Grouping and Binning Data

Dynamic grouping allows you to create your own groups, such as to group countries with negligible sales to an "Others" group. In addition to grouping categories together, you can also create bins (buckets or bands) from numerical and time fields, such as to segment customers by revenue or create aging buckets.

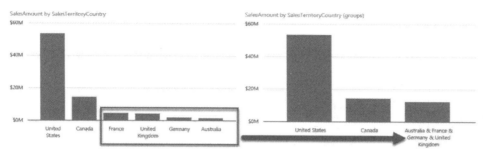

Figure 8.27 The second visual on the right groups European countries together.

Implementing groups
Consider the two visualizations shown in **Figure 8.27**. The visual on the left is a column chart that shows sales by country. Because European countries have less sales you might want to group them together, as shown on the right. Follow these steps to implement the group:

1. Create a Stacked Column Chart with SalesTerritoryCountry (SalesTerritory table) in the Axis area and SalesAmount (ResellerSales table) in the Values area.

2. Hold the Ctrl key and click each of the data categories you want to group.

3. Right-click any of the selected categories and click Group from the context menu. Power BI Desktop adds a new SalesTerritoryCountry (group) field to the SalesTerritory table. This field represents the group and it's prefixed with a special double-square icon. Power BI Desktop also adds the field to the Legend area.

4. In the Fields pane, click the ellipsis button next to SalesTerritoryCountry (group). Click Rename and change the field name to *European Countries*.

5. Click the ellipsis button next to the European Countries field and then click Edit Groups.

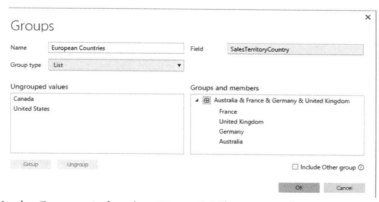

Figure 8.28 Use the Groups window to view the grouped values and control how the ungrouped values are shown.

6. In the Groups window (see **Figure 8.28**), you can change and group name and see the grouped and ungrouped members. If the "Include Other group" checkbox is checked (default setting), the rest of the data categories (Canada and United States) will be grouped into an "Other" group. Uncheck the "Include Other group" checkbox so that they show as separate data categories. Click OK.

7. Back to the report, remove SalesTerritoryCountry from the Axis area. Move the European Countries field from the Legend to the Axis area to create the right visualization shown in **Figure 8.27**.

 TIP Although Power BI Desktop doesn't support lassoing for a faster selection of categories, you can use the Groups window to select and add values to group. Instead of clicking elements on the chart, right-click the corresponding field in the Fields pane and then click Group to open the Groups window. Select the values in the "Ungrouped values" (you can hold the Shift key for extended selection) and then click the Group button to create a new group.

Binning data

Besides grouping categories, Power BI Desktop is also capable of discretizing numeric values or dates in equally sized ranges called bins. Suppose you want to know how many customers exist in different bin sizes based on the customer's overall sales, such as $0-$99, $100-$200, and so on (see **Figure 8.29**).

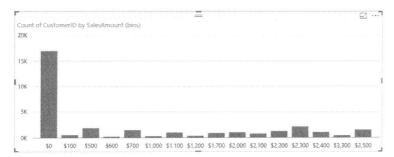

Figure 8.29 This report counts customers in bin sizes of $100 based on the overall sales.

This report counts distinct values of the CustomerID field (Count Distinct aggregation function) in the Customer table which is related to the InternetSales table. However, this requires traversing the relationship because the SalesAmount field in the InternetSales table will become the "dimension" while the measure (Count of Customers) would come from the Customer table.

1. In the Relationships View, if the InternetSales[CustomerKey] ⇨ Customer[CustomerKey] relationship has a single arrow (cross filter direction is Single), double-click it to open Edit Relationship window and change the "Cross filter direction" drop-down to Both. Click OK.

2. Switch to the Report View (or Data View). In the Fields pane, click the ellipsis button next to the SalesAmount field in the InternetSales table and then click New Group.

3. In the Groups window, change the bin size to 100 (you're grouping customers in bins of $100). Rename the group if you wish and then click OK.

4. Add a Stacked Column Chart visualization. Add the SalesAmount (bins) field that you've just created to the Axis area of the Visualizations pane since you'll be grouping the chart data on it.

5. Add the CustomerID field from the Customer table to the Value area. Expand the field drop-down in the Value area and switch the aggregation to Count (Distinct). Compare your results with **Figure 8.29**.

 TIP The built-in binning feature creates equal bins based on the bin size you specify in the Groups window. If you need more control over the bin ranges, consider either using Query Editor to add a conditional column, as I explained in Section 7.1.1, or creating a separate lookup (dimension) table for the bins and then join this table to the fact table.

Clustering data

Currently in preview (recall that you can enable preview features from the File ⇨ "Options and settings" menu), clustering (also called segmentation) is another way for dynamic grouping that lets you quickly find groups of similar data points in a subset of your data. You must use a scatter chart to detect clusters.

1. Create a scatter chart report with ProductName (Product table) in the Details area, SalesAmount (ResellerSales) in the X Axis area, and StandardCost (Product table) in the Y Axis area. This chart seeks a correlation between the product standard cost and its sales.

2. Hover the visualization, click the ellipsis menu in the top-right corner, and then click "Automatically find clusters". In the Clusters window, leave the defaults to auto-detect clusters to let Power BI automatically find clusters that make the most sense with your data.

3. Click OK. The algorithm finds three clusters and shows them in different colors (see **Figure 8.30**).

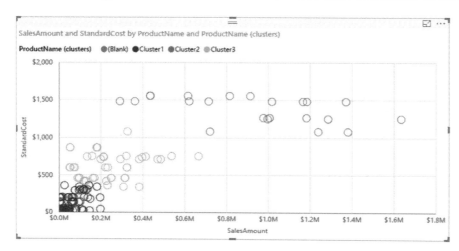

Figure 8.30 Automatic clustering found three clusters.

After the clustering algorithm runs, it creates a new categorical field called "Product name (clusters)" with the different cluster groups in it. This new field is added to your scatter chart's Legend field.

4. In the Fields pane, click the ellipsis next to "Product name (clusters)" and then click "Edit clusters". This bring you to the Clusters window where you can review the clusters and make changes, such as to increase the number of clusters. Now you understand that the first cluster (the one with low sales) has 99 products, the second cluster has 22 products, and the third cluster has 45 products.

5. (Optional) Create another visualization that uses the new "Product name (clusters)" field. Although you must use a scatter chart to detect clusters, you can then use the clusters just like any other field.

8.5   Summary

Once you import the initial set of tables, you should spend time exploring the model data and refining the model schema. The Data View supports various column operations to help you explore the model data and to make the necessary changes. You should make your model more intuitive by having meaningful table and column names. Revisit each column and configure its data type and formatting properties.

Relationships are the cornerstone of self-service data modelling that involves multiple datasets. You must have table relationships in order to integrate data across multiple tables.

As Power BI Desktop evolves, it adds more features to address popular analytical needs. Hierarchies let you explore data following natural paths. Data categories help Power BI Desktop interpret the field content. Use quick calculations to implement common measures without writing DAX code. Define forecast lines to implement time series forecasting. Use groups to analyze data across categories that you specify.

You've come a long way in designing the Adventure Works model! Next, let's make it even more useful by extending it with business calculations.

Chapter 9

Implementing Calculations

Power BI promotes rapid personal business intelligence (BI) for essential data exploration and analysis. Chances are, however, that in real life you might need to go beyond just simple aggregations. Business needs might require you to extend your model with calculations. Data Analysis Expressions (DAX) gives you the needed programmatic power to travel the "last mile" and unlock the full potential of Power BI.

DAX is a big topic that deserves much more attention, and this chapter doesn't aim to cover it in depth. However, it'll lay down the necessary fundamentals so that you can start using DAX to extend your models with business logic. The chapter starts by introducing you to DAX and its arsenal of functions. Next, you'll learn how to implement custom calculated columns and measures. I'll also show you how to handle more advanced scenarios with DAX. And you'll create various visualizations to test the sample calculations.

9.1   Understanding Data Analysis Expressions

Data Analysis Expressions (DAX) is a formula-based language in Power BI, Power Pivot, and Tabular that allows you to define custom calculations using an Excel-like formula language. DAX was introduced in the first version of Power Pivot (released in May 2010) with two major design goals:

- Simplicity – To get you started quickly with implementing business logic, DAX uses the Excel standard formula syntax and inherits many Excel functions. As a business analyst, Martin already knows many Excel functions, such as SUM and AVERAGE. When he uses Power BI, he appreciates that DAX has the same functions.

- Relational – DAX is designed with data models in mind and supports relational artifacts, including tables, columns, and relationships. For example, if Martin wants to sum up the SalesAmount column in the ResellerSales table, he can use the following formula: =SUM(ResellerSales[SalesAmount]).

DAX also has query constructs to allow external clients to query organizational Tabular models. As a data analyst, you probably don't need to know about these constructs. This chapter focuses on DAX as an expression language to extend self-service data models. If you need to know more about DAX in the context of organizational BI, you might find my book "Applied Microsoft SQL Server 2012 Analysis Services: Tabular Modeling" useful.

You can use DAX as an expression language to implement custom calculations that range from simple expressions, such as to concatenate two columns together, to complex measures that aggregate data in a specific way, such as to implement weighted averages. Based on the intended use, DAX supports two types of calculations: calculated columns and measures.

9.1.1 Understanding Calculated Columns

A calculated column is a table column that uses a DAX formula to compute the column values. This is conceptually similar to a formula-based column added to an Excel list, although DAX formulas reference columns instead of cells.

How calculated columns are stored

When a column contains a formula, the storage engine computes the value for each row and saves the results, just like it does with a regular column. To use a techie term, values of calculated columns get "materialized" or "persisted". The difference is that regular columns import their values from a data source, while calculated columns are computed from DAX formulas and saved after the regular columns are loaded. Because of this, the formula of a calculated column can reference regular columns and other calculated columns.

The storage engine might not compress calculated columns as much as regular columns (they don't participate in the row re-ordering algorithm that optimizes the compression). So, if you have a large table with a calculated column that has many unique values, this column might have a larger memory footprint.

Understanding row context

Every DAX formula is evaluated in a specific context. The formulas of calculated columns are evaluated for each row (row context). Let's look at a calculated column called FullName that's added to the Customer table, and it uses the following formula to concatenate the customer's first name and last name:

FullName=[FirstName] & " " & [LastName]

Because its formula is evaluated for each row in the Customer table (see **Figure 9.1**), the FullName column returns the full name for each customer. Again, this is very similar to how an Excel formula works when applied to multiple rows in a list, so this should be easy to understand.

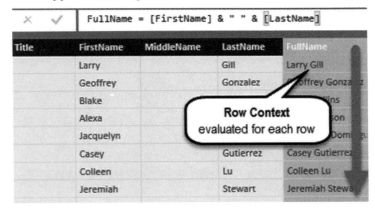

Figure 9.1 Calculated columns operate in row context, and their formulas are evaluated for each table row.

In terms of reporting, you can use calculated columns to group and filter data, just like you can use regular columns. For example, you can add a calculated column to any area of the Visualizations pane.

When to use calculated columns

In general, use a calculated column when you need to use a DAX formula to derive the column values. Because DAX formulas can reference other tables, a good usage scenario might be to look up a value from another table, just like you can use Excel VLOOKUP to reference values from another sheet. For example, to calculate the profit for each line item in ResellerSales, you might need to look up the product cost from the Product table. In this case, using a calculated column might make sense because its results are stored for each row in ResellerSales.

When shouldn't you use calculated columns? I mentioned that because calculated columns don't compress, they require more storage than regular columns. Therefore, if you can perform the calculation at the data source or in the model query, I recommend you do it there instead of using calculated columns. This is especially true for high-cardinality calculated columns in large tables because they require more memory for storage. For example, you might need to concatenate a carrier tracking number from its distinct parts in a large fact table. It's better to do so in the data source or in the table query before the data is imported. Continuing this line of thought, the example that I gave for using a calculated column for the customer's full name should probably be avoided in real life because you can perform the concatenation in the query.

Sometimes, however, you don't have a choice. For example, you might need a more complicated calculation that can be done only in DAX, such as to calculate the rank for each customer based on sales history. In these cases, you can't easily apply the calculation at the data source or the query. This is a good scenario for using DAX calculated columns.

9.1.2 Understanding Measures

Besides calculated columns, you can use DAX formulas to define measures. Unlike calculated columns, which might be avoided by using other implementation approaches, measures typically can't be replicated in other ways – they have to be written in DAX. DAX measures are very useful because they are used to produce aggregated values, such as to summarize a SalesAmount column or to calculate a distinct count of customers who have placed orders. Although measures are associated with a table, they don't show in the Data View's data preview pane, as calculated columns do. Instead, they're accessible in the Fields pane. When used on reports, measures are typically added to the Value area of the Visualizations pane.

Understanding measure types
Power BI Desktop supports two types of measures:

■ Implicit measures – To get you started as quickly as possible with data analysis, Microsoft felt that you shouldn't have to write formulas for basic aggregations. Any field added to the Value area of the Visualizations pane is treated as an implicit measure and is automatically aggregated, based on the column data type. For example, numeric fields are summed while text fields are counted. You can think of quick calculations that I discussed in the previous chapter as another type of implicit measures.

■ Explicit measures – You'll create explicit measures when you need an aggregation behavior that goes beyond the standard aggregation functions and quick calculations. For example, you might need a year-to-date (YTD) calculation. Explicit measures are measures that have a custom DAX formula you specify. **Table 9.1** summarizes the differences between implicit and explicit measures.

Table 9.1   Comparing implicit and explicit measures.

Criterion	Implicit Measures	Explicit Measures
Design	Automatically generated	Manually created
Accessibility	Can be changed on the report	Become a part of the model
DAX support	Standard aggregation formulas only	Can use DAX functions

Implicit measures are automatically generated by Power BI Desktop when you add a field to the Value area of the Visualizations pane. By contrast, you must specify a custom formula for explicit measures. Once the implicit measure is created, you can use the Visualizations pane to change its aggregation function. By contrast, explicit measures become a part of the model, and they can't be changed on the report. Implicit measures can only use the DAX standard aggregation functions: Sum, Count, Min, Max, Average, DistinctCount, Standard Deviation, Variance, and Median. By contrast, explicit measures can use any DAX function, such as to define a custom aggregation behavior.

Understanding filter context

Unlike calculated columns, DAX measures are evaluated *at run time* for each report *cell* as opposed to once for each table row. DAX measures are always dynamic and the result of the measure formula is never saved. Moreover, measures are evaluated in the filter context of each cell, as shown in **Figure 9.2**.

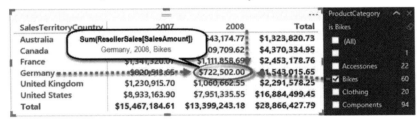

Figure 9.2 Measures are evaluated for each cell, and they operate in filter context.

This report summarizes the SalesAmount measure by countries on rows and by years on columns. The report is further filtered to show only sales for the Bikes product category. The filter context of the highlighted cell is the Germany value of the SalesTerritory[SalesTerritoryCountry] fields (on rows), the 2008 value of the Date[CalendarYear] field (on columns), and the Bikes value of the Product[ProductCategory] field (used as a filter).

If you're familiar with the SQL language, you can think of the DAX filter context as a WHERE clause that's determined dynamically and then applied to each cell on the report. When Power BI calculates the expression for that cell, it scopes the formula accordingly, such as to sum the sales amount from the rows in the ResellerSales table where the SalesTerritoryCountry value is Germany, the CalendarYear value is 2008, and the ProductCategory value is Bikes.

When to use measures

In general, measures are most frequently used to aggregate data. Explicit measures are typically used when you need a custom aggregation behavior, such as for time calculations, aggregates over aggregates, variances, and weighted averages. Suppose you want to calculate year-to-date (YTD) of reseller sales. As a first attempt, you might decide to add a SalesAmountYTD calculated column to the ResellerSales table. But now you have an issue because each row in this table represents an order line item. It's meaningless to calculate YTD for each line item.

As a second attempt, you could create a summary table in the database that stores YTD sales at a specific grain, such as product, end of month, reseller, and so on. While this might be a good approach for report performance, it presents issues. What if you need to lower the grain to include other dimensions? What if your requirements change and now YTD needs to be calculated as of any date? A better approach would be to use an explicit measure that's evaluated dynamically as users slice and dice the data. And don't worry too much about performance. Thanks to the memory-resident nature of the storage engine, most DAX calculations are instantaneous!

 NOTE The performance of DAX measures depends on several factors, including the complexity of the formula, your knowledge of DAX (whether you write inefficient DAX), the amount of data, and even the hardware of your computer. While most measures, such as time calculations and basic filtered aggregations, should perform very well, more involved calculations, such as aggregates over aggregates or the number of open orders as of any reporting date, are more intensive.

9.1.3 Understanding DAX Syntax

As I mentioned, one of the DAX design goals is to look and feel like the Excel formula language. Because of this, the DAX syntax resembles the Excel formula syntax. The DAX formula syntax is case-insensitive. For example, the following two expressions are both valid:

=YEAR([Date])
=year([date])

That said, I suggest you have a naming convention and stick to it. I personally prefer the first example where the function names are in uppercase and the column references match the column names in the model. This convention helps me quickly identify functions and columns in DAX formulas, and so that's what I use in this book.

Understanding expression syntax

A DAX formula for calculated columns and explicit measures has the following syntax:

Name=expression

Name is the name of the calculated column or measure. The expression must evaluate to a scalar (single) value. Expressions can contain operators, constants, or column references to return literal or Boolean values. The FullName calculated column that you saw before is an example of a simple expression that concatenates two values. You can add as many spaces as you want to make the formula easier to read.

Expressions can also include functions to perform more complicated operations, such as aggregating data. For example, back in **Figure 9.2**, the DAX formula references the SUM function to aggregate the SalesAmount column in the ResellerSales table. Functions can be nested. For example, the following formula nests the FILTER function to calculate the count of line items associated with the Progressive Sports reseller:

=COUNTROWS(FILTER(ResellerSales, RELATED(Reseller[ResellerName])="Progressive Sports"))

DAX supports up to 64 levels of function nesting, but going beyond two or three levels makes the formulas more difficult to understand. When you need to go above two or three levels of nesting, I recommend you break the formula into multiple measures. This also simplifies testing complex formulas.

Understanding operators

DAX supports a set of common operators to support more complex formulas, as shown in **Table 9.2**. DAX also supports TRUE and FALSE as logical constants.

Table 9.2 DAX supports the following operators.

Category	Operators	Description	Example
Arithmetic	+, -, *, /, ^	Addition, subtraction, multiplication, division, and exponentiation	=[SalesAmount] * [OrderQty]
Comparison	>, >=, <, <=, <>	For comparing values	=FILTER(RELATEDTABLE(Products),Products[UnitPrice]>30))
Logical	||, &&	Logical OR and AND	=FILTER(RELATEDTABLE(Products),Products[UnitPrice]>30 && Products[Discontinued]=TRUE())
Concatenation	&	Concatenating text	=[FirstName] & " " & [LastName]
Unary	+, -, NOT	Change the operand sign	= - [SalesAmount]

Referencing columns

One of DAX's strengths over regular Excel formulas is that it can traverse table relationships and reference columns. This is much simpler and more efficient than referencing Excel cells and ranges with the VLOOKUP function. Column names are unique within a table. You can reference a column using its fully qualified name in the format <TableName>[<ColumnName>], such as in this example:

ResellerSales[SalesAmount]

If the table name includes a space or is a reserved word, such as Date, enclose it with single quotes:

'Reseller Sales'[SalesAmount] or 'Date'[CalendarYear]

When a calculated column references a column from the same table, you can omit the table name. The AutoComplete feature in the formula bar helps you avoid syntax errors when referencing columns. As **Figure 9.3** shows, the moment you start typing the fully qualified column reference in the formula bar, it displays a drop-down list of matching columns. The formula bar also supports color coding, and it colors the function names in a blue color.

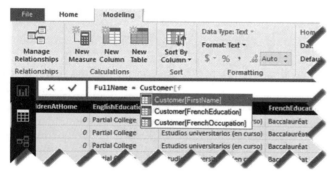

Figure 9.3 AutoComplete helps you with column references in the formula bar.

9.1.4 Understanding DAX Functions

DAX supports over a hundred functions that encapsulate a prepackaged programming logic to perform a wide variety of operations. If you type in the function name in the formula bar, AutoComplete shows the function syntax and its arguments. For the sake of brevity, this book doesn't cover the DAX functions and their syntax in detail. For more information, please refer to the DAX language reference by Ed Price (this book's technical editor) at http://bit.ly/daxfunctions, which provides a detailed description and examples for most functions. Another useful resource is "DAX in the BI Tabular Model Whitepaper and Samples" by Microsoft (http://bit.ly/daxwhitepaper).

Functions from Excel

DAX supports approximately 80 Excel functions. The big difference is that DAX formulas can't reference Excel cells or ranges. References such as A1 or A1:A10, which are valid in Excel formulas, can't be used in DAX functions. Instead, when data operations are required, the DAX functions must reference columns or tables. **Table 9.3** shows the subset of Excel functions supported by DAX with examples.

Aggregation functions

As you've seen, DAX "borrows" the Excel aggregation functions, such as SUM, MIN, MAX, COUNT, and so on. However, the DAX counterparts accept a table column as an input argument instead of a cell range. Since only referencing columns can be somewhat limiting, DAX adds X-version of these functions: SUMX, AVERAGEX, COUNTAX, MINX, MAXX. These functions take two arguments. The first one is a table and the second is an expression.

Table 9.3 DAX borrows many functions from Excel.

Category	Functions	Example
Date and Time	DATE, DATEVALUE, DAY, EDATE, EOMONTH, HOUR, MINUTE, MONTH, NOW, SECOND, TIME, TIMEVALUE, TODAY, WEEKDAY, WEEKNUM, YEAR, YEARFRAC	=YEAR('Date'[Date])
Information	ISBLANK, ISERROR, ISLOGICAL, ISNONTEXT, ISNUMBER, ISTEXT	=IF(ISBLANK('Date'[Month]), "N/A", 'Date'[Month])
Logical	AND, IF, NOT, OR, FALSE, TRUE	=IF(ISBLANK(Customers[MiddleName]),FALSE(),TRUE())
Math and Trigonometry	ABS,CEILING, ISO.CEILING, EXP, FACT, FLOOR, INT, LN, LOG, LOG10, MOD, MROUND, PI, POWER, QUOTIENT, RAND, RANDBETWEEN, ROUND, ROUNDDOWN, ROUNDUP, SIGN, SQRT, SUM, SUMSQ, TRUNC	=SUM(ResellerSales[SalesAmount])
Statistical	AVERAGE, AVERAGEA, COUNT, COUNTA, COUNTBLANK, MAX, MAXA, MIN, MINA	=AVERAGE(ResellerSales[SalesAmount])
Text	CONCATENATE, EXACT, FIND, FIXED, LEFT, LEN, LOWER, MID, REPLACE, REPT, RIGHT, SEARCH, SUBSTITUTE, TRIM, UPPER, VALUE	=SUBSTITUTE(Customer[Phone],"-", "")

Suppose you want to calculate the total order amount for each row in the ResellerSales table using the formula [SalesAmount] * [OrderQuantity]. You can accomplish this in two ways. First, you can add an OrderAmount calculated column that uses the above expression and then use the SUM function to summarize the calculated column. However, a better approach is to perform the calculation in one step by using the SUMX function, as follows:

=SUMX(ResellerSales, ResellerSales[SalesAmount] * ResellerSales[OrderQuantity])

Although the result in both cases is the same, the calculation process is very different. In the case of the SUM function, DAX simply aggregates the column. When you use the SUMX function, DAX will compute the expression for each of the detail rows behind the cell and then aggregate the result. What makes the X-version functions flexible is that the table argument can also be a function that returns a table of values. For example, the following formula calculates the simple average (arithmetic mean) of the SalesAmount column for rows in the InternetSales table whose unit price is above $100:

=AVERAGEX (FILTER(InternetSales, InternetSales[UnitPrice] > 100), InternetSales[SalesAmount])

This formula uses the FILTER function, which returns a table of rows matching the criteria that you pass in the second argument.

Statistical functions
DAX adds new statistical functions. The COUNTROWS(Table) function is similar to the Excel COUNT functions (COUNT, COUNTA, COUNTX, COUNTAX, COUNTBLANK), but it takes a table as an argument and returns the count of rows in that table. For example, the following formula returns the number of rows in the ResellerSales table:

=COUNTROWS(ResellerSales)

Similarly, the DISTINCTCOUNT(Column) function, counts the distinct values in a column. DAX includes the most common statistical functions, such as STDEV.S, STDEV.P, STDEVX.S, STDEVX.P, VAR.S, VAR.P, VARX.S, and VARX.P, for calculating standard deviation and variance. Similar to Count, Sum, Min, Max, and Average, DAX has its own implementation of these functions for better performance instead of just using the Excel standard library.

Filter functions

This category includes functions for navigating relationships and filtering data, including the ALL, ALLEXCEPT, ALLNOBLANKROW, CALCULATE, CALCULATETABLE, DISTINCT, EARLIER, EARLIEST, FILTER, LOOKUPVALUE, RELATED, RELATEDTABLE, and VALUES functions. Next, I'll provide examples for the most popular filter functions.

You can use the RELATED(Column), RELATEDTABLE(Table), and USERELATIONSHIP (Column1, Column2) functions for navigating relationships in the model. The RELATED function follows a many-to-one relationship, such as from a fact table to a lookup table. Consider a calculated column in the ResellerSales table that uses the following formula:

=RELATED(Product[StandardCost])

For each row in the ResellerSales table, this formula will look up the standard cost of the product in the Product table. The RELATEDTABLE function can travel a relationship in either direction. For example, a calculated column in the Product table can use the following formula to obtain the total reseller sales amount for each product:

=SUMX(RELATEDTABLE(ResellerSales), ResellerSales[SalesAmount])

For each row in the Product table, this formula finds the corresponding rows in the ResellerSales table that match the product and then it sums the SalesAmount column across these rows. The USERELATIONSHIP function can use inactive role-playing relationships, as I'll demonstrate in section 9.4.1.

The FILTER (Table, Condition) function is useful to filter a subset of column values, as I've just demonstrated with the AVERAGEX example. The DISTINCT(Column) function returns a table of unique values in a column. For example, this formula returns the count of unique customers with Internet sales:

=COUNTROWS(DISTINCT(InternetSales[CustomerKey]))

When there is no table relationship, the LOOKUPVALUE (ResultColumn, SearchColumn1, SearchValue1 [, SearchColumn2, SearchValue2]...) function can be used to look up a single value from another table. The following formula looks up the sales amount of the first line item bought by customer 14870 on August 1st, 2007:

=LOOKUPVALUE(InternetSales[SalesAmount],[OrderDateKey],"20070801",[CustomerKey],"14870", [SalesOrderLineNumber],"1")

If multiple values are found, the LOOKUPVALUE function will return the error "A table of multiple values was supplied where a single value was expected". If you expect multiple values, use the FILTER function instead.

The CALCULATE(Expression, [Filter1],[Filter2]..) function is a very popular and useful function because it allows you to overwrite the filter context. It evaluates an expression in its filter context that could be modified by optional filters. Suppose you need to add a LineItemCount calculated column to the Customer table that computes the count of order line items posted by each customer. On a first attempt, you might try the following expression to count the order line items:

=COUNTROWS(InternetSales)

However, this expression won't work as expected (see the top screenshot in **Figure 9.4**). Specifically, it returns the count of all the rows in the InternetSales table instead of counting the line items for each customer. To fix this, you need to force the COUNTROWS function to execute in the current row context. To do this, I'll use the CALCULATE function as follows:

=CALCULATE(COUNTROWS(InternetSales))

The CALCUATE function determines the current row context and applies the filter context to the formula. Because the Customer table is related to InternetSales on CustomerKey, the value of CustomerKey for each row is passed as a filter to InternetSales. For example, if the CustomerKey value for the first row is 11602, the filter context for the first execution is COUNTROWS(InternetSales, CustomerKey=11602).

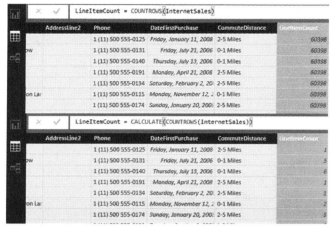

Figure 9.4 This calculated column in the second example uses the CALCULATE function to pass the row context to the InternetSales table.

The CALCULATE function can also take one or more filters as optional arguments. The filter argument can be a Boolean expression or a table. The following expression returns the transaction count for each customer for the year 2007 and the Bikes product category:

=CALCULATE(COUNTROWS(InternetSales), 'Date'[CalendarYear]=2007, Product[ProductCategory]="Bikes")

The following expression counts the rows in the InternetSales table for each customer where the product category is "Bikes" or is missing:

=CALCULATE(COUNTROWS(InternetSales), FILTER(Product, Product[ProductCategory]="Bikes" || ISBLANK(Product[ProductCategory])))

The FILTER function returns a table that contains only the rows from the Product table where ProductCategory="Bikes". When you pass the returned table to the CALCULATE function, it'll filter away any combination of column values that doesn't exists in the table.

 TIP When the expression to be evaluated is a measure, you can use the following shortcut for the CALCULATE function: =MeasureName(<filter>). For example, =[SalesAmount1]('Date'[CalendarYear]=2006)

Time intelligence functions
One of the most common analysis needs is implementing time calculations, such as year-to-date, parallel period, previous period, and so on. The time intelligence functions require a Date table. The Date table should contain one row for every date that might exist in your data. You can add a Date table using any of the techniques I discussed in Chapter 6. DAX uses the Data table to construct a set of dates for each calculation depending on the DAX formula you specify. For more information about how DAX uses a date table, read the blog post, "Time Intelligence Functions in DAX" by Microsoft's Howie Dickerman (http://bit.ly/daxtifunctions).

NOTE Readers familiar with Excel data modeling might know that you need to explicitly mark a date table. Power BI Desktop doesn't require you to do so as long as the relationships to the date table join on a column of a Date data type.

As I mentioned in the previous chapter, Power BI doesn't limit you to a single date table. For example, you might decide to import three date tables so you can do analysis on order date, ship date, and due date. As long as they are all related to the ResellerSales table, you can implement calculations such as:

SalesAmountByOrderDate = TOTALYTD(SUM(ResellerSales[SalesAmount]), 'OrderDate'[Date])
SalesAmountByShipDate = TOTALYTD(SUM(ResellerSales[SalesAmount]), 'ShipDate'[Date])

DAX has about 35 functions for implementing time calculations. The functions that you'll probably use most often are TOTALYTD, TOTALQTD, and TOTALMTD. For example, the following formula calculates the YTD sales. The second argument tells DAX which Date table to use as a reference point:

= TOTALYTD(SUM(ResellerSales[SalesAmount]), 'Date'[Date])
-- or the following expression to use fiscal years that end on June 30th
= TOTALYTD(SUM(ResellerSales[SalesAmount]), 'Date'[Date], ALL('Date'), "6/30")

Another common requirement is to implement variance and growth calculations between the current and previous time period. The following formula calculates the sales amount for the previous year using the PREVIOUSYEAR function:

=CALCULATE(SUM(ResellerSales[SalesAmount]), PREVIOUSYEAR('Date'[Date]))

There are also to-date functions that return a table with multiple periods, including the DATESMTD, DATESQTD, DATESYTD, and SAMEPERIODLASTYEAR. For example, the following measure formula returns the YTD reseller sales:

=CALCULATE(SUM(ResellerSales[SalesAmount]), DATESYTD('Date'[Date]))

Finally, the DATEADD, DATESBETWEEN, DATESINPERIOD, and PARALLELPERIOD functions can take an arbitrary range of dates. The following formula returns the reseller sales between July 1st 2005 and July 4th 2005.

=CALCULATE(SUM(ResellerSales[SalesAmount]), DATESBETWEEN('Date'[Date], DATE(2005,7,1), DATE(2005,7,4)))

Ranking functions

You might have a need to calculate rankings. DAX supports ranking functions. For example, the RANK.EQ(Value, Column, [Order]) function allows you to implement a calculated column that returns the rank of a number in a list of numbers. Consider the Rank calculated column in the SalesTerritory table (see **Figure 9.5**).

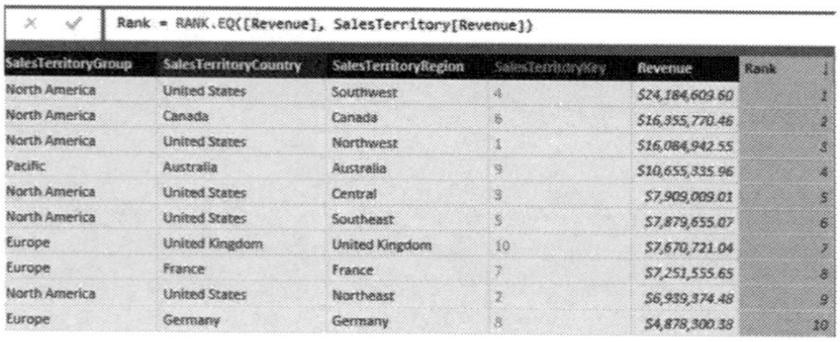

	Rank = RANK.EQ([Revenue], SalesTerritory[Revenue])					
SalesTerritoryGroup	SalesTerritoryCountry	SalesTerritoryRegion	SalesTerritoryKey	Revenue	Rank	
North America	United States	Southwest	4	$24,184,609.60	1	
North America	Canada	Canada	6	$16,355,770.46	2	
North America	United States	Northwest	1	$16,084,942.55	3	
Pacific	Australia	Australia	9	$10,655,335.96	4	
North America	United States	Central	3	$7,909,009.01	5	
North America	United States	Southeast	5	$7,879,655.07	6	
Europe	United Kingdom	United Kingdom	10	$7,670,721.04	7	
Europe	France	France	7	$7,251,555.65	8	
North America	United States	Northeast	2	$6,939,374.48	9	
Europe	Germany	Germany	8	$4,878,300.38	10	

Figure 9.5 The RANK.EQ function ranks each row based on the value in the REVENUE column.

The formula uses the RANK.EQ function to return the rank of each territory, based on the value of the Revenue column. If multiple territories have the same revenue, they'll share the same rank. However, the presence of duplicate numbers affects the ranks of subsequent numbers. For example, had Southwest and Canada had the same revenue, their rank would be 1, but the Northwest rank would be 3. The function can take an Order argument, such as 0 (default) for a descending order or 1 for an ascending order.

Creating calculated tables

An interesting Power BI Desktop feature is creating calculated tables using DAX. A calculated table is just like a regular table, but it's populated with a DAX function that returns a table instead of using a query.

You can create a calculated table by clicking the New Table button in the ribbon's Modeling tab. For example, you can add a SalesSummary table (see **Figure 9.6**) that summarizes reseller and Internet sales by calendar year using the following formula:

SalesSummary = SUMMARIZE(ResellerSales, 'Date'[CalendarYear], "ResellerSalesAmount", SUM(ResellerSales[SalesAmount]), "InternetSalesAmount", SUM(InternetSales[SalesAmount]))

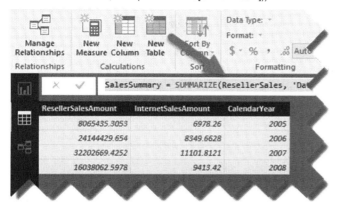

Figure 9.6 You can use the New Table button in the ribbon's Modeling tab to create a calculated table that uses a DAX formula.

This formula uses the SUMMARIZE function which works similarly to the SQL GROUP BY clause. It summarizes the ResellerSales table by grouping by Date[CalendarYear] and computing the aggregated ResellerSales[SalesAmount] and InternetSales[SalesAmount]. Unlike SQL, you don't have to specify joins because the model has relationships from the ResellerSales and InternetSales tables to the Date table.

Now that I've introduced you to the DAX syntax and functions, let's practice creating DAX calculations. You'll also practice creating visualizations in the Report View to test the calculations, but I won't go into the details because you've already learned about visualizations in Chapter 3. If you don't want to type in the formulas, you can copy them from the dax.txt file in the \Source\ch09 folder.

9.2   Implementing Calculated Columns

As I previously mentioned, calculated columns are columns that use DAX formulas for their values. Unlike the regular columns you get when you import data, you add calculated columns after the data is imported, by entering DAX formulas. When you create a report, you can place a calculated column in any area of the Visualizations pane, although you'd typically use calculated columns to group and filter data on the report.

9.2.1   Creating Basic Calculated Columns

DAX includes various operators to create basic expressions, such as expressions for concatenating strings and for performing arithmetic operations. You can use these operators to create simple expression-based columns.

Concatenating text
Suppose you need a visualization that shows sales by employee (see **Figure 9.7**). Since you'd probably need to show the employee's full name, which is missing in the Employee table, let's create a calculated column that shows the employee's full name:

1. Open the Adventure Works file with your changes from the previous chapter.
2. Click the Data View icon in the navigation bar. Click the Employee table in the Fields pane to select it.

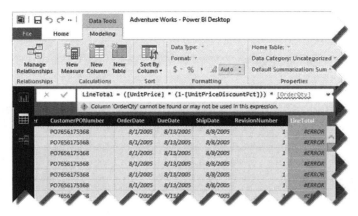

Figure 9.7 This visualization shows sales by the employee's full name.

3. In the Modeling bar, click the New Column button. This adds a new column named "Column" to the end of the table and activates the formula bar.

4. In the formula bar, enter the following formula:

FullName = [FirstName] & " " & [LastName]

This formula changes the name of the calculated column to *FullName*. Then, the DAX expression uses the concatenation operator to concatenate the FirstName and LastName columns and to add an empty space in between them. As you type, AutoComplete helps you with the formula syntax, although you should also follow the syntax rules, such as that a column reference must be enclosed in square brackets.

5. Press Enter or click the checkmark button to the left of the formula bar. DAX evaluates the expression and commits the formula. Power BI Desktop adds the FullName field to the Employee table in the Fields pane and prefixes it with a special *fx* icon.

Working with date columns

Instead of DAX calculated columns, you can implement simple expression-based columns in table queries. This is the technique you'll practice next.

1. Right-click the Customer table in the Fields pane and then click Edit Query.

2. Add a FullName custom column (in the ribbon's Add Column tab, click Custom Column) to the Customer query with the following formula:

=[FirstName] & " " & [LastName]

3. In the Queries pane, select the Date query. Add the custom columns shown in **Table 9.4** to assign user-friendly names to months, quarters, and semesters.

Table 9.4   Add the following calculated columns in the Date query.

Column Name	Expression	Example
MonthNameDesc	=[MonthName] & " " & Text.From([CalendarYear])	July 2007
CalendarQuarterDesc	="Q" & Text.From([CalendarQuarter]) & " " & Text.From([CalendarYear])	Q1 2008
FiscalQuarterDesc	="Q" & Text.From([FiscalQuarter]) & " " & Text.From([FiscalYear])	Q3 2008
CalendarSemesterDesc	="H" & Text.From([CalendarSemester]) & " " & Text.From([CalendarYear])	H2 2007
FiscalSemesterDesc	="H" & Text.From([FiscalSemester]) & " " & Text.From([FiscalYear])	H2 2007

In case you're wondering, the Text.From() function is used to cast a number to text. An explicit conversion is required because the query won't do an implicit conversion to text, and so the formula will return an error.

4. Click the "Close & Apply" button to apply the changes to the data model.

5. In the Fields pane, expand the Date table, and click the MonthNameDesc column to select it in the Data View. Click the "Sort By Column" button (ribbon's Modeling tab) to sort the MonthNameDesc column by the MonthNumberOfYear column. You do this so that month names are sorted in the ordinal order when MonthNameDesc is used on a report.

6. To reduce clutter, hide the CalendarQuarter, CalendarSemester, FiscalQuarter and FiscalSemester columns in the Date table. These columns show the quarter and semester ordinal numbers, and they're not that useful for analysis.

7. In the Reports tab, create a Bar Chart using the SalesAmount field from the ResellerSales table (add it to Value area) and the FullName field from the Employee table (add it to the Axis area).

8. Hover on the chart and click the ellipsis (…) menu in the upper-right corner. Sort the visualization by SalesAmount in descending order. Compare your results with **Figure 9.8** to verify that the FullName calculated column is working. Save the Adventure Works model.

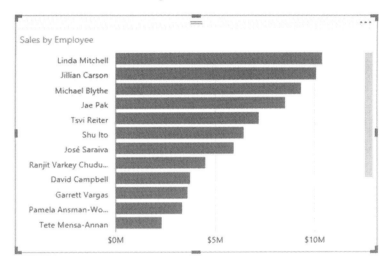

Figure 9.8 The formula bar displays an error when the DAX formula contains an invalid column reference.

Performing arithmetic operations

Another common requirement is to create a calculated column that performs some arithmetic operations for each row in a table. Follow these steps to create a LineTotal column that calculates the total amount for each row in the ResellerSales table by multiplying the order quantity, discount, and unit price:

1. Another way to add a calculated column is to use the Fields pane. In the Fields pane, right-click the ResellerSales table, and then click New Column.

2. In the formula bar, enter the following formula and press Enter. I've intentionally misspelled the OrderQty column reference to show you how you can troubleshoot errors in formulas.

```
LineTotal = [UnitPrice] * (1-[UnitPriceDiscountPct]) * [OrderQty]
```

This expression multiplies UnitPrice times UnitPriceDiscountPrc times OrderQty. Notice that when you type in a recognized function in the formula bar and enter a parenthesis "(", AutoComplete shows the function syntax. Notice that the formula bar shows an error "Column 'OrderQty' cannot be found or may be used in this expression". In addition, the LineTotal column shows "Error" in every cell.

3. In the formula bar, replace the OrderQty reference with OrderQuantity as follows:

LineTotal = [UnitPrice] * (1-[UnitPriceDiscountPct]) * **[OrderQuantity]**

4. Press Enter. Now, the column should work as expected.

9.2.2 Creating Advanced Calculated Columns

DAX supports formulas that allow you to create more advanced calculated columns. For example, you can use the RELATED function to look up a value from a related table. Another popular function is the SUMX function, with which you can sum values from a related table.

Implementing a lookup column

Suppose you want to calculate the net profit for each row in the ResellerSales table. For the purposes of this exercise, you'd calculate the line item net profit by subtracting the product cost from the line item total. As a first step, you need to look up the product cost in the Product table.

1. In the Fields pane, add a new NetProfit calculated column to the ResellerSales table that uses the following expression:

NetProfit = RELATED(Product[StandardCost])

This expression uses the RELATED function to look up the value of the StandardCost column in the Product table. Since a calculated column inherits the current row context, this expression is evaluated for each row. Specifically, for each row DAX gets the ProductKey value, navigates the ResellerSales[ProductKey] ⇨ Product[ProductKey] relationship, and then retrieves the standard cost for that product from the Product[StandardCost] column.

2. To calculate the net profit as a variance from the line total and the product's standard cost, change the expression as follows:

NetProfit = [LineTotal] - RELATED(Product[StandardCost])

Note that when the line item's product cost exceeds the line total, the result is a negative value.

Aggregating values

You can use the SUMX function to aggregate related rows from another table. Suppose you need a calculated column in the Product table that returns the reseller sales for each product:

1. Add a new ResellerSales calculated column to the Product table with the following expression:

ResellerSales = SUMX(RELATEDTABLE(ResellerSales), ResellerSales[SalesAmount])

The RELATEDTABLE function follows a relationship in either direction (many-to-one or one-to-many) and returns a table containing all the rows that are related to the current row from the specified table. In this case, this function returns a table with all the rows from the ResellerSales table that are related to the current row in the Product table. Then, the SUMX function sums the SalesAmount column.

2. Note that the formula returns a blank value for some products because these products don't have any reseller sales.

Ranking values

Suppose you want to rank each customer based on the customer's overall sales. The RANKX function can help you implement this requirement:

1. In the Fields pane, right-click the Customer table and click New Column.

2. In the formula bar, enter the following formula:

SalesRank = RANKX(Customer, SUMX(RELATEDTABLE(InternetSales), [SalesAmount]),,,Dense)

This function uses the RANKX function to calculate the rank of each customer, based on the customer's overall sales recorded in the InternetSales table. Similar to the previous example, the SUMX function is used to aggregate the [SalesAmount] column in the InternetSales table. The Dense argument is used to avoid skipping numbers for tied ranks (ranks with the same value).

9.3   Implementing Measures

Measures are typically used to aggregate values. Unlike calculated columns whose expressions are evaluated at design time for each row in the table, measures are evaluated at run time for each cell on the report. DAX applies the row, column, and filter selections when it calculates the formula. DAX supports implicit and explicit measures. An implicit measure is a regular column that's added to the Value area of the Visualizations pane. An explicit measure has a custom DAX formula. For more information about the differences between implicit and explicit measures, see Table 9.1 again.

9.3.1   Implementing Implicit Measures

In this exercise, you'll work with implicit measures. This will help you understand how implicit measures aggregate and how you can control their default aggregation behavior.

Changing the default aggregation behavior

I explained before that by default, Power BI Desktop aggregates implicit measures using the SUM function for numeric columns and the COUNT function for text-based columns. When you add a column to the Value area, Power BI Desktop automatically creates an implicit measure and aggregates it based on the column type. For numeric columns Power BI Desktop uses the DAX SUM aggregation function. If the column date type is Text, Power BI Desktop uses COUNT. Sometimes, you might need to overwrite the default aggregation behavior. For example, the CalendarYear column in the Date table is a numeric column, but it doesn't make sense to sum it up on reports.

1. Make sure that the Data View is active. In the Fields pane, click the CalendarYear column in the Date table. This shows the Date table in the Data View and selects the CalendarYear column.

2. In the ribbon's Modeling tab, expand the Default Summarization drop-down and change it to "Do Not Summarize". As a result, the next time you use CalendarYear on a report, it won't get summarized.

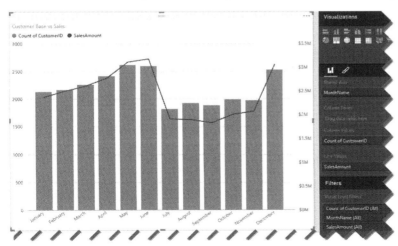

Figure 9.9 Implemented as a combo chart, this visualization shows the correlation between count of customers and sales.

Working with implicit measures

Suppose you'd like to check if there's any seasonality impact to your business. Are some months slower than others? If sales decrease, do fewer customer purchase products? To answer these questions, you'll create the report shown in **Figure 9.9**. Using the Line and Clustered Column Chart visualization, this report shows the count of customers as a column chart and the sales as a line chart that's plotted on the secondary axis. You'll analyze these two measures by month.

Let's start with visualizing the count of customers who have purchased products by month. Traditionally, you'd add some customer identifier to the fact table and you'd use a Distinct Count aggregation function to only count unique customers. But the InternetSales table doesn't have a CustomerID column, and your chances to get IT to add it to the data warehouse are probably slim. Can you count on the CustomerID column in the Customer table?

 NOTE Why not count on the CustomerKey column in InternetSales? This will work if the Customer table handles Type 1 changes only. A Type 1 change results in an in-place change. When a change to a customer is detected, the row is simply overwritten. However, chances are that business requirements necessitate Type 2 changes as well, where a new row is created when an important change occurs, such as when the customer changes a state. Therefore, counting on CustomerKey (called a surrogate key in dimensional modeling) is often a bad idea because it might lead to overstated results. Instead, you'd want to do a distinct count on a customer identifier that is not system generated, such as the customer's account number.

1. Switch to the Report View. From the Fields pane, drag the CustomerID column from the Customer table, and then drop it on an empty area in the report canvas.
2. Power BI Desktop defaults to a table visualization that shows all customer identifiers. Switch the visualization type to "Line and Clustered Column Chart".
3. In the Visualizations pane, drag CustomerID from the Shared Axis area to the Column Values area.
4. Expand the dropdown in the "Count of CustomerID" field. Note that it uses the Count aggregation function, as shown in **Figure 9.10**.

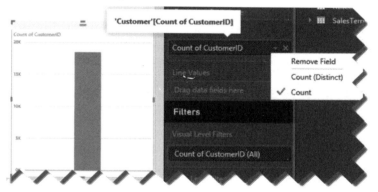

Figure 9.10 Text-based implicit measures use the Count function by default.

5. A product can be sold more than once within a given time period. If you simply count on CustomerID, you might get an inflated count. Instead, you want to count customers uniquely. Change the aggregation function of "Count of CustomerID" to Count (Distinct).
6. (Optional) Use the ribbon's Modeling tab to change the CustomerID default summarization to Count (Distinct) so you don't have to overwrite the aggregation function every time this field is used on a report.
7. With the new visualization selected, check the MonthName column of the Date table in the Fields pane to add it to the Shared Axis area of the Visualizations pane.

At this point, the results might be incorrect. Specifically, the count of customers might not change across months. The issue is that the aggregation happens over the InternetSales fact table via the Date ⇔ InternetSales ⇨ Customer path (notice that the relationship direction changes). Furthermore, the cardinality of the Date and Customer tables is Many-to-Many (there could be many customers who purchased something on the same date, and a repeating customer could buy multiple times). So, in case you skipped the change in the previous chapter (the binning example), make sure that the InternetSales ⇨ Customer relationship is bidirectional in the next step.

8. Switch to the Relationships View. Double-click the InternetSales ⇨ Customer relationship. In the Advanced Options properties of the relationship, change the cross filter direction to Both.

9. Switch to the Report View. Note that now the results vary by month.

10. Drag the SalesAmount field from the InternetSales table to the Line Values area of the Visualizations pane.

Note that because SalesAmount is numeric, Power BI Desktop defaults to the SUM aggregation function. Note also that indeed, seasonality affects sales. Specifically, the customer base decreases during the summer. And as the number of customers decreases, so do sales.

9.3.2 Implementing Explicit Measures

Explicit measures are more flexible than implicit measures because you can use custom DAX formulas. Similar to implicit measures, explicit measures are typically used to aggregate data and are usually placed in the Value area in the Visualizations pane.

 TIP DAX explicit measures can get complex and it might be preferable to test nested formulas step by step. To make this process easier, you can test measures outside Power BI Desktop by using DAX Studio. DAX Studio (http://daxstudio.codeplex.com) is a community-driven project to help you write and test DAX queries connected to Excel Power Pivot models, Tabular models, and Power BI Desktop models. DAX Studio features syntax highlighting, integrated tracing support, and exploring the model metadata with Dynamic Management Views (DMVs). If you're not familiar with DMVs, you can use them to document your models, such as to get a list of all the measures and their formulas.

Implementing a basic explicit measure

A common requirement is implementing a measure that filters results. For example, you might need a measure that shows the reseller sales for a specific product category, such as Bikes. Let's implement a BikeResellerSales measure that does just that.

1. In Fields pane (Data View or Report View), right-click the ResellerSales table, and click New Measure.

2. In the formula bar, enter the following formula and press Enter:

BikeResellerSales = CALCULATE(SUM(ResellerSales[SalesAmount]), 'Product'[ProductCategory]="Bikes")

Power BI Desktop adds the measure to the ResellerSales table in the Fields pane. The measure has a special calculator icon in front of it.

 TIP Added a measure to a wrong table? Instead of recreating the measure in the correct table, you can simply change its home table. To do this, click the measure in the Fields pane to select it. Then, in the ribbon's Modeling tab, use the Home Table dropdown (Properties group) to change the table. Because measures are dynamic, they can be anchored to any table.

3. (Optional) Add a map visualization to show the BikeResellerSales measure (see **Figure 9.11**). Add both SalesTerritoryCountry and SalesTerritoryRegion fields from the SalesTerritory table to the Location area of the Visualizations pane. This enables the drill down buttons on the map and allows you to drill down sales from country to region!

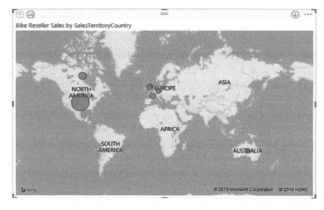

Figure 9.11   This map visualization shows the "Sum of Bike Reseller Sales" measure.

Implementing a percent of total measure

Suppose you need a measure for calculating a ratio of current sales compared to overall sales across countries. In the previous chapter, you did this using the "Percent of Grand Total" quick calculation. But what if you want a slightly different behavior? Instead of a percent of the grand total, you might need a percent of the column total. For example, for "United States", the measure calculates the ratio between the sales for United States and the sales across all the territories (see **Figure 9.12**). Let's create this calculated measure.

SalesTerritoryCountry	2005	2006	2007	2008	Total
Australia			2.63 %	4.66 %	1.98 %
Canada	18.76 %	19.98 %	17.55 %	14.90 %	17.87 %
France		3.55 %	7.37 %	8.58 %	5.73 %
Germany			3.41 %	5.52 %	2.47 %
United Kingdom		3.49 %	6.71 %	7.96 %	5.32 %
United States	81.24 %	72.99 %	62.33 %	58.37 %	66.63 %
Total	100.00 %	100.00 %	100.00 %	100.00 %	100.00 %

Figure 9.12   The PercentOfTotal measure shows the contribution of the country sales to the overall sales.

1. Another way to create a measure is to use the New Measure button. Make sure that the Data View is selected. In the Fields pane, click the ResellerSales table.
2. Click the New Measure button in the Modeling ribbon.
3. In the Formula field, enter the following formula:

   PercentOfTotal = DIVIDE (SUM(ResellerSales[SalesAmount]), CALCULATE (SUM(ResellerSales[SalesAmount]), ALL(SalesTerritory)))

   To avoid division by zero, the expression uses the DAX DIVIDE function, which performs a safe divide and returns a blank value when the denominator is zero. The SUM function sums the SalesAmount column for the current country. The denominator uses the CALCULATE and ALL functions to ignore the current context so that the expression calculates the overall sales across *all* the sales territories.
4. Click the Check Formula button to verify the formula syntax. You shouldn't see any errors. Press Enter.
5. In the Formatting section of the ribbon's Modeling tab, change the Format property to Percentage, with two decimal places.
6. (Optional). In the Report View, add a matrix visualization that uses the new measure (see **Figure 9.12** again). Add the SalesTerritoryCountry to the Rows area and CalendarYear to the Columns area to create a crosstab layout.
7. (Optional) Add a "Percent of Grand Total" quick calculation to the report and notice the difference in the results between the quick calculation and the PercentOfTotal measure.

Implementing a YTD calculation

DAX supports many time intelligence functions for implementing common date calculations, such as YTD, QTD, and so on. These functions require a column of the Date data type in the Date table. The Date table in the Adventure Works model includes a Date column that meets this requirement. Also remember that for the DAX time calculations to work, relationships to the Date table must use the Date column and not the DateKey column. Let's implement an explicit measure that returns year-to-date (YTD) sales:

1. In the Fields pane, right-click the ResellerSales table, and then click New Measure.
2. In the formula bar, enter the following formula:

SalesAmountYTD =TOTALYTD(Sum(ResellerSales[SalesAmount]), 'Date'[Date])

This expression uses the TOTALYTD function to calculate the SalesAmount aggregated value from the beginning of the year to date. Note that the second argument must reference the column of the Date data type in the date table.

3. To test the SalesAmountYTD measure, create the matrix visualization shown in **Figure 9.13**. Add CalendarYear and MonthName fields from the Date table in the Rows area and SalesAmount, and SalesAmountYTD fields in the Values area.

CalendarYear	MonthName	SalesAmount	SalesAmountYTD
2005	July	$489,328.58	$489,328.5787
	August	$1,538,408.31	$2,027,736.8909
	September	$1,165,897.08	$3,193,633.9687
	October	$844,721.00	$4,038,354.965
	November	$2,324,135.80	$6,362,490.7625
	December	$1,702,944.54	$8,065,435.3053
	Total	$8,065,435.31	$8,065,435.3053
2006	January	$713,116.69	$713,116.6943
	February	$1,900,788.93	$2,613,905.6247
	~rch	1,455~0.41	$4,0~186.0~2

Figure 9.13 The SalesAmountYTD measure calculates the year-to-date sales as of any date.

If the SalesAmountYTD measure works correctly, its results should be running totals. For example, the SalesAmountYTD value for 2005 ($8,065,435) is calculated by summing the sales of all the previous months since the beginning of the year 2005. Moreover, notice that the formula works for any date. It also works with any field from the Date table. For example, if you add the Date field to the report, then YTD will be calculated as of any day. This brings a tremendous flexibility to reporting!

9.4   Implementing Advanced Relationships

Besides regular table relationships where a lookup table joins the fact table directly, you might need to model more advanced relationships, including role-playing, parent-child, and many-to-many relationships. Next, I'll show you how to meet such requirements with DAX.

9.4.1 Implementing Role-Playing Relationships

In Chapter 6, I explained that a lookup table can be joined multiple times to a fact table. The dimensional modeling terminology refers to such a lookup table as a role-playing dimension. For example, in the Adventure Works model, both the InternetSales and ResellerSales tables have three date-related columns: OrderDate, ShipDate, and DueDate. However, you only created relationships from these tables to the OrderDate column. As a result, when you analyze sales by date, DAX follows the InternetSales[OrderDate] ⇨ Date[Date] and ResellerSales[OrderDate] ⇨ Date[Date] paths.

Creating inactive relationships

Suppose that you'd like to analyze InternetSales by the date the product was shipped (ShipDate):

1. Click the Manage Relationships button. In the Manage Relationships window, click New.

2. Create the InternetSales[ShipDate] ⇨ Date[Date] relationship, as shown in **Figure 9.14**. Note that this relationship will be created as inactive because Power BI Desktop will discover that there's already an active relationship (InternetSales[OrderDate] ⇨ Date[Date]) between the two tables.

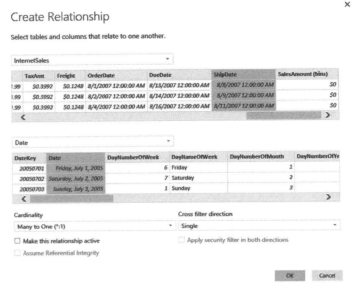

Figure 9.14   The InternetSales[ShipDate] ⇨ Date[Date] relationship will be created as inactive because there is already a relationship between these two tables.

3. Click OK and then click close.

4. In the Relationships View, confirm that there's a dotted line between the InternetSales and Date tables, which signifies an inactive relationship.

Navigating relationships in DAX

Let's say that you want to compare the ordered sales amount and shipped sales amount side by side, such as to calculate a variance. To address this requirement, you can implement measures that use DAX formulas to navigate inactive relationships. Follow these steps to implement a ShipSalesAmount measure in the InternetSales table:

1. Switch to the Data View. In the Fields pane, right-click InternetSales, and then click New Measure.

2. In the formula bar, enter the following expression:

ShipSalesAmount = CALCULATE(SUM([SalesAmount]), USERELATIONSHIP(InternetSales[ShipDate], 'Date'[Date]))

The formula uses the USERELATIONSHIP function to navigate the inactive relationship between the ShipDate column in the InternetSales table and the Date column in the Date table.

3. (Optional) Add a Table visualization with the CalendarYear (Date table), SalesAmount (InternetSales table) and ShipSalesAmount (InternetSales table) fields in the Values area. Notice that the ShipSalesAmount value is different than the SalesAmount value. That's because the ShipSalesAmount measure is aggregated using the inactive relationship on ShipDate instead of OrderDate.

9.4.2 Implementing Parent-Child Relationships

A parent-child relationship is a hierarchical relationship formed between two entities. Common examples of parent-child relationships include an employee hierarchy, where a manager has subordinates who in turn have subordinates, and an organizational hierarchy, where a company has offices and each office has branches. DAX includes functions that are specifically designed to handle parent-child relationships.

Understanding parent-child relationships

The EmployeeKey and ParentEmployeeKey columns in the Employee table have a parent-child relationship, as shown in **Figure 9.15**. Specifically, the ParentEmployeeKey column points to the EmployeeKey column for the employee's manager. For example, Kevin Brown (EmployeeKey = 2) has David Bradley (EmployeeKey=7) as a manager, who in turn reports to Ken Sánchez (EmpoyeeKey=112). (Ken is not shown in the screenshot.) Ken Sánchez's ParentEmployeeKey is blank, which means that he's the top manager. Parent-child hierarchies might have an arbitrary number of levels. Such hierarchies are called *unbalanced* hierarchies.

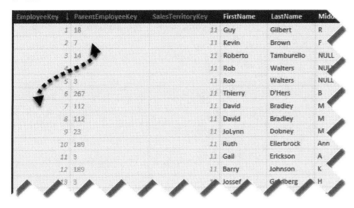

Figure 9.15 The ParentEmployeeKey column contains the identifier for the employee's manager.

Implementing a parent-child relationship

Next, you'll use DAX functions to flatten the parent-child relationship before you can create a hierarchy to drill down the organizational chart:

1. Start by adding a Path calculated column to the Employee table that constructs the parent-child path for each employee. For the Path calculated column, use the following formula:

Path = PATH([EmployeeKey], [ParentEmployeeKey])

> **NOTE** At this point, you might get an error "The columns specified in the PATH function must be from the same table, have the same data type and that type must be Integer or Text". The issue is that the ParentEmployeeKey column has a Text data type. This might be caused by a literal text value "NULL" for Ken Sánchez's while it should be a blank (null) value. To fix this, open the Query Editor (right-click the Employee table and click Query Editor), right-click the ParentEmployeeKey column, and then click Replace Values. In the Replace Value dialog, replace NULL with blank. Then, in the Query Editor (Home ribbon tab), change the column type to Whole Number and click the "Close & Apply" button.

The formula uses the PATH DAX function, which returns a delimited list of IDs (using a vertical pipe as the delimiter) starting with the top (root) of a parent-child hierarchy and ending with the current employee identifier. For example, the path for Kevin Brown is 112|7|2. The rightmost part is the ID of the employee on that row and each segment to the right follows the organizational path.

The next step is to flatten the parent-child hierarchy by adding a column for each level. This means that you need to know beforehand the maximum number of levels that the employee hierarchy might have. To be on the safe side, add one or two more levels to accommodate future growth.

2. Add a Level1 calculated column that has the following formula:

```
Level1 = LOOKUPVALUE(Employee[FullName], Employee[EmployeeKey], VALUE(PATHITEM([Path],1)))
```

This formula uses the PATHITEM function to parse the Path calculated column and return the first identifier, such as 112 in the case of Kevin Brown. Then, it uses the LOOKUPVALUE function to return the full name of the corresponding employee, which in this case is Ken Sánchez. The VALUE function casts the text result from the PATHITEM function to Integer so that the LOOKUPVALUE function compares the same data types.

3. Add five more calculated columns for Levels 2-6 that use similar formulas to flatten the hierarchy all the way down to the lowest level. Compare your results with **Figure 9.16**. Note that most of the cells in the Level 5 and Level 6 columns are empty, and that's okay because only a few employees have more than four indirect managers.

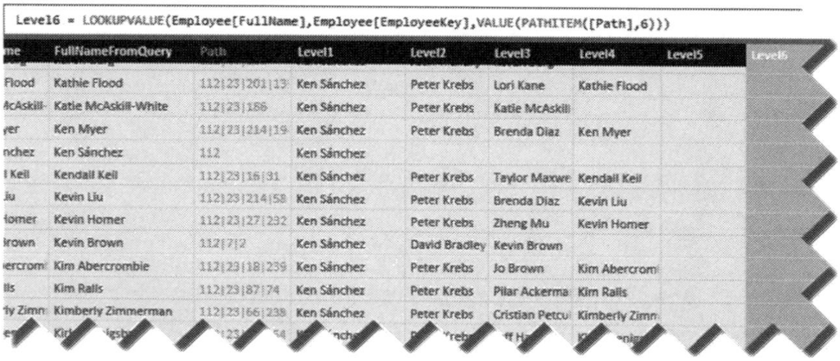
Level6 = LOOKUPVALUE(Employee[FullName],Employee[EmployeeKey],VALUE(PATHITEM([Path],6)))

me	FullNameFromQuery	Path	Level1	Level2	Level3	Level4	Level5	Level6
Flood	Kathie Flood	112|23|201|13	Ken Sánchez	Peter Krebs	Lori Kane	Kathie Flood		
lcAskill-	Katie McAskill-White	112|23|186	Ken Sánchez	Peter Krebs	Katie McAskill			
yer	Ken Myer	112|23|214|19	Ken Sánchez	Peter Krebs	Brenda Diaz	Ken Myer		
nchez	Ken Sánchez	112	Ken Sánchez					
l Keil	Kendall Keil	112|23|16|31	Ken Sánchez	Peter Krebs	Taylor Maxwe	Kendall Keil		
iu	Kevin Liu	112|23|214|58	Ken Sánchez	Peter Krebs	Brenda Diaz	Kevin Liu		
omer	Kevin Homer	112|23|27|232	Ken Sánchez	Peter Krebs	Zheng Mu	Kevin Homer		
rown	Kevin Brown	112|7|2	Ken Sánchez	David Bradley	Kevin Brown			
ercrom	Kim Abercrombie	112|23|18|239	Ken Sánchez	Peter Krebs	Jo Brown	Kim Abercrom		
lls	Kim Ralls	112|23|87|74	Ken Sánchez	Peter Krebs	Pilar Ackerma	Kim Ralls		
ly Zimm	Kimberly Zimmerman	112|23|66|238	Ken Sánchez	Peter Krebs	Cristian Petcu	Kimberly Zimm		

Figure 9.16 Use the PATHITEM function to flatten the parent-child hierarchy.

4. Hide the Path column in the Employee table as it's not useful for analysis.
5. (Optional) Create an Employees hierarchy consisting of six levels based on the six columns.
6. (Optional) Create a table visualization to analyze sales by any of the Level1-Level6 fields.
7. (Optional) Deploy the Adventure Works model to Power BI Service. To do this, click the Publish button in the ribbon's Home tab, or use the File ⇨ Publish ⇨ "Publish to Power BI" menu. This will add an Adventure Works dataset and Adventure Works report to the navigation bar in the Power BI portal. Once the model is published, go to Power BI Service (powerbi.com) and test the visualizations you've created. Use your knowledge from Part 1 of this book to explore and visualize the Adventure Works dataset.

9.4.3 Implementing Many-to-Many Relationships

Typically, a row in a lookup table relates to one or more rows in a fact table. For example, a given customer has one or more orders. This is an example of a one-to-many relationship that most of our tables have used so far. Sometimes, you might run into a scenario where two tables have a logical many-to-many relationship. As you've seen in the case of the Customer distinct count example, handling many-to-many is easy, thanks to the DAX bi-directional relationships. But what if you need to report closing balances (common for financial reporting)?

Understanding many-to-many relationships

The M2M.pbix sample in the \Source\ch09 folder demonstrates a popular many-to-many scenario that you might encounter if you model joint bank accounts. Open it in another Power BI Desktop and examine its Relationship View. It consists of five tables, as shown in **Figure 9.17**. The Customer table stores the bank's customers. The Account table stores the customers' accounts. A customer might have multiple bank accounts, and a single account might be owned by two or more customers, such as a savings account.

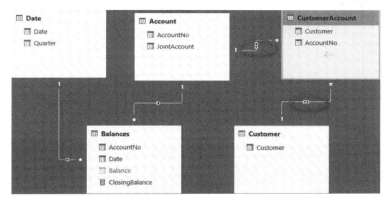

Figure 9.17 The M2M model demonstrates joint bank accounts.

The CustomerAccount table is a bridge table that indicates which accounts are owned by which customer. The Balances table records the account balances over time. Note that the relationships CustomerAccount[AccountNo] ⇨ Account[AccountNo] and CustomerAccount[Customer] ⇨ Customer[Customer] are bi-directional.

Implementing closing balances

If the Balance measure is fully additive (can be summed across all lookup tables that are related to the Balances table), then you're done. However, semi-additive measures, such as account balances and inventory quantities, are trickier because they can be summed across all the tables except for the Date table. To understand this, take a look at the report shown in **Figure 9.18**.

Quarter	Q1 2011				Q2 2011			Total
Customer	1/1/2011	2/1/2011	3/1/2011	Total	4/1/2011	5/1/2011	Total	
Alice	100	200	300	300				300
Bob	600	700	300	300				300
John	100	200		200				200
Sam		100	100	100	200	50	50	50
Total	700	1000	400	400	200	50	50	50

Figure 9.18 This report shows closing balances per quarter.

If you create a report that simply aggregates the Balance measure (hidden in Report View), you'll find that the report produces wrong results. Specifically, the grand totals at the customer or account levels are correct, but the rest of the results are incorrect. Instead of using the Balance column, I added a ClosingBalance explicit measure to the Balances table that aggregates his account balance correctly. The measure uses the following formula:

```
ClosingBalance = CALCULATE(SUM(Balances[Balance]), LASTNONBLANK('Date'[Date], CALCULATE(SUM(Balances[Balance]))))
```

This formula uses the DAX LASTNONBLANK function to find the last date with a recorded balance. This function travels back in time, to find the first non-blank date within a given time period. For John and Q1 2011, that date is 2/1/2011 when John's balance was 200. This becomes the first quarter balance for John, as you can see in the Matrix visualization. He didn't have an account balance for Q2 (perhaps, his account was closed) so the Q2 balance is empty. His overall balance matches the Q1 balance of 200.

9.5 Implementing Data Security

Do you have a requirement to allow certain end users to see only a subset of data that they're authorized to access? For example, as a model author Martin can see all the data he imported. However, when he deploys the model to Power BI Service, he wants Elena to see only sales for a specific geography. This is where the Power BI data security (also known as row-level security or RLS) can help. Data security is a Power BI Pro feature so users who access published secured models must have Power BI Pro licenses.

9.5.1 Understanding Data Security

Data security is supported for models that import data and that connect live to data, except when connecting live to Analysis Services, which has its own security model. At a high level, implementing data security is a two-step process:

- Modeling step – This involves defining roles and table filters inside the model to restrict access to data. Because more involved security scenarios require DAX knowledge for filters, I discuss data security in this chapter.
- Operational step – Once roles are defined, you need to deploy the model to Power BI Service in order to assign members to roles. Configuring membership is the operational aspect of RLS that needs be done in Power BI Service.

It's important to understand that data security is only enforced in Power BI Service, that is when the model is deployed and shared with other users who have view-only rights (they don't have Admin or Edit Content permissions to a workspace) to shared content. Such users won't be able to access any data unless they are assigned to a role. However, if you email the Power BI Desktop file to another user and he opens it in Power BI Desktop, data security is *not* enforced and the user can see all the data.

Understanding roles
A role allows you to grant other users restricted access to data in a secured model. **Figure 9.19** is meant to help you visualize a role.

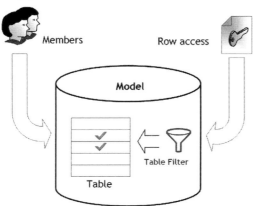

Figure 9.19 A role grants its members permissions to a table, and it optionally restricts access to table rows.

In a nutshell, a role gives its members permissions to view the model data. To create a new role, click the Manage Roles button in the ribbon's Modeling tab. Then click the Create button in the "Manage roles" window and name the role. As I mentioned, after you deploy the model to Power BI Service, you must assign members to the role. You can type in email addresses of individual users, security groups, and workspace groups.

What happens if a user with view-only rights to shared content in Power BI Service attempts to view a report in a secured model, and the user is not assigned to a role, either individually or via a group membership? When they view a report, all report visualizations show errors (see **Figure 9.20**).

Figure 9.20 If a user with view-only rights is not added to a role when data security is enabled, report visualizations show errors with details "Couldn't load the data for this visual".

Understanding table filters

By default, a role can access all the data in all tables in the model. However, the whole purpose of implementing data security is to limit access to a subset of data, such as to allow Maya to see only sales for the United States. This is achieved by specifying one or more table filters. As its name suggests, a table filter defines a filter expression that evaluates which table rows the role is allowed to see. To set up a row filter in Role Manager, enter a DAX formula next to the table name. The DAX formula must evaluate to a Boolean condition that returns TRUE or FALSE. For example, when the user connects to the published model and the user is a member of the role, Power BI applies the row filter expression to each row in the SalesTerritory table. If the row meets the criteria, the role is authorized to see that row.

Figure 9.21 This table filter grants the US role access to rows in the SalesTerritory table where SalesTerritoryCountry is United States.

Roles are additive. If a user belongs to multiple roles, the user will get the superset of all the role permissions. For example, suppose Maya is a member of both the Sales Representative and Marketing roles. The Sales Representative role grants her rights to United States, while the Marketing role grants her access to all countries. Because roles are additive, Maya can see data for all countries.

 TIP As it stands, Power BI doesn't support object security to hide entire tables. Even if the table filter qualifies no rows, the table will show in the model metadata. The simplest way to disallow a role from viewing any rows in a table is to set up a table filter with a FALSE() expression. If no table filter is applied to a table, TRUE() is assumed and the user can see all of its data.

How table filters affect related tables

From an end-user perspective, rows the user isn't authorized to view and their related data in tables on the many side of the relationship simply don't exist in the model. Imagine that a global WHERE clause is applied to the model that selects only the data that's related to the allowed rows of all the secured tables.

Figure 9.22 A table filter can propagate to related tables depending on the relationship type and cross filter direction.

Given the model shown in **Figure 9.22**, the user can't see any other sales territories in the SalesTerritory table except United States. Moreover, because of the SalesTerritory ⇨ ResellerSales one-to-many relationship, the user can't see sales for these territories in the ResellerSales table or in any other tables that are directly or indirectly (via cascading relationships) related to the SalesTerritory table. In other words, Power BI propagates data security to related tables following the existing one-to-many relationships.

What about the Reseller table? Should the user see only Resellers with sales in the United States? The outcome depends on the relationship cross-filter direction. If it's Single (there is a single arrow pointing from Reseller to ResellerSales), the security filter is not propagated to the Reseller table and the user can see all resellers. To clarify, the user can see the list of all resellers but he can see only sales for the US resellers because sales come from the filtered ResellerSales table. However, if the cross filter direction is Both and the "Apply security filter in both directions" setting (see **Figure 8.16**) is checked, then the security filter propagates to the Reseller table and the user can see only resellers with sales in the United States.

 NOTE If you don't see the "Apply security filter in both directions" checkbox, the feature is probably still in preview. To enable it, check "Enable cross filtering in both directions for DirectQuery" in the File ⇨ Options and settings ⇨ Options menu ("Preview features" tab).

9.5.2 Implementing Basic Data Security

In the exercise that follows, you'll add a role that allows the user to view only the United States. Then, I'll show you how to test the role on the desktop and how to add members to the role after you deploy your model to Power BI Service.

Creating a role
Start by creating a new role in the Adventure Works model.
1. In the ribbon's Modeling tab, click the Manage Roles button.
2. In the Manage Roles window, click the Create button. Rename the new role to *US*.
3. Click the ellipsis button next to the SalesTerritory table, and then click "Add filter…" ⇨ [SalesTerritoryCountry] to filter the values in this column.
4. Change the "Table Filter DAX Expression" content with the following formula (see again **Figure 9.21**):

[SalesTerritoryCountry] = "United States"
5. Click Save.

 TIP Consider adding an Open Access role that doesn't have any table filter. This role is for users who need full access to data. Recall that by default a role has unrestricted access unless you defined a table filter.

Testing data security

You don't have to deploy the model to Power BI Service to test the role. Power BI Desktop lets you do this conveniently on the desktop. Recall that you can add yourself to a role in Power BI Desktop (even if you were able to you'll still gain unrestricted access as a model author). However, you can test the role as though you're a user who is a member of the role.

1. In the ribbon's Modeling tab, click the "View as Roles" button.
2. In the "View as roles" window, make sure that that US role is selected (see **Figure 9.23**). Click OK.

Figure 9.23 The "View as roles" lets you test a role inside Power BI Desktop.

3. You should see a status bar showing "Now viewing report as: US". Create a report that includes the SalesTerritoryCountry column from the SalesTerritory table, such as the one shown in **Figure 9.24**. The report should show only data for US.

Figure 9.24 The report shows only data for United States.

4. (Optional) Add a Table visualization showing the ResellerName column from the Reseller table. You should see all resellers. However, if you add a measure from the ResellerSales table, you should see only resellers with sales in the USA. If you want to prevent the role to see non-US resellers, change the cross filter direction of the ResellerSales[ResellerKey] ⇨ Reseller[ResellerKey] to Both.

Defining membership

Now that the role is defined, it becomes a part of the model but its setup is not complete yet. Next, you'll deploy the model to Power BI Service and add members to the role.

1. In the ribbon's Home tab, click Publish. If prompted, log in to Power BI and deploy the Adventure Works model to My Workspace.
2. Open your browser and navigate to Power BI Service (powerbi.com). Click My Workspace.
3. In the workspace content page, click the Datasets tab. Click the ellipsis button next to the Adventure Works dataset, and then click Security from the drop-down menu.

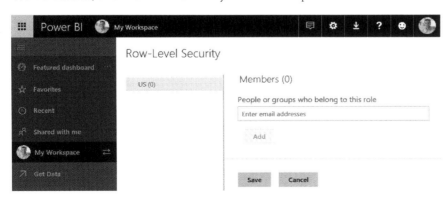

Figure 9.25 You set up the role membership in Power BI Service.

4. In the "Row-Level Security" window, add the emails of individuals or groups who you want to add to the role (**Figure 9.25**). Click Save.

5. (Optional) Create a dashboard that uses visualizations from the Adventure Works report, and share the dashboard with users who belong and don't belong to the role (users must have Power BI Pro subscriptions). Ask them to view the dashboard and report their results.

6. (Optional) Republish the Adventure Works model. Power BI Desktop will ask you to replace the dataset. In Power BI Service, go to the Adventure Works dataset security settings and notice that the role membership is preserved. That's because the role membership is external to the Adventure Works model and republishing the file doesn't overwrite it. However, if you delete the dataset in Power BI Service, you'll lose its role membership.

 NOTE As a model author, you always have admin rights to model so don't be surprised that you see all the data irrespective of your role membership. If you publish the model to a workspace (workspaces are discussed in the next chapter), the workspace administrators and members who can edit content also gain unlimited access.

9.5.3 Implementing Dynamic Data Security

The row filter example securing on a territory that I've just shown you returns a fixed (static) set of allowed rows. This works well if you have a finite set of unique permissions. For example, if there are three regions, you can build three roles. Static filters are simple to implement and work well when the number of roles is relatively small. However, suppose you must restrict managers to view only the sales data of the employees that are reporting directly or indirectly to them. If static filters were the only option, you'd have no choice except to set up a database role for each manager. This might lead to a huge number of roles and maintenance issues. This is why Power BI supports dynamic data security.

Understanding dynamic data security

Dynamic security relies on the identity of the interactive user to filter data. For example, if Maya logs in to Power BI as maya@adventure-works.com, you can filter the Employee table to allow Maya to access herself and her subordinates. You need only a single role with the following table filter applied to the Employee table:

PATHCONTAINS(Employee[Path], LOOKUPVALUE(Employee[EmployeeKey], Employee[EmailAddress], USERPRINCIPALNAME()))

This expression uses the USERPRINCIPALNAME() DAX function (specifically added to support Power BI) which returns the user principal name (UPN) in both Power BI Service and Power BI. If you have set up dynamic security with Analysis Services Multidimensional or Tabular, you have probably used the USERNAME() function. However, this function returns the user domain login in Power BI Desktop (see **Figure 9.26**). You can use the WhoAmI.pbix Power BI Desktop file in the \Source\ch09 folder to verify the results.

Figure 9.26 USERPRINCIPALNAME() and USERNAME() return different results on the desktop.

To avoid using an OR filter to support both Power BI and Power BI Desktop, use USERPRINCIPALNAME() but make sure that the EmailAddress column stores the user principal name (typically but not always UPN corresponds to the user's email address) and not the user's Windows login (domain\login). To explain the rest of the filter, the DAX expression uses the DAX LOOKUPVALUE function to retrieve the value of the EmployeeKey column that's matching the user's login. Then, it uses the PATHCONTAINS function to parse the Path column in the Employee table in order to check if the parent-child path includes the employee key. If this is the case, the user is authorized to see that employee and the employee's related data because the user is the employee's direct or indirect manager.

 NOTE If your computer is not joined to a domain, both USERPRINCIPALNAME() and USERNAME() would return your login (NetBIOS name) in the format MachineName\Login in Power BI Desktop. In this case, you'd have to use an OR filter so that you can test dynamic security in both Power BI Service and Power BI Desktop.

Setting up the test environment
Next, I'll walk you through the steps required to implement dynamic data security for the manager-subordinate scenario. Ideally, you would have two Power BI accounts to test dynamic security in Power BI. Since you're not on the adventure-works domain, start by making changes to the Employee table:

1. In the Adventure Works model, right-click the Employee table in the Fields pane, and then click Edit Query to open the Query Editor.
2. Find the row for Stephen Jiang (EmployeeKey = 272). Right-click the EmailAddress cell for that row and click Copy to copy his email (it should be stephen0@adventure-works.com). In the next step, you'll replace this email with your email address.
3. Right-click the EmailAddress column and then click "Replace Values…". In the Replace Values window, paste the copied email address in the "Value to Find" field. In the "Replace With" field, type in your email address (the one you use to log in to Power BI).
4. (Optional) Right-click the EmailAddress column and then click "Replace Values…" again. In the Replace Values window, enter *amy0@adventure-works.com* in the "Value to Find" field. In the "Replace With" field, type in the email address of someone else in your organization that has a Power BI Pro subscription.
5. In the ribbon's Home tab, click Close & Apply to reload the Employee table.

Creating a new role
Next, you'll create a new role that will filter the Employee table.

1. In the ribbon's Modeling tab, click Manage Roles.
2. In the "Manage roles" window create a new *Employee* role.
3. In the Table section, select the Employee table. Enter the following expression in the "Table Filter DAX Expression" field:

PATHCONTAINS(Employee[Path], LOOKUPVALUE(Employee[EmployeeKey], Employee[EmailAddress], USERPRINCIPALNAME()))

4. Click the checkmark button in the top right corner of the window to check the expression syntax. If there are no errors, click Save to create the role.

Figure 9.27 The "View as roles" window lets you test specific roles and impersonate users.

Testing the role
Now that the Employee role is in place, let's make sure it works as expected.

1. In the ribbon's Modeling tab, click "View As Roles".

2. In the "View as roles" window (**Figure 9.27**), check the Employee role to simulate that you're a member of the role.

3. If you'd like to impersonate another user to test his permissions, check the "Other user" checkbox and type in the user's UPN. As a result, USERPRINCIPALNAME() will return whatever you typed in. Click OK.

4. (Optional) Create a Table report that uses the Employees hierarchy (or Level1-Level6 fields), as shown in **Figure 9.28**. Notice that the report lets you access Stephen Jiang and his direct or indirect subordinates.

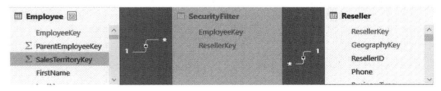

Figure 9.28 The "View as roles" window lets you test specific roles and impersonate users.

9.5.4 Externalizing Security Policies

The final progression of data security is externalizing security policies in another table. Suppose that Adventure Works uses a master data management application, such as Master Data Services (MDS), to associate a sales representative with a set of resellers that she oversees. Your task is to enforce a security role that restricts the user to see only her resellers. This would require importing a table that contains the employee-reseller associations.

 REAL LIFE This approach builds upon the factless fact table implementation that I demonstrated in my "Protect UDM with Dimension Data Security, Part 2" article (http://bit.ly/YBcu1d). I've used this approach in real-life projects because of its simplicity, performance, and ability to reuse the security filters across other applications, such as across operational reports that source data directly from the data warehouse.

Implementing the security filter table
A new SecurityFilter table is required to store the authorized resellers for each employee (see **Figure 9.29**).

Figure 9.29 The Security-Filter bridge table stores the authorized resellers for each employee.

This table is related to the Reseller and Employee tables. If an employee is authorized to view a reseller, a row is added to SecurityFilter table. In real life, business users or IT pros will probably maintain the security associations in a database or external application. For the sake of simplicity, you'll import the security policies from a text file (you can also enter the data directly using the Enter Data button in the ribbon's Home tab).

1. In the ribbon's Home tab, click Get Data. Choose CSV.

2. Navigate to the \Source\ch09 folder and select the SecurityFilter.csv file. Click Open.

3. Preview the data and compare your results with **Figure 9.30**. Click Load. Power BI Desktop adds a SecurityFilter table to the model.

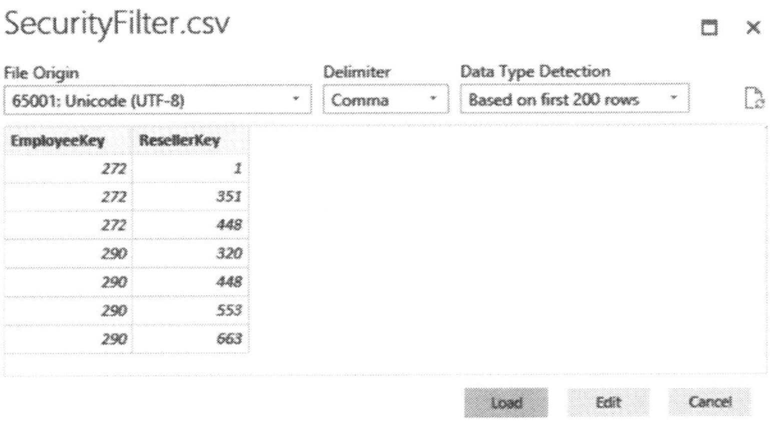

SecurityFilter.csv □ ×

File Origin	Delimiter	Data Type Detection
65001: Unicode (UTF-8) ▾	Comma ▾	Based on first 200 rows ▾

EmployeeKey	ResellerKey
272	1
272	351
272	448
290	320
290	448
290	553
290	663

Load   Edit   Cancel

Figure 9.30 The SecurityFilter datasets specifies the resellers that an employee can access.

4. Because users shouldn't see this table, right-click the SecurityFilter table in the Fields pane (Data View) and click "Hide in Report View".

5. In the Relationships View, double-click the ResellerSales[ResellerKey]⇨Reseller[ResellerKey] relationship. If the "Apply security filter in both directions" checkbox is checked, uncheck it because it will conflict with the new relationships.

6. In the Relationships View, verify that the SecurityFilter[EmployeeKey]⇨Employee[EmployeeKey] and SecurityFilter[ResellerKey]⇨Reseller[ResellerKey] relationships exist and that they are active. If that's not the case, make the necessary changes to create these two relationships.

 REAL LIFE Although in this case the SecurityFilter table is related to other tables, this is not a requirement. DAX is flexible and it allows you to filter tables using the FILTER() function even if they can't be related. For example, a real-life project required defining application security roles and granting them access to any level in an organization hierarchy. The DAX row filter granted the role access to a parent without explicit access to its children. The security table didn't have relationships to the tact table.

Implementing the Reseller role

Next, you'll add a role that will enforce the security policy. Follow these steps to set up a new Reseller role:

1. In the ribbon's Modeling tab, click Manage Roles.

2. In the "Manage roles" window create a new *Reseller* role.

3. In the Table section, select the Reseller table. Enter the following expression in the "Table Filter DAX Expression" field (you can copy it from \Source\ch09\dax.txt file):

```
CONTAINS(RELATEDTABLE(SecurityFilter), SecurityFilter[EmployeeKey], LOOKUPVALUE(Employee[EmployeeKey],
Employee[EmailAddress], USERPRINCIPALNAME())))
```

Let's digest this expression one piece at a time. As you already know, the LOOKUPVALUE function is used to obtain the employee key associated with the email address. Because the table filter is set on the Reseller table, for each reseller, the CONTAINS function attempts to find a match for that reseller key and employee key combination in the SecurityFilter table. Notice the use of the RELATEDTABLE function to pass the current reseller. The net effect is that the CONTAINS function returns TRUE if there is a row in the SecurityFilter table that matches the ResellerKey and EmployeeKey combination.

Testing the Reseller role

Let's follow familiar steps to test the role:

1. In the ribbon's Modeling tab, click "View As Roles".

2. In the "View as roles" window, check the Reseller role.

3. If you'd like to impersonate another user to test his permissions, check the "Other user" checkbox and type in the user's UPN. As a result, USERPRINCIPALNAME() will return whatever you typed in. Click OK.

4. (Optional) Create a Table report that uses the ResellerName field from the Reseller table. The report should show only the three resellers associated with Stephen.

5. (Optional) Deploy the Adventure Works model to Power BI Service. Add members to the Employee and Reseller roles. Ask the role members to view reports and report results.

9.6   Summary

One of the great strengths of Power BI is its Data Analysis Expressions (DAX) language, which allows you to unlock the full power of your data model and implement sophisticated business calculations. This chapter introduced you to the DAX calculations, syntax, and formulas. You can use the DAX formula language to implement calculated columns and measures.

Calculated columns are custom columns that use DAX formulas to derive their values. The column formulas are evaluated for each row in the table, and the resulting values are saved in the model. The practices walked you through the steps for creating basic and advanced columns.

Measures are evaluated for each cell in the report. Power BI Desktop automatically creates an implicit measure for every column that you add to the Value area of the Visualizations pane. You can create explicit measures that use custom DAX formulas you specify.

More complex models might call for role-playing, parent-child, and many-to-many relationships. You can use DAX formulas to navigate inactive relationships, to flatten parent-child hierarchies, and to change the measure aggregation behavior.

Power BI supports a flexible data security model that can address various security requirements, ranging from simple filters, such as users accessing specific countries, to externalizing security policies and dynamic security based on the user's identity. You define security roles and table filters in Power BI Desktop and role membership in Power BI Service.

PART

Power BI for Pros

BI and IT pros have much to gain from Power BI. Information technology (IT) pros are concerned with setting up and maintaining the necessary environment that facilitates self-service and organizational BI, such as providing access to data, managing security, data governance, and other services. On the other hand, BI pros are typically tasked to create backend services required to support organizational BI initiative, including data marts and data warehouses, cubes, ETL packages, operational reports, and dashboards.

We're back to Power BI Service now. This part of the book gives IT pros the necessary background to establish a trustworthy and collaborative environment! You'll learn how Power BI security works. You'll see how you can create workspaces and groups to promote team BI where multiple coworkers can work on the same BI artifacts. Finally, you'll learn how to create organizational content packs so that you can push BI content to a larger audience and even to the entire company. And you'll discover how the on-premises data gateway can help you centralize data management and implement hybrid solutions where your data remains on-premises but you can still enjoy Power BI interactive reports dashboards and reports that connect to the data via the gateway.

I'll show BI pros how to integrate popular organizational BI scenarios with Power BI. If you've invested in on-premises Analysis Services models, you'll see how you can create reports and dashboards connected to these models without moving data to the cloud. If you plan to implement real-time BI solutions, I'll show how you can do that with Azure Stream Analytics Service and Power BI. Most of the features discussed in this part of the book require the Power BI Pro edition. And if you're interested in predictive analytics, you'll see how you can integrate Power BI with Azure Machine Learning!

Chapter 10

Enabling Team BI

We all need to share information, and this is even more true with BI artifacts that help an organization understand its business. To accomplish this, an IT department (referred to as "IT" in this book) must establish a trustworthy environment where users have secure access to the BI content and data they need. While traditionally Microsoft has promoted SharePoint for sharing all your documents, including BI artifacts, Power BI doesn't have dependencies on SharePoint Server or SharePoint Online. Power BI has its own sharing and collaboration capabilities! Although these capabilities are available to all users, establishing a cooperative environment should happen under the guidance and supervision of IT. This is why sharing and collaboration are discussed in this part of the book.

Currently, Power BI doesn't have all the SharePoint data governance capabilities, such as workflows, taxonomy, self-service BI monitoring, versioning, retention, and others. Although a large organization might be concerned about the lack of such management features now, Power BI gains in simplicity and this is a welcome change for many who have struggled with SharePoint complexity, and for organizations that haven't invested in SharePoint. This chapter starts by laying out the Power BI management fundamentals. Next, it discusses workspaces and groups, and then explains how members of a department or a group can share Power BI artifacts. Next, it shows you how IT can leverage Power BI content packs to bundle and publish content across your organization, and how to centralize data management.

10.1 Power BI Management Fundamentals

Recall from Chapter 2 that Power BI makes it easy for users to sign up to Power BI Service. When the first user signs up, Power BI creates an unmanaged "shadow" tenant (yourcompany.onmicrosoft.com) in Azure AD. It's unmanaged because it's under Microsoft's management, not yours. I refer to this stage as "The Wild West". Everyone can sign up without any supervision. The next progression is to take over the unmanaged tenant in Office 365. This allows the Office 365 admins to manage certain aspects of the user enrollment and enables the Power BI Admin Portal. The final step is to federate your organizational Active Directory to Azure Active Directory to achieve a single sign-on between your on-premises AD and Azure Active Directory. To accomplish this, you can use the DirSync tool to synchronize your on-premises AD with Azure, or you can federate (extend) your corporate AD to Azure.

 NOTE If you deploy models with imported data, your data will be stored in a Microsoft data center in a specific geography. When the first user signs up, Power BI will ask the user which country your company is located in. Based on the country selection, Power BI will choose a data center. Unfortunately, once that data center is selected and associated with the tenant, it can't be changed although there are good scenarios to do so, such as a multinational company that prefers a data center closer to where most of the Power BI users will be located. For more information about Power BI data regions, read the "How the Power BI Data Region is selected" blog by Adam Saxton at https://guyinacube.com/2016/08/power-bi-data-region-selected.

10.1.1 Managing User Access

If your tenant is still unmanaged, I strongly suggest your system administrator takes it over so that it can be actively managed. I said "system administrator" because the takeover process requires knowledge of your organization's domain setup and small changes to the domain registration so that Power BI can verify domain ownership. For more information about the specific takeover steps, refer to the blog "How to perform an IT Admin Takeover with O365" by Adam Saxton at https://powerbi.microsoft.com/en-us/blog/how-to-perform-an-it-admin-takeover-with-o365.

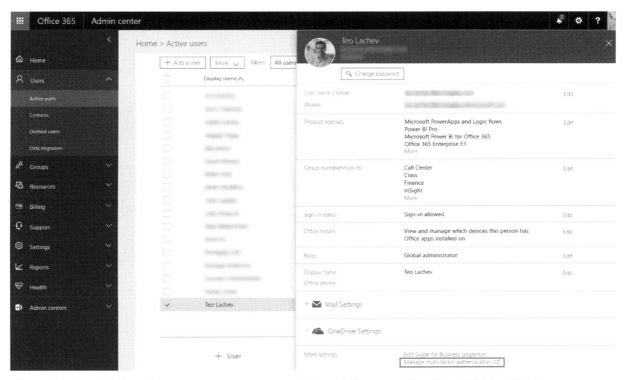

Figure 10.1 The global administrator can manage users and Power BI licenses in the Office 365 Admin Center.

Managing users
Once the admin takeover is completed, the Office 365 global administrator can use the Office 365 Admin Center (https://portal.office.com) to manage users and licenses (see **Figure 10.1**). Another way to navigate to the Office 365 Admin Center is to click the "Office 365 Application Launcher" icon in the top left corner of the Power BI portal and then click the Admin button. Only Office 365 global admins can see the Admin button. Finally, a third option to navigate directly to the "Active Users" section of the Office 365 Admin Center is from the "Manage users" area in the Power BI Admin Portal (discussed in the "Using the Admin Portal" section later in this chapter).

 TIP You can promote users to O365 global administrators by clicking Edit next to the Roles item in the user properties and then assigning the user to the "Global administrator" role. This will grant the user rights to manage all aspects of the Office 365 tenant, including Power BI licenses.

Unless you extend or synchronize your on-premises AD, the user chooses a password when the user signs up with Power BI. The Power BI password is independent of the password he uses to log in to the corporate network. As a best practice, it's a good idea to expire passwords on a regular basis. Switching to a managed client gives you a limited control over the password policy, which you can find under the Settings menu in the left toolbar ⇨ "Security & privacy". You can turn on the password expiration policy using the "Days before password expire" setting. You can also specify if the users will be able to reset their passwords.

Managing licenses

From a Power BI standpoint, one important task that the administrator will perform is managing Power BI Pro licenses. Users don't need a license to access Power BI Free features. Yet, your organization might have concerns about indiscriminate enrolling to Power BI and uploading corporate data. Solutions can be found in the "Power BI in your organization" document by Microsoft at http://bit.ly/1IY87Qt.

Power BI Pro features require a license. The Product Licenses section of the user properties (see again **Figure 10.1**) show what licenses the user has. Click the Edit link to grant the user a Power BI Pro license. This of course will entail a monthly subscription fee unless your organization is on the Office 365 E5 business plan which includes Power BI Pro.

Enabling conditional access

The cloud nature of Power BI could be both a blessing and a curse. Users can access Power BI reports and dashboards from anywhere and on any device as long as they're connected to Internet. However, unless you take additional steps, Power BI security hinges only on the user's password since the user email is not secure. One of the most important steps you can take to enforce an additional level of security to restrict access to Power BI (and your organization's data) by enabling conditional access.

A multifactor authentication (MFA) is a security configuration that requires more than one method of authentication to verify the user's identity. For example, Office 365 could send an application password to the user's mobile device. The user will have to enter it in addition to the Power BI password when signing in to Power BI. You can enable MFA for all Office 365 services (see the corresponding link in the "More settings" section on the user properties page in **Figure 10.1**) or just for Power BI.

 NOTE Depending on the O365 business plan your organization has, tenant-level MFA might require an additional fee, or it might be included in the plan. For more information about MFA, read the "Getting started with Azure Multi-Factor Authentication in the cloud" article by Kelly Gremban at https://docs.microsoft.com/en-us/azure/multi-factor-authentication/multi-factor-authentication-get-started-cloud.Configuring application-level access (also known as conditional rules) requires a subscription to Azure Active Directory Premium. In addition, it requires a federated or managed Azure Active Directory tenant.

Follow these steps to enable MFA for Power BI only:

1. As of this time, you have to use the old Azure portal as the new one (portal.azure.com) doesn't support conditional rules per application yet. Navigate to manage.windowsazure.com and sign-in with your account (you need to be an admin on the tenant).
2. In the left navigation bar, click Active Directory. Then, click your organization.
3. In your AD organization page, click the Applications menu.
4. Click the arrow next to Microsoft Power BI (see **Figure 10.2**).
5. In the next page, click the Configure link.

prologika

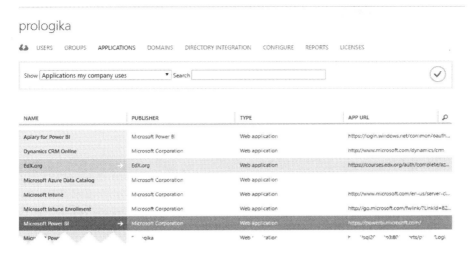

NAME	PUBLISHER	TYPE	APP URL	
Apiary for Power BI	Microsoft Power BI	Web application	https://login.windows.net/common/oauth...	
Dynamics CRM Online	Microsoft Corporation	Web application	http://www.microsoft.com/dynamics/crm	
EdX.org	EdX.org	Web application	https://courses.edx.org/auth/complete/az...	
Microsoft Azure Data Catalog	Microsoft Corporation	Web application		
Microsoft Intune	Microsoft Corporation	Web application	http://www.microsoft.com/en-us/server-cl...	
Microsoft Intune Enrollment	Microsoft Corporation	Web application	http://go.microsoft.com/fwlink/?LinkId=82...	
Microsoft Power BI	Microsoft Corporation	Web application	https://powerbi.microsoft.com/	
Micr... Pow...	...ogika	Web ...ation	...'sql2... ...n3:80 ...rts/p... ...Logi...	

Figure 10.2 Use the Azure Portal to enable MFA for Power BI.

6. In the next page, set "Enable Access Rules" to On (see **Figure 10.3**).

multi-factor authentication and location based access rules

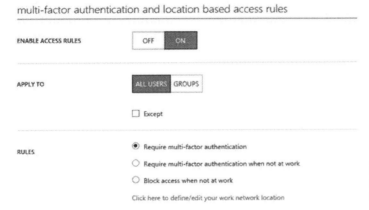

Figure 10.3 Enable conditional access rules, such as MFA and block access when not at work.

Understanding conditional rules

The rules section deserves more explanation.

■ Require Multi-factor authentication – Users to whom access rules apply will be required to complete multi-factor authentication before accessing the application affected by the rule.

■ Require Multi-factor authentication when not at work – Users trying to access the application from a trusted IP address won't be required to perform multi-factor authentication. Click the link below to enter the trusted IP address ranges that define your work location.

■ Block access when not at work – Users trying to access the application from outside your corporate network will not be able to access the application.

 REAL LIFE I helped a large organization to evaluate and adopt Power BI. One of the first questions their review committee asked was if they can limit access to Power BI only from the corporate network and from approved devices. I didn't have a good answer then. Conditional access can help you meet this requirement.

Once the rules are configured, Azure will apply them when a user attempts to sign in to Power BI. For example, let's say that Elena (Office 365 admin) has configured conditional access policy requiring MFA for only Power BI. When Maya visits the Office 365 portal to check her email, she can log in (or automatically sign in if the active directory is federated to Azure) without using MFA. But when Maya tries to navigate to Power BI, she'll be asked to complete an MFA challenge irrespective of the device she uses. And if the "Block access when not at work" rule is enabled, she can access Power BI only from the corporate network.

 TIP You can secure access to Power BI even further by enabling these conditional access policies alongside Risk Based Conditional Access policy available with Azure AD Identity Protection. Azure Identity Protection detects risk events involving identities in Azure Active Directory that indicate that the identities may have been compromised. For more information, read the "AzureAD Identity Protection adds support for federated identities" at bit.ly/2gwdTGu.

10.1.2 Using the Admin Portal

Power BI provides an admin portal to allow the administrator to view usage statistics and control tenant wide settings. To access the Admin Portal, log in to Power BI Service, expand the Settings menu in the top-right corner, and then click Admin Portal.

Understanding portal access
To see the Admin Portal menu, you have a member of one of these roles:

- Office 365 Global Administrator – The Office 365 global administrator can manage all aspects of Office 365, including Power BI.
- Power BI Service Administrator – The Office 365 global administrator can delegate access to Admin Portal to other users. Since currently there isn't a user interface for this task, the global administrator would need to run a PowerShell command (before you run the command, install Azure PowerShell from https://docs.microsoft.com/en-us/powershell/).

For example, to grant Martin Power BI Administrator rights to the Adventure Works Power BI tenant, Elena would execute the following command:

Add-MsolRoleMember -RoleMemberEmailAddress "martin@adventureworks.com" -RoleName "Power BI Service Administrator"

Now Martin can access the Power BI Admin Portal, which is shown in **Figure 10.4**. Currently, the portal has four management areas (Usage metrics, Manage Users, Audit logs, and Tenant settings).

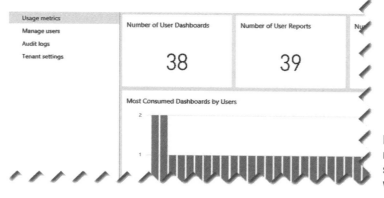

Figure 10.4 Use the Admin Portal to view usage statistics and control tenant wide settings.

Monitoring usage metrics
The "Usage metrics" management area provides insights into the usage of Power BI within your organization. It opens a dashboard that has two sections of tiles:

- User-level information – The top three rows provide usage statistics for individual users, including the total number of dashboards, reports, and datasets, top users with most dashboards and reports, most consumed dashboards, and most consumed content packs.

- Group-level information – The bottom three rows provide the same information but for groups (I'll discuss workspaces and groups in the next section).

The "Usage metrics" is a good starting point to help you understand Power BI utilization but much more is needed to make it really useful. I hope Microsoft extends it in future with additional health monitoring features to help you proactively manage Power BI, such as CPU and memory utilization, data quotas, refresh failures, and others.

Managing users

The second management area (Manage users) includes a shortcut that brings to the Office 365 Admin Center (see again **Figure 10.1**). Recall that you can use the Office 365 Admin Center to manage users, licenses, and groups.

Auditing logs

The "Audit logs" management area provides another shortcut to the Office 365 portal where you view tenant activity and export the audit logs. I'll discuss auditing user activity in the next section.

Managing tenant settings

Go to the "Tenant settings" section of the Admin Portal to manage tenant-wide settings (see **Figure 10.5**).

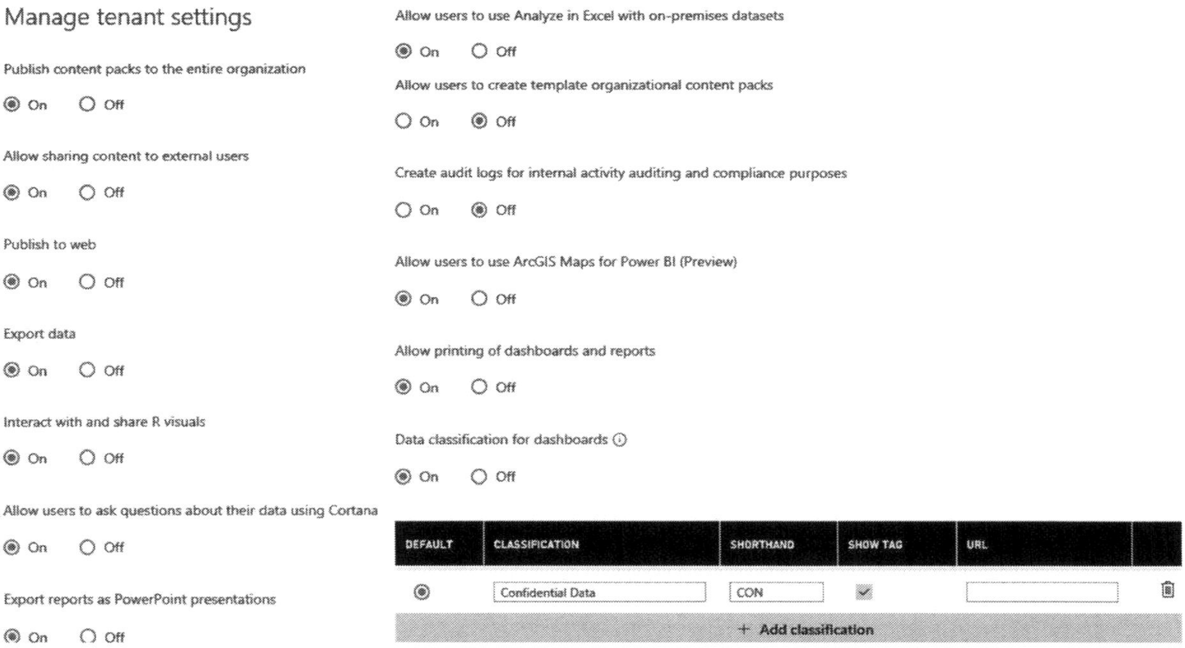

Figure 10.5 Use the "Manage tenant settings" area to manage important tenant-wide security and functionality settings.

Let's go quickly through these settings. "Publish content packs to the entire organization" controls the allowed audience when creating organizational content packs (discussed in the "Packaging and Publishing Content" section later on in this chapter). If you turn it off, users can publish content packs to specific groups only.

The "Allow sharing content to external users" controls whether users can share dashboards to users external to your organization. By default, your users can share dashboards by email (simple sharing) to both internal and external users so consider disabling this setting for added data security. The "Publish to web" setting is even more dangerous. By default, your users will be able to share reports anonymously to anyone on the Internet! Strongly consider turning this setting off.

The "Export data" setting controls if users would be able to export data from report visualizations. By default, users would be able to export summarized and underlying data. "Interact with and share R visuals" is for custom visuals designed with R. R visuals can be created in Power BI Desktop, and then published to the Power BI service. Unless this setting is off, for the most part R visuals behave like any other visual in the Power BI service; users can interact, filter, slice, and pin them to a dashboard, or share them with others.

When off, the "Allow users to ask questions about their data using Cortana" setting effectively disables Power BI integration with Cortana. Consequently, a Windows 10 user can't use Cortana to ask Power BI questions on the desktop (they must go to Power BI Service). When off, the "Export reports as PowerPoint presentations" disables exporting to PowerPoint.

Recall that the "Analyze in Excel" feature allows users to create pivot reports in Excel Desktop connected to Power BI datasets, just like they'd use Excel to connect to cubes. Users can publish the Excel reports to Power BI Service dashboards. When off, this setting disables this feature for datasets that connect directly to on-premises databases.

Unless "Allow users to create template organizational content packs" is off, when a user creates an organizational content with imported data they can decide to remove the data and package the content as a template content pack. This works conceptually similar to Power BI Desktop templates. When turned on, "Create audit logs for internal activity auditing and compliance purposes" enables logging.

When off, "Allow users to use ArcGIS Maps for Power BI" removes this visual from the Visualizations pane in Power BI Service. When off, "Allow printing of dashboards and reports" disables the corresponding menus.

When on, "Data classifications for dashboards" allow you tag dashboards. For example, your users might have dashboards that show some sensitive information and they might request a mechanism to inform the users about it. As the administrator, you can use the Admin Portal to create a "Confidential Data" tag. Then, your users can go to the dashboard settings in Power BI Service and select the tag from the "Data classification" dropdown. Once they choose a tag, it'll show next to the dashboard name when the user views the dashboard in the Power BI portal (see **Figure 10.6**).

Figure 10.6 Users can use the data classification tags defined in the Admin Portal to tag dashboards.

If you mark a tag as a default tag in the Admin Portal (see again **Figure 10.5**), all new and existing dashboards will show this tag. To avoid this, create a dummy tag, set it as a default tag, and clear the "Show Tag" setting. Also, when setting up a tag, consider providing a tag URL so that users can click on the dashboard tag and learn more about why the dashboard was classified this way.

10.1.3 Auditing User Activity

Regulatory and compliance requirements are typically met with audit policies. Power BI can log certain user activities, such as creating, editing, printing, exporting, sharing reports and dashboards, and creating groups and content packs (for the full list, see "List of activities audited by Power BI" at bit.ly/2gAfawk).

Getting started with Power BI auditing

You can turn on Power BI auditing by flipping the "Create audit logs for internal activity auditing and compliance purposes" setting to On in the Power BI Admin Portal (see again **Figure 10.5**). Be patient though because audit logs can take up to 24 hours to show after you enable them. To see the actual logs, you need to use the Office 365 Admin Center again. A convenient shortcut is available in the "Audit Logs" area of the Power BI Admin Portal and it brings you directly to the "Audit search" page in the Office 365 Admin Center.

 NOTE Auditing is a Power BI Pro feature and auditing events are only available for Power BI Pro users. Users with Power BI (free) licenses will be displayed as Free User when you view the audit logs. In addition, to enable auditing for Power BI, you need at least one Exchange mailbox license in your tenant.

Viewing audit logs

The "Audit log search" page (see **Figure 10.7**) allows you to view and search all Office 365 audit logs. To view only the Power BI logs, expand the Activities drop-down and then select "Power BI activities" or choose specific Power BI activities, such as "Viewed Power BI dashboard". To search logs for a particular user, start typing in the user name and Power BI will show a drop-down to help you locate the user (you can enter multiple users). You can also subscribe to receive an alert that meets the search criteria.

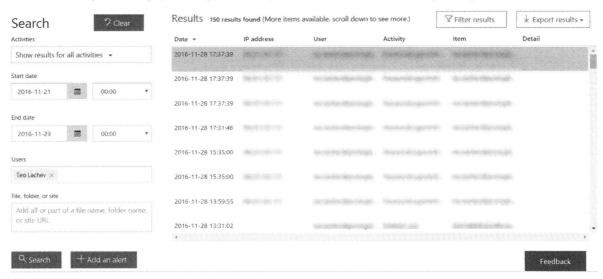

Figure 10.7 Use the "Audit log search" page to view Office 365 audit logs, including logs for Power BI.

If the search criteria result matches existing logs, the logs will be shown in the Results pane. You can see the date, the user IP address, user email, activity (corresponds to the items in the Activities drop-down), item (the object that was created or modified as a result of the corresponding activity) and Detail (some activities have more details). You can click a row to see more details, such as to see if the activity succeeded or failed. You can click the "Export results" to export the results as a CSV file.

10.2 Understanding Workspaces and Groups

Oftentimes, BI content needs to be shared within an organizational unit or with members of a project group. Typically, the group members require write access so that they can collaborate on the artifacts they produce and create new content. This is where Power BI workspaces and groups can help. Remember that Power BI workspaces and groups are features of Power BI Pro.

For example, now that Martin has created a self-service data model with Power BI Desktop, he would like to share it with his coworkers from the Sales department. Because his colleagues also intend to produce self-service data models, Martin approaches Elena to set up a workspace for the Sales department. The workspace would only allow the members of his unit to create and share BI content. To support similar department or project needs, Elena can set up groups and add the appropriate members to these groups. Then she can create workspaces and grant the groups access to their workspaces.

10.2.1 Understanding Groups

Power BI groups offer a simplified sharing and collaborative experience built on Office 365 groups. Groups bring together people, information, and applications to facilitate sharing and collaboration in a secure environment.

What is a group?
From an implementation standpoint, a Power BI group is a record in Azure Active Directory (AAD) that has a shared membership. To understand why you need groups consider that today every Office 365 online application (Exchange, SharePoint, OneDrive for Business, Skype for Business, Yammer, and others) has its own security model, making it very difficult to restrict and manage security across applications. Microsoft introduced groups in Office 365 to simplify this and to foster sharing and collaboration.

 NOTE Conceptually, an Office 365 group is similar to a Windows AD group; both have members and can be used to simplify security. However, an Office 365 group has shared features (such as a mailbox, calendar, task list, and others) that Windows groups don't have. Unlike Windows groups, Office 365 groups can't be nested. To learn more about Office 365 groups, read the "Find help about groups in Office 365" document by Microsoft at http://bit.ly/1BhDecS.

Although Power BI groups use Office 365 groups behind the scenes, they don't require an Office 365 plan. However, if you have an Office 365 subscription or if you're an administrator of your organization's Office 365 tenant, you can use both Power BI and the Office 365 portal to create and manage groups. Currently, you have to use Office 365 to manage some aspects of the group, such as the group description, to see the group email address, and to find which groups a user is a member of.

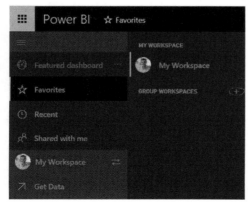

Figure 10.8 Click the Create Group (+) button to create a new group.

Creating groups

Currently, any Power BI Pro user can create a group. The user who creates the group becomes the administrator of the group. The administrator can add other Power BI Pro users as members of the group. Power BI groups have two roles: Admins and Members. Admins can add or remove group members. Creating a group from Power BI Service only takes a few mouse clicks:

1. Once you log in to Power BI Service, click the "Switch your workspace" button next to My Workspace.
2. Click the Create Group (+) button next to the Group Workspaces section, as shown in **Figure 10.8**.
3. In the "Create a Group" window (see **Figure 10.9**), enter the group details and members, and click Save.

Figure 10.9 When creating a group, specify the group name, privacy, member access and membership.

When creating a group, you need to specify the group name, such as *Sales Department*. Every group has a unique identifier which Power BI auto-generates from the group name but you can change it if you need something more descriptive. A group can have one of the following privacy settings:

■ Private (default) – Only the group members can access the group content.

■ Public – Every Power BI Pro user can become a member and gain access to the group content.

> **TIP** A public group doesn't grant access to everyone. Users still have to discover and join the group. One way for users to discover public groups is to use Outlook, as explained in more detail in "Join a group in Outlook" at bit.ly/2fAlQtn.

Note that you can also specify a privacy level: edit or only view content. It's important to understand that the privacy level is granted at a group level and not at the user level. If you change the group privacy to "Members can only view Power BI content", all the group members will get read-only rights to the group's content. Now all the members of this group can only view the Power BI dashboards and reports that the group shares. They can't create or edit content. They can't even view the datasets in the workspace. However, admin users always have the rights to create and edit content. It's important to consider content security when you can plan your groups.

4. If you want to add members right away, enter a name or email alias in the "Add group members" field. You can separate multiple members with a comma (,) or a semi-colon (;). Currently, Power BI doesn't support membership via Office 365 or AD groups so you must enumerate all members. If this is an issue, consider sharing content via organizational content packs, which can be distributed to groups.

Once the group is created, a welcome page opens that's very similar to the Get Data page, so that you can start adding content the group can work on.

NOTE It might take a while for Office 365 to fully provision a group and enable its collaboration features. When the group is ready, the members will receive an email explaining that they've joined the new group. The email includes useful links to get the members started with the collaboration features, including access to group files, a shared calendar, and conversations.

Disabling group creation

One of the benefits of groups is that it enables users to create shared workspaces without relying on IT. At the same time, IT might want to prevent indiscriminate use of this feature. Currently, the only way to disable creating new groups is to use a PowerShell script that applies a policy to the user Exchange mail account. For more information and the steps required to disable groups across the board or for specific users, read the "Disable Group creation" document by Microsoft at http://bit.ly/1MvPGF0.

10.2.2 Understanding Workspaces

A Power BI workspace is a container of BI content (datasets, reports, and dashboards) that the group members share and collaborate on. By default, all the content you create goes to the default workspace called "My Workspace". Think of My Workspace as your private desk – no one can see its content unless you share it. By contrast, a group workspace is shared by all the group members.

Once you create a group, Power BI creates a workspace that has the same name as the group. Currently, there's a one-to-one relationship between groups and workspaces: one Power BI group has one corresponding workspace. Members who belong to the group will see the group workspace added to the Power BI navigation bar. A Power BI user can be added to multiple groups and can access their workspaces. For example, **Figure 10.10** shows that besides My Workspace, I'm a member of four other groups and I can access their workspaces.

Figure 10.10 Each group has a workspace associated with it and any Power BI Pro user can create workspaces.

Besides creating an organizational content pack, currently there isn't another way to move or copy content from one workspace, such as My Workspace, to another. Therefore, it makes sense to create a workspace before you start adding content to Power BI. If you a Power BI Pro user, think of who you want to share the content with and create a group that includes these people. You can use the default My Workspace to publish content that you want to share with people that don't have Power BI Pro rights (remember that simple dashboard sharing works with the Power BI Free edition) as long as the underlying reports don't use Power BI Pro features.

Understanding collaboration features

Because the primary goal of Power BI groups is to facilitate communication and collaboration, groups go beyond BI and support collaborative features. Group members can access these features from the workspace page by clicking the ellipsis (…) in the top-right corner, as shown in **Figure 10.11**. Let's review the available collaboration features:

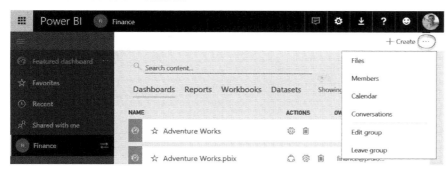

Figure 10.11 Group members have access to a set of features that allows them to communicate and share files.

- Files – Brings you to the OneDrive for Business file storage that's dedicated to the group. While you can save all types of files to OneDrive, Excel workbooks used to import data to Power BI are particularly interesting. As I mentioned, that's because Power BI automatically refreshes the datasets you import from Excel files stored to OneDrive every ten minutes or when the file is updated.

- Members – This menu allows you to manage the group membership, such as to view, add, or remove members.

- Calendar – This brings you to a shared group calendar that helps members coordinate their schedules. Everyone in the group sees meeting invites and other events posted to the group calendar. Events that you create in the group calendar are automatically added and synchronized with your personal calendar. For events that other members create, you can add the event from the group calendar to your personal calendar. Changes you make to those events automatically synchronize with your personal calendar.

- Conversations – Think of a conversation as a real-time discussion list. The conversations page displays each message. If you use Outlook, conversations messages are delivered to a separate folder dedicated to the group. You can either use Outlook or the conversation page to reply to messages and you can include attachments.

- Edit Group – This allows you to change the group name and manage the group members. You can also delete the group. Deleting a group deletes the workspace and its content so be very careful!

- Leave Group – Use this menu if you want to be removed from the group.

Understanding data security

The main goal of workspaces is to allow all group members to access the same data. When the group members explore datasets with imported data, everyone sees the same data. An interesting scenario exists when the group member connects to an on-premises Analysis Services model. In this case, the user identity is carried over to Analysis Services. If the Analysis Services model applies data security based on the user identity, the data will still be secured and the user can only see the data he's authorized to see. So, in this case there are two levels of security: workspace security and model data security.

Remember that when you import data, Power BI datasets cache a copy of the data. However, a user can schedule a data refresh to periodically synchronize the Power BI dataset with changes that occur in the data source. What happens if you need to make changes to the data refresh but this user goes on vacation or leaves the company? Fortunately, another user can take over maintaining the data refresh. To do so, the group member would click the ellipsis button (…) next to the dataset to go to the dataset properties, and then click Schedule Refresh. Then the user clicks Take Over (see **Figure 10.12**) to take ownership of the data refresh and to overwrite the refresh settings if needed.

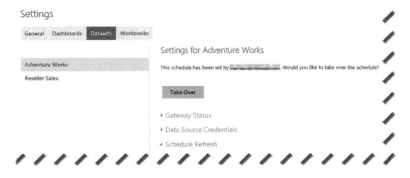

Figure 10.12 A group member can take over the data refresh settings.

10.2.3 Working with Group and Workspaces

We're back to Martin, a data analyst from Adventure Works. Martin approached Elena, who oversees data analytics, to help him set up a workspace for the Sales Department. This workspace will be accessed only by members of his unit, and it'll contain BI content produced by Martin and his colleagues.

> **NOTE** Unless IT has disabled Office 365 group creation, currently there's nothing stopping Martin from creating a group on his own (if he has a Power BI Pro subscription) and becoming the new group's admin. However, I do believe that someone needs to coordinate groups and workspaces, because creating groups indiscriminately could quickly become as useful as having no groups at all. It would be impossible for IT to maintain security over groups they didn't know existed.

Creating a group
As a first step, you need to create a Sales Department group:

1. Open your web browser and navigate to http://powerbi.com. Log in to Power BI Service.
2. In the left navigation bar, click the "Switch your workspace" next to My Workspace.
3. Click the plus (+) sign next to the Group Workspaces section.
4. In the "Create a Group" window, enter *Sales Department* as a group name.
5. In the "Add group members" field, enter the email addresses of some of your coworkers, or leave the field blank for now. You don't have to add your email because your membership is applied when you create the group, and you'll be the group admin.
6. Click Save to create the group.

In the navigation bar, the Group Workspaces section now includes the Sales Department workspace.

Uploading content
As you create a group, Power BI opens a "Welcome to the Sales Department group" page so that you can start adding content immediately. Let's add the Adventure Works model (that you previously created) to the Sales Department workspace:

1. In the welcome page, click the Get button in the Files section (**Figure 10.13**). If you close your web browser and go back to Power BI, make sure that you expand My Workspace and select Sales Department so that content is added to this workspace and not to your personal workspace.

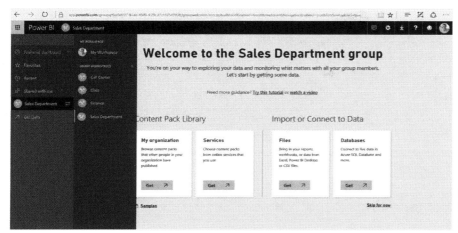

Figure 10.13 This page allows you to add content to a workspace.

2. In the Files page, click Local File.

3. Navigate to the Adventure Works.pbix file you worked on in the previous part of the book, and upload it in Power BI.

4. Using your knowledge from reading this book, view and edit the existing reports, and create some new reports and dashboards. For example, open the Adventure Works.pbix dashboard. Click the Adventure Works.pbix tile to navigate to the underlying report, and then pin some tiles to the dashboard. Back to the dashboard, delete the Adventure Works.pbix tile, and rename the dashboard to *Adventure Works Sales Dashboard.*

Scheduling data refresh

Once a business user uploads content to the workspace, the user might want to schedule an automatic data refresh. As a prerequisite, they need to install and configure the Power BI Personal Gateway.

NOTE As its name suggests, the Personal Power BI Gateway is for your personal use. The idea here is to allow business users to refresh imported data without bothering IT. You can install the gateway on your computer or another machine that has access to the data source you want to refresh the data from. Each personal gateway installation is tied to the user who installs it and it can't be shared with other users. By contrast, the On-premises Data Gateway (discussed in section 10.4) allows IT to centralize and manage access to on-premises data.

1. From the Power BI portal, expand the Downloads menu in the top-right corner, and click Data Gateway. In the next page, click the "Download gateway" button (both gateways are included in the same setup).

2. Once the setup program starts, select "Personal gateway" when the setup asks you what type of gateway you want to install. Then follow the steps to install the gateway. When the gateway is installed, a configuration utility pops up. It asks you to specify what Windows account the gateway will run under. By default, it'll use your account so that it can access the data sources on your behalf. The configuration utility will ask you to enter your Windows password. Remember that if your password expires, you'll need to reconfigure the gateway. To do so, click the Power BI Personal Gateway icon in the Windows taskbar or open the application with the same name.

3. Back in Power BI Service, click the ellipsis (…) button next to the Adventure Works dataset. In the properties window, click Schedule Refresh to open the Settings page.

NOTE Depending on the account permissions (admin versus regular user), the Personal Gateway installs either as a service or as an application. If you have administrator access to your computer, it will install as a service (Data Management Gateway Service) and run unattended, even if you log out of the computer. If you change your password, you need to update the service password as well. If you don't have administrator rights, the gateway will run as an application using your current account and password, but you need to be logged in. For more information about these setup scenarios, read the "Power BI Personal Gateway" topic in the Power BI documentation at https://support.powerbi.com/knowledgebase/articles/649846-power-bi-personal-gateway.

4. In the Settings page (Datasets tab), expand the Data Source Credentials section, which should look like the one shown in **Figure 10.14**.

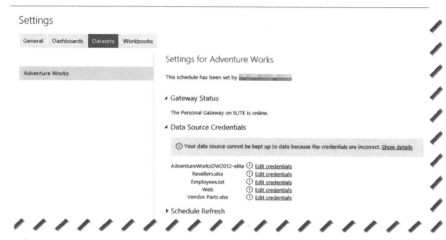

Figure 10.14 The data settings page allows you to configure data refresh.

5. The Gateway Status should show that the personal gateway is online on the computer where it's installed.

 NOTE If you use the on-premises data gateway to schedule the refresh, make sure that the data sources in your Power BI Desktop model have the same connection settings as the data sources registered in the on-premises data gateway. For example, if you have imported an Excel file, make sure that the file path in the underlying query matches the file path in the gateway data source. If the connection settings differ, you won't be able to use the on-premises data gateway.

6. The "Data Source Credentials" section shows that the credentials are incorrect. Although this might look alarming, it's easy to fix, and you only need to do it once per data source. Power BI simply requires you to restate how you want to connect. Click the "Edit Credentials" link for each data source, specify Windows authentication as the authentication method, and then click the "Sign In" button (see **Figure 10.15**).

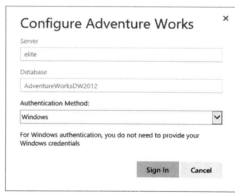

Figure 10.15 The first time you configure scheduled data refresh, you need to reset the authentication method.

7. (Optional) Specify a schedule interval. Back in the Datasets tab of the Settings page (see **Figure 10.14** again), expand the Schedule Refresh section, and update your settings, such as turning on the refresh, refresh frequency, your time zone, time of the refresh, and whether you want refresh failure email notifications. When you're finished, click Apply.

Now the Adventure Works is scheduled for an automatic refresh. When the schedule is up, Power BI will connect to the Personal Gateway, which in turn will connect to all the data sources in the model and will reload the data. Currently, there isn't an option to refresh specific data sources or to specify data source-specific schedules. Once a model is enabled for refresh, Power BI will refresh all the data on the same schedule.

8. (Optional) If another member in your group has scheduled a dataset refresh, go to the dataset Settings page and discover how you can take over the data refresh when you need to. Once you take over, you can overwrite the data source and the schedule settings.

10.3 Packaging and Publishing Content

You saw how workspaces foster collaboration across members of a group. But what if you want to package and publish content to a broader audience, such as across multiple departments or even to the entire organization? Enter Power BI organizational content packs. Your users no longer need to wait for someone else to share content and will no longer be left in the dark without knowing what BI content is available in your company! Instead, users can discover and open content packs from a single place - the Power BI Content Gallery.

10.3.1 Understanding Organizational Content Packs

In Chapter 2, I explained that Power BI comes with content packs that allow your information workers to connect to a variety of online services, such as Google Analytics, Dynamics CRM, QuickBooks, and many more. Microsoft and its partners provide these content packs to help you analyze data from popular cloud services. Not only do content packs allow you to connect easily to external data, but they also include pre-packaged reports and dashboards that you can start using immediately! Similar to Power BI content packs, organizational content packs let data analysts and IT/BI pros package and distribute BI content within their organization. Organizational content packs are a Power BI Pro feature.

What's an organizational content pack?
An organizational content pack is a way for any company to distribute Power BI content to anyone who's interested in it. A content pack includes specific dashboards, reports, and datasets. Packaging an item publishes dependent items as well, so that the dependencies are included and the package content is functional.

For example, if you publish a dashboard, the content pack will also include the dependent reports and datasets. And if you publish a report, the content pack will include the report dataset. You create a content pack from the Power BI Settings ⇨ "Create Content Pack" menu. Use the "Create content pack" to specify which items you want to publish from the workspace you selected.

For example, if you're in your private workspace (My Workspace), you can publish any dashboard, report, or dataset that exists there. However, if you select the Sales Department workspace, you can only publish content from that workspace. Because I was in the Sales Department workspace before creating the content pack, I can choose items from this workspace only (see **Figure 10.16**).

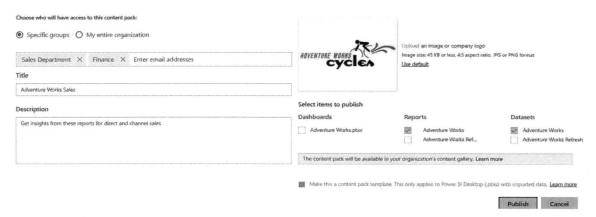

Figure 10.16 An organizational content pack can include dashboards, reports, and dataset references.

I've checked the Adventure Works report. The content pack will automatically include the Adventure Works dataset because that's the dataset that this report uses. If I've decided to publish the Adventure Works dashboard that uses the Adventure Works report, the content pack will include that report and the Adventure Works dataset. If I decide to publish only the datasets, users won't get access to my reports but they can create their own reports from these datasets.

An organizational content pack packages *links* to the original content that you publish. Going back to the example, the consumers of my content pack will gain read-only access by default to the Adventure Works report and its dataset. But what if they want to make changes?

Understanding content access
In the process of creating an organizational content pack, you specify which users will have access to it. You can publish the content pack to the entire organization, or restrict it to specific individuals, Office 365 unified groups, or AD groups. As shown back in **Figure 10.16**, I've decided to publish the "Adventure Works Sales" content pack to the Sales Department and Finance Office 365 groups.

 NOTE Notice that unlike workspaces, content packs support distributing content to groups. You can just start typing the group name and a pick list should show up. In **Figure 10.16**, I've decided to distribute content to two Office 365 unified groups but you can distribute to AD groups too.

Any Power BI Pro user can create an organizational content pack. The content pack author can view and manage the content packs he published by going to the Power BI Settings ⇨ "View content pack" menu. This opens a page that shows the content packs you published for the active workspace. For example, if you have selected the Sales Department workspace, you'll see the content packs you've published from that workspace (see **Figure 10.17**). The Edit link sends you to the "Update Content Pack" page, which is similar to the "Create Content Package" page. You can click the Delete link to delete a content pack.

On the consumer side of things, any Power BI Pro user can consume a content pack. If the content pack is restricted to specific groups, the user must be a member of one or more of these groups. By default, consumers get read-only access to the content. However, a consumer can customize the included dashboards and reports without affecting other users and the original content. When a consumer indicates that he wants to change a BI artifact that's included in a content pack, Power BI creates a copy of the content pack. This copies the original report or dashboard. However, consumers can never modify datasets or change the dataset refresh settings. Only the content pack author can make dataset changes.

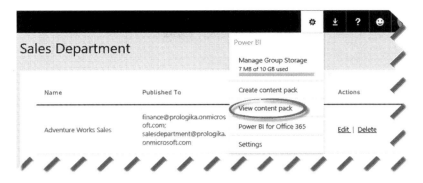

Figure 10.17 Click Power BI Settings ⇨ View Content Pack to view and manage the content packs that you've published.

Understanding data security

Content pack data security is similar to workspace data security. If Elena creates and publishes the Adventure Works self-service model created by Martin, every consumer of the content pack will have access to all the data that Martin imported. In other words, Martin and the content pack consumers have the same access to the content pack data. If Martin has scheduled the Adventure Works model for data refresh, the consumers will also see the new data.

What if you want consumers to have different access rights to the data? For example, you might want Martin to have unrestricted access but want Maya to see data for only a subset of your customers. One option is to implement an Analysis Services model that applies data security, based on the user identity. In Power BI, you need to create a dataset that connects live to the Analysis Services model. You can create this dataset by using Get Data in the Power BI Portal or by using Power BI Desktop and publishing the model to Power BI Service. Now when Maya uses the content pack, her identity will be passed to Analysis Services, and she'll get restricted access depending on how the SSAS security is set up.

If you prefer to keep your model in Power BI Desktop, another option is to extend the model with row-level security (RLS), which I discussed in Chapter 10. This accomplishes the same level of security as using Analysis Services. Of course, there are factors that might influence your decision to choose Analysis Services, such as planning for a centralized data model, scalability, and others.

Discovering organizational content packs

The Power BI AppSource gallery allows users to discover and consume organizational content packs. You can access AppSource from the Get Data ⇨ My Organization section. The "My organization" area in AppSource shows the organizational content packs and allows users to search on the content pack name and description. Users can only see content packs that they have permissions to access, via their group membership, unless the content pack is published to the entire organization.

 NOTE It's important to be in the right workspace before the user consumes a content pack. If the user is in My Workspace, the content will be added to My Workspace (this is the most common usage case). However, if the user plans to share the content with other members, the user needs to be in the appropriate workspace before going to AppSource.

Figure 10.18 shows that the user has permissions to use two content packs. When the user selects a content pack, a popup section is displayed with more information about the content pack, including the author, the created date, and the description. Once the user connects to the pack by clicking Get, the user can access its content.

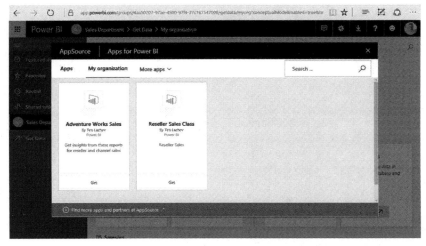

Figure 10.18 The Power BI AppSource (My Organization area) allows consumers to discover and use content packs.

10.3.2 Understanding the Content Pack Lifecycle

Let's go through a few scenarios that will help you understand the lifecycle of a content pack. The lifecycle includes initial publishing, consumer access and changes, as well as changes by the content pack author. In this scenario, Elena is the content pack author, and Maya is the consumer.

Initial publishing and access
The content pack lifecycle starts when the content pack is published and available for access:

1. Elena belongs to the Sales Department workspace via a Power BI group membership. Martin has informed Elena that the Sales Department has added some BI content that could benefit the finance group and even the entire organization!

2. Elena creates and publishes an Adventure Works Sales content pack that includes some dashboards, reports, and datasets. When Elena uses the "Create Content Pack" page, she grants access to a group that Maya belongs to.

3. Maya logs in to Power BI and navigates to AppSource. Maya discovers the Adventure Works Sales content pack and connects to it. Now Maya has read-only access to the dashboard and reports that are packaged in the Adventure Works Sales content pack.

Changes by consumers
Consumers can personalize content that's included in an organizational content pack. However, consumers never modify the original content. Instead, to make a change, they need to create a personal copy of the content pack. At this point, the content exists in two places: the original content as published by the report author and a personal copy for the consumer. Let's follow Maya as she makes some changes:

1. Maya analyzes the reports and dashboards in the Adventure Works Sales dashboard.

2. Maya wants to change a dashboard (or a report), such as to add a new dashboard tile, but she can't because the dashboard and underlying reports are read only. Upon examining the content included in the content pack, Maya sees a copy icon next to the dashboard (or report) name.

3. Maya clicks the icon, and she's asked whether or not she wants to get a personal copy of the content pack (see **Figure 10.19**).

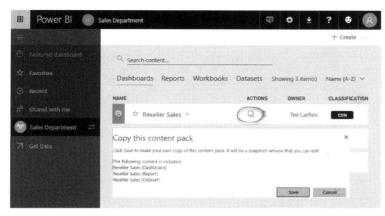

Figure 10.19 Consumers can personalize dashboards and reports included in a content pack by cloning the content pack.

4. Maya clicks the Save button. Power BI clones the content of the organizational content pack. Maya looks at the content and sees another set of reports, dashboards, and datasets with the same names as the ones included in the content pack but prefixed with " – Copy", such as "Adventure Works – Copy". Now she can change her personal copy of the pack content. Her changes never affect other users or the original content.

Changes by the content pack publisher
Content packs are likely to undergo changes. For example, as the business evolves, Elena might want to make changes to the content pack reports and dashboards:

1. Elena opens the Adventure Works dashboard (or report) and makes a change. For example, she changes an existing visualization or adds a visualization.

2. Power BI pops up the message shown in **Figure 10.20**

Figure 10.20 Power BI shows this message when the publisher changes content included in an organizational content pack.

3. Now Elena has to decide if she wants to push the changes to all the consumers. If she wants to do that, she can click the "View Content Packs" button or go to "Power BI Settings" ⇨ "View Content Pack".

4. This action shows all content packs she created (see again **Figure 10.17**). However, this time the Adventure Works Sales content pack has a warning icon next to its name. When Elena hovers her mouse over the warning icon, a message pops up to let her know that she needs to update the content pack, as shown in **Figure 10.21**.

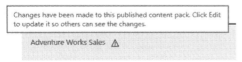

Figure 10.21 Power BI informs the content pack publisher about pending changes.

5. Elena updates the content pack.

6. The next time that Maya views the original dashboards and reports that are included in the content pack, she sees Elena's changes. However, Maya's personalized content doesn't change. When Maya opens her personal copy, she sees a warning message that the content pack has been updated. Maya knows that her personal copy might be outdated because a new version of the content pack has been published.

Deleting content packs

Consumers can delete content that was pushed to them from a content pack. When they remote a content pack item, such as a dashboard, they'll see a prompt that the item is a part of a content pack. If they confirm the prompt, the entire content pack is removed from the workspace. A content pack might also reach the end of its lifecycle and it's no longer needed. Then, the content pack owner can remove the content pack. Deleting a content pack removes the shared content from all consumers.

1. The Adventure Works Sales content pack is outdated, and Elena needs to remove it. When she attempts to delete it, she's prompted to confirm her intention and warned that anyone who's connected to the content pack will no longer be able to access it.

2. Elena confirms the prompt, and Power BI removes the content pack.

3. When Maya opens the Power BI portal, she notices that the original reports and datasets are gone. Her personalized reports are also gone because the underlying datasets have been removed. The cloned dashboards are still there but all the original tiles are removed.

10.3.3 Comparing Sharing Options

To recap, Power BI supports three ways of sharing BI content: simple dashboard sharing, workspaces, and organizational content packs. Because having that many options could be confusing, **Table 10.1** summarizes their key characteristics and usage scenarios.

Table 10.1 This table compares the sharing options supported by Power BI.

	Dashboard Sharing	Group Workspaces	Organizational Content Packs
Purpose	Ad hoc dashboard sharing	Team collaboration	Broader content delivery
Discovery	Invitation email or direct sharing to another user's workspace	Workspace content	Content Gallery
Target audience	Selected individuals (lie your boss)	Groups (your team)	Anyone who might be interested
Content permissions	Read-only dashboards	Read/edit to all workspace content	Read only by default and edit for a personalized copy
Membership	Individuals	Individuals	Individuals and groups
Communication		Calendar, conversations, files	
License	Power BI Free	Power BI Pro	Power BI Pro

Dashboard sharing

The primary purpose of dashboard sharing is the ad hoc sharing of dashboards only by sending an email to selected individuals or direct sharing to their workspace. For example, you might want to share your dashboard with your boss or a teammate. Consumers can't edit the shared dashboards. Dashboard sharing is the only sharing option supported by the free version of Power BI (Power BI Free).

Group workspaces

Group workspaces foster team collaboration and communication. They're best suited for departments or project teams. Based on Office 365 groups, group workspaces allow all the members of a group to edit and view the workspace content. Group workspaces are the only option that supports shared communication features, including OneDrive for Business file sharing, a shared calendar, and conversations.

Organizational content packs
Organizational content packs are designed for broader content delivery, such as across groups or even across the entire organization. Consumers discover content packs in Power BI AppSource. By default, consumers get read-only access to the published content, but they can create personalized copies.

10.3.4 Working with Organizational Content Packs

Several departments at Adventure Works have expressed interest in the content that the Sales Department has produced, so that they can have up-to-date information about the company's sales performance. Elena decides to create an organizational content pack in order to publish these artifacts to a broader audience.

Creating an organizational content pack
As a prerequisite, Elena needs to discover if there are any existing Active Directory, Exchange Distribution Lists, or Office 365 groups that include the authorized consumers. This is an important step from a security and maintenance standpoint. Elena doesn't want the content pack to reach unauthorized users. She also doesn't want to create a new group if she can reuse what's already in place. Elena needs to be a member of the Sales Department Power BI group so that she has access to this workspace.

1. Elena discusses this requirement with the Adventure Works system administrator, and she discovers that there's already an AD group for the Finance Department. Since the rest of the users come from other departments, the system administrator recommends Elena creates an Office 365 group for them.

2. Elena uses Power BI Service (she can also use the Office 365 Admin Center) to set up a new group. Now she has two groups to distribute the content to. Elena records the group email aliases. At this point, Elena might want to make sure the target users have Power BI Pro licenses so that they can consume the pack.

3. In Power BI Service, Elena clicks "Switch your workspace" next to "My Workspace" in the navigation bar and selects the Sales Department workspace. She does this so that, when she creates a content pack, she'll only see the Sales Department workspace content.

4. In Power BI Service, Elena expands the Settings menu in the top-right corner, and then she clicks "Create Content Pack".

5. In the "Create Content Pack" page (see **Figure 10.16** again), Elena enters the authorized groups. She fills in the content pack name and enters a useful description about the content pack's purpose. Then she selects the dashboards and reports that she wants to distribute, and she clicks Publish.

At this point, the Adventure Works Sales content pack is published and ready for authorized consumers.

Consuming an organizational content pack
Maya learns about the availability of the sales content pack, and she wants to use it. Maya belongs to one of the groups that's authorized to use the pack.

1. Maya logs in to Power BI and clicks Get Data ⇨ My Organization.

 TIP If Maya wants to share the content pack with members of a group workspace she belongs to, Maya can expand My Workspace and select that workspace. Then when she imports the content pack, all the group members will have access to the content pack.

2. If there many content packs available, Maya uses the search box to search for "sales".

3. Maya discovers the Adventure Works Sales content pack. She selects it and clicks Connect. Power BI adds all dashboards, reports, and datasets included in the content pack to Maya's My Workspace. Maya can now gain insights from the prepackaged content.

4. (Optional) Review and practice the different steps of the content pack lifecycle, such as to make changes and republish the pack.

10.4 Centralizing Data Management

Because it's a cloud platform, Power BI requires special connectivity software to access on-premises data. You've seen how the Personal Gateway allows end users to refresh datasets connected to on-premises data sources, such as relational databases and files. However, this connectivity mechanism doesn't give IT the ability to centralize and sanction data access. Moreover, Personal Gateway is limited to refreshing datasets with imported data, and it doesn't support DirectQuery to on-premises databases. The On-premises Data Gateway fills in these gaps.

10.4.1 Understanding the On-premises Data Gateway

The On-premises Data Gateway supports the following features:

- Serving many users – Unlike the Personal Gateway, which serves the needs of individuals, the administrator can configure one or more on-premises gateways for entire teams and even the organization.

- Centralizing management of data sources, credentials, and access control – The administrator can use one gateway to delegate access to multiple databases and can authorize individual users or groups to access these databases.

- Providing DirectQuery access from Power BI Service to on-premises data sources – Once Martin creates a model that connects directly to a SQL Server database, Martin can publish the model to Power BI Service and its reports will just work.

- Cross-application support – Besides Power BI, the On-premises Data Gateway can be used by other applications, including PowerApps, Flow, and Azure Logic Apps.

Table 10.2 This table compares the two gateways.

	On-premises Data Gateway	Personal Gateway
Purpose	Centralized data management	Isolated access to data by individuals
Audience	IT	Business users
DirectQuery	Yes	No
Data refresh	Yes	Yes
User access	Users and groups managed by IT	Individual user
Data sources	Multiple data sources (DirectQuery and refreshable)	All refreshable data sources
Data source registration	Must register data sources	Registration is not required
High availability	Yes (multiple gateways can service the same data source)	No
User license	Power BI Pro	Power BI Pro

Comparing connectivity options
Thanks to Microsoft unifying gateways (the Analysis Services Connector has been discontinued), deciding which gateway to use is much simpler. In a nutshell, the Personal Gateway is meant for a business user

who wants to set up automated data refresh without bothering IT by installing the gateway on his computer. By contrast, the On-premises Data Gateway will be used by IT for centralizing data access to both refreshable and DirectQuery data sources. **Table 10.2** compares the two gateways.

10.4.2 Getting Started with the On-Premises Data Gateway

Next, I'll show you how to install and use the On-Premises Data Gateway. While you can install the gateway on any machine, you should install it on a dedicated server within your corporate network. You can install multiple gateways if needed, such as to assign department-level admin access.

Installing the On-Premises Data Gateway
For your convenience, Microsoft has packaged both gateways in a single installation package. Follow these steps to download the gateway:

1. Remote in to the server where you want to install the gateway. This server should have a fast connection to the on-premises databases that the gateway will access. Verify that you can connect to the target databases.

2. Open the web browser and log in to Power BI Service.

3. In the Application Toolbar located in the upper-right corner of the Power BI portal, click the Download menu, and then click "Data Gateway". You can also access the download page directly at https://powerbi.microsoft.com/gateway/.

4. In the next page, click "Download gateway".

5. Once you download the setup executable, run it. On the "Choose the type of the gateway you need", leave the default option of "On-premises data gateway" selected.

6. Select the installation folder, read and accept the agreement, and then click Install. The gateway installs and runs as a Windows service called "On-premises data gateway service" (PBIEgwService) and its default location is the "C:\Program Files\On-premises data gateway" folder. The setup program configures the service to run under a low-privileged NT SERVICE\PBIEgwService Windows account.

What's interesting about the gateway is that it doesn't require any inbound ports to be open in your corporate firewall. Data transfer between the Power BI service and the gateway is secured through Azure Service Bus (relay communication). The gateway communicates on outbound ports 443 (HTTPS), 5671, 5672, 9350 thru 9354. By default, the gateway uses port 443, which is used for all secure socket layer (SSL) connections (every time users request HTTPS pages). If this port is congested, consider allowing outbound connections through the other outbound ports (my experience has been that port 443 is sufficient). What all this means is that in most cases the gateway should just work with no additional configuration.

 REAL LIFE I helped a large organization to implement a Power BI hybrid architecture to keep their data on premises. In this case, the gateway failed to register after installation. The reason was that this organization used a web proxy server. Had the proxy supported Windows Authentication, we could have solved the issue by just changing the gateway service account to an account that had rights to the proxy. However, their proxy server was configured for Basic Authentication so we had to pass the account password to the proxy. We had to change the gateway configuration file to specify the account credentials. For more technical details, read my "Power BI Hybrid Architecture" blog at http://prologika.com/power-bi-hybrid-architecture.

Configuring the on-premises data gateway
Next, you need to configure the gateway:

1. Once the setup program installs the gateway, it'll ask you to sign in to Power BI.

2. In the next step, leave the default option of "Register a new gateway on this computer". Notice that the second option is to migrate, restore, or take over an existing gateway.

3. Specify the gateway name and a recovery key (see **Figure 10.22**). Save the recovery key in a safe place. Someone might need it to restore the gateway if admin access is lost or the gateway needs to be moved to another server.

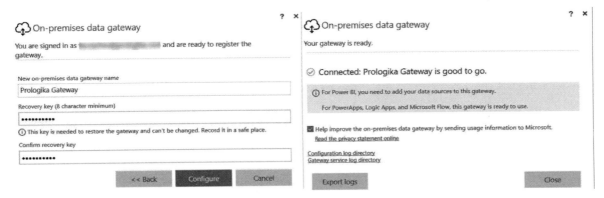

Figure 10.22 When you configure the on-premises gateway, you need to give it a name and provide a recovery key.

4. Click Configure. This registers the gateway with Power BI. You should see a message that the gateway is connected.

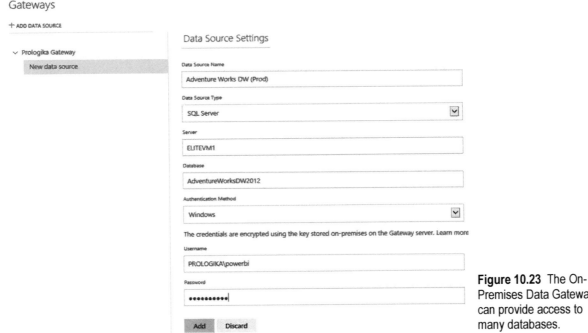

Figure 10.23 The On-Premises Data Gateway can provide access to many databases.

Registering data sources
Now that the gateway is connected, it's time to add one or more data sources to the gateway. Note that unlike the Personal Gateway which doesn't require data source registration, the On-premises Data Gateway

requires you to register all data sources that the gateway serves. This needs to be done in Power BI Service, as follows:

1. Log in to Power BI Service. Click the Settings menu in the Application Toolbar in the upper-right corner, and then click "Manage gateways".

2. In the Gateways page, select your gateway and notice that you can enter additional gateway settings, such as the department and description. Moreover, you can specify additional administrators who can manage the gateway (the person who installs the gateway becomes the first administrator).

3. Next, add one or more data sources that the gateway will delegate access to. Suppose you want to set up DirectQuery to the AdventureWorksDW2012 database (I'll show how to connect to SSAS in the next chapter). In the Gateways page, click "Add Data Source" (see **Figure 10.23**).

4. Fill in the data source settings to reflect your database setup.

5. The Authentication method allows you to specify the credentials of a trusted Windows account or a standard SQL Server login that has access to the database. Remember to grant this account at least read credentials to the database, such by assigning it to the SQL Server db_reader role. Note that all queries from all users will use these credentials to connect to the database, so grant the account only the minimum set of permissions it needs to the SQL Server database. This might result in different data permissions than the permissions a data analyst had when he used Power BI Desktop to connect to SQL Server under *his* credentials.

 NOTE The gateway uses asymmetric encryption to encrypt the credentials so that they cannot be decrypted in the cloud. Power BI sends the credentials to the gateway server, which decrypts the credentials when the data sources are accessed.

6. Once you add a data source and click the data source in the Gateways page, you'll see a new Users tab. For an added level of security, all users who will be publishing reports that will connect to this data source, must be added to the Users tab. Note that you need to add *only* the publishers and not the rest of the users who will be just viewing reports.

 TIP If you have issues with the On-premises Data Gateway setup or data source access, you can configure it for troubleshooting. You can find the troubleshooting steps in the "Troubleshooting the On-Premises Data Gateway" article by Adam Saxton at https://powerbi.microsoft.com/en-us/documentation/powerbi-gateway-enterprise-tshoot.

That's almost all you need to know about the gateway. There are special considerations that apply when connecting to Analysis Services but I'll discuss them in the next chapter. Let's now put our business user's hat on and see how you can create reports that connect to on-premises data via the gateway.

10.4.3 Using the On-Premises Data Gateway

Once the On-premises Data Gateway is set up and functional, you can use it for setting up automated data refresh and for reports that connect directly to on-premises data sources. In Chapter 2, I showed you how a business user can connect to an on-premises Analysis Services model via the gateway. Next, I'll show you how to use the gateway to connect directly to an on-premises SQL Server database. With the exception of Analysis Services, setting up DirectQuery connections to on-premises databases is currently only available in Power BI Desktop, so you must create a data model.

 NOTE The gateway is completely transparent to Power BI Desktop. You never specify a gateway when you connect to a data source in Power BI Desktop. Instead, you connect as usual by entering the server name and database. Only after you publish the Power BI Desktop file, Power BI Service examines the connections and determines which gateway services the data source(s). So, gateways are only for Power BI Service and don't apply to Power BI Desktop.

Connecting directly to SQL Server

Follow these steps to create a simple data model that you can use to test the gateway:

1. Open Power BI Desktop and expand the Get Data button in the ribbon's Home tab. Select SQL Server.
2. In the SQL Server Database prompt, specify the name of the SQL Server instance.
3. In the Navigator Window, expand the database the gateway delegates access to, select one or more tables, and then click Load.
4. In the Connection Settings window, select DirectQuery and click OK to create the dataset.
5. (Optional) Create a report that shows some data. If you skip this step, you can create the report in Power BI Service.
6. Publish the model to Power BI Service by clicking the Publish button in the ribbon's Home page.

Testing connectivity

Next, test that you can create reports from Power BI Service:

1. Log in to Power BI.
2. In the navigation bar, click My Workspace, and then click the dataset to explore it. Note that it's not enough to see the model metadata showing in the Fields pane because the list comes from the Tabular backend database where the model is hosted. You need to visualize the data to verify that the gateway is indeed functional.
3. In the Fields pane, check a field to create a visualization. If you see results on the report, then the gateway works as expected. You can also use the SQL Server Profiler to verify that the report queries are sent to the SQL Server database.

10.5 Summary

Power BI has comprehensive features for establishing a trustworthy environment. As an administrator, you can use the Office 365 Admin Center to manage users and grant them access to Power BI. You can use the Power BI Admin Portal to monitor utilization and configure tenant-wide settings.

Power BI allows teams to collaborate and share BI artifacts via dashboard sharing, group workspaces, and organizational content packs. Dashboard sharing is available on the free version of Power BI, but you'll need the Power BI Pro license for group workspaces and organizational content packs. This chapter started by introducing you to group workspaces. Based on Office 365 groups, workspaces allow a team to collaborate and share Power BI content. In addition, group workspaces include communication features, such as calendar, files, and conversations, which allow the group to share information.

Organizational content packs are designed to complement group workspaces by letting content producers share their insights with other teams and even with the entire organization. Authorized users can discover content packs in Power BI AppSource. When consumers connect to a content pack, they can view all the published content, but they can't edit the content. However, they can create personalized copies without affecting other content pack consumers or the original content.

This chapter compared the three sharing and collaboration options and recommended usage scenarios. It also walked you through a few exercises to help you practice the new concepts. It also showed you how the On-premises Data Gateway is positioned to centralize and simplify access to on-premises data.

Now that you know about sharing, the next chapter will show you how you can create more advanced BI solutions that integrate with Power BI!

Chapter 11

Organizational BI

So far, the main focus of this book has been the self-service and team flavors of Power BI, which empower business users and data analysts to gain insights from data and to share these insights with other users. Now it's time to turn our attention to BI pros who implement organizational BI solutions. Back in Chapter 2, I compared self-service and organizational BI at a high level. I defined organizational BI as a set of technologies and processes for implementing an end-to-end BI solution where the implementation effort is shifted to BI professionals.

This chapter shows BI pros how to build common organizational BI solutions. You'll understand the importance of having an organizational semantic layer, and you'll learn how to integrate it with Power BI. Implementing real-time BI solutions is one of the fastest growing BI trends. I'll show you how this can be done using the Power BI real-time API and Azure Stream Analytics Service, while you use Power BI for real-time dashboards. Because predictive analytics is another popular scenario, I'll show you how you can integrate Power BI with predictive models that you publish to Azure Machine Learning.

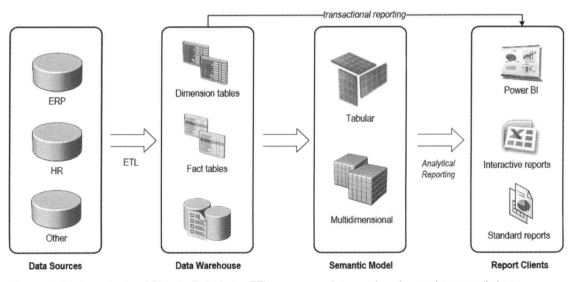

Figure 11.1 Organizational BI typically includes ETL processes, data warehousing, and a semantic layer.

11.1 Implementing Classic BI Solutions

In Chapter 2, I introduced you at a high level to what I refer to as a classic BI solution (see **Figure 11.1**). This diagram should be familiar to you. Almost every organization nowadays has a centralized data repository, typically called a data warehouse or a data mart, which consolidates cleaned and trusted data from operational systems.

REAL LIFE Data warehousing might mean different things to different people. In my consulting practice, I've seen data warehouse "flavors" ranging from normalized operational data stores (ODS) to hub-and-spoke architectures. If they work for you then that's all that matters. I personally recommend and implement a consolidated data repository designed in accordance with Ralph Kimball's dimensional modeling (star schema), consisting of fact and dimension tables. For more information about dimensional modeling, I recommend the book "The Data Warehouse Toolkit" by Ralph Kimball and Margy Ross.

You might not have an organizational semantic layer that sits between the data warehouse and users, and you might not know what it is. In general, semantics relates to discovering the meaning of the message behind the words. In the context of data and BI, semantics represents the user's perspective of data: how the end user views the data to derive knowledge from it. As a BI pro, your job is to translate the machine-friendly database structures and terminology into a user-friendly semantic layer that describes the business problems to be solved. In Microsoft BI, the role of this layer is fulfilled by Microsoft BI Semantic Model (BISM).

11.1.1 Understanding Microsoft BISM

Microsoft BISM is a unifying name for several Microsoft technologies for implementing semantic models, including self-service models implemented with Excel Power Pivot or Power BI Desktop, and organizational Microsoft Analysis Services models. From an organizational BI standpoint, BI pros are most interested in Microsoft Analysis Services modeling capabilities.

NOTE Besides the necessary fundamentals, this chapter doesn't attempt to teach you Multidimensional or Tabular. To learn more about Analysis Services, I covered implementing Analysis Services Multidimensional models in my book "Applied Microsoft Analysis Services 2005" and Tabular models in "Applied Microsoft SQL Server 2012 Analysis Services: Tabular Modeling".

Introducing Multidimensional and Tabular
Since its first release in 1998, Analysis Services has provided Online Analytical Processing (OLAP) capabilities so that IT professionals can implement Multidimensional OLAP cubes for descriptive analytics. The OLAP side of Analysis Services is referred to as *Multidimensional*. Multidimensional is a mature model that can scale to large data volumes. For example, Elena can build a Multidimensional cube on top of a large data warehouse with billions of rows, while still providing an excellent response time where most queries finish within a second!

Starting with SQL Server 2012, Microsoft expanded the Analysis Services capabilities by adding a new path for implementing semantic models, where entities are represented as relational-like constructs, such as two-dimensional tables, columns, and relationships. Referred to as *Tabular*, this technology uses the same xVelocity engine that powers Power BI Desktop, Excel Power Pivot, Power BI, and SQL Server columnstore indexes. Although not as scalable as Multidimensional, Tabular gains in simplicity and flexibility. And because Tabular uses the same storage engine, if you know how to create self-service data models in Power BI Desktop or Excel, you already know 90% of Tabular! That's right, while you were learning how to build self-service data models with Power BI Desktop you were also learning how to implement Tabular models.

Understanding implementation paths

Microsoft organizational BISM can be visualized as a three-tier model that consists of data access, business logic, and data model layers (see **Figure 11.2**). The data model layer is exposed to external clients. Clients can query BISM by sending Multidimensional Expressions (MDX) or Data Analysis Expressions (DAX) queries. For example, Excel can connect to both Multidimensional and Tabular and send MDX queries, while Power BI and Power View send DAX queries.

The business logic layer allows the modeler to define business metrics, such as variances, time calculations, and key performance indicators (KPIs). In Multidimensional, you can implement this layer using Multidimensional Expressions (MDX) constructs, such as calculated members, named sets, and scope assignments. Tabular embraces the same Data Analysis Expressions (DAX) that you've learned about in Chapter 9 when you added business calculations to the Adventure Works model.

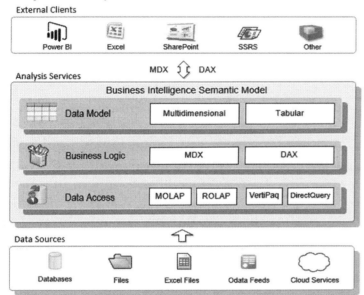

Figure 11.2 BISM has two organizational BI implementation paths: Multidimensional and Tabular.

The data access layer interfaces with external data sources. By default, both Multidimensional and Tabular import data from the data sources and cache the dataset on the server for best performance. The default multidimensional storage option is Multidimensional OLAP (MOLAP), where data is stored in a compressed disk-based format. The default Tabular storage option is xVelocity, where data is initially saved to disk but later loaded in memory when users query the model.

Both Multidimensional and Tabular support real-time data access by providing a Relational OLAP (ROLAP) storage mode for Multidimensional and a DirectQuery storage mode for Tabular. When a Multidimensional cube is configured for ROLAP, Analysis Services doesn't process and cache the data on the server. Instead, it auto-generates and sends native queries to the database. Similarly, when a Tabular model is configured for DirectQuery, Analysis Services doesn't keep data in xVelocity; it sends native queries directly to the data source. As I mentioned in Chapter 6, the DirectQuery mode of Tabular enables DirectQuery connections in Power BI Desktop.

Understanding the BISM advantages

Having a semantic model is very valuable for organizational BI for the following main reasons:

- Larger data volumes – Remember that Power BI Service currently limits imported files to 250 MB each, including Power BI Desktop models. This size limit won't be adequate for organizational solutions that are typically built on top of corporate data warehouses. By contrast, BISM can scale to billions of rows and terabytes of data!

- Great performance – BISM is optimized to aggregate data very fast. Queries involving regular measures and simple calculations should be answered within seconds even, when aggregating millions of rows!

- Single version of the truth – Business logic and metrics can be centralized in the semantic model instead of being defined and redefined in the database or in reports.

> **REAL WORLD** The BI department of a retail company included some 20 report developers on staff whose sole responsibility was creating operational reports from stored procedures. Over time, stored procedures have grown in complexity, and developers have defined important business metrics differently. Needless to say, operational reports didn't tally. Although the term "a single version of the truth" is somewhat overloaded, a centralized semantic model can get pretty close to it.

- Data security – Similar to row-level security (RLS) in Power BI Desktop, BISM models can apply data security based on the user's identity, such as to allow Maya to only see the data for the customers she's authorized to access.

- Implicit relationships – In the process of designing the semantic layer, the modeler defines relationships between entities, just like a data analyst does when creating a self-service model. As a result, end users don't need to join tables explicitly because the relationships have already been established at design time. For example, you don't have to know how to join the Product table to the Sales table. You simply add the fields you need on the report, and then the model knows how to relate them!

- Interactive data analysis – From an end-user perspective, data analysis is a matter of dragging and dropping attributes on the report to slice and dice data. A "smart" client, such as Power BI, auto-generates report queries, and the server takes care of aggregating data, such as to summarize sales at the year level.

- Good client support – There are many reporting tools, including Power BI, Excel, Reporting Services, and third-party tools, that support BISM and address various reporting needs, including standard reports, interactive reports, and dashboards.

When should you upgrade to organizational BI?

You might have started your BI journey with a self-service model in Excel or Power BI Desktop. Why can't this be your semantic model given that it could be as feature-rich as a Tabular model. At what point should you consider switching to an organizational solution? What would you gain?

> **REAL WORLD** Everyone wants quick and easy BI solutions, ideally with a click of a button. But the reality is much more difficult. I often find that companies have attempted to implement organizational BI solutions with self-service tools, like Power BI Desktop, Excel, or some other third-party tools. The primary reasons are cutting cost and misinformation (that's why it's important to know who you listen to). The result is always the same – sooner or later the company finds that it's time to "graduate" to organizational BI. Don't get me wrong, though. Self-service BI has its important place, as I explain in Chapter 2. But having trusted organizational-level solutions will require the right architecture, toolset, and investment.

You should consider moving to an organizational solution when the following happens:

- Data integration – The requirements call for extracting data from several systems and consolidating data instead of implementing isolated self-service data models.

- Data complexity – You realize that the data complexity exceeds the capabilities of the Power BI Desktop queries. For example, the integration effort required to clean and transform corporate data typically exceeds the simple transformation capabilities of self-service models.

- Data security – Security requirements might dictate leaving data on premises without compromising report performance. This excludes deploying data extracts to the cloud.

- Enterprise scalability – Power BI Desktop and Excel models import data in files. Once you get beyond a few million rows, you'll find that you stretch the limits of these tools. For example, it'll take a while to save and load the file. It'll take even longer to upload the file to Power BI. Moreover, Power BI Service limits you currently to a maximum file size of 1 GB for published files. By contrast, organizational models must be capable of handling larger data volumes. Just by deploying the model to an Analysis Services instance, you gain better scalability that's boosted by the hardware resources of a dedicated server. Also, to reduce the data load window and to process data incrementally, you can divide large tables in partitions.

- Faster data refresh – Unlike the Power BI Desktop sequential data refresh, organizational models support processing tables and partitioned tables in parallel, in order to better utilize the resources of a dedicated server.

- Richer model – Tabular supports additional features that might be appealing to you, including international translations, drillthrough actions, display folders, and programmatically generating the model schema. Because you'll be using Visual Studio to design your BISM, you can enjoy all the Visual Studio IDE features, including source control integration, and add-ons (such as the community BIDS Helper tool) that add even more features.

NOTE What if you have started with Power BI Desktop but want to upgrade to Tabular? Currently, Tabular supports upgrading from Excel Power Pivot only. There's no officially supported upgrade path from Power BI Desktop models. That's because Microsoft updates Power BI Desktop on a monthly basis, and it can get ahead of Tabular, which is included in the SQL Server box product and only releases a new version every few years. However, I outlined an unsupported way in my blog "Upgrading Power BI Desktop Models to Tabular" at http://prologika.com/upgrading-power-bi-desktop-models-to-tabular. Use it at you your own risk!

Comparing self-service and organizational models

Since you're reading this book, the logical transition path is from Power BI Desktop (or Excel) to Tabular. Then you'll discover that you can seamlessly transition your knowledge to organizational projects. Indeed, an organizational Tabular model has the same foundation as Power Pivot or Power BI Desktop, but it adds enterprise-oriented and advanced features, such as options for configuring security, scalability, and low latency. **Table 11.1** provides a side-by-side comparison between self-service and organizational features.

Table 11.1 This table highlights the differences between self-service and organizational semantic models.

Feature	Self-service Models	Organizational Models
Target users	Business users	Professionals
Environment	Power BI Desktop or Excel	Visual Studio (SSDT)
xVelocity Engine	Out of process (local in-memory engine)	Out of process (dedicated Analysis Services instance)
Size	One file (up to 1 GB to publish to Power BI)	Large data volumes, table partitions
Refreshing data	Sequential table refresh	Parallel table refresh, incremental processing (parallel partition refresh in SQL Server 2016)
Data transformation	Power Query in Excel, queries in PBI Desktop	Not available (typically ETL processes are in place)
Development	Ad-hoc development	Project (business case, plan, dates, hardware, source control)
Lifespan	Weeks or months	Years

How Power BI Service connects to on-premises Analysis Services

Now that you understand the benefits of an organizational semantic model, let's see how Power BI integrates with Analysis Services. Currently in preview, Azure Analysis Services allows you to deploy Tabular models to the cloud. In this case, no gateways are needed because Power BI can connect directly to cloud data sources. Power BI can access on-premises Analysis Services models with the Power BI On-premises Data Gateway.

NOTE Currently, the gateway doesn't support connecting to Tabular in SharePoint integration mode (Power Pivot for Share-Point uses this mode). I hope this limitation is lifted soon so that you can connect Power BI to cubes and to Power Pivot models deployed to SharePoint if you have invested in Power Pivot. Unfortunately, Power BI doesn't support HTTP access to Analysis Services using a special component called data pump (HTTP access to SSAS is discussed in the "Configure HTTP Access to Analysis Services on Internet Information Services (IIS) 8.0" article at https://msdn.microsoft.com/library/gg492140.aspx). So, you can't avoid using a gateway to access on-premises SSAS models.

From the Power BI standpoint, the BISM integration scenario that will inspire the most interest is the hybrid architecture shown in **Figure 11.3**. This architecture will be also appealing for companies that prefer to keep data on premises but want to host only report and dashboard definitions to on Power BI. Elena has implemented an Analysis Services Tabular model layered on top of the Adventure Works data warehouse, and she deployed it to an on-premises server. "On premises" could mean any model that is not hosted in Azure Analysis Services, such as a server hosted in the company's data center or on an Azure virtual machine. So Power BI can connect to the model, Elena installs the On-premises Data Gateway on a machine that can connect to the Analysis Services instance. Elena has granted Maya access to the model.

Live dashboards
and exploration

Live query

Analysis Services
on-premises

Figure 11.3 You can implement a hybrid architecture by connecting Power BI to on-premises Analysis Services models.

Maya logs in to Power BI and uses Get Data to connect to Analysis Services. Maya selects the Adventure Works model. Power BI establishes a live connection. Now Maya can create reports and dashboards, as I demonstrated in Chapter 2. If the model is configured for data security, Maya can only see the data that the model security authorizes her to access. When she explores the data, Power BI auto-generates DAX queries and sends them to the Adventure Works model. The model sends results back. No data is hosted on Power BI!

11.1.2 Understanding Setup Requirements

Because Power BI needs to connect to the on-premises model and pass the user identity, IT needs to take care of certain prerequisites for both on premises and in the cloud. The exact setup steps depend on how your company is set up for Microsoft Azure.

Understanding domain considerations

The following special considerations apply when setting up a gateway data source that connects to SSAS.

1. Analysis Services must be installed on a domain-joined machine. That's because Analysis Services supports only Windows security.

2. The Windows account that you specify in the data source properties of the On-premises Data Gateway, must have admin rights to the Analysis Services instance. That's because behind the scenes the gateway passes the user identity by appending an EffectiveUserName setting to the connection string. This connectivity mechanism requires admin rights.

NOTE Behind the scenes, the gateway appends a special EffectiveUserName connection setting when it connects to an on-premises SSAS. If Maya connects to the Analysis Services server, then EffectiveUserName will pass Maya's email, such as EffectiveUserName=maya@adventureworks.com. To verify or grant the account admin rights to SSAS, open SQL Server Management Studio (SSMS) and connect to your SSAS instance. Right-click on the instance, and then click Properties. In the Security tab of the Analysis Services Properties page, add the account to the server administrators list.

3. Without special mapping (see next section), the end user and Analysis Services must be on the same domain or trusted domains. For example, if I log in to Power BI as teo@adventureworks.com, Analysis Services must be on the adventureworks.com domain, or on a domain that has a trust relationship.

Checking access

Follow these steps to verify whether the On-premises Data Gateway can delegate the user identity:

1. Make sure that you have administrator access to the Analysis Services instance.

2. Open SQL Server Management Studio (SSMS). In Object Explorer, expand the Connect drop-down, and then click Connect ⇨ Analysis Services.

3. In the "Connect to Server", enter your Analysis Services instance name. Don't click Connect yet.

4. Click Options. In the Additional Connection Parameters tab, enter EffectiveUserName, followed by the Universal Principal Name (UPN) of the user who you want to test (see **Figure 11.4**). Typically, UPN is the same as the user's email address. If you're not sure, ask the user to open the command prompt and enter the following command: whoami /upn.

Figure 11.4 Use SSMS to verify if the interactive user will gain access to Analysis Services by passing the EffectiveUserName setting.

5. Click Connect. If you are able to connect successfully, the gateway should be able to delegate the user identity. If you get an error, see the next section.

Mapping user names

If you get an error, more than likely there isn't a trust relationship between the two domains. For example, Adventure Works might have acquired Acme and the Acme employees might still be on the acme.com domain. This will cause an issue when these employees attempt to connect to Analysis Services and the connection will fail. If you follow the steps to test EffectiveUserName and open SQL Server Profiler to monitor connections to Analysis Services, you'll see the error "The following system error occurred: The user name or password is incorrect."

Fortunately, Power BI has a simple solution. When setting up a data source to Analysis Services in the On-premises Data Gateway, the Users tab has a "Map user names" button, which brings you to the "Map user names" window (see **Figure 11.5**).

Figure 11.5 Map users names when users and Analysis Services are on different domains.

You can set up a simple mapping rule to replace some text in the user's email, such as to replace "acme" with "adventureworks" assuming that Analysis Services is installed on somedomain.com domain. Make sure to click the Add button to add the rule to the grid. There is also a convenient feature that allows you to test the rule.

> **TIP** What is the CustomData setting? When USERNAME isn't enough, another option that's less frequently used for dynamic data security is to use the CustomData setting. A client can append a CustomData setting to the connection string in order to pass some custom text, such as CustomData=Partner to indicate that the user requesting the report belongs to a partner organization. Then, the row filter can use the CUSTOMDATA DAX function to obtain the identifier. For example, the expression IF(CUSTOMDATA()="Partner", TRUE, FALSE) allows the user to see all rows when the CustomData setting is set to "Partner".

11.1.3 Using Analysis Services in Power BI Service

Once you register Analysis Services with the On-Premises Data Gateway, users can go to Power BI and connect live to Analysis Services. However, users still might not be able to connect if they don't have rights to access the Analysis Services models. As you can see, there are multiple levels of security so be patient.

Granting user access

By default, users don't have access to Analysis Services models. To grant users access, you need an Analysis Services database role. For the purposes of this exercise, you'll use SQL Server Management Studio (SSMS) to add users to a role. Let's grant user access to the Adventure Works Tabular model:

 TIP As a best practice, the BI developer should use SQL Server Data Tools (SSDT) to define role membership in the Analysis Services project, instead of using SSMS. This way the role membership becomes a part of the project and can be deployed together with the project. But we're using SSMS here for the sake of simplicity.

1. Open SQL Server Management Studio (SSMS) and connect to the Analysis Services instance.
2. In the Object Explorer in the left pane, expand the Analysis Services instance, and then expand the Databases node.
3. Expand the "AdventureWorks Tabular Model SQL 2012" database, and then expand the Roles folder.
4. The Adventure Works SSAS database includes an Analysts role that grants access to the model. For the purposes of this exercise, you'll use this role. Double-click the Analysts role.
5. In the Role Properties window (see **Figure 11.6**), select the Membership tab and add the users.

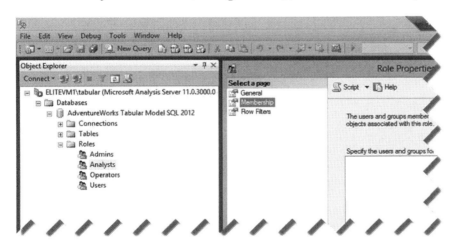

Figure 11.6 You must grant users access to the SSAS model by assigning users to a database role.

Verifying user connectivity

Once you grant the users access to the model, they should be able to run reports in Power BI Service that connect to SSAS. I showed you how they do this back in Chapter 2. From an administrator standpoint, you need to know how to troubleshoot connectivity issues.

Ask the user to go to Power BI Service and connect to SSAS (Get Data ⇨ Databases ⇨ SQL Server Analysis Services). The user will see all the registered gateways (see **Figure 11.7**), even though he might not have rights to access any of the databases. Power BI Service will make the actual connection only when the user selects a gateway and click Connect. At this point, the user will only see the SSAS databases they are allowed to access on that instance.

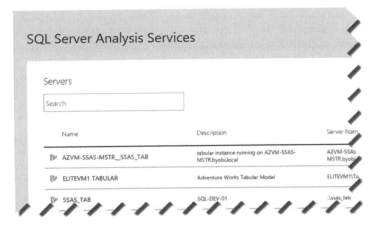

Figure 11.7 Power BI lists all the registered gateways, regardless if the user has permissions to any of the databases hosted on that SSAS instance.

If the connection fails, the best way to verify what identity the user connects under is to use the SQL Server Profiler connected to the SSAS instance. Many events, such as Discover Begin or Query Begin, have a PropertyList element that includes the EffectiveUserName property (see **Figure 11.8**).

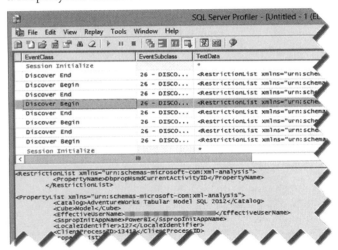

Figure 11.8 The EffectiveUserName property includes the identity of the interactive user.

The EffectiveUserName should match the work email that the user typed to log in to Power BI, such as maya@adventureworks.com. If you need data security, you can set up row filters in your Tabular model to filter the SSAS model data, based on the user identity, just like you can set up roles in Power BI Desktop.

11.1.4 Integrating Reporting Services

If your organization has invested in SQL Server Reporting Services (SSRS), you can integrate SSRS with Power BI. In fact, SQL Server 2016 has three integration options between Reporting Services (SSRS) and Power BI. In this section, I'll review these options and provide some important considerations to help you decide when to use them.

Understanding integration options
Here are the three integration options and the value they add to your users:

- Deploy Power BI Desktop files to the SSRS portal – Currently, SSRS doesn't support online rendering of Power BI reports. This feature is expected in mid-2017 (see the "Power BI reports in SQL Server Reporting Services" blog at bit.ly/ssrs_pbi). Ability to deploy Power BI reports on premises has been one of the most requested features. Currently, SSR 2016 supports uploading Power BI Desktop files but when the end user clicks the report, the Power BI Desktop file is downloaded locally. Consequently, the user needs to have Power BI Desktop installed to view reports. Once Microsoft adds this feature, clicking the file will render the Power BI report online.

- View SSRS mobile reports in Power BI Mobile – Microsoft has extended the Power BI mobile apps to support viewing SSRS mobile reports and KPIs. Mobile reports are a new report type in SSRS 2016. A BI developer creates them using Microsoft SQL Server Mobile Report Publisher. This integration option doesn't require any special setup but your users must be on the corporate network to view mobile reports (I walked you through an example in Chapter 4).

- Pin report items to Power BI dashboards – Your users can pin image-generating report items, such as charts, gauges, maps, and images, to a Power BI dashboard. When the user clicks a dashboard tile that is pinned from a report item, the user is navigated by default to the underlying report (you can change the URL in the tile properties to navigate the user elsewhere). Consequently, the user must be on the corporate network to navigate to the report (the user doesn't have to be on the corporate network to view the tile).

Understanding limitations for pinning report items

Pinning report items requires specific setup steps that are well documented by Microsoft at bit.ly/2g0vHW0. Microsoft had done a good job documenting the limitations but I'd like to add a few comments for you to consider before you enable this feature. First, the source reports must use stored credentials. This is because the underlying mechanism for refreshing pinned items rely on individual subscriptions. SSRS individual subscriptions are scheduled and run unattended with SQL Server Agent. What this limitation means is that when configuring the report data source, you must specify user name and password of a login that has read rights to the data source.

This limitation has been a personal frustration of mine since the early days of SSRS because it's impractical when connecting to data sources that require Windows authentication, such as Analysis Services. For example, it's a common requirement to implement dynamic security in SSAS models to restrict data depending on the user identity. But now you have a predicament because you must store the user credentials and the data security won't work.

 REAL LIFE Reporting Services uses individual subscriptions to refresh the Power BI tiles. Because individual subscriptions are associated with the user who pinned the item, Microsoft could have implemented a mechanism to pass the user identity without requiring the password, similar to how Power BI uses EffectiveUserName.

Continuing the list of limitations, you can't pin tables and matrices, which happen to be the most popular report items. Another thing to watch for is that deleting a dashboard tile with a pinned report item doesn't remove the individual subscriptions. So, if 10 users pin a report item and all users decide that they don't need that tile anymore and delete it from their dashboards, you still have 10 scheduled subscriptions that will continue running on report-specific schedules! Since currently SSRS doesn't give the administrator an easy way to view what individual subscriptions exist, it might not be long before your report server starts experiencing performance issues.

Finally, I don't know why Microsoft prioritized mobile reports to show up in the Power BI native apps. As I explain in my blog "Choosing a reporting tool" at http://prologika.com/choosing-a-reporting-tool, I have reservations about this report type. In my opinion, it would have been much more useful to start with traditional (now referred to as paginated) reports, which is the most popular report type.

11.2 Implementing Real-time BI Solutions

The growing volume of real-time data and the reduced time for decision making are driving companies to implement real-time operational intelligence systems. You might have heard the term "Internet of Things" (IoT), which refers to sensors, devices, and systems that constantly generate data. Unlike the classic descriptive BI architecture (which is all about analyzing the past), real-time data analytics is concerned about what happens now. For example, Adventure Works might be interested in sentiment analysis, based on customer feedback that was shared on popular social networks, such as Twitter. A descriptive approach would require you to import customer data, transform it, and then analyze it.

But what if you're interested in what customers are saying *now*? Your implementation approach might depend on your definition of "now", and what data latency is acceptable. Perhaps, you can run ETL more often and still address your requirements with the classic BI architecture? However, if you need to analyze data as it streams, then you'll need a different approach. Fortunately, Power BI supports streaming API, that makes it easy to push data to Power BI and show the data in a dashboard that changes as the new data streams in. You can meet more advanced requirements with complex event processing (CEP) solutions. Microsoft StreamInsight, which ships with SQL Server, allows you to implement on-premises real-time BI solutions. And Microsoft Azure Stream Analytics is its cloud-based counterpart.

11.2.1 Using the Streaming API

The simplest way to stream data in Power BI is to use its real-time API – a lightweight, simple way to get real-time data onto a Power BI dashboard. It only takes a few lines of code to write a custom app that programmatically access the data as it streams in and then pushes the data to Power BI! For example, you might have a requirement to show call center statistics real-time as calls are handled. The phone system might provide a TCP socket, which your application can connect to in order to get the data stream. Then your app can push some statistics, such as the count of handled calls, to a Power BI dashboard. Let's cover quickly the implementation steps.

 REAL LIFE Before streaming datasets, a developer had to programmatically create a dataset using the Power BI API (discussed in Chapter 12), define a table, and then call the "Add Rows to Table" API to populate the dataset. This approach doesn't require much code and it's still supported but Power BI has subsequently made data streaming even easier with streaming datasets and streaming tiles.

To help you get started with the real-time streaming API, Microsoft has provided a sample C# console app PBIRealTimeStreaming (you can download the source from bit.ly/2fWv3xJ). For your convenience, I included the source code in the \Source\Ch11\Real-time folder. The app pushes the current date and a random integer to the Power BI REST API every second. As a first step to implementing a real-time dashboard, you need to create a streaming dataset.

Implementing a streaming dataset
A streaming dataset is a special dataset that has a push URL attached to it. Your app calls this URL using HTTP POST to push the data. Follow these steps to create a streaming dataset:

1. Log in to Power BI Service. If you want to create the dataset in a specific workspace so it can be shared with other people, navigate to that workspace. Otherwise, click My Workspace to go to the workspace content page.

2. In the upper-right corner, expand the Create menu and then click "Streaming dataset".

New streaming dataset
Choose the source of your data

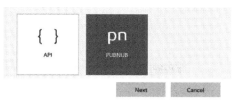

Figure 11.9 Power BI supports API and PubNub as sources for pushing data into a streaming dataset.

3. On the "Choose the source of your data" page (see **Figure 11.9**), you choose where the streaming data will come from. Currently, Power BI supports the streaming API and PubNub as streaming sources (see **Figure 11.9**). Leave API selected and click Next.

 NOTE What's PubNub? PubNub (https://www.pubnub.com) is a cloud service that allows developers to build real-time web, mobile, and IoT apps. With Power BI's PubNub integration, you can connect your PubNub data streams to Power BI in seconds, in order to create low latency visualizations on streaming data.

4. In the dataset properties page (**Figure 11.10**), enter *Real-time API* as the dataset name. Our dataset will have only two fields: *ts* (DateTime data type) and *value* (Text data type).

New streaming dataset

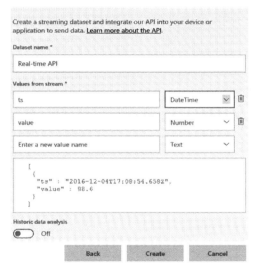

Figure 11.10 Specify the dataset name, fields, and retention policy.

The "Historic data analysis" slide corresponds to the dataset's defaultRetentionPolicy setting (discussed in Chapter 12). To explain it quickly, the dataset will store up to 200,000 rows. After that, as new rows come in, old rows will be removed from the dataset. If you turn the slider on, the dataset won't remove old rows and it will grow until its maximum allowed size of 1 GB.

5. Click Create. The Real-time API dataset is added to the workspace.

The next page (API info on Real-time API) shows the Push URL and different ways to load the dataset (Raw, Curl, and PowerShell). For example, your app can submit the following raw payload to insert the value 98.6 for a specific date in the dataset.

[{"ts" :"2016-12-04T18:17:01.020Z", "value" :98.6}]

6. Copy the Push URL and click Done.

7. Locate the dataset in the Datasets tab and notice that its Streaming property shows Yes.

Implementing a real-time tile
Now that we have a place to store the streamed data, let's visualize it in a real dashboard.

1. Back to the workspace content page, expand the Create menu again and create a new dashboard. Type in *Real-time API* as the dashboard name, and then click Create.

2. In the Real-time API dashboard, click "+Add Tile" in the upper-right corner.

3. In the Add Tile page, select the "Real-time Data" source.

4. In the "Choose a streaming dataset" page, select the Real-time API dataset. Notice if you don't have a streaming dataset, you can use this page to create one by clicking the "+Add streaming dataset" button.

5. In the "Visualization design" page (**Figure 11.11**), leave the Card visualization preselected. You can also show data as a chart or gauge. Each visualization type requires different fields. For example, if you want to show the streaming data as a line chart, you can bind the timestamp (ts) field to the Axis area and the value field to the Values area. By contrast, the Card visualization can show a single field. Expand the Fields dropdown and select the value field.

6. Click the Format tab (the one with the pencil icon). Notice that you can specify basic format settings, including display units and the number of the decimal places. Click Next.

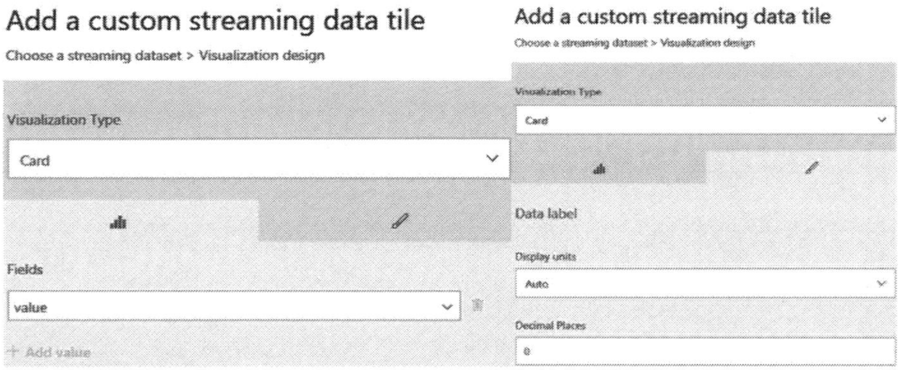

Figure 11.11 When configuring the real-time tile, specify the visualization type and fields to show.

7. In the Tile Details page, enter *Real-time API* as the tile name. Notice that you can specify additional tile properties, such as a URL to navigate the user to a report when then click the tile. Click Apply to add the tile to the dashboard.

Streaming data
The last piece left is to stream the actual data. This is where the PBIRealTimeStreaming sample comes in.

1. Open the PBIRealTimeStreaming.sln solution file in Visual Studio (if you don't have Visual Studio, install the free Visual Studio Community Edition from https://www.visualstudio.com/vs/community.

2. In the Solution Explorer, double-click the Program.cs file.

3. Locate the realTimePushURL variable and paste the push URL of the Real-time API dataset.

4. Press Ctrl+F5 to run the application. Switch to Power BI Service and notice that the Real-time API tile updates every second with new data.

Behind the scenes, the sample uses the .NET WebRequest class to create a new POST request for each new row. The sample then sends the request to the dataset Push URL. You now have a real-time dashboard!

11.2.2 Using Azure Stream Analytics

As you've seen, it's easy to meet basic real-time BI needs with the Power BI streaming API. But, what if your solution needs to ingest thousands of events per seconds and scale on demand. Or, what if you need to aggregate data as it streams in, such as to calculate the average count of calls for a given duration. Such requirements call for a complex event processing (CEP) solution, which you can implement with Azure Stream Analytics.

Understanding Microsoft Azure Stream Analytics

Traditionally, implementing a complex event processing (CEP) solution has been difficult because...well, it's complex, and it requires a lot of custom code. Microsoft sought to change this by introducing Azure Stream Analytics as a fully managed stream-processing service in the cloud. Stream Analytics provides low latency and real-time processing of millions of events per second in a highly resilient service (see its architecture in **Figure 11.12**).

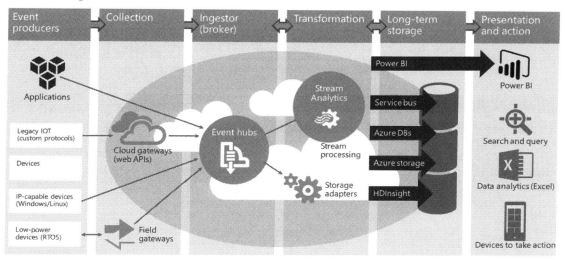

Figure 11.12   Stream Analytics is a cloud-based service and it's capable of processing millions of events per second.

Common real-time BI scenarios that will benefit from Stream Analytics include fraud detection, identity protection, real-time financial portfolio analysis, click-stream analysis, and energy smart grid utilization. Stream Analytics integrates with Azure Event Hubs, which is a highly scalable service for ingesting data streams. It enables the collection of event streams at high throughput from a diverse set of devices and services.

For example, Event Hubs is capable of processing millions of events per second via HTTP(S) or Advanced Message Queuing Protocol (AMQP) protocols. Once data is brought into Event Hubs, you can then use Stream Analytics to apply a standing SQL-like query for analyzing the data as it streams through, such as to detect anomalies or outliers. The query results can also be saved into long-term storage destinations, such as Azure SQL Database, HDInsight, or Azure Storage, and then you can analyze that data. Similar to the Power BI streaming API, Stream Analytics can output query results directly to Power BI streaming datasets, which in turn can update dashboard streaming tiles! This allows you to implement a real-time dashboard that updates itself constantly when Stream Analytics sends new results.

Now that you've learned about real-time BI, let me walk you through a sample solution that demonstrates how Azure Stream Analytics and Power BI can help you implement CEP solutions. Suppose that Adventure Works is interested in analyzing customer sentiment from messages that are posted on Twitter. This is immediate feedback from its customer base, which can help the company improve its products and services. And so Adventure Works wants to monitor the average customer sentiment about specific topics in real time. **Figure 11.13** shows you the process flow diagram.

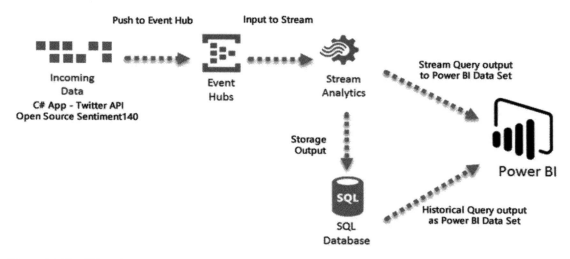

Figure 11.13   This solution demonstrates how you can integrate Stream Analytics with Power BI.

Instead of building the entire solution from scratch, I decided to use the Real-time Twitter sentiment analysis sample by Microsoft. You can download the code from GitHub (https://github.com/Azure/azure-stream-analytics/tree/master/DataGenerators/TwitterClient) and read the documentation from https://github.com/Azure/azure-content/blob/master/articles/stream-analytics/stream-analytics-twitter-sentiment-analysis-trends.md. You can also read the documentation online at https://azure.microsoft.com/en-us/documentation/articles/stream-analytics-twitter-sentiment-analysis-trends.

 NOTE   This sample demonstrates how remarkably simple it is to implement CEP cloud solutions with Stream Analytics. You only need to write custom code to send events to Events Hub. By contrast, a similar StreamInsight-based application would require much more coding on your part, as the Big Data Twitter Demo (http://twitterbigdata.codeplex.com) demonstrates. That's because you'd need to write the plumbing code for observers, adapters, sinks, and more.

Understanding the client application

Designed as a C# console application, the client app uses the Twitter APIs to filter tweets for specific keywords that you specify in the app.config file. To personalize the demo for our fictitious bike manufacturer, (Adventure Works), I used the keywords "Bike" and "Adventure". In the same file, you must specify the Twitter OAuth settings that you obtain when you register a custom application with Twitter. For more information about registering an application with Twitter and about obtaining the security settings, read the "Tokens from dev.twitter.com" topic at https://dev.twitter.com/oauth/overview/application-owner-access-tokens.

Note that the client app (as coded by Microsoft) doesn't have any error handling. If you don't configure it correctly, it won't show any output and won't give you any indication what's wrong. To avoid this and to get the actual error, I recommend that you re-throw errors in every catch block in the EventHubObserver.cs file.

```
catch (Exception ex)
{
    throw ex;
}
```

The application integrates with an open source tool (Sentiment140) to assign a sentiment value to each tweet (0: negative, 2: neutral, 4: positive). Then the tweet events are sent to the Azure Event Hubs. Therefore, to test the application successfully, you must first set up an event hub and configure Stream Analytics. If all is well, the application shows the stream of tweets in the console window as they're sent to the event hub.

Configuring Stream Analytics

The documentation that accompanies the sample provides step-by-step instructions to configure the Azure part of the solution. You can perform the steps using the old Azure portal (https://manage.windowsazure.com) or the new Azure portal (http://portal.azure.com). Instead of reiterating the steps, I'll just emphasize a few points that might not be immediately clear:

1. Before setting up a new Stream Analytics job, you must create an event hub that ingests that data stream.

2. After you create the hub, you need to copy the connection information from the hub registration page and paste it in the EventHubConnectionString setting in the client application app.config file. This is how the client application connects to the event hub.

3. When you set up the Stream Analytics job, you can use sample data to test the standing query. You must have run the client application before this step so that the event hub has some data in it. In addition, make sure that the date range you specify for sampling actually returns tweet events.

4. This is the standing query that I used for the Power BI dashboard:

```
SELECT System.Timestamp as Time, Topic, COUNT(*), AVG(SentimentScore), MIN(SentimentScore),
Max(SentimentScore), STDEV(SentimentScore)
FROM TwitterStream TIMESTAMP BY CreatedAt
GROUP BY TUMBLINGWINDOW(s, 5), Topic
```

This query divides the time in intervals of five seconds. A tumbling window is one of the windows types that's supported by both Stream Analytics and SQL Server StreamInsight (read about windowing at https://msdn.microsoft.com/en-us/library/azure/dn835055.aspx). Within each interval, the query groups the incoming events by topic and calculates the event count, minimum, maximum, average sentiment score, and the standard deviation. Because stream analytics queries are described in a SQL-like grammar, you can leverage your SQL query skills.

 NOTE Unlike SQL SELECT queries, which execute once, Stream Analytics queries are standing. To understanding this, imagine that the stream of events passes through the query. As long as the Stream Analytics job is active, the query is active and it's always working. In this case, the query divides the stream in five-second intervals and calculates the aggregates on the fly.

Outputting data to Power BI

A Stream Analytics job can have multiple outputs, such as to save the query results to a durable storage for offline analysis and to display them on a real-time dashboard. **Figure 11.14** shows that I selected Power BI as an output (other input types include SQL Database, Blob Storage, DocumentDB, Azure Data Lake, and more). Follow these steps to configure Stream Analytics to send the output to Power BI.

1. In the "Add an output to your job" step, select Power BI. Click the Authorize button to sign in to Power BI.

2. In "Output details" (see again **Figure 11.14**), enter the name of the Power BI dataset and table names. You can send results from different queries to separate tables within the same dataset. If the table with the same name exists, it'll be overwritten.

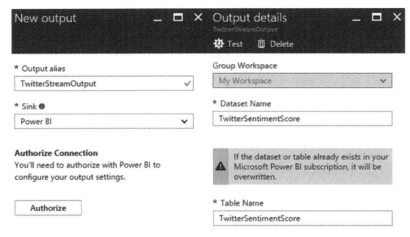

Figure 11.14   Specify Power BI as a sink and then the names of the dataset and table where the results will be loaded.

Creating a real-time dashboard

Now that all the setup steps are behind us, we're ready to have fun with the data:

1. Run the Stream Analytics job. It might take a while for the job to initiate, so monitor its progress on the Stream Analytics dashboard page.

2. Once the job is started, it'll send the query results to Power BI, assuming there are incoming events that match the query criteria. Power BI will create a dataset with the name you specified.

> **NOTE**   Outputting the results from Azure Stream Analytics to a streaming dataset is currently in preview. Once this goes to production, you should be able to follow the steps to create a streaming tile from the streaming dataset. This will allow you to implement the two most common real-time requirements: 1) showing the latest value and 2) showing values on a line chart over a time window. Currently, Azure Stream Analytics creates a regular dataset that you have to explore to create a report and then a real-time dashboard.

3. Now you log in to Power BI Service and explore the dataset.

4. To show the data in real time, you need to create a dashboard by pinning the report visualization. The dashboard tile in **Figure 11.15** is based on a report visualization that uses a Combo Chart. It shows the count of events as columns and the average sentiment score as a line. Time is measured on the shared axis.

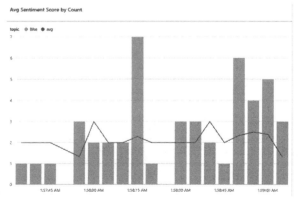

Figure 11.15   Power BI updates a real-time dashboard as Stream Analytics streams the events.

5. Watch the dashboard update itself as new data is coming in, and you gain real-time insights from your CEP solution!

11.3 Implementing Predictive Solutions

Predictive analytics (based on data mining and machine learning algorithms) is an increasingly popular requirement. It also happens to be one of the least understood because it's usually confused with slicing and dicing data. However, predictive analytics is about discovering patterns that aren't easily discernible. These hidden patterns can't be derived from traditional data exploration, because data relationships might be too complex or because there's too much data for a human to analyze.

Typical data mining tasks include forecasting, customer profiling, and basket analysis. Data mining can answer questions, such as, "What are the forecasted sales numbers for the next few months?", "What other products is a customer likely to buy along with the product he or she already chose?", and "What type of customer (described in terms of gender, age group, income, and so on) is likely to buy a given product?"

11.3.1 Understanding Azure Machine Learning

Predictive analytics isn't new to Microsoft. Microsoft extended Analysis Services with data mining back in SQL Server 2000. Besides allowing BI pros to create data mining models with Analysis Services, Microsoft also introduced the Excel Data Mining add-in to let business users perform data mining tasks in Excel.

 NOTE With the focus shifting to Azure ML and R, we probably won't see future investments from Microsoft in SSAS Data Mining (and the Excel data mining add-in for that matter) which is currently limited to nine algorithms.

SQL Server 2016 added R Services that allow you to integrate the power of R with your T-SQL code. You've already seen that Power BI includes Quick Insights, time-series forecasting, and clustering as built-in predictive features.

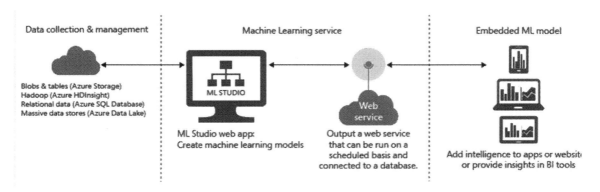

Figure 11.16 The diagram demonstrates a common flow to implement predictive models with AzureML.

Introducing Azure Machine Learning
In 2014, Microsoft unveiled a cloud-based service for predictive analytics called Azure Machine Learning or AzureML, which also originated from Microsoft Research. In a nutshell, Azure Machine Learning makes it easy for data scientists to quickly create and deploy predictive models. The Azure ML value proposition includes the following appealing features:

■ It provides an easy-to-use, comprehensive, and scalable platform without requiring hardware or software investments.

- It supports workflows for transforming and moving data. For example, AzureML supports custom code, such as R or Python code, to transform columns. Furthermore, it allows you to chain tasks, such as to load data, create a model, and then save the predictive results.

- It allows you to easily expose predictive models as REST web services, so that you can incorporate predictive features in custom applications. **Figure 11.16** shows a typical AzureML implementation.

Understanding workflows

Because it's a cloud service, AzureML can obtain the input data directly from other cloud services, such as Azure tables, Azure SQL Database, or Azure HDInsight. Alternatively, you can export on-premises data as a file and upload the dataset to AzureML.

Then you use ML Studio to build a workflow for creating and training a predictive model. ML Studio is a browser-based tool that allows you to drag, drop, and connect the building blocks of your solution. You can choose from a large library of Machine Learning algorithms to jump-start your predictive models! You can also extend the workflow with your own custom R and Python scripts.

Similar to Stream Analytics and Power BI, AzureML is an integral component of the Cortana Analytics Suite, although you can also use it as a standalone service. The Cortana Analytics Gallery (http://gallery.cortanaanalytics.com) is a community-driven site for discovering and sharing predictive solutions. It features many ready-to-go predictive models that have been contributed by Microsoft and the analytics community. You can learn more about Azure Machine Learning at its official site (https://azure.microsoft.com/en-us/services/machine-learning).

11.3.2 Creating Predictive Models

Next, I'll walk you through the steps to implement an AzureML predictive model for a familiar scenario. Our bike manufacturer, Adventure Works, is planning a marketing campaign. The marketing department approaches you to help them target a subset of potential customers who are the most likely to purchase a bike. You need to create a predictive model that predicts the purchase probability, based on past history.

Understanding the historical dataset

To start, you'd need to obtain an order history dataset that you'd use to train the model:

1. In SQL Server Management Studio (SSMS), connect to the AdventureWorksDW2012 database and execute the following query:

```
SELECT
  Gender,YearlyIncome,TotalChildren,NumberChildrenAtHome,
  EnglishEducation,EnglishOccupation,HouseOwnerFlag,
  NumberCarsOwned,CommuteDistance,Region,Age,BikeBuyer
FROM [dbo].[vTargetMail]
```

This query returns a subset of columns from the vTargetMail view that Microsoft uses to demonstrate the Analysis Services data mining features. The last column, BikeBuyer, is a flag that indicates if the customer has purchased a bike. The model will use the rest of the columns as an input to determine the most important criteria that influences a customer to purchase a bike.

 NOTE   The Adventure Works Analysis Services Multidimensional cube includes a Targeted Mailing data mining structure, which uses this dataset. The mining models in the Targeted Mailing structure demonstrate how the same scenario can be addressed with an on-premises Analysis Services solution.

2. Export the results to a CSV file. For your convenience, I included a Bike Buyers.csv file in the \source\ch11\AzureML folder.

Creating a predictive model

Next, you'll use AzureML to create a predictive model, using the Bike Buyers.csv file as an input:

1. Go to https://studio.azureml.net and sign in. If you don't have an Azure subscription, you can start a trial subscription, or just use the free version!

2. Once you are in Microsoft Azure Machine Learning (Azure ML) Studio, click New on the bottom of the screen, and then create a dataset by uploading the Bike Buyers.csv file. Name the dataset *Bike Buyers*.

3. Click the New button again and create a new experiment. An Azure ML experiment represents the workflow to create and train a predictive model (see **Figure 11.17**).

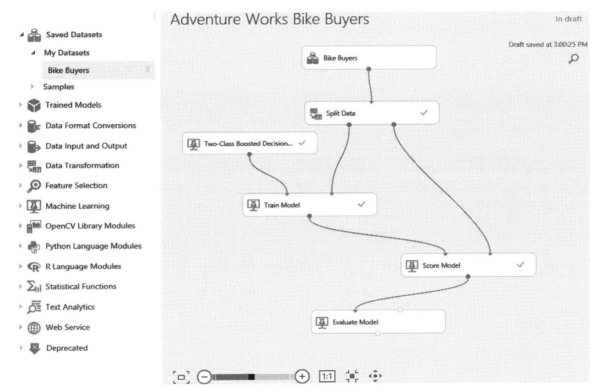

Figure 11.17   The Adventure Works Bike Buyer predictive model.

4. From the Saved Datasets section in the navigation bar, drag and drop the Bike Buyers dataset.

5. Using the search box, search for each of the workflow nodes shown in **Figure 11.17** by typing its name, and then drop them on the workflow. Join them as shown in **Figure 11.17**. For example, to find the Split Data task, type "Split" in the search box. From the search results, drag the Split Data task and drop it onto the workflow. Then connect the Bike Buyer dataset to the Split Data task.

6. The workhorse of the model is the Two-Class Boosted Decision Tree algorithm, which generates the predictive results. Click the Split Data transformation and configure its "Fraction of rows in the first output dataset" property for a 0.8 split. That's because you'll use 80% of the input dataset to train the model and the remaining 20% to evaluate the model accuracy.

Setting up a web service

A great AzureML feature is that it can easily expose an experiment as a REST web service. The web service allows client applications to integrate with AzureML and use the model for scoring. Setting up a web service is remarkably easy.

1. Click the Run button to run the experiment.

2. (Optional) Right-click the output (the small circle at the bottom) of the Evaluate Model task, and then click Visualize to analyze the model accuracy. For example, the Lift graph shows the gain of the model, compared to just targeting all the customers without using a predictive model.

3. At the bottom of the screen, click "Set up Web Service". AzureML creates a new experiment because it needs to remove the unnecessary tasks from the web service, such as the task to train the model. **Figure 11.18** shows the workflow of the predictive experiment after AzureML sets up the web service.

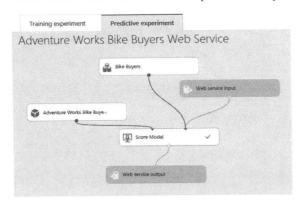

Figure 11.18   The predictive experiment is optimized for scoring.

4. Run the predictive experiment.

5. At the bottom of the screen, click "Deploy Web Service" to create the REST API endpoint.

6. In the navigation bar, click Web Services, and then click the new web service that you just created.

7. AzureML opens the web service page (see **Figure 11.19**).

adventure works bike buyers web service

DASHBOARD   CONFIGURATION

General

Published experiment
View snapshot   View latest

Description
No description provided for this web service.

API key

Default Endpoint

API HELP PAGE	TEST
REQUEST/RESPONSE	Test
BATCH EXECUTION	

Figure 11.19   The web service page allows you to obtain the API key and test the web service.

Your application will use the API key to authenticate against ML. Think of it as a password. Copy the API key because you'll need it later. The Request/Response link is for calling the web service in a singleton manner (one row at a time). The Batch Execution link is for scoring multiple rows in one batch.

TIP The Microsoft Azure ML team has provided an Excel Azure Machine Learning Add-in (bit.ly/2g0oAgc) that allows you to integrate the Azure ML predictive web service with Excel. The add-in supports scoring multiple rows from an Excel range by calling the Azure ML batch API.

8. Click the Request/Response link to see the web service developer documentation and to test the web service. The documentation page includes the web service endpoint, which should look like this following example (I excluded the sensitive information):

https://ussouthcentral.services.azureml.net/workspaces/<...>/execute?api-version=2.0&details=true

The page also shows a simple POST request and response described in JSON (see **Figure 11.20**).

Sample Request


```
{
  "Inputs": {
    "input1": {
      "ColumnNames": [
        "Gender",
        "YearlyIncome",
        "TotalChildren",
        "NumberChildrenAtHome",
        "EnglishEducation",
        "EnglishOccupation",
        "HouseOwnerFlag",
        "NumberCarsOwned",
        "CommuteDistance",
        "Region",
        "Age",
        "BikeBuyer"
      ],
      "Values": [
        [
```


Sample Response


```
{
  "Results": {
    "output1": {
      "type": "DataTable",
      "value": {
        "ColumnNames": [
          "Gender",
          "YearlyIncome",
          "TotalChildren",
          "NumberChildrenAtHome",
          "EnglishEducation",
          "EnglishOccupation",
          "HouseOwnerFlag",
          "NumberCarsOwned",
          "CommuteDistance",
          "Region",
          "Age",
          "BikeBuyer",
          "Scored Labels"
```


Figure 11.20 This figure shows a simple request and response from the Adventure Works Bike Buyers predictive web service.

Operationalizing the predictive service

While creating a web service is easy, Microsoft has left some ground for improvement when it comes to operationalizing it. For example, you might be interested in automating your predictive solution, such as scheduling your experiment for retraining, but Azure ML doesn't have a scheduling feature. You need to integrate with the experiment's web service either programmatically or by using Azure Data Factory.

Continuing on the list of limitations, executing the batch endpoint requires either custom code (see the Microsoft Azure Machine Learning Samples on CodePlex at https://mamls.codeplex.com) or using an Azure Data Factory pipeline. Either of these scenarios would require an intervention from your fellow programmer or Azure Data Factory expert. While we're waiting for Microsoft to add these features, learn how to implement an Azure Data Factory pipeline to automate Azure ML in my blog "AzureML – Current State of Affairs" at http://prologika.com/azureml-current-state-of-affairs.

11.3.3 Integrating Machine Learning with Power BI

Currently, Power BI doesn't include a connector to connect directly to Azure Machine Learning. This leaves you with two integration options:

- Instead of publishing to a web service, save the predictive results to Azure Storage, such as to an Azure SQL Database. Then use Power BI Service's Get Data to visualize the predictive results.

- Publish the predictive model as a web service, and then use Power BI Desktop or Power Query to call the web service.

The second option allows you to implement flexible integration scenarios, such as to call the web service for each customer from a dataset you imported in Power BI Desktop. Moreover, it demonstrates some of the advanced capabilities of Power BI Desktop queries and Power Query. This is the integration option I'll demonstrate next.

EMailAddress	Gende	YearlyIncoi	TotalChildr	NumberChi	EnglishEducation	EnglishOccupation	HouseOwn	NumberC	CommuteDistance	Region	Age	BikeBuyer
jon24@adventur	M	90000	2	0	Bachelors	Professional	1	0	1-2 Miles	Pacific	49	0
eugene10@adve	M	60000	3	3	Bachelors	Professional	0	1	0-1 Miles	Pacific	50	0
ruben35@adveni	M	60000	3	3	Bachelors	Professional	1	1	2-5 Miles	Pacific	50	0
christy12@adver	F	70000	0	0	Bachelors	Professional	0	1	5-10 Miles	Pacific	47	0
elizabeth5@advi	F	80000	5	5	Bachelors	Professional	1	4	1-2 Miles	Pacific	47	0
julio1@adventur	M	70000	0	0	Bachelors	Professional	1	1	5-10 Miles	Pacific	50	0
janet9@adventu	F	70000	0	0	Bachelors	Professional	1	1	5-10 Miles	Pacific	49	0
marco14@adven	M	60000	3	3	Bachelors	Professional	1	2	0-1 Miles	Pacific	51	0
rob4@adventure	F	60000	4	4	Bachelors	Professional	1	3	10+ Miles	Pacific	51	0
shannon38@advi	M	70000	0	0	Bachelors	Professional	0	1	5-10 Miles	Pacific	51	0
jacquelyn20@ad	F	70000	0	0	Bachelors	Professional	0	1	5-10 Miles	Pacific	51	0
curtis9@adventu	M	60000	4	4	Bachelors	Professional	1	4	10+ Miles	Pacific	51	0
lauren41@adven	F	100000	2	0	Bachelors	Management	1	2	1-2 Miles	North Ame	47	0
ian47@adventuri	M	100000	2	0	Bachelors	Management	1	3	0-1 Miles	North Ame	47	0
sydney23@adver	F	100000	3	0	Bachelors	Management	0	3	1-2 Miles	North Ame	47	0
chloe23@advent	F	30000	0	0	Partial College	Skilled Manual	0	1	5-10 Miles	North Ame	36	0
wyatt32@advent	M	30000	0	0	Partial College	Skilled Manual	1	1	5-10 Miles	North Ame	36	0
shannon1@adve	F	20000	4	0	High School	Skilled Manual	1	2	5-10 Miles	Pacific	71	0
clarence32@advi	M	30000	2	0	Partial College	Clerical	1	2	5-10 Miles	Pacific	71	0
luke18@adventu	M	40000	0	0	High School	Skilled Manual	0	2	5-10 Miles	Europe	37	0

Figure 11.21 The New Customers Excel file has a list of customers that need to be scored.

Understanding the input dataset

Let's get back to our Adventure Works scenario. Now that the predictive web service is ready, you can use it to predict the probability of new customers who could purchase a bike, provided that you have the customer demographics details. The marketing department has given you an Excel file with potential customers, which they might have downloaded from the company's CRM system.

1. In Excel, open the New Customers.xlsx file, which includes 20 new customers (see **Figure 11.21**).
2. Note that the last column BikeBuyer is always zero. That's because at this point you don't know if the customer could be a potential bike buyer. That's what the predictive web service is for.

The predictive web service will calculate the probability for each customer to purchase a bike. This requires calling the web service for each row in the input dataset by sending a predictive query (a data mining query that predicts a single case is called a singleton query). To see the final solution, open the Predict Buyers.pbix file in Power BI Desktop.

Creating a query function

You already know from Chapter 7 how to use query functions. Similar to other programming languages, a query function encapsulates common logic so that it can be called repeatedly. Next, you'll create a query function that will invoke the Adventure Works predictive web service:

1. In Power BI Desktop, click Edit Queries to open the Query Editor.
2. In Query Editor, expand the New Source button and click Blank Query. Then in the ribbon's View tab, click Advanced Editor.
3. Copy the function code from the \source\ch11\real-time\fnPredictBuyer.txt file and paste in the query. The query function code follows:

```
1.   let
2.   PredictBikeBuyer = (Gender, YearlyIncome, TotalChildren, NumberChildrenAtHome, EnglishEducation, EnglishOccupation,
     HouseOwnerFlag, NumberCarsOwned, CommuteDistance, Region, Age, BikeBuyer) =>
```

```
3.   let
4.   //replace service Uri and serviceKey with your own settings
5.   serviceUri="https://ussouthcentral.services.azureml.net/workspaces/.../execute?api-version=2.0&details=true",
6.   serviceKey="<your service key>"
7.   RequestBody = "
8.   {
9.   ""Inputs"": {
10.  ""input1"": {
11.  ""ColumnNames"": [
12.  ""Gender"", ""YearlyIncome"", ""TotalChildren"", ""NumberChildrenAtHome"", ""EnglishEducation"", ""EnglishOccupation"",
13.  ""HouseOwnerFlag"", ""NumberCarsOwned"", ""CommuteDistance"", ""Region"", ""Age"", ""BikeBuyer""
14.  ],
15.  ""Values"": [
16.  [
17.  """"&Gender&"""", """"&Text.From(YearlyIncome)&"""", """"&Text.From(TotalChildren)&"""",
     """"&Text.From(NumberChildrenAtHome)&"""", """"&EnglishEducation&"""", """"&EnglishOccupation&"""",
     """"&Text.From(HouseOwnerFlag)&"""", """"&Text.From(NumberCarsOwned)&"""", """"&Text.From(CommuteDistance)&"""",
18.  """"&Region&"""", """"&Text.From(Age)&"""", """"&Text.From(BikeBuyer)&""""
19.  ]]}},
20.  ""GlobalParameters"": {}
21.  }
22.  ",
23.  Source=Web.Contents(serviceUri,
24.  [Content=Text.ToBinary(RequestBody),
25.  Headers=[Authorization="Bearer "&serviceKey,#"Content-Type"="application/json; charset=utf-8"]]),
26.  #"Response" = Json.Document(Source),
27.  #"Results" = Record.ToTable(#"Response")
28.  in
29.  #"Results"
30.  in
31.  PredictBikeBuyer
```

The code in line 2 defines a PredictBikeBuyer function with 12 arguments that correspond to the columns in the input dataset. Remember to update lines 5 and 6 with your web service URI and service key. Then the code creates a request payload described in JSON, as per the web service specification (see **Figure 11.20** again). Notice that the code obtains the actual values from the function arguments. Lines 23-25 invoke the web service. Line 26 reads the response, which is also described in JSON. Line 27 converts the response to a table.

4. Rename the query to *fnPredictBuyer* and save it.

Creating a query

Now that you have the query function, let's create a query that will load the input dataset from the New Customers Excel file, and then call the function for each customer:

1. In Query Editor, expand New Source again and then click Excel.

2. Navigate to New Customers.xlsx and load Table1. Table1 is the Excel table that has the new customers.

3. Rename the query to *PredictedBuyers*.

4. Add a custom column called PredictedScore, as shown in **Figure 11.22**. This column calls the fnPredict-Buyer function and passes the customer demographic details from each row in the input dataset.

Add Custom Column

New column name

PredictedScore

Custom column formula:

```
= fnPredictBuyer([Gender],[YearlyIncome],[TotalChildren],
[NumberChildrenAtHome],[EnglishEducation],[EnglishOccupation],
[HouseOwnerFlag],[NumberCarsOwned],[CommuteDistance],[Region],
[Age],[BikeBuyer])
```

Available columns:

EMailAddress
Gender
YearlyIncome
TotalChildren
NumberChildrenAtHome
EnglishEducation
EnglishOccupation

<< Insert

Learn about Power BI Desktop formulas

✓ No syntax errors have been detected.

OK   Cancel

Figure 11.22 The PredictedScore custom column calls the fnPredictBuyer function.

5. The results of the custom column will be a table, which includes other nested tables, as per the JSON response specification (see **Figure 11.23**). You need to click the "expand" button four times until you see "List" showing in the PredictedScore column.

Region	Age	BikeBuyer	PredictedScore
Pacific	49	0	Table
Pacific	50	0	Table
Pacific	50	0	Table
Pacific	47	0	Table
Pacific	47	0	Table
Pacific	50	0	Table

Figure 11.23 Expand the PredictedScore column four times until you get to the list of values.

6. Once you get to the list, add another custom column to get the last value of the list. Because you have 12 input columns, the last value will be always at position 13. This value represents the score:

[PredictedScore.Value.output1.value.Values]{0}{13}

7. The final steps are to rename the column, change the column type to Decimal Number, and remove any errors.

8. Create a table report that shows the customer e-mail and the probability for each customer to purchase a bike, as shown in **Figure 11.24**.

EMailAddress	PredictedScore
jon24@adventure-works.com	0.97
julio1@adventure-works.com	0.94
janet9@adventure-works.com	0.94
clarence32@adventure-works.com	0.88
lauren41@adventure-works.com	0.71
christy12@adventure-works.com	0.48
ian47@adventure-works.com	0.40
jacquelyn20@adventure-works.com	0.32

Figure 11.24 A table report that shows the predicted results.

11.4 Summary

As a BI pro, you can meet more demanding business requirements and implement versatile solutions with Power BI and Azure cloud services. You can preserve the investments you've made in classic BI by integrating Power BI with Analysis Services. This allows you to implement a hybrid scenario, where data remains on premises, and Power BI reports and dashboards connect live to Analysis Services.

If you need to implement real-time solutions that analyze data streams, you'll save significant effort by using the Power BI Streaming API. And, when requirements call for complex event processing (CEP) solutions, Azure Stream Analytics Service will make your task much easier. It's capable of ingesting millions of events per second. You can create a standing query to analyze the data stream and send the results to a real-time Power BI dashboard.

Your Power BI solutions can do more than descriptive analytics. If you need to predict future outcomes, you can implement on-premises or cloud-based predictive models. Azure Machine Learning lets business users and professionals build experiments in the cloud. You can save the predictive results to Azure, or you can publish the experiment as a predictive REST web service. Then Power BI Desktop and Power Query can call the predictive web service so that you can create "smart" reports and dashboards that transcend traditional data slicing and dicing!

Thanks to its open architecture, Power BI supports other integration scenarios that application developers will find very appealing, as you'll see in the next part of this book.

PART

Power BI for Developers

O ne of Power BI's most prominent strengths is its open APIs, which will be very appealing to developers. When Microsoft architected the Power BI APIs, they decided to embrace popular industry standards and formats, such as REST, JSON, and OAuth2. This allows any application on any platform to integrate with the Power BI APIs. This part of the book shows developers how they can extend Power BI and implement custom solutions that integrate with Power BI.

I'll start by laying out the necessary programming fundamentals for programming with Power BI. Once I introduce you to the REST APIs, I'll walk you through the Power BI developer site, which is a great resource to learn and test the APIs. I'll explain how Power BI security works. Then I'll walk you through a sample application that uses the REST APIs to programmatically retrieve Power BI content and to load datasets with application data.

Chances are that your organization is looking for ways to embed insightful BI content on internal and external applications. Thanks to the embedded APIs, Power BI supports this scenario, and I'll walk you through the implementation details of embedding dashboards and reports. Then you'll see how the Power BI Embedded cloud service makes report embedding even easier.

As you've likely seen, Power BI has an open visualization framework. Web developers can implement custom visuals and publish them to the Power BI visuals gallery. If you're a web developer, you'll see how you can leverage your experience with popular JavaScript-visualization frameworks, such as D3, WebGL, Canvas, or SVG, to create custom visuals that meet specific presentation requirements, and if you wish, you can contribute your custom visualizations to the community!

Chapter 12

Programming Fundamentals

Developers can build innovative solutions around Power BI. In the previous chapter, I've showed examples of descriptive, predictive, and real-time BI solutions that use existing Microsoft products and services. Sometimes, however, developers are tasked to extend custom applications with data analytics features, such as to implement real-time dashboards for operational analytics. Because of the open Power BI APIs, you can integrate any modern application on any platform with Power BI!

If you're new to Power BI development, this chapter is for you. I'll start by introducing you to the Power BI REST APIs. To jump start your programming journey, you'll see how to use the Power BI Developer Center to learn and test the APIs. You'll find how to register your custom applications so that they can access the Power BI APIs. I'll demystify one of the most complex programming topics surrounding Power BI programming: OAuth authentication. Finally, I'll walk you through a sample application that demonstrates how a custom application can integrate with the Power BI APIs.

12.1 Understanding Power BI APIs

When Microsoft worked on the Power BI APIs, they adopted the following design principles:

- Embrace industry standards – Instead of implementing proprietary interfaces, the team looked at other popular cloud and social platforms, and decided to adopt already popular open standards, such as Representational State Transfer (REST) programming (https://en.wikipedia.org/wiki/Representational_state_transfer), OAuth authorization (https://en.wikipedia.org/wiki/OAuth), and JavaScript Object Notation (JSON) for describing object schemas and data (https://en.wikipedia.org/wiki/JSON).

- Make it cross platform – Because of the decision to use open standards, the Power BI APIs are cross platform. Any modern native or web application on any platform can integrate with Power BI.

- Make it consistent – If you have experience with the above-mentioned industry specifications, you can seamlessly transfer your knowledge to Power BI programming. Consistency also applies within Power BI so that the APIs reflect the same objects as the ones the user interacts with in the Power BI portal.

- Easy to get started – Nobody wants to read tons of documentation before writing a single line of code. To help you get up to speed, the Power BI team created a Power BI Developer Center site where you can try the APIs as you read about them!

12.1.1 Understanding Object Definitions

As I've just mentioned, one of the design goals was consistency within Power BI. To understand this better, let's revisit the three main Power BI objects: *datasets*, *reports*, and *dashboards*. Please refer to the diagram shown in **Figure 12.1**, which shows their relationships.

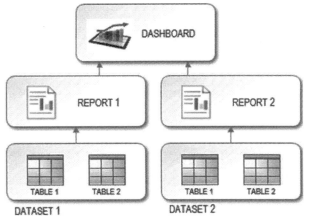

Figure 12.1 The main Power BI objects are datasets, reports, and dashboards.

Understanding dataset definitions

As you might know by now, the dataset object is the gateway to Power BI. A dataset connects to the data, and the other two main objects (reports and dashboards) get data from datasets. Specifically, a report can reference a single dataset. A dashboard can include visualizations from multiple reports, and thus display data from multiple datasets. From a developer standpoint, the dataset object has a simple JSON definition:

```
{
   "id": "<guid>",
   "name": "<dataset name>"
}
```

As you can see, a dataset has a unique identifier of a GUID data type and a name. The JSON name property returns the dataset name you see in the Power BI portal's navigation bar.

Understanding table definitions

In the previous chapter, I briefly touched on the fact that a dataset is just a logical container. The actual data is exposed as tables. When you import the data, a table stores the schema and the cached data. When you use DirectQuery, the table has just the schema. A dataset could have multiple tables, such as when you use Get Data in Power BI Service or Power BI Desktop to import multiple Excel sheets. Each table has a collection of columns. Here's what the JSON definition of a hypothetical Product table might look like (the definition is split into three columns to conserve space):

```
{                              {                                   {
 "name": "Product",              "name": "Name",                     "name": "ManufacturedOn",
 "columns": [                    "dataType": "string"                "dataType": "DateTime"
  {                            }, {                                },
   "name": "ProductID",          "name": "IsCompete",              {
   "dataType": "Int64"           "dataType": "bool"                 "name": "Category",
  },                           },                                   "dataType": "string"   } ]}
```

The Product table has five columns. Each column has a name and a data type. As far as column data types are concerned, Power BI supports a subset of the Entity Data Model (EDM) data types. but with some restrictions, as shown in **Table 12.1**.

Table 12.1 Power BI supports the following subset of EDM data types for table columns.

Data type	Purpose	Restrictions
Int64	A whole integer number	Int64.MaxValue and Int64.MinValue aren't allowed
Double	A decimal number	Double.MaxValue and Double.MinValue are not allowed. NaN isn't supported.
Boolean	A Boolean TRUE/FALSE value	
Datetime	A datetime value	Precision to 3.33 ms
String	A text value	Up to 128K characters

12.1.2 Understanding the REST APIs

The Power BI APIs are evolving! Because of the importance of datasets, the initial set of APIs was centered around dataset manipulation. Later on, the team added APIs to list and manage groups, dashboards, reports, imported datasets, and gateways. In this section, you'll learn about the capabilities of the existing methods.

 NOTE Currently, some REST APIs are in preview, and their method signatures show you this, such as "beta" in the URL: https://api.powerbi.com/**beta**/myorg/dashboards. Remember to update your code when the beta methods move to production. For example, when the "Get All Dashboards" method is production ready, its method signature will include the version number, such as https://api.powerbi.com/**v1.0**/myorg/dashboards.

Understanding the verbs
As I mentioned, the Power BI APIs are based on a programming specification for method invocation over HTTP, called Representational State Transfer (or REST for short). Because the same API can serve different purposes, REST supports a set of HTTP verbs to indicate the purpose of the method invocation. For example, to get the list of existing datasets, you'll use the GET verb. Power BI supports the most common HTTP verbs, as shown in **Table 12.2**.

Table 12.2 Power BI supports four HTTP verbs.

Verb	Operation	Success Response Codes	Error Response Codes
GET	Read	200 (OK)	404 (Not Found) or 400 (Bad Request).
POST	Create	201 (Created)	404 (Not Found), 409 (Conflict) if resource already exists
PUT	Update	200 (OK) (or 204 if not returning any content in response body)	404 (Not Found) if ID is not found
DELETE	Delete	200 (OK)	404 (Not Found) if ID is not found

The HTTP GET method is used to retrieve a representation of a resource, such as a dataset collection. When executed successfully, GET returns the JSON representation in the response body. POST is used to create a new resource, such as a new dataset. Upon successful completion, it returns the HTTP status 201 and a Location header with a link to the newly created resource.

You typically use the PUT verb to update an existing resource by using the unique identifier of the resource. Upon a successful update, you'll get a response code of 200 (or 204 if the API doesn't return any content in the response body). Finally, given an identifier, DELETE removes the specified resource, such as a given row in a dataset table.

Understanding the dataset methods

The dataset-related methods are centered around the manipulation of datasets and tables, as shown in **Table 12.3**. Using the Power BI Rest API's, you can programmatically create new datasets, and you can add or remove rows to and from the tables in those datasets.

Table 12.3 This table shows the dataset-related methods.

Purpose	Verb	Method Signature	Parameters
List all datasets	GET	https://api.powerbi.com/v1.0/myorg/datasets	
Create a dataset	POST	https://api.powerbi.com/v1.0/myorg/datasets	defaultRetentionPolicy (None, basicFIFO)
List all tables	GET	https://api.powerbi.com/v1.0/myorg/datasets/<id>/tables	id (the dataset identifier)
Update table schema	PUT	https://api.powerbi.com/v1.0/myorg/datasets/<id>/tables/<tableName>	id (the dataset identifier), tableName
Add rows to table	POST	https://api.powerbi.com/v1.0/myorg/datasets/<id>/tables/<tableName>/rows	id (the dataset identifier), tableName
Clear all rows	DELETE	https://api.powerbi.com/v1.0/myorg/datasets/<id>/tables/<tableName>/rows	id (the dataset identifier), tableName
Get sequence numbers	GET	https://api.powerbi.com/v1.0/myorg/datasets/<id>/tables/<tableName>/sequenceNumbers	id (the dataset identifier), tableName
List all data sources	GET	https://api.powerbi.com/v1.0/myorg/datasets/<id>/dataSources	id (the dataset identifier)
Update connection strings	POST	https://api.powerbi.com/v1.0/myorg/datasets/<id>/Default.SetAllConnections	id (the dataset identifier)
Discover Gateway data sources	GET	https://api.powerbi.com/v1.0/myorg/datasets/<id>/Default.GetBoundGatewayDataSources	id (the dataset identifier)

As you can see, the verb indicates the intended action. For example, if I use the GET verb when I call the dataset API, I'll get a list of all the datasets, exactly as they're listed in the Power BI Service navigation bar under My Workspace. If I call the same API with a POST verb, I instruct Power BI to create a new dataset. In the latter case, I can specify an optional *defaultRetentionPolicy* parameter. This controls the store capacity of the dataset. The retention policy becomes important when you start adding rows to the dataset, such as to supply data to a real-time dashboard. By default, the dataset will accumulate all the rows. However, if you specify *defaultRetentionPolicy=basicFIFO*, the dataset will store up to 200,000 rows. Once this limit is reached, Power BI will start purging old data as new data comes in (see **Figure 12.2**).

Figure 12.2 The basic FIFO dataset policy stores up to 200,000 rows and removes old data as new data flows in.

Currently, the last three APIs apply to datasets that use DirectQuery connections. For example, your application can call "Discover Gateway Data Sources" to obtain the connection string for a DirectQuery dataset and then call "Update Connection Strings" to change it.

NOTE Besides creating tables, the "Create a dataset" method also supports specifying relationships programmatically, DAX calculations, and additional modeling properties. This allows you to create datasets programmatically with the same features as in Power BI Desktop. For more information about these features, refer to the "New features for the Power BI Dataset API" blog by Josh Caplan at https://powerbi.microsoft.com/en-us/blog/newdatasets.

Understanding the dashboard methods

Currently in preview, the dashboard methods allow you to retrieve dashboards and tiles. This is useful if you need to embed a dashboard tile on a custom application, as I'll cover in the next chapter. **Table 12.4** shows you the dashboard methods.

Table 12.4   This table shows the dashboard-related methods.

Purpose	Verb	Method Signature	Parameters
List all dashboards	GET	https://api.powerbi.com/beta/myorg/dashboards	
List tiles	GET	https://api.powerbi.com/beta/myorg/dashboards/<id>/tiles	id (dashboard identifier)
Get a tile	GET	https://api.powerbi.com/beta/myorg/dashboards/<id>/tiles/<tileID>	id (dashboard identifier), tileID (tile identifier)

The "List all dashboards" method returns a list of dashboards as they appear in the Power BI portal's navigation bar. Every dashboard element in the response body has a GUID identifier, name, and an *isReadOnly* property that indicates whether the dashboard is read-only, such as when it's shared with you by someone else, and you're given read-only access. The "List Tiles" method takes the dashboard identifier, and returns a collection of the dashboard tiles. Here's a sample JSON format that describes the "This Year's Sales" tile of the Retail Analysis Sample dashboard:

```
{
    "id": "b2e4ef32-79f5-49b3-94bc-2d228cb97703",
    "title": "This Year's Sales",
    "subTitle": "by Chain",
    "embedUrl": "https://app.powerbi.com/embed?dashboardId=<dashboard id>&tileId=b2e4ef32-79f5-49b3-94bc-2d228cb97703"
}
```

From a content embedding standpoint, the most important element is *embedUrl*, because your application needs it to reference a tile. Finally, the "Get a tile" method returns the same information for a specific tile.

Understanding the report methods

Currently in preview, the report API allows you to retrieve reports. This is useful if you need to embed a report in a custom application, as I'll cover in the next chapter. **Table 12.5** shows the "List All Reports" method that allows you to programmatically retrieve your reports.

Table 12.5   This table shows the dashboard-related methods.

Purpose	Verb	Method Signature	Parameters
List all reports	GET	https://api.powerbi.com/beta/myorg/reports	

The "List all reports" method returns a list of reports as they appear in the navigation bar. Every report element in the response body has a GUID-based identifier (*id*), name, *webUrl*, and *embedUrl*. The *webUrl* link navigates to the report in Power BI Service. The *embedUrl* link is used to embed the report in a custom application. Here's a sample JSON format that describes the Retail Analysis Sample report that you implemented in Chapter 4.

```
{
"id":"22454c20-dde4-46bc-9d72-5a6ea969339e",
"name":"Retail Analysis Sample",
"webUrl":"https://app.powerbi.com/reports/22454c20-dde4-46bc-9d72-5a6ea969339e",
"embedUrl":"https://app.powerbi.com/reportEmbed?reportId=22454c20-dde4-46bc-9d72-5a6ea969339e"
}
```

Understanding the group methods

As I explained in the previous chapter, a user can access other workspaces besides its private My Workspace. Therefore, to present the user with all the objects he has access to, a custom app must enumerate not only the user's My Workspace but also all other groups he's a member of. Currently, Power BI defines only one group method (see **Table 12.6**).

Table 12.6 This table shows the List all Groups method.

Purpose	Verb	Method Signature	Parameters
List all groups	GET	https://api.powerbi.com/v1.0/myorg/groups	

This method returns all groups the sign-in user belongs to. Each group element has an identifier and name properties. Here's an example that returns the Sales Department and Finance groups that I belong to:

```
"value": [
  {
    "id": "42e3a472-2855-4a78-aec7-387d2e8722ae",
    "name": "Sales Department"
  },
  {
    "id": "e6e4e5ab-2644-4115-96e0-51baa89df249",
    "name": "Finance"
  }
```

 TIP What if you want to retrieve objects from another workspace that you're a part of through your group membership, such as to list the datasets from the Finance workspace, or to create a new dataset that's shared by all the members of a group? Fortunately, the dataset, dashboard, and report methods support specifying a group. For example, to list all of the dataset for a specific group, you can invoke https://api.PowerBI.com/v1.0/myorg/**groups/{group_id}**/datasets, where *group_id* is the unique group identifier that you can obtain by calling the "List all groups" method. As it stands, the developer's console doesn't allow you to change the method signature, so you can't use the group syntax in the Power BI Developer Center, but you can use this syntax in your applications.

Understanding the import methods

The import APIs lets you programmatically upload a Power BI Desktop file (*.pbix) or an Excel file to a user's workspace. This could be useful if you want to automate the deployment process of uploading datasets and reports but remember that organizational content packs might be an easier and more flexible option to distribute content to many users. **Table 12.7** shows the method signatures.

Table 12.7 This table shows the Imports methods.

Purpose	Verb	Method Signature	Parameters
List all imports	GET	https://api.powerbi.com/v1.0/myorg/imports	
Import File	POST	https://api.powerbi.com/v1.0/myorg/imports	
Get import status	GET	https://api.powerbi.com/v1.0/myorg/imports/<id>	Id (import id>

The "List all imports" method lists all Excel and Power BI Desktops files that were imported. For each file, the method returns the import state (Succeeded or Failed), when the dataset was created and updated, and the datasets and reports that were included in the file. The "Import File" method is for automating the task for importing a file. To call this method, you must create a "POST" request whose body includes a filePath parameter that points to the file to be uploaded.

The actual import operation executes asynchronously. When you invoke the POST method, you'll get back a GUID identifier for the import task, such as:

{"id" : "12e3a412-2855-4a78-aec7-387d2e1234ae"}

You can use this identifier to check the status of the import task by using the "Get import status" method and pass the *importID* identifier. You'll get back a JSON response, such as the one shown in **Figure 12.3**.

```
{
    "id":"1db51a3d-94ea-4a43-9df2-10ab08c1922a",
    "importState":"Succeeded",
    "createdDateTime":"2015-08-10T16:44:35.087",
    "updatedDateTime":"2015-08-10T16:44:35.087",
    "reports":[
        {
            "id":"a53ad8ae-7c7f-4c28-8de4-f1c4e58f2482",
            "name":"AdventureWorks",
            "webUrl":"https://api.powerbi.com/reports/a53ad8ae-7c7f-4c28-8de4-f1c4e58f2482"
        }
    ],
    "datasets":[
        {
            "id":"c6ee6c94-08a4-40a1-a34a-21e20f8e189e",
            "name":"AdventureWorks",
            "tables":[
            ]
        }
    ],
    "name":"AdventureWorks"
}
```

Figure 12.3 The response of the GET verb invocation shows the status of the operation.

Your code can inspect the *importState* property to determine if the import task has completed.

12.1.3 Using Power BI Developer Center

Now that you've learned about the Power BI REST APIs, you're probably eager to try them out. But hold off writing code in Visual Studio. As it turns out, Microsoft created a very useful site, Power BI Developer Center, to get you started with Power BI programming!

Getting started with Power BI Developer Center
You can access the Power BI Developer Center in three different ways:

1. Navigate to http://powerbi.com. Scroll all the way to the bottom of the page and then click Developers in the Learn section.
2. Log in to Power BI. Expand the "Help & Support" (?) menu and then click "Power BI for Developers".
3. Navigate directly to https://powerbi.microsoft.com/developers.

Figure 12.4 Power BI Developer Center is your one-stop resource for programming with Power BI.

The Power BI Developer Center (see **Figure 12.4**) is your one-stop resource for all your Power BI developer needs. It has links to useful resources, including developer documentation and step-by-step guides of how to accomplish specific tasks.

4. Since I'm on the subject of REST APIs, scroll all the way down the Developer Center page and then click the "Try the API" link in the "REST API and real time" section. This opens the Power BI REST API site, where you can read the API documentation.

Testing the APIs

A great feature of the Power BI REST API site is that it includes a testing console where you can try the APIs without writing a single line of code! Follow these steps to test the dataset APIs:

1. In the Power BI REST API site, click the Datasets link in the navigation page to expand the section.
2. Click the Datasets Collection item. This shows you the documentation of the dataset-related APIs.
3. Click the "List all Datasets" section. The right pane shows an example of the method call, including a sample request and a sample raw JSON response (see **Figure 12.5**).

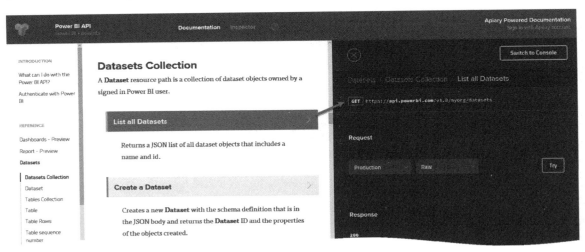

Figure 12.5 The Power BI REST API site shows an example of the method invocation.

4. To get a code example written in your preferred programming language, expand the drop-down menu to the left of the Try button (that says "Raw"), and then select your targeted language, such as C#, Visual Basic, JavaScript, Node.js, and others. The default Raw option shows only the request and response payloads that your application needs to invoke the API and process the results. Another good use of the Raw option is that you copy the Request code, and then use it to make direct method invocations with network tools, such as Fiddler, when you want to test or troubleshoot the APIs.

5. To try the API, click the Try button. This switches you to an interactive console, as shown in **Figure 12.6**.

6. Click the Get Resource button. If you haven't signed in to Power BI, this is when you'll be asked to do so. That's because all the API calls happen under the identity of the signed user.

7. After some delay, you'll get the actual request/response pair as a result of the method invocation.

If you examine the request body, you'll see an Authorization header. The obfuscated setting after "Bearer" is where the OAuth authorization token will go with an actual method invocation. The Response pane shows the result of the call. As you know already, the "200" response code means a successful invocation. Next, the Response section displays the response headers and the response body (not shown in **Figure**

12.6). The response body includes the JSON definition of the dataset collection, with all the datasets in My Workspace.

Figure 12.6   The console lets you invoke APIs and shows the request and the response.

Working with parameters

Now let's use the console to get a list of tables in a given dataset:

1. Scroll down the response pane and copy the GUID of the id property of the Retail Analysis Sample dataset.
2. In the navigation pane, click the Tables Collection tab. On the Tables Collection page, click the "List all Tables" link.
3. In the Console pane (see **Figure 12.7**), click the URI Parameters button. This method takes an id parameter, which in this case is the dataset identifier.

Figure 12.7   The console lets you pass parameters to the method, such as the dataset identifier in this example.

4. Paste the dataset identifier next to the id parameter, and then click Call Resource.
5. If the method invocation succeeds, you should get a "200" response. Then the response body should show the JSON definition of a table collection with five tables.
6. (Optional) Experiment with calling other methods, such as to create a new dataset, create a new table, and add rows to a table.

12.2 Understanding OAuth Authentication

The Console makes it easy to understand and test the Power BI REST APIs. However, it hides an important and somewhat complex part of Power BI programming, which is security. You can't get much further beyond the console if you don't have a good grasp of how Power BI authentication and authorization works. And security is never easy. In fact, sometimes implementing security can be more complicated than the application itself. The good news is that Power BI embraces another open security standard, OAuth2, which greatly reduces the plumbing effort to authenticate users with Power BI! As you'll see in this chapter and the next one, OAuth2 is a flexible standard that supports various security scenarios.

REAL LIFE   I once architected a classic BI solution consisting of a data warehouse, cube, and reports, for a card processing company. After a successful internal adoption, their management decided to allow external partners to view their own data. One of the security requirements was federating account setup and maintenance to the external partners. This involved setting up an Active Directory subdomain, a web application layer, and countless meetings. At the end, the security plumbing took more effort than the actual BI system!

12.2.1 Understanding Authentication Flows

OAuth2 allows a custom application to access Power BI Service on the user's behalf, after the user consents that this is acceptable. Next, the application gets the authorization code from Azure AD, and then exchanges it for an access token that provides access to Power BI.

Understanding the OAuth parties
There are three parties that are involved in the default three-leg authentication flow:

- User – This is the Power BI user.
- Application – This is a custom native client application or a web application that needs to access Power BI content on behalf of the user.
- Resource – In the case of Power BI, the resource is some content, such as a dataset or a dashboard, which the user has access to.

With the three-leg flow, the custom application never has the user's credentials because the entire authentication process is completely transparent to the application. However, OAuth opens a sign-in window so that the user can log in to Power BI. In the case when the application knows the user credentials, OAuth2 supports a two-leg flow where the application directly authenticates the user to the resource. The two-leg flow bypasses the sign-in window, and the user isn't involved in the authentication flow. I'll demonstrate the two-leg scenario in the next chapter.

Understanding the web application flow
Figure 12.8 shows the OAuth flow for web applications. By "web application", I mean any browser-based application, such as a custom ASP.NET application.

The typical authentication flow involves the following steps:

1. The user opens the Web browser and navigates to the custom application in order to request a Power BI resource, such as to view a report.
2. The web application calls to and passes the application client ID and Reply URL (AD). Azure Active Directory uses the client ID to identify the custom application. You obtain the client ID when you register your application with Azure AD. The Reply URL is typically a page within your application where Azure AD will redirect the user after the user signs in to Power BI.
3. Azure AD opens the Power BI sign-in page.

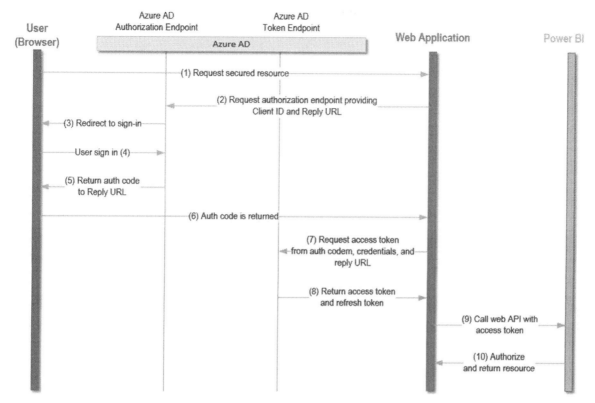

Figure 12.8 This sequence diagram shows the OAuth2 flow for web applications.

4. The user signs in using valid Power BI credentials. Note that the actual authentication is completely transparent to the application. The user might sign in using his Power BI credentials or, if the organization policy requires it, the user might use a smart card to authenticate. Azure AD determines the authentication mechanism depending on the AD corporate policy.

> **NOTE** The first time the user signs in, he will be asked to authorize the custom app for all the permissions you granted the app when you register it in the Azure AD. To see the authorized custom apps, the user can open the Power BI portal, and then click the Office 365 Application Launcher button (at the top-left corner of the portal) ⇨ "View all my apps". The user can use this menu to remove authorized custom applications at any point, and then see the granted permissions.

5. The Azure AD Authorization Endpoint service redirects the user to the page that's specified by the Reply URL, and it sends an authorization code as a request parameter.

6. The web application collects the authorization code from the request.

7. The web application calls down to the Azure AD Token Endpoint service to exchange the authorization code with an access token. In doing so, the application presents credentials consisting of the client id and client secret (also called a key). You can specify one or more keys when you register the application with Azure AD. The access token is the holy grail of OAuth because this is what your application needs in order to access the Power BI resources.

8. The Azure AD Token Endpoint returns an access token and a refresh token. Because the access token is short-lived, the application can use the refresh token to request additional access tokens instead of going again through the entire authentication flow.

9. Once the application has the access token, it can start making API calls on behalf of the user.

10. When you register the application, you specify an allowed set of Power BI permissions, such as "View all datasets". Power BI will evaluate these permissions when authorizing the call. If the user has the required permission, Power BI executes the API and returns the results.

Understanding the native client flow

A native client is any installed application that doesn't require the user to use the Web browser. A native client could be a console application, desktop application, or an application installed on a mobile device. **Figure 12.9** shows the OAuth sequence flow for native clients.

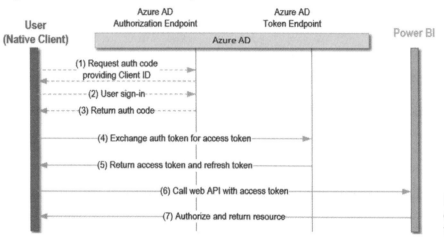

Figure 12.9 This sequence diagram shows the OAuth2 flow for native clients.

As you can see, the authentication flow for native clients is somewhat simpler than the flow for web apps.

1. Before making a Power BI API call, the native client app calls to the Azure AD Authorization Endpoint and presents the client id. A native client application probably won't have a redirect page. However, because Azure AD requires a Redirect URI, a native client app can use any URI, as long as it matches the one you specified when you register the app with Azure AD. Or, if you're running out of ideas of what this artificial URI might be, you can use the Microsoft suggested URI for native clients, which is https://login.live.com/oauth20_desktop.srf.

2. As with the web application flow, Azure AD will open the Web browser so that the user can sign in to Power BI. Again, the sign-in experience depends on how the organization is set up with Azure AD, but typically the user is asked to enter credentials in the Power BI sign-in page.

3. The Azure AD Authorization Endpoint returns an authorization code. The dotted lines in the **Figure 12.9** represent that this handshake happens within a single call. All a .NET application needs to do is call the *AcquireToken* method of the *AuthenticationContext* class to get the user to sign in, and then acquire the authorization code. In fact, the *AquireToken* method also performs the next step (step 4) on the same call.

4. A handshake takes place between the native client and the Azure AD Token Endpoint to exchange the authorization code for an access token.

5. The Azure AD Token Endpoint returns an access token and a refresh token.

6. The client calls the Power BI resource passing the access token.

7. Power BI authorizes the user and executes the call if the user has the required permissions.

12.2.2 Understanding Application Registration

As a prerequisite of integrating custom applications with Power BI, you must register the app with Azure AD. In the process of registering the application, you specify the OAuth2 details, including the type of the application (web or native client), keys, Redirect URL, and permissions. The easiest way to register a custom application is to use the Power BI registration page. You can also use the Azure Management Portal to register your application, but the process is more involved.

Note that although you can use the Power BI registration page for the initial registration process, you still need to use the Azure Management Portal to make subsequent changes, such as to change the Redirect URL. Next, I'll walk you through the steps to register web and native client applications using the Power BI registration page and Azure Management Portal.

Getting started with registration

The application registration page helps you create a new application in Azure AD that has all the information required to connect to Power BI. Anyone can register a custom application. You can find the Power BI registration page in the Power BI Developer Center, as follows:

1. Open your Web browser, navigate to Power BI Service (http://powerbi.com), and log in.
2. In the Application Toolbar at the top-right corner of the screen, click the Help & Support menu, and then click "Power BI for developers".
3. In the Power BI Developer Center, scroll down the page and then click the "Register your app" link found in the Web section.
4. Or instead of these three steps, you can go directly to the Power BI Registration Page at http://dev.powerbi.com/app.

Registering your application using the Power BI registration page

Figure 12.10 shows the Power BI registration page (to preserve space, steps 3 and 4 are shown on the right). Registering a custom application takes four simple steps:

1. Sign in to Power BI.
2. Specify the application details (see **Table 12.8**).

Table 12.8   This table describes the application registration details.

Setting	Explanation	Example
App Type	Choose "Server-side Web app" for browser-based web apps, and choose "Native app" for an installed application, such a console app	
Redirect URL	The web page where Azure AD will redirect the user after the Power BI sign-in completes	http://localhost:999/powerbiwebclient/redirect (for web apps) https://login.live.com/oauth20_desktop.srf (for native apps)
Home Page URL (web apps only)	The URL for the home page of your application (used by Azure AD to uniquely identify your application)	http://prologika.com/powerbiwebclient

3. Specify which Power BI REST APIs your application needs permissions to call. For example, if the custom app needs to push data to a dataset table, you'll have to check the "Read and Write All Dataset permissions". As a best practice, grant the app the minimum set of permissions it needs. You can always change this later if you need to.

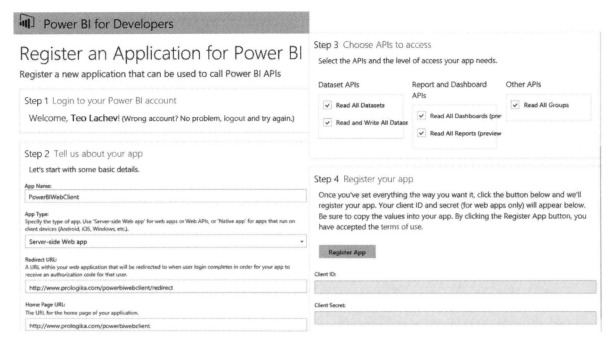

Figure 12.10 Register your custom app in four steps, using the Power BI registration page.

4. Click the Register App button to register your app. If all is well, you'll get back the client ID. For web apps, you'll also get a client secret (also called a key). As I mentioned, your custom web app needs the client secret to exchange the authorization code for an access token.

> **TIP** Because Power BI currently doesn't let you update the registration details (you need to use the Azure Management Portal for this), if you develop a web app I recommend you put some thought in the Redirect URL. Chances are that during development, you would use the Visual Studio Development Server or IIS Express. The Redirect URL needs to match your development setup, such as to include localhost. Once the application is tested, your Azure administrator can use the Azure Management Portal to change your web app and to add a production Redirect URL, such as http://www.prologika.com/powerbiwebclient/redirect.

Because managing registered applications can't be done in Power BI, next I'll show you how you can use the Azure Management Portal to view, register, and manage custom apps. You must have Azure AD admin rights to your organization's Active Directory in order to register an application. In addition, although the basic features of Azure Active Directory are free, you need an Azure subscription to use the portal and this subscription must be associated with your organizational account.

Registering web applications using Azure Management Portal
Follow these steps to register a custom web application in the Azure Management Portal:

1. Navigate to the Azure Management Portal (at https://portal.azure.com) and sign in with your organizational account. Again, the account you use must be associated with an Azure subscription.

2. In the navigation bar on the left, select Azure Active Directory. In the next page, click "App registrations" to view the registered applications (see **Figure 12.11**).

3. On the top of the page, click Add to register a new app. In the "What do you want to do?" window, and then click the default option of "Add an application my organization is developing".

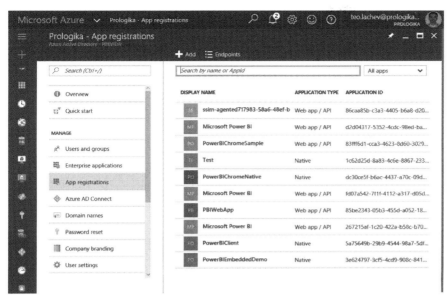

Figure 12.11 Select the "App registrations" tab to view and register custom applications.

4. In the Create blade, enter the name of your application, such as *PowerBIWebClient* (see **Figure 12.12**). The name must be unique across the registered application within your organization. Because this is a web application, leave the default type of "Web app / API" selected. Enter the application Sign-on URL (same as "Home Page URL" in the Power BI registration page). This is the address of a web page where users can sign in to use your app, such as http://prologika.com/powerbiwebclient. Azure AD doesn't validate this URL but it's required. Click Create to create the application. Once Azure creates the app, it adds it to the list of the registered apps.

Figure 12.12 Specify the application name, application type (web or native), and sign-on URL.

5. In the app registrations, select the app you just registered to show its settings. The Settings blade is where you can configure the rest of the application registration details. It has Properties, Reply URLs, Owners, "Required permissions", and Keys tabs (see **Figure 12.13**).

Figure 12.13 Use the Settings blade to configure the rest of the application registration details.

For example, in the Properties tab you can configure if the app has a multi-tenant scope. By default, the application isn't multi-tenant, meaning that only users on your domain can access the app. The "Reply URLs" tab allows you to specify one or more reply URLs (fulfill the same role as the redirect URL in the Power BI registration page) where Azure AD will redirect the user after the user signs in to Power BI. Enter a valid URL, such as http://www.prologika.com/powerbiwebclient/redirect. The Owners tab lets you register additional owners who can change the app settings.

6. So that Power BI can authorize your application, use the "Required permissions" tab to grant your app permissions to Power BI. To do this, select the "Power BI Service" API and then click "Select permissions". If you don't see "Power BI Service" in the list of applications, make sure that at least one user has signed up for and accessed Power BI. **Figure 12.14** shows you the permissions that Power BI currently supports or that are currently in preview.

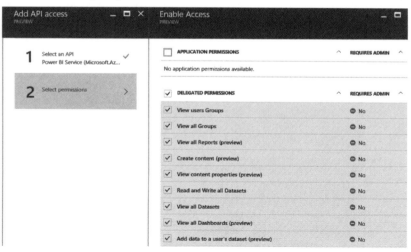

Figure 12.14 You must grant your application permissions to Power BI.

Some of these permissions correspond to the available REST APIs that you see in the Power BI registration page. For example, if the application wants to get a list of the datasets available for the signed user, it needs to have the "View all Datasets" permission. As a best practice, grant the application the minimum permissions it needs.

7. Use the Keys tab to create a key(s) (same as the client secret in the Power BI registration page) that you can use as a password when the application exchanges the authorization code for an access token. Currently, the maximum duration for the key validity is two years.

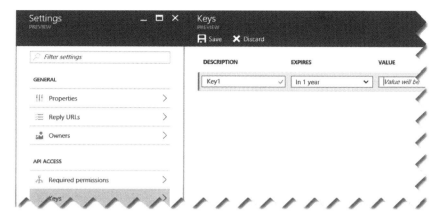

Figure 12.15 Create one or more client keys that your app will use to authenticate with Power BI.

Registering native clients

The native client registration is much simpler. The only required properties are the application name and Redirect URI. As I mentioned, you can use https://login.live.com/oauth20_desktop.srf as a Redirect URI. **Figure 12.16** shows a sample configuration for a native client application. As with registering a web app, you need to grant the native app permissions to Power BI (not shown in **Figure 12.16**).

Figure 12.16 Registering a native client application requires a name and Redirect URI.

Viewing and removing registered applications

The user can view which applications are registered to use Power BI and what permissions they have by following these steps:

1. Log in to Power BI Service (http://www.powerbi.com).

2. Click the Office 365 Application Launcher button in the top-left corner.

3. At the bottom of the window that shows the Office 365 applications, click the "View all my apps" link.

4. On the "My apps" screen, find your application, hover on it, and then click the ellipsis (…) button. A menu will pop up and show you the permissions granted to the application.

Sometimes, the application might stop working. You can use the ellipsis menu to remove the application from the tenant. The next time you launch the application, it'll ask you to register it with Power BI.

12.3 Working with Power BI APIs

Now that you know about the Power BI REST APIS and how to configure custom applications for OAuth, let's practice what's you've learned. Next, I'll walk you through a sample application that will help you get started with Power BI programming. While I was considering writing a sample from scratch, as it turned out Microsoft has already provided a sample app.

Implemented as a .NET console application, the PBIGettingStarted application demonstrates how a native client can authenticate and integrate with Power BI. You can download it from GitHub at https://github.com/Microsoft/PowerBI-CSharp/tree/master/samples/consoleapp/getting-started-for-dotnet, or by clicking the Sample link on the Power BI Developer Center under the "Client app" section. For your convenience, I included the sample in the \Source\ch12 folder. To run the sample, you'll need Visual Studio 2010 or a higher version (and valid Power BI credentials).

12.3.1 Implementing Authentication

Let's start with understanding how the application uses OAuth2 to authenticate the user before she makes calls to Power BI. As a prerequisite, you'll need to register a native client application in Azure AD.

Configuring the application
Before running the application, you need to change a few class-level variables to reflect your setup.

1. Open the PBIGettingStarted application in Visual Studio.
2. In Solution Explorer, double click Program.cs to open it.
3. Change the following variables:

```
private static string clientID = "<client_id>";
private static string redirectUri = "https://login.live.com/oauth20_desktop.srf";
private static string datasetName = "SalesMarketing";
private static string groupName = "Finance";
```

Replace the *clientID* variable with the Client ID of your application when you register it with Azure AD (see **Figure 12.15** again). Replace the *redirectUri* variable with the Redirect URI of your application or leave it set to https://login.live.com/oauth20_desktop.srf if this is the Redirect URI that you register. One of the tasks that the application demonstrates is programmatically creating a new "SalesMarketing" dataset. If the dataset name isn't what you want, change it accordingly. The application demonstrates working with groups. To try this feature, use Power BI Service to create a workspace group, such as "Finance". Then change the *groupName* variable to the name of the group. If you use Power BI Free, which doesn't support groups, you can just skip this part of the application.

Implementing OAuth
Every API invocation calls the *AccessToken* method, which performs the actual authentication. **Figure 12.17** shows the *DatasetRequest* method that is used by all dataset-related examples, such as when the application lists datasets (the *GetDatasets* method). The *DatasetRequest* method creates a web request object as required by the Power BI API specification. It adds an Authorization header with a Bearer property that specifies the access token. In case you're wondering, the access token is a base64-encoded hash that looks something like this "eyJ0eXAiOiJKV1QiLCJhbGciOiJSUzI1N…".

Remember that you need the access token to authenticate successfully with OAuth. The application obtains the token by calling the *AccessToken* method. Line 551 constructs a .NET *AuthenticationContext* class, passing the URL of the Azure AD Token Endpoint and an instance of a *TokenCache* class. I separated the original code to call *AcquireToken* into two lines, so you can gain a better understanding what happens next. Line 553 calls *AcquireToken*. It passes the URL of the resource that needs to be authorized. In your case, the resource is Power BI and its resource URI is https://analysis.windows.net/powerbi/api. The code also passes the Client ID and the redirect URI.

```
543    static string AccessToken()
544    {
545        if (token == String.Empty)
546        {
547            //Get Azure access token
548            // Create an instance of TokenCache to cache the access token
549            TokenCache TC = new TokenCache();
550            // Create an instance of AuthenticationContext to acquire an Azure access token
551            authContext = new AuthenticationContext(authority, TC);
552            // Call AcquireToken to get an Azure token from Azure Active Directory token issuance endpoint
553            AuthenticationResult result = authContext.AcquireToken(resourceUri, clientID, new Uri(redirectUri), PromptBehavior.RefreshSessic
554            token = result.AccessToken;
555        }
556        else
557        {
558            // Get the token in the cache
559            token = authContext.AcquireTokenSilent(resourceUri, clientID).AccessToken;
560        }
561
562        return token;
563    }
593    private static HttpWebRequest DatasetRequest(string datasetsUri, string method, string accessToken)
594    {
595        HttpWebRequest request = System.Net.WebRequest.Create(datasetsUri) as System.Net.HttpWebRequest;
596        request.KeepAlive = true;
597        request.Method = method;
598        request.ContentLength = 0;
599        request.ContentType = "application/json";
600        request.Headers.Add("Authorization", String.Format( "Bearer {0}", accessToken));
601
602        return request;
603    }
604    }
605 }
```

Figure 12.17   The AccessToken method performs the OAuth authentication flow.

When the application calls *AcquireToken*, you'll be required to sign in to Power BI. Once you type in your credentials and Power BI authenticates you successfully, you'll get back an instance of the *AuthenticationResult* class. *AuthenticationResult* encapsulates important details, including the access token, its expiration date, and refresh token. On line 554, the application stores the access token so that it can pass it with subsequent API calls without going through the authentication flow again. As it stands, the application doesn't use the refresh token flow, but you can enhance it to do so. For example, you can check if the access token is about to expire and then call the *authContext.AquireAccessTokenByRefreshToken* method.

12.3.2 Invoking the Power BI APIs

Once the application authenticates the interactive user, it's ready to call the Power BI APIs. The next sample demonstrates calling various APIs to create a dataset, adding and deleting rows to and from a dataset table, changing the dataset table schema, and getting the groups that the user belongs to. I'll walk you through the PBIGettingStarted code for creating datasets and loading a dataset table with data.

Creating datasets
A custom application can create a Power BI dataset to store data from scratch. The sample application demonstrates this with the *CreateDataset* method (see **Figure 12.18**). Line 213 constructs the API method signature for creating datasets by using the POST verb. Line 216 calls the *GetDatasets* method (not shown in **Figure 12.18**), which in turn calls the "List all datasets" Power BI API.

```
207    static void CreateDataset()
208    {
209        //In a production application, use more specific exception handling.
210        try
211        {
212            //Create a POST web request to list all datasets
213            HttpWebRequest request = DatasetRequest(String.Format("{0}/datasets", datasetsUri), "POST", AccessToken());
214
215            //Get a list of datasets
216            dataset ds = GetDatasets().value.GetDataset(datasetName);
217
218            if (ds == null)
219            {
220                //POST request using the json schema from Product
221                Console.WriteLine(PostRequest(request, new Product().ToDatasetJson(datasetName)));
222            }
223            else
224            {
225                Console.WriteLine("Dataset exists");
226            }
227        }
228        catch (Exception ex)
229        {
230            Console.WriteLine(ex.Message);
231        }
232    }
```

Figure 12.18 The CreateDataset method demonstrates how to programmatically create a dataset.

Line 221 passes an instance of the Product object, and it serializes the object to the JSON format. As a result, the request body contains the JSON representation of a dataset that has a single table called Product with five columns (ProductName, Name, Category, IsComplete, and ManufacturedOn). Once the call completes, you should see the SalesMarketing dataset in the Power BI Service navigation bar.

At this point, the dataset Product table contains no data. However, I recommend you take a moment now to create a table report for it, and then pin a visualization from the report to a dashboard. This will allow you to see in real time the effect of loading the dataset with data. Next, the code loads some data.

Loading data

The custom application can programmatically push rows to a dataset table. This scenario is very useful because it allows you to implement real-time dashboards, similar to the one we've implemented with Azure Stream Analytics Service in the previous chapter. The difference is that in this case, it's your application that pushes the data and you have full control over the entire process, including how the data is shaped and how often it pushes data to Power BI. The *AddRows* method demonstrates this (see **Figure 12.19**).

```
375    static void AddRows(string datasetId, string tableName)
376    {
377        //In a production application, use more specific exception handling.
378        try
379        {
380            HttpWebRequest request = DatasetRequest(String.Format("{0}/datasets/{1}/tables/{2}/rows", datasetsUri, datasetId, tableName), "POST", AccessToken());
381
382            //Create a list of Product
383            List<Product> products = new List<Product>
384            {
385                new Product{ProductID = 1, Name="Adjustable Race", Category="Components", IsCompete = true, ManufacturedOn = new DateTime(2014, 7, 30)},
386                new Product{ProductID = 2, Name="LL Crankarm", Category="Components", IsCompete = true, ManufacturedOn = new DateTime(2014, 7, 30)},
387                new Product{ProductID = 3, Name="HL Mountain Frame - Silver", Category="Bikes", IsCompete = true, ManufacturedOn = new DateTime(2014, 7, 30)},
388            };
389
390            //POST request using the json from a list of Product
391            //NOTE: Posting rows to a model that is not created through the Power BI API is not currently supported.
392            //      Please create a dataset by posting it through the API following the instructions on http://dev.powerbi.com.
393            Console.WriteLine(PostRequest(request, products.ToJson(JavaScriptConverter<Product>.GetSerializer())));
394        }
395        catch (Exception ex)
396        {
397            Console.WriteLine(ex.Message);
398        }
399    }
```

Figure 12.19 The AddRows method demonstrates how your custom app can load a dataset table.

On line 380, the code creates the API method signature for creating rows using the POST verb. Then the code creates a list collection with three products. This collection will be used to add three rows to the dataset. On line 393, the code calls the *PostRequest* method and passes the collection (serialized as JSON). This JSON output will be included in the request body. Once this method completes, three rows will be added to the Product table in the *SalesMarketing* dataset. If you watch the Power BI dashboard, you should see its tile data updating in real time. Now you have a real-time BI solution!

12.4 Summary

The Power BI APIs are based on open industry standards, such as REST, JSON, and OAuth. These APIs allow you to automate content management and data manipulation tasks, including creating and deleting datasets, loading dataset tables with data, changing the dataset schema, and determining the user's group membership. You can use the Power BI Developer Center to learn and try the APIs.

As a trustworthy environment, Power BI must authenticate users before authorizing them to access the content. The cornerstone of the Power BI authentication is the OAuth2 protocol. By default, it uses a three-leg authentication flow that asks the user to sign in to Power BI. As a prerequisite to integrating a custom app with Power BI, you must register the custom app with Azure AD.

The PBIGettingStarted sample app demonstrates how a native client can authenticate and call the Power BI REST APIs. I walked you through the code that creates a new dataset and loads it with data. This allows you to implement real-time dashboards that display data as the data streams from your application.

Another very popular integration scenario that the Power BI APIs enable is embedding reports in custom applications. This is the subject of the next chapter.

Chapter 13

Embedding Reports

I mentioned before that because Power BI generates HTML5, users can enjoy insightful reports on any platform and on any device. Wouldn't it be nice to bring this experience to your custom apps? Fortunately, Power BI includes REST APIs that allow you to embed reports and dashboards in any web-enabled application, so that you don't have to navigate your users out of your application and into Power BI Service. Moreover, embedded reports preserve their interactive features and offer the same engaging experience as viewing them in Power BI Service. Tasked to embed reports for external customers? It gets even better thanks to Power BI Embedded – a Microsoft Azure service that enables developers to add interactive Power BI reports into their applications without requiring a Power BI license!

As with the previous chapter, this is a code-intensive chapter, so be prepared to wear your developer's hat. I'll start by introducing you to the Power BI dashboard REST APIs that let you embed dashboard tiles and interactive reports. I'll walk you through some sample code that demonstrates how your intranet and Internet apps can use these features. You can find the sample web applications in the \Source\ch13 folder.

13.1 Understanding the Embedded Tile API

Embedded reporting is a common requirement for both internal and external (customer-facing) applications. Typically, the application presents a list of reports or dashboards to the user, so the user can pick which one to view. Then the application embeds the content in the presentation layer, so that reports and dashboards appear to be a part of the application itself (as opposed to redirecting the user to Power BI).

13.1.1 Understanding Embedded Tiles

Power BI includes dashboard APIs that allow you to embed specific dashboard tiles in your apps. The benefit of tile embedding is that the end users can decide what tiles they want to see on a consolidated dashboard, without having to use Power BI Service. This way your app can mimic the dashboard features of Power BI Service. It can allow the user to compile its own dashboards from Power BI dashboard tiles, and even from tiles that are located in different Power BI dashboards!

Understanding embedded features
From the end user standpoint, embedded tiles look the same as the ones hosted in Power BI Service. **Figure 13.1** shows the "Sales vs Orders" tile from the Internet Sales dashboard, which you implemented in Chapter 3.

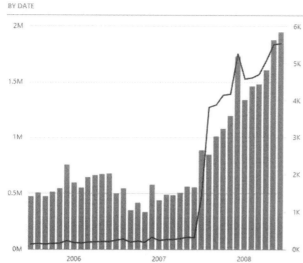

Sales vs Orders
BY DATE

Figure 13.1 This tile is embedded in an iframe element that's hosted by a web page.

The difference between Power BI Service dashboards and embedding tiles in your app is that, by default, clicking a tile doesn't do anything. You need to write code for something to happen, such as to navigate the user to the underlying report (from which the visualization was pinned). On the upside, your custom code has more control over what happens when the end user clicks a tile.

Understanding implementation steps
At a high level, the embedding tile workflow consists of the following steps:

- Obtain the tile identifier – You need to gain access programmatically to a dashboard before you get to a tile. So you'd need to find the dashboards available for the user, and then enumerate the dashboard tiles. Once the user chooses a tile, then you work with the tile identifier.

- Embed a tile – Embed the tile in your application, such by using an iframe.

- (Optional) Handle tile interaction – For example, you might want to open the underlying report when the user clicks a tile.

Of course, security needs to be addressed as well. I'll explain special considerations related to integrating custom application security with Power BI when I walk you through the sample code in section 13.3. Now let's dig deeper into the implementation steps.

13.1.2 Enumerating Dashboards and Tiles

I mentioned in the previous chapter that Power BI includes APIs for enumerating dashboards and tiles. Your application can call these APIs to present the users with a list of tiles that they might want to see in your application.

Enumerating dashboards
The "List All Dashboards" method returns the dashboards available in the user's My Workspace. This method has the following signature:

https://api.powerbi.com/beta/myorg/dashboards

Similar to listing datasets, this method supports enumerating dashboards in another workspace by passing the group identifier. For example, if the group identifier of the Finance workspace is e6e4e5ab-2644-4115-96e0-51baa89df249 (remember that you can obtain the groups that the user belongs to by calling the "List All Groups" method), you can get a list of dashboards available in the Finance workspace by using this signature:

https://api.powerbi.com/beta/myorg/**groups/e6e4e5ab-2644-4115-96e0-51baa89df249**/dashboards

Enumerating tiles

Once you retrieve the list of dashboards, you can present the user with a list of tiles from a specific dashboard by calling the "List All Tiles" method. This method takes an *id* parameter that corresponds to the dashboard identifier, which you obtain from the "List All Dashboards" method. Here is a sample "List All Tiles" method invocation:

https://api.powerbi.com/beta/myorg/dashboards/**id**/tiles

The result of this method is a JSON collection of all the tiles hosted in that dashboard. The following snippet shows the definition of the "Daily Sales" tile:

```
{
"id": "255d89b5-75b4-439d-8776-40f5de0463f0",
"title": "Daily Sales",
"subTitle": "By day",
"embedUrl": "https://app.powerbi.com/embed?dashboardId=d0b9e383-7b84-4bbf-8f55-9094efdca212&tileId=255d89b5-75b4-439d-8776-40f5de0463f0"
}
```

The *embedUrl* element is what you need to embed the tile in your app.

13.1.3 Embedding Tiles

Once you have the embed URL, the next step it to embed the tile on a web page. When sending the tile URL, you'd need to also send the OAuth access token to the Power BI Service.

 NOTE Currently, the tile embedded API doesn't support real-time updates when other applications push rows to a dataset. As a workaround, you can use the tile API to refresh the tile data, and then refresh your iframe to load updated data periodically.

Requesting a tile

In the most common scenario, you'd probably report-enable a web application. You can display the tile in an iframe element. To do so, you must write client-side JavaScript to communicate with the Power BI Service. As a first step, you'd need to reference the iframe element and handle its events:

```
var iframe = document.getElementById("iFrameEmbedTile');
var embedTileUrl = document.getElementById('tb_EmbedURL').value;
iframe.src = embedTileUrl;
// iframe.src = embedTileUrl + "&width=" + width + "&height=" + height;
iframe.onload = postActionLoadTile;
```

When making this call, you can specify the width and height that you want the tile to have. You must handle the *onload* event in your code by defining an event handler for the *iframe.onload* event. In this case, the *postActionLoadTile* function is the event handler function. If you don't handle the *iframe.onload* event, the user will see a spinning progress image, and the tile won't load.

Handling client-side authentication

Once the iframe triggers the load event, you have to send the access token to Power BI Service. The *postActionLoadTile* function takes care of this:

```
function postActionLoadTile() {
    // get the access token
    accessToken = '<%=Session["authResult"]==null? null:
        ((Microsoft.IdentityModel.Clients.ActiveDirectory.AuthenticationResult)Session["authResult"]).AccessToken%>';

    if ("" === accessToken)  return;

    var h = height;
    var w = width;
    // construct the push message structure
    var m = { action: "loadTile", accessToken: accessToken, height: h, width: w };
    message = JSON.stringify(m);
    // push the message.
    iframe = document.getElementById('iFrameEmbedTile');
    iframe.contentWindow.postMessage(message, "*");;
}
```

First, the code obtains the access token from a session variable that stores the authentication result from the OAuth flow. Normally, the browser would reject cross-domain frame communication. However, the HTML5 specification introduces the *window.postMessage()* method (see https://developer.mozilla.org/en-US/docs/Web/API/Window/postMessage) as a secure mechanism to circumvent this restriction. The code creates a JSON push message structure to instruct Power BI Service to load the tile, and then it passes the access token and tile dimensions.

Next, the code posts the message. At this point, the tile should render on the page. Power BI visualizations use HTML5 and JavaScript to render visualizations on the client (read the next chapter for more detailed information about how this works). The tile will automatically scale to fit within the iframe, based on the height and width you provide.

Filtering tile content

Dashboard tiles support limited filtering capabilities. This could be useful when you want to further filter the content based on some user-specified filter. You can pass a filter on the embed URL using this syntax:

```
https://app.powerbi.com/embed?dashboardId=<dashboard_id>&tileId=<tile_id>&$filter={FieldName} eq '{FieldValue}'
```

You can filter on any field in the underlying model, even though the field might not be used in the tile. Fields are contained in tables so the FieldName must be specified as TableName/FieldName. The filter is added as "AND" filter to any existing filters that are already applied to the tile, report, or Q&A.

Suppose that the user has indicated that they want to see the sales for Canada only. To meet this requirement, you can filter the SalesTerritoryCountry field in the SalesTerritory table. The embed URL that specifies this filtering condition might look like this:

```
embedTileUrl += "&$filter=SalesTerritory/SalesTerritoryCountry eq 'Canada'
```

Currently, the filter syntax supports only a single value and you can't specify multiple filtering conditions. When you use a filter, the *navigationUrl* property of the tile will be updated to include the filter. This allows you to pass on the filter to the underlying report if your code opens the report when the user clicks the tile.

Handling user interaction

Remember that Power BI Service allows the user to click a tile and opens the underlying report (from which the tile was pinned). You can add a similar feature to your app with the following code:

```
if (window.addEventListener) {
        window.addEventListener("message", receiveMessage, false);
    } else {
        window.attachEvent("onmessage", receiveMessage);
}
function receiveMessage(event) {
   if (event.data) {
        messageData = JSON.parse(event.data);
        if (messageData.event === "tileClicked") {
          // code to do something with the report URL
        }
```

The code defines an event handler that will listen for messages posted to the iframe content. For example, when the tile is loaded, the message is "tileLoaded", and when the tile is clicked, the message is "tileClicked". It's up to you what you want to do with the *navigationUrl* property, which you obtain from the event parameter. One option is to open a separate window that shows the entire dashboard or the underlying report. Another option (demonstrated by my sample code) is to show the underlying report in the same iframe.

13.2   Understanding the Embedded Report API

For years, Microsoft hasn't had a good story about embedded interactive reporting. If developers wanted to distribute interactive reports with their applications, they had to use third-party components. The good news is that Power BI supports this scenario! The bad news is that, at least for now, report embedding is limited to Reading View. This means that users can enjoy report interactive features, such as filtering and highlighting, but they can't change the report layout, such as to add new fields or to change the visualizations. Regardless of this limitation, many scenarios will benefit from embedding Power BI reports.

 NOTE Supporting Editing View for embedded reports (to allow the user to change the report layout) is high on the Power BI wish list, and Microsoft is working on implementing this feature!

13.2.1 Understanding Embedded Reports

Power BI includes report APIs that allow you to embed specific reports in your applications. For example, your application can present the user with a list of reports that he's authorized to see. When the user selects a report, the application can embed the report on a web page.

Understanding embedded features
Figure 13.2 shows the Internet Sales Report, from which the "Sales vs Orders" tile was pinned. When the user clicks the "Sales vs Orders" tile, the app embeds the report in the same iframe element. Note that the report supports the same features as when you open the report in Reading View in Power BI Service. For example, you can sort data in visualizations that support sorting.

To demonstrate that interactive highlighting works, I clicked a bar in the "Sales Amount by Product" chart, and this action cross filters the other visualizations. The Filters pane is also available to allow me to apply page-level and visualization-level filters. If the report has multiple pages, I can navigate through the report pages. Users can also pop out visualizations to examine them in more detail. Currently, embedded reports don't support interactive events, such as to do something when the user clicks a visualization on the report.

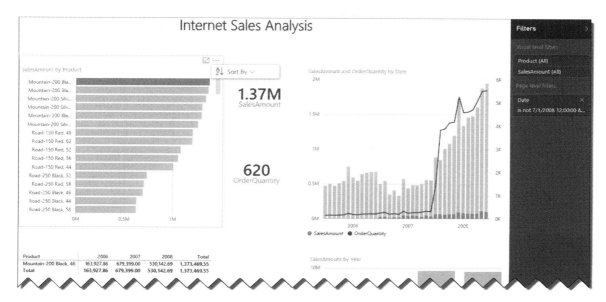

Figure 13.2 The Internet Sales Analysis report is embedded on a web page.

Understanding implementation steps

Embedding reports involves similar steps as embedding dashboard tiles:

- Obtain the report identifier – Your app can call the "List All Reports" method to present a list of reports to the end user. Once the user selects a report, the app has the report identifier.

- Embed the report – Once you have the report identifier, you can embed the report in your app, such as by showing the report content in an iframe.

Next, I'll explain the two implementation steps in more details.

13.2.2 Enumerating Reports

Remember from the previous chapter that Power BI includes a REST API method for enumerating reports. Your application can call this method to show a list of reports that the user can access.

Enumerating reports in My Workspace

The "List All Reports" method returns all the reports that are available in the user's My Workspace. It has the following signature:

https://api.powerbi.com/beta/myorg/reports

The resulting JSON response is a collection of report elements. Each report element has *id* (report identifier), *name*, *webUrl*, and *embedUrl* properties. Here's the definition of the Internet Sales Analysis report:

```
{
    "id":"b605950b-4f18-4eba-9292-82720f215693",
    "name":"Internet Sales Analysis",
    "webUrl":"https://app.powerbi.com/reports/b605950b-4f18-4eba-9292-82720f215693",
    "embedUrl":"https://app.powerbi.com/reportEmbed?reportId=b605950b-4f18-4eba-9292-82720f215693"
}
```

Enumerating reports in another workspace

Chances are that your users will share their content. Similar to the "List All Dashboards" method, the "List All Reports" method supports enumerating reports in another workspace by passing the group identifier. For example, if the group identifier of the Finance workspace is e6e4e5ab-2644-4115-96e0-51baa89df249 (remember that you can obtain the group identifier by calling the "List All Groups" method), you can get a list of the reports available in the Finance workspace by using this signature:

https://api.powerbi.com/beta/myorg/**groups/e6e4e5ab-2644-4115-96e0-51baa89df249**/reports

 TIP   To show all the reports that the user can access, you need to enumerate the reports in the user's My Workspace and the reports from all the groups (workspaces) that the user belongs to.

13.2.3 Embedding Reports

When the user picks a report, your application can use client-side JavaScript to embed the report. This is very similar to embedding dashboard tiles.

Requesting a report

If you report-enable a web application, you can display the report in an iframe element. You need to use client-side JavaScript to communicate with Power BI Service and to pass the access token. As a first step, you need to reference the iframe element and handle its events:

```
var iframe = document.getElementById("iFrameEmbedReport');
var embedTileUrl = document.getElementById('tb_EmbedURL').value;
iframe.src = embedTileUrl;
// iframe.src = embedTileUrl + "&width=" + width + "&height=" + height;
iframe.onload = postActionLoadReport;
```

You must handle the *onload* event in your code by defining an event handler for *iframe.onload*. In this case, the *postActionLoadReport* function is the event handler.

Handling client-side authentication

Once the iframe triggers the load event, you need to send the access token to Power BI Service:

```
function postActionLoadReport() {
    // get the access token.
    accessToken = '<%=Session["authResult"]==null? null:
        ((Microsoft.IdentityModel.Clients.ActiveDirectory.AuthenticationResult)Session["authResult"]).AccessToken%>';
    // return if no access token
    if ("" === accessToken) return;
    // construct the push message structure
    var m = { action: "loadReport", accessToken: accessToken};
    message = JSON.stringify(m);

    // push the message.
    iframe = document.getElementById('iFrameEmbedReport');
    iframe.contentWindow.postMessage(message, "*");;
}
```

First, the code obtains the access token from a session variable that stores the authentication result from the OAuth flow. The code creates a JSON push message structure to instruct Power BI Service to load the report, and then it passes the access token. Then the code posts the message to Power BI Service. At this point, the report should render on the page.

Filtering the report data

Similar to tiles, reports support limited filtering capabilities. This could be useful when you want to further filter the report content based on some user-specified filter, after the report filters are applied. You can pass a filter on the embed URL by using this syntax:

https://app.powerbi.com/reportEmbed?reportId=<report_id>&$filter={FieldName} eq '{FieldValue}'

Again, you can filter on any field in the underlying model, even though the field might not be used in the report itself.

13.3   Report-enabling Intranet Applications

Now that you've learned how to embed Power BI content, let me walk through sample code to help you report-enable your intranet applications.

 NOTE   You can use this code to embed Power BI reports in intranet applications when your end users already have Power BI licenses. If you plan to embed reports in external apps, skip to the next section where I discuss Power BI Embedded.

The code demonstrates the following features:

- Authenticating users – The sample code shows both a three-leg authentication flow (a Power BI sign-on page opens) and a two-leg authentication flow (the application authenticates directly with Power BI on behalf of the user).
- Embedding dashboard tiles – The sample code uses the "List All Dashboards" and "List Tiles" methods to present dashboards and tiles to the end user. Then once the user chooses a tile, JavaScript code embeds the tile on a web page.
- Embedding reports – The application shows a list of reports to the end user. Once the user picks a report, the JavaScript code embeds the report on a web page.

13.3.1 Understanding the Sample Application

The book source code includes a sample PBIWebApp ASP.NET application in the \Source\ch13\Intranet\ folder. The code is based on Microsoft's PBIWebApp sample (https://github.com/Microsoft/PowerBI-CSharp/tree/master/samples/webforms/get-started-web-app-asp.net), but I've made numerous changes to it, including handling the two-leg OAuth flow, and navigating the user to the underlying report when the user clicks a tile.

Table 13.1   The registration settings for the PBIWebApp sample.

Setting	Value	Notes
Name*	PBIWebApp	Defines the name of the application
Sign-on URL	http://prologika.com/pbiwebapp	The URL of the sign-on page (not used by PBIWebApp)
Application is multi-tenant	No	The application won't need access to data owned by other organizations
Keys	Auto-generated	Create a key that will be used by the two-leg OAuth
Reply URL*	http://localhost:13528/Redirect	The redirect page for three-leg authentication (make sure that the port number matches your development setup)
Permissions*	Power BI Service (all permissions)	Grant all Power BI Service permissions to your application

Registering the application

I mentioned in the previous chapter that any custom application that integrates with Power BI must be registered in Azure Active Directory. Follow the steps in the previous chapter to register PBIWebApp using the settings in **Table 13.1**. For the sake of completeness, the table lists all settings that you need if you register the application using the Power BI registration page or Azure Management Portal (the settings you need for the Power BI registration page are suffixed with an asterisk).

Configuring the application

Before you run the application, you need to change a few configuration settings to match your setup:

1. Open the PBIWebApp project in Visual Studio (version 2012 or higher). If you don't have Visual Studio, you can download and install the free Visual Studio 2016 Community Edition.

2. In Solution Explorer, right-click the project, and then click Properties ⇨ Settings (see **Figure 13.3**).

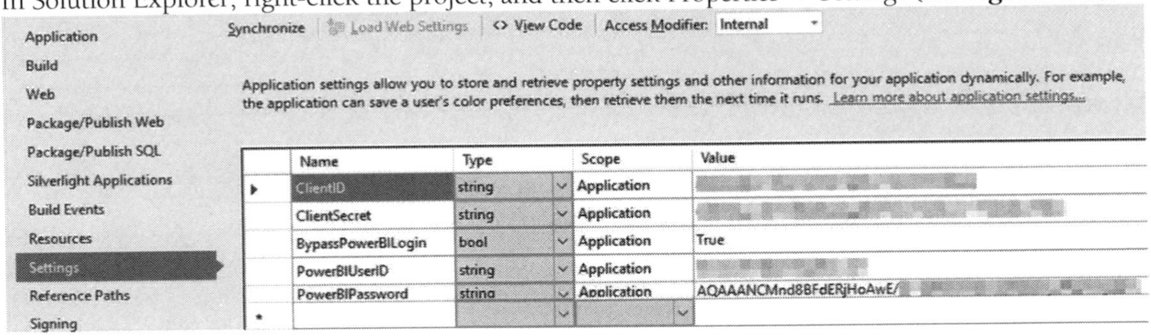

Figure 13.3 Update the PBIWebApp settings to match your setup before you run the application.

3. Change the *ClientID* setting to match the client ID of your application that you obtain after you register it.

4. Change the *ClientSecret* setting to match the *Client Secret* setting of the registered application.

5. When set to True, *BypassPowerBILogin* forces the application to authenticate the user with the two-leg OAuth flow. When this setting is False, PBIWebApp will open the Power BI sign-on page. Change the setting, depending on which authentication flow you want to test.

6. To test the two-leg authentication flow, change the *PowerBIUserID* setting to the email of your Power BI account (or a test user account that can access the Power BI Service).

7. To test the two-leg authentication flow, change the *PowerBIUserPassword* setting to your Power BI password (or the password of a test user account). This setting is encrypted using the Windows Data Protection API (DPAPI). For your convenience, I included a helper Util class in the PBIWebApp application, and you can use its *EncryptString* method to encrypt the password. In real life, your app would probably retrieve the Power BI credentials of the provisioned user from a profile store, such as a database.

13.3.2 Authenticating Users

One of the Power BI integration challenges that you'll encounter is authenticating your intranet users with Power BI. To recap from the previous chapter, you have two choices:

- Three-leg flow – The app doesn't collect or store the user password. Instead, the app redirects the user to the Power BI sign-on page to authenticate the user and return a token.

- Two-leg flow – The app either has or prompts the user to enter the Power BI credentials using its own login form. The app then authenticates the user with Power BI *without* redirecting the user to the Power BI sign-on page.

Implementing three-leg OAuth flow

If the *BypassPowerBILogin* setting is False, the app authenticates the user with Power BI with the three-leg OAuth flow, which I explained in detail in the previous chapter. **Figure 13.4** shows the relevant code from the /Reports/Report.aspx Page_Load event assuming you want to embed a Power BI report (if you want to embed a dashboard, you can find the same code in the /Reports/Dashboard.aspx page).

```
77  //perform three-leg OAuth
78  string authorityUri = "https://login.windows.net/common/oauth2/authorize/";
79  //Create a query string
80  //Create a sign-in NameValueCollection for query string
81  var @params = new NameValueCollection
82  {
83      //Azure AD will return an authorization code.
84      //See the Redirect class to see how "code" is used to AcquireTokenByAuthorizationCode
85      {"response_type", "code"},
86
87      //Client ID is used by the application to identify themselves to the users that they are requesting perm:
88      //You get the client id when you register your Azure app.
89      {"client_id", Properties.Settings.Default.ClientID},
90
91      //Resource uri to the Power BI resource to be authorized
92      {"resource", "https://analysis.windows.net/powerbi/api"},
93
94      //After user authenticates, Azure AD will redirect back to the web app http://localhost:13528/Redirect
95      {"redirect_uri", String.Format("{0}://{1}/Redirect", HttpContext.Current.Request.Url.Scheme,
96          HttpContext.Current.Request.Url.Authority)}
97  };
98  //Create sign-in query string
99  var queryString = HttpUtility.ParseQueryString(string.Empty);
100 queryString.Add(@params);
101 Session["redirectUrl"] = "/Reports/Report.aspx";
102 Response.Redirect(String.Format("{0}?{1}", authorityUri, queryString));
```

Figure 13.4   The three-leg OAuth flow redirects the user to the Power BI sign-on page.

The application creates a JSON request that includes the client id, the Power BI API authorization URL, and the Redirect URI that you specified when you registered the application. Line 140 sends the request to the authorization endpoint, which redirects the user to the Power BI sign-on page. Once the user authenticates with Power BI, the user is redirected to the Redirect.aspx page. The Redirect page saves the authentication result (the access token, refresh token, and other details) into a session variable (see line 38 in **Figure 13.5**) and redirects the user back to the report page.

```
23  string authorityUri = "https://login.windows.net/common/oauth2/authorize/";
24
25  // Get the auth code
26  string code = Request.Params.GetValues(0)[0];
27
28  // Get auth token from auth code
29  TokenCache TC = new TokenCache();
30
31  AuthenticationContext AC = new AuthenticationContext(authorityUri, TC);
32
33  ClientCredential cc = new ClientCredential(Properties.Settings.Default.ClientID, Properties.Settings.Default.ClientSecret);
34  AuthenticationResult AR = AC.AcquireTokenByAuthorizationCode(code,
35      new Uri(new Uri(HttpContext.Current.Request.Url.OriginalString).GetLeftPart(UriPartial.Path)), cc);
36
37  //Set Session "authResult" index string to the AuthenticationResult
38  Session["authResult"] = AR;
39  if (Session["user"] != null) Response.Redirect(Session["redirectUrl"].ToString());
```

Figure 13.5   This code saves the authentication results into an AuthenticationContext object.

Implementing the two-leg OAuth flow

Your end users probably won't want to have to authenticate twice. If your organization provisions users within your organization (or partner organization) with Power BI, then you already know the Power BI login credentials and you can avoid the Power BI sign-on page. For example, if your company does business with Acme1 and Acme2, you could register acme1@yourorg.com and acme2@yourorg.com with Power BI. When an external user authenticates with your web application, your app can retrieve the user credentials from somewhere and send them to Power BI.

OAuth is a very flexible security mechanism, and it supports different flows via the *grant_type* parameter. One of the flows that it supports is the "grant_type=password" flow that allows you to avoid the Power BI sign-in step, if you know the user credentials. This is conceptually similar to how Basic Authentication works. The OAuth2 "grant_type=password" scenario is also referred to as two-leg authentication. PBIWebApp demonstrates this flow when you set the BypassPowerBILogin setting to True. The relevant code from the Login.aspx page is shown in **Figure 13.6**.

Line 95 instructs OAuth to use the "grant_type=password" flow. Besides the client ID and client secret, the code adds the Power BI user name and password to the request payload. When Power BI authenticates the user, it'll immediately return the OAuth access token in the JSON response. So that the application can save the results in the *AuthenticationResult* object (as it does with the three-leg scenario), the code replaces some settings to match the serialized *AuthenticationResult* format (lines 84-86). Finally, the code saves the *AuthenticationResult* object in a session variable, as it does in the case of the three-leg flow.

 NOTE Remember that the access token has a limited lifespan, and your code needs to catch errors that are caused by expired tokens. Although PBIWebApp doesn't demonstrate this workflow, your code can use the refresh token to extend the user session when the access token expires.

```
79   Session["user"] = userID;
80   Session["redirectUrl"] = FormsAuthentication.GetRedirectUrl(userID, false);
81   bool bypassPowerBILogin = Properties.Settings.Default.BypassPowerBILogin;
82   if (bypassPowerBILogin)
83   {
84   // As it stands, Power BI doesn't support custom security so the user must be registered with Power BI
85   // After you authenticate the user, you need to retrieve the Power BI user credentials
86   string powerBIUserID = Properties.Settings.Default.PowerBIUserID;
87   System.Security.SecureString powerBIPassword = Util.DecryptString(Properties.Settings.Default.PowerBIPassword);
88
89   // perform two-leg OAuth
90       System.Net.WebRequest request = System.Net.WebRequest.Create("https://login.microsoftonline.com/e7b81d0a-a949-4103-83dc-feff
91       request.ContentType = "application/x-www-form-urlencoded";
92       request.Method = WebRequestMethods.Http.Post;
93       using (StreamWriter streamWriter = new StreamWriter(request.GetRequestStream()))
94       {
95           string payload = String.Format("grant_type=password&client_id={0}&client_secret={1}&resource=https%3a%2f%2fanalysis.wind
96               WebUtility.UrlEncode(Properties.Settings.Default.ClientID), WebUtility.UrlEncode(Properties.Settings.Default.Client
97               WebUtility.UrlEncode(powerBIUserID), WebUtility.UrlEncode(Util.ToInsecureString(powerBIPassword)));
98           streamWriter.Write(payload);
99       }
00       using (HttpWebResponse response = (HttpWebResponse)request.GetResponse())
01       {
02           using (StreamReader streamReader = new StreamReader(response.GetResponseStream()))
03           {
04               string payload = streamReader.ReadToEnd();
05               payload = payload.Replace("access_token", "AccessToken");
06               payload = payload.Replace("refresh_token", "RefreshToken");
07
08               AuthenticationResult ar = AuthenticationResult.Deserialize(payload);
09               Session["authResult"] = ar;
```

Figure 13.6   The two-leg OAuth flow avoids the Power BI sign-on page.

13.3.3 Implementing Embedded Tiles

Next, I'll walk you through the sample code for embedding tiles in a custom application. This includes retrieving the list of dashboards available to the authenticated user, getting a list of tiles in the selected dashboard, and embedding the selected tile on a web page.

Configuring the Dashboard web page

The Dashboard.aspx page in the Reports folder demonstrates how to embed tiles:

1. In the project properties, select the Web tab and change the "Specific Page" setting in the Start Action section to Reports/Dashboard.aspx, as shown in **Figure 13.7**.

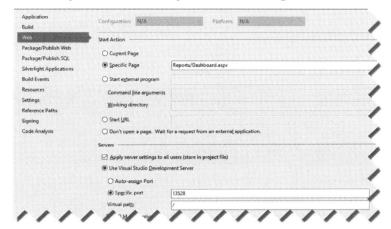

Figure 13.7 Configure the PBI-WebApp application to start with the Dashboard.aspx page.

2. Run the application. You can press Ctrl-F5 to run the application or F5 to start it in Debug mode.
3. On the logon step, click the Logon button to authenticate with Power BI. Once the authentication flow completes, PBIWebApp opens the Dashboards.aspx page.

Getting dashboards

The Dashboard.aspx page demonstrates a typical flow that your application could adopt to embed a tile. As a first step, the application would show the users a list of dashboards that they have access to, as shown in **Figure 13.8**.

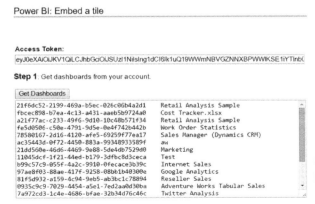

Figure 13.8 PBIWebApp shows a list of dashboards available in the user's My Workspace.

Although PBIWebApp only shows the dashboards from the user's My Workspace, you can easily extend it to enumerate all the workspaces that the user belongs to and append the dashboards from these groups.

Remember that to do this, you can call the "List All Groups" method. Then you can call the "List All Dashboard" method and specify the group identifier. **Figure 13.9** shows the code that constructs the request and processes the response to show the dashboards in the list.

```
52  protected void getDashboardsButton_Click(object sender, EventArgs e)
53  {
54      string responseContent = string.Empty;
55
56      //Configure datasets request
57      System.Net.WebRequest request = System.Net.WebRequest.Create(String.Format("{0}dashboards", baseUri)) as System.Net.HttpWebRequest;
58      request.Method = "GET";
59      request.ContentLength = 0;
60      request.Headers.Add("Authorization", String.Format("Bearer {0}", authResult.AccessToken));
61
62      //Get datasets response from request.GetResponse()
63      using (var response = request.GetResponse() as System.Net.HttpWebResponse)
64      {
65          //Get reader from response stream
66          using (var reader = new System.IO.StreamReader(response.GetResponseStream()))
67          {
68              responseContent = reader.ReadToEnd();
69
70              //Deserialize JSON string
71              PBIDashboards PBIDashboards = JsonConvert.DeserializeObject<PBIDashboards>(responseContent);
72
73              tb_dashboardsResult.Text = string.Empty;
74              //Get each Dataset from
75              foreach (PBIDashboard db in PBIDashboards.value)
76              {
77                  tb_dashboardsResult.Text += String.Format("{0}\t{1}\n", db.id, db.displayName);
78              }
```

Figure 13.9 This code retrieves and shows the list of dashboards.

Lines 57-60 create the web request to invoke the "List All Dashboards" method. Line 60 adds the access token to authorize the user. Line 63 sends the request and obtains the response from the method invocation. Line 68 saves the response, which is described in JSON. Line 71 creates a collection of *PBIDashboard* objects from the response, for easier navigation through the dashboard elements. Lines 75-78 populate the list with the dashboard identifier and dashboard name.

Getting tiles
Next, you can specify a dashboard so that you get a list of its tiles:

1. Copy one of the dashboard identifiers, such as the one for the Internet Sales dashboard, and paste it in the text box in the Step 2 section.

2. Click the Get Tiles button to get the tile list (see **Figure 13.11**).

Figure 13.10 PBIWebApp shows a list of tiles from the selected dashboard.

Figure 13.11 shows the code that populates the tile list. Lines 96-100 create the request to invoke the "List Tiles" method for the dashboard identifier you specified. Once the method is invoked, PBIWebApp saves the response in a collection of *PBITile* objects. Then the code enumerates through the collection to show the tile identifier, tile name, and the embed URL.

```
84 ⊟        protected void getTilesButton_Click(object sender, EventArgs e)
85          {
86              string responseContent = string.Empty;
87              string dashboardId = string.Empty;
88
89              if (string.Empty == inDashboardID.Text)
90              {
91                  tb_tilesResult.Text = "Please enter a dashboard id above"; return;
92              }
93              dashboardId = inDashboardID.Text;
94
95              //Configure datasets request
96              System.Net.WebRequest request = System.Net.WebRequest.Create(String.Format("{0}Dashboards/{1}/Tiles",
97                      baseUri, dashboardId)) as System.Net.HttpWebRequest;
98              request.Method = "GET";
99              request.ContentLength = 0;
100             request.Headers.Add("Authorization", String.Format("Bearer {0}", authResult.AccessToken));
101
102             using (var response = request.GetResponse() as System.Net.HttpWebResponse)
103             {
104                 //Get reader from response stream
105                 using (var reader = new System.IO.StreamReader(response.GetResponseStream()))
106                 {
107                     responseContent = reader.ReadToEnd();
108                     //Deserialize JSON string
109                     PBITiles PBITiles = JsonConvert.DeserializeObject<PBITiles>(responseContent);
110                     tb_tilesResult.Text = string.Empty;
111                     foreach (PBITile tile in PBITiles.value)
112                     {
113                         tb_tilesResult.Text += String.Format("{0}\t{1}\t{2}\n", tile.id, tile.title, tile.embedUrl);
114                     }
```

Figure 13.11 This code retrieves the list of tiles that are hosted in the selected dashboard.

Embedding a tile
Next, you can specify which tile you want to embed on the web page:

1. Copy the embed URL (starts with https) of one of the tiles shown in Step 2. For example, copy the embed URL of the "Sales vs Orders" tile.
2. Paste the embed URL in the Step 3 text box, and then click Embed Tile to render the tile on the web page, as shown in **Figure 13.12**.

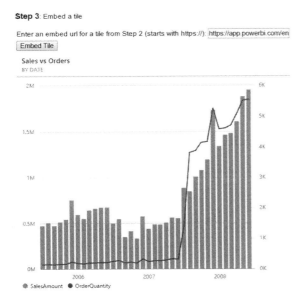

Figure 13.12 Specify the tile embed URL to embed the tile on the web page.

3. (Optional) Click the tile to open the underlying report. Remember that the web page has some JavaScript code that handles tile embedding and report navigation, as I've mentioned in section 13.1.

13.3.4 Implementing Embedded Reports

The Report.aspx page demonstrates the embedding report workflow. Make sure to open the project properties and change the Start Action setting to Reports/Report.aspx.

Getting reports

The Report.aspx page demonstrates how a custom app can embed a report. As a first step, the application would show the user a list of reports the user has access to, as shown in **Figure 13.13**.

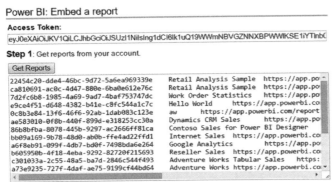

Power BI: Embed a report
Access Token:
eyJ0eXAiOiJKV1QiLCJhbGciOiJSUzI1NiIsIng1dCI6Ik1uQ19WWmNBVGZNNXBPWWIKSE1iYTInbC

Step 1: Get reports from your account.
`Get Reports`

```
22454c20-dde4-46bc-9d72-5a6ea969339e   Retail Analysis Sample   https://app.po
ca810691-ac0c-4d47-880e-6ba0e612e76c   Retail Analysis Sample   https://app.po
7d2fc6b8-1985-4a69-9ad7-4baf753747dc   Work Order Statistics    https://app.po
e9ce4f51-d648-4382-b41e-c8fc544a1c7c   Hello World   https://app.powerbi.co
0c8b3e84-13f6-46f6-92ab-1dab083c123e   aw      https://app.powerbi.com/report
ae583010-0f8b-440f-899d-e318253cc30a   Dynamics CRM Sales       https://app.po
86b8bfba-8078-445b-9297-ac2666ff81ca   Contoso Sales for Power BI Designer
bb09a169-9b78-48d0-ab0b-ffe4ad22ffd1   Internet Sales  https://app.powerbi.co
a6f8eb91-099f-4db7-bd0f-7498bda6e264   Google Analytics         https://app.po
b605950b-4f18-4eba-9292-82720f215693   Reseller Sales  https://app.powerbi.co
c301033a-2c55-48a5-ba7d-2846c544f493   Adventure Works Tabular Sales   https:
a73e9235-727f-4daf-ae75-9199cf44bd64   Adventure Works https://app.powerbi.co
```

Figure 13.13   In Step 1, PBIWebApp shows the reports in the user's workspace.

Although PBIWebApp only shows the reports in the user's workspace, you can easily extend it to enumerate the groups that the user belongs to and to append the reports from these groups. Remember that to do this, you can call the "List all groups" method to obtain all the groups that the user belongs to. Then you can call "List all reports" for each group and specify the group identifier in the method signature.

```
46  protected void getReportsButton_Click(object sender, EventArgs e)
47  {
48      string responseContent = string.Empty;
49      //Configure datasets request
50      System.Net.WebRequest request = System.Net.WebRequest.Create(String.Format("{0}reports", baseUri))
51          as System.Net.HttpWebRequest;
52      request.Method = "GET";
53      request.ContentLength = 0;
54      request.Headers.Add("Authorization", String.Format("Bearer {0}", authResult.AccessToken));
55
56      //Get datasets response from request.GetResponse()
57      using (var response = request.GetResponse() as System.Net.HttpWebResponse)
58      {
59          //Get reader from response stream
60          using (var reader = new System.IO.StreamReader(response.GetResponseStream()))
61          {
62              responseContent = reader.ReadToEnd();
63
64              //Deserialize JSON string
65              PBIReports PBIReports = JsonConvert.DeserializeObject<PBIReports>(responseContent);
66
67              tb_reportsResult.Text = string.Empty;
68              //Get each Dataset from
69              foreach (PBIReport rpt in PBIReports.value)
70              {
71                  //https://wabi-staging-us-east-redirect.analysis.windows.net
72                  tb_reportsResult.Text += String.Format("{0}\t{1}\t{2}\n", rpt.id, rpt.name,
73                      "https://app.powerbi.com/reportEmbed?reportId="+rpt.id);
```

Figure 13.14   This code retrieves the list of reports from the user's workspace.

Figure 13.14 shows the code that retrieves the list of reports. Lines 49-54 create the request to invoke the "List All Reports" method. Then, the code invokes the method and saves the response as a collection of *PBIReport* objects. Finally, the code enumerates through the collection and shows the report identifier, name, and the embed URL.

Embedding a report

Next, you can choose a report to embed it on the web page:

1. Copy the embed URL (starts with https) of one of the reports shown in Step 2. For example, copy the embed URL for the Reseller Sales report.

2. Paste the embed URL in the Step 2 text box and click Embed Report to render the report on the web page, as shown in **Figure 13.15**. Clicking the Embed Report button executes client-side JavaScript code that handles report embedding, as I've discussed in section 13.2.

3. (Optional) Test some of the report's interactive features, such as highlighting, sorting, and filtering. All of these features should work because embedded reports preserve their interactive features. Currently, you can't open the embedded report in Editing View to make layout changes to the report. Embedded reports are limited to Reading View.

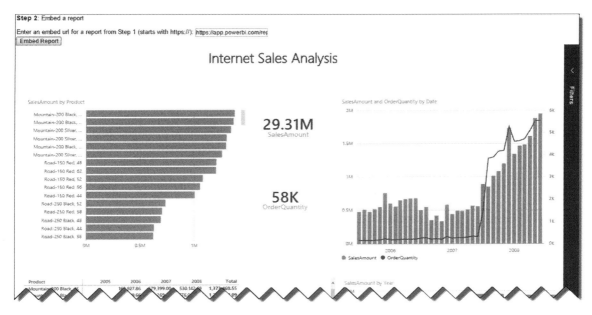

Figure 13.15 The Internet Sales Analysis report is embedded on a web page.

13.4 Report-enabling Internet Applications

Requiring users to have Power BI subscriptions to see embedded reports might be fine for intranet applications but it's impractical for Internet apps. An Internet-facing app typically authenticates users with Forms Authentication, by showing a login form to let the users enter application credentials. Then the application verifies the credentials against a profile store, such as a table in a SQL Server database. If you plan a large number of external users, you'd want to avoid registering your users twice: with your application and with

Power BI (Azure Active Directory). Moreover, it would be cost prohibitive to cover hundreds and thousands of users with Power BI Pro licenses when your app requires pro features, such as when reports connect to an on-premises Analysis Services model. If you're tasked to report-enable a custom app that will be used by many external users, you should strongly consider Power BI Embedded.

> **NOTE** Think of Power BI Embedded as a subset of Power BI. As with embedded API, Power BI Embedded is all about allowing end users to view embedded reports (reports must be created with Power BI Desktop). Currently, Power BI Embedded doesn't support other Power BI Service features, such as Q&A and Quick Insights. Further, Power BI Embedded doesn't allow the end user to edit the report (the Power BI Edit Report feature and Field List are not available).

13.4.1 Understanding Power BI Embedded

Power BI Embedded is a Microsoft Azure service that allows developers and Independent Software Vendors (ISV) to add interactive Power BI reports in their custom apps for third party. As other Azure services, Power BI Embedded requires an Azure subscription (not Power BI subscription).

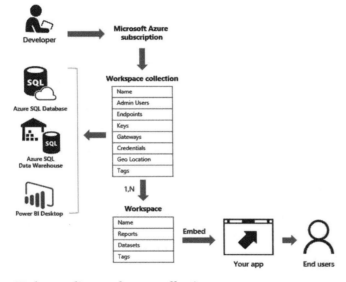

Figure 13.16 Power BI Embedded is an Azure service and organizes content in workspace collections and workspaces.

Understanding workspace collections
Figure 13.16 shows the Power BI Embedded conceptual model. Once you have your Azure subscription, you need to log in to the Azure portal and create a new Power BI Embedded Service. This provisions a single workspace collection, which is a top-level container for resources. These resources include standard Azure properties (name, endpoints, and tags) and resources specific to Power BI Embedded, such as:

- Access keys – Similar to a password, your app authenticates with Power BI Embedded using an access key, just like the intranet custom app in the previous example used an access key to authenticate with Power BI Service.
- Admin users – Azure Active Directory (AAD) users who can manage the Power BI Embedded Service
- Region – The Azure geographical region where the service will be hosted

Because each workspace collection has its own access keys and admin users, a collection isolates its content and represents the top-level security and administration boundary. Conceptually, a workspace collection to Power BI Embedded is what a tenant is to Power BI Service.

NOTE Although Power BI Embedded uses the Power BI APIs and backend services for report embedding, it doesn't deploy content to Power BI Service, meaning that you can't log in to powerbi.com to see the content you've deployed to Power BI Embedded. Instead, you must programmatically access and manage the Power BI Embedded content.

Understanding workspaces

You use Power BI Desktop to create datasets and reports that you plan to deploy to Power BI Embedded. Once you are done with the reports, you upload the Power BI Desktop file to a workspace. Just like you can use workspaces and groups to organize content in Power BI Service, you can use a Power BI Embedded workspace to deploy Power BI Desktop files. Initially, your workspace collection has no workspaces. You can create one or more workspaces. How many do you need? Consider a custom app that connects to a multi-tenant database and uses Power BI row-level security (RLS) to isolate data among customers. You can provision just one workspace that will host a single Power BI Desktop file.

What if you want to physically separate data by providing each customer with a data extract as a separate (*.pbix) file. Then, you might create a workspace per customer and deploy each file to a separate workspace. You'll end up having as many workspaces as customers that you want to support (with all the maintenance headaches to support that many files). It's really up to you how you want to organize the content across workspaces. Since you're not charged per workspace, you can have as many as you want.

Currently, the Azure Portal doesn't have UI for creating workspaces and uploading content. You must do so programmatically by calling the Azure API (more on this in the "Understanding APIs" section).

Understanding data access

Because Power BI Embedded is an Azure service, it can connect directly to other cloud data sources, such as Azure SQL Database, Azure SQL Data Warehouse, Spark on HDInsight and soon Azure Analysis Services, without requiring gateways. To support this data access scenario, choose DirectQuery when you connect Power BI Desktop to these data sources. As of this time, Power BI Embedded doesn't support on-premises sources or Azure Analysis Services, but adding more connectivity options is on the roadmap.

Besides cloud data sources, you can import your data into a Power BI Desktop model and deploy both reports and the data when you upload the file to a workspace. However, currently Power BI Embedded doesn't include refresh APIs (refresh APIs are also on the roadmap). So, you must refresh your data manually on the desktop and re-upload the files periodically, or use one of the unsupported ways to "automate" refreshing of Power BI Desktop files that I mention in my blog "Automating Power BI Desktop Refresh" (http://prologika.com/automating-power-bi-desktop-refresh). Continuing down the list of limitations, similar to Power BI, the Power BI Desktop file size can't exceed one gigabyte. So, if you plan to scale beyond that size, you need to move the data out of Power BI Desktop and to an external database.

Understanding licensing

To support cost-effective options for delivering reports to a large number of users, Power BI Embedded has its own licensing model. Unlike the Power BI Service per-user and per-month licensing model, Power BI Embedded introduces per-session pricing. With the current licensing model, a session associates a user with a report and it includes all interactions with that report up to an hour. So, when the app issues a token granting the user rights to view a report, Power BI Embedded initiates a new session and starts the session clock. All user interactions with that report (filtering, sorting, and page navigation) are included in the session and are not charged separately.

The session ends when the user closes the report, or when one hour is over, whichever comes first. Currently, a session costs five cents and the first 100 sessions per month are free! As far as service level agreements, Microsoft guarantees 99.9% availability for Power BI Embedded.

 NOTE As the pricing details page states, Power BI Embedded is primarily intended for report-enabling external apps for a third party and it can't be used as a cheaper substitute to Power BI Service for internal apps. For more details, read the Pricing Details page at https://azure.microsoft.com/en-us/pricing/details/power-bi-embedded.

REAL LIFE I've helped a few ISVs integrate their apps with Power BI Embedded. All of them have considered other vendors and third-party libraries for reports, but were attracted to Power BI Embedded because of its rich code-free visualizations and very cost-effective licensing model.

13.4.2 Understanding APIs

Power BI Embedded has three programing interfaces to help developers automate content management, report embedding, and client-side programming (see **Figure 13.17**).

Understanding Azure APIs
Starting from the left, the first programming interface is Azure API, which is also known as Azure Resource Manager. It includes a set of REST APIs to manage Azure resources. In the case of Power BI Embedded, you can call the Azure API to manage content, such as to create workspace collection and workspaces, import a Power BI Desktop file, update connection strings, and enumerate datasets.

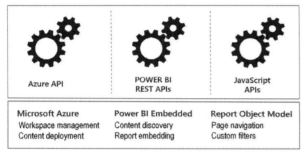

Figure 13.17 Power BI Embedded supports three application programming interfaces.

Understanding Power BI APIs
You're already familiar with the Power BI REST APIs, which I discussed in this and previous chapters. Your app will call the Power BI REST APIs to enumerate and embed reports. Embedding a Power BI report in your application is done with an iframe, which is hosted as part of the app. The iframe acts as a boundary between your application and the Power BI report.

Understanding JavaScript APIs
To support additional customization scenarios, Power BI Embedded includes a JavaScript API. Without this API, your app won't be able to manipulate the report on the client side. This is because your app won't be able to pass information through the iframe, the report cannot interact with your application and your application can't interact with the report. At the same time, there are scenarios where client-side interaction without reposting the page can be beneficial, such as when you want to implement your own filtering features instead of relying on the built-in Filter pane.

The JavaScript API exposes a report object model which is documented at http://bit.ly/pbijavascriptapi.It allows you to programmatically perform an action in a report and listen for events from actions that users make from within the reports themselves. The current API supports the following features:

- Manage reports – Embed a report on a page, configure report settings (enable or disable the Filter pane and page navigation, set defaults for pages and filters), enter and exist full screen mode.
- Navigate pages – Discover what pages exist in a report and navigate the user to a specific page.
- Filter reports – Apply basic and advanced filters.
- Handle events – Your application can react to certain user events, such as when the user navigates to a page and the report is loaded.

13.4.3 Using Power BI Embedded

To help you get started with Power BI Embedded, Microsoft provided a sample ASP.NET MVP application, which you can download from http://bit.ly/2fPMQma. For your convenience, I included the app in the book source code in the \Source\ch13\Internet folder. As a prerequisite, follow the steps in the "Get started with Microsoft Power BI Embedded" blog at http://bit.ly/2fGnutJ to create a Power BI Service and a workspace collection. Once the service is provisioned, obtain the following items: subscription id, resource group, workspace collection name, and access key (you need only one of the two).

 TIP Don't know ASP.NET? To get you started without using the sample app, Microsoft has also provided a nice online sample (http://bit.ly/pbiembeddeddemo) that walks you through the necessary steps to authorize with Power BI Embedded, embed a report, and use the JavaScript APIs to interact with the report. Check it out!

Provisioning Power BI Embedded
You'll use the ProvisionSample console app included in the solution to create a new workspace and upload the Adventure Works Power BI Desktop file.

1. In the ProvisionSample app, open the App.config file and update the following configuration settings to reflect your setup: *subscriptionId*, *resourceGroup*, *workspaceCollectionName*, and *accessKey*.

2. In the Solution Explorer, right-click the ProvisionSample app and then click "Set as Startup Project".

3. Right-click the app again and then click Build. The app should build successfully. If it doesn't, you're probably missing some dependencies. To fix this, right-click the app, click "Manage NuGet Packages", and then install all dependencies the app requires.

4. Press Ctrl+F5 to run the app. You should see the output shown in **Figure 13.18**. The different options call the corresponding Azure APIs to deploy and manage content.

```
C:\WINDOWS\system32\cmd.exe

What do you want to do?
================================================================
1. Provision a new workspace collection
2. Get workspace collection metadata
3. Retrieve a workspace collection's API keys
4. Get list of workspaces within a collection
5. Provision a new workspace in an existing workspace collection
6. Import PBIX Desktop file into an existing workspace
7. Update connection string info for an existing dataset
8. Retrieve a list of Datasets published to a workspace
9. Delete a published dataset from a workspace
```

Figure 13.18 Use the ProvisionSample app to manage Power BI Embedded content.

5. Press 5 to provision a workspace. If you have specified the correct configuration settings, the app will create a new workspace with the name you specify and return the workspace identifier. Copy this identifier.

6. Press 6 to import a PBIX file. You'll be asked to provide a dataset name (that's the Power BI Desktop file). Type in *AdventureWorks* (the name you provide will show in the app menu so choose a descriptive name).

7. You'll be asked for a file path to the PBIX file. Enter the path to the Adventure Works file that you implemented in Part 3 of this book. If all is well, the file should upload successfully.

8. (Optional) Press 8 to see a list of the datasets that you've published to the workspace and make sure that the AdventureWorks dataset is listed. Close the console window.

Running the EmbedSample app
Next, let's test the EmbedSample app.

1. Back to Visual Studio, in the EmbedSample app, open the Web.config file and update the following configuration settings to reflect your setup: *AccessKey*, *WorkspaceCollectionName*, and *WorkspaceId*.

2. In the Solution Explorer, right-click the EmbedSample app, and then click "Set as Startup Project". Press Ctrl+F5 to build the app and then press Ctrl+F5 to run it.

3. In the left navigation bar, expand the reports section. You should see AdventureWorks in the menu.

4. Click the AdventureWorks menu. The app should show the report embedded on the page (see **Figure 13.19**). Take some time to test interactive features. The Page Navigation menu demonstrates the JavaScript API (more on this in a moment).

Next, let me walk you through some important implementation details to help you understand how the app integrates with Power BI Embedded.

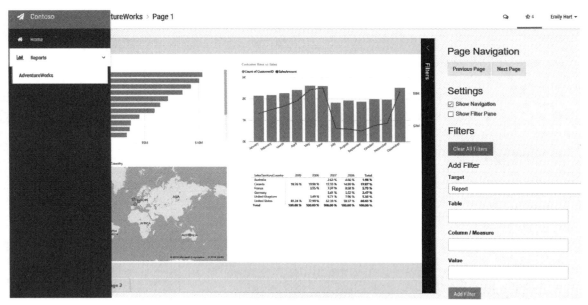

Figure 13.19   The EmbedSample app shows the AdventureWorks report embedded on a web page.

Enumerating reports
The EmbedSample app is an ASP.NET MVC application. The Power BI Embedded integration code is remarkably simple. **Figure 13.20** shows the server-side code in the DashboardController class. The Reports method is responsible for enumerating reports that are available in a workspace (recall that a workspace can have multiple Power BI Desktop files and each file can include a report). The GetReports call on line 38 is a wrapper on top of the Power BI "List all Reports" API. As you know by now, this API returns a collection of reports and each report element has a report id, embed URL, name, and web URL. The web UI adds a menu for each report in the left navigation bar.

When the user selects a report, the application calls the Report method (line 46). This method is responsible for generating a token for the user by calling the CreateReportEmbedToken method (line 52). This is similar to working with OAuth tokens. The difference is that the application generates the tokens on the behalf of the user. The application is responsible for authenticating and authorizing the user. If all users will see the same data, there is no need to propagate the user context to Power BI Embedded. On line 57, the application generates the access token using the Power BI access key. On line 54, the app returns the report object and access token so it's available to the JavaScript client-side code.

Embedding reports
The actual report embedding takes place on the client side in the view file (Report.cshtml file) with just one line of code:

```
@Html.PowerBIReportFor(m => m.Report, new { id = "pbi-report", style = "height:85vh", powerbi_access_token = Model.AccessToken })
```

PowerBIReportFor is a wrapper on top of the report embedding API and it's implemented in the powerbi.js script. Make sure to include powerbi.js in every page that needs to embed reports or include it in the master page (_layout.cshtml) as the sample demonstrates. PowerBIReportFor passes the report object and the access token generated by the server code. As a result, Power BI Embedded generates an iframe with the specified height that contains the embedded reports.

```
33 [ChildActionOnly]
34 public ActionResult Reports()
35 {
36     using (var client = this.CreatePowerBIClient())
37     {
38         var reportsResponse = client.Reports.GetReports(this.workspaceCollection, this.workspaceId);
39         var viewModel = new ReportsViewModel
40         {
41             Reports = reportsResponse.Value.ToList()
42         };
43         return PartialView(viewModel);
44     }
45 }
46 public async Task<ActionResult> Report(string reportId)
47 {
48     using (var client = this.CreatePowerBIClient())
49     {
50         var reportsResponse = await client.Reports.GetReportsAsync(this.workspaceCollection, this.workspaceId);
51         var report = reportsResponse.Value.FirstOrDefault(r => r.Id == reportId);
52         var embedToken = PowerBIToken.CreateReportEmbedToken(this.workspaceCollection, this.workspaceId, report.Id);
53
54         var viewModel = new ReportViewModel
55         {
56             Report = report,
57             AccessToken = embedToken.Generate(this.accessKey)
58         };
59         return View(viewModel);
60     }
61 }
```

Figure 13.20 The server-side code in the MVC controller enumerates reports and authenticates the user.

Working with the report object model

The Reports.cshtml page also demonstrates the JavaScript APIs. You can use the Page Navigation pane (see again **Figure 13.20**) to practice some of these options, including page navigation, controlling the visibility of page navigation and filter pane, custom page navigation and report filtering. The most interesting of these is the ability to control report filtering, such as in the case where your app needs to provide a custom user interface for filters.

The Page Navigation pane allows you to select the filter type (report or page) and specify which column or measure you want to filter. For example, to filter all the visuals on the report (across all pages) to show only sales for United States, leave the Target field set to Report, enter *SalesTerritory* in the Table field, *SalesTerritoryCounty* in the Column/Measure field, and *United States* in the Value field. Clicking the Add Filter button invokes the addFilter function (see **Figure 13.21**). The function obtains the values specified by the user. Then, it defines a basic IN filter, appends the filter to the report object and calls setFilters to apply the filter.

Similar to the Filter pane, the JavaScript API also supports advanced filters, such as to apply multiple OR/AND filter conditions. For more information about the filtering capabilities, see the Filters page in the JavaScript API documentation at https://github.com/Microsoft/PowerBI-JavaScript/wiki/Filters.

```
130 // For a complete guide to setting filters see the following wiki page
131 // https://github.com/Microsoft/PowerBI-JavaScript/wiki/Filters
132 function addFilter() {
133     var target = $('#filter-target').val();
134     var table = $('#filter-table').val();
135     var column = $('#filter-column').val();
136     var value = $('#filter-value').val();
137
138     var basicFilter = {
139         $schema: "http://powerbi.com/product/schema#basic",
140         target: {
141             table: table,
142             column: column
143         },
144         operator: 'In',
145         values: [value]
146     };
147
148     var filterTarget = target === 'page' ? currentPage : report;
149     // Get existing filters and append a new filter
150     // https://microsoft.github.io/PowerBI-JavaScript/interfaces/_src_ifilterable_.ifilterable.html#getfilters
151     filterTarget.getFilters().then(function (allTargetFilters) {
152         allTargetFilters.push(basicFilter);
153
154         // Set filters
155         // https://microsoft.github.io/PowerBI-JavaScript/interfaces/_src_ifilterable_.ifilterable.html#setfilters
156         filterTarget.setFilters(allTargetFilters);
157     });
158
159     $('#filter-form')[0].reset();
160 }
```

Figure 13.21   The addFilter function uses the JavaScript API to append a filter specified by the end user.

Working with row-level security (RLS)

In Chapter 9, I showed you how to implement row-level security (RLS) in Power BI Desktop models. As you know by now, Power BI Embedded users are authenticated and authorized by your application, and your app is responsible for issuing tokens to grant that user access to a specific Power BI Embedded report. However, Power BI Embedded doesn't have any information about the user identity. For RLS to work, your server-side code needs to call a special overload of the CreateReportEmbedToken method, which takes the username and one or more roles that you want to apply. For example, the following code generates a token for teo.lachev@prologika.com and applies the US and Reseller roles:

```
var embedToken = PowerBIToken.CreateReportEmbedToken(this.workspaceCollection, this.workspaceId, report.Id,
    "teo.lachev@prologika.com", new string[] { "US", "Reseller" });
```

If RLS uses dynamic security, USERNAME() and USERPRINCIPALNAME() will return whatever username your app passes to this method. Typically, this will be the login name that the user enters to authenticate with the app, but it can be whatever is required for dynamic security to work (recall that with Power BI Embedded users don't sign to Power BI Service. so the username can be anything). The roles that you pass to the method must exist in the Power BI Desktop file. If the app passes multiple roles, the user will get the superset of all the role permissions.

13.5 Summary

Developers can enrich custom applications with embedded BI content. Thanks to the Power BI open architecture, you can report-enable any web-enabled application on any platform! You can use the Power BI embedded tiles API to assemble dashboards from tiles published to Power BI. And your code can handle tile click events to open the underlying report or another web page. You can leverage the embedded reports API to embed Power BI reports. Embedded reports preserve their interactive features, such as filtering, highlighting, and sorting. Currently, embedded reports are limited to Reading View.

One of the most challenging aspects of report-enabling custom applications is security. If you're tasked to report-enable internal business app and your users have Power BI licenses, your app can pass the user identity to Power BI with OAuth and then call the Power BI embed APIs. As you saw, OAuth is a flexible security framework that supports different authentication flows. The default (three-leg) flow navigates the user to a sign-on page, while the two-leg flow lets you authenticate the user directly with Power BI, if you know the user name and password.

External (Internet-facing) apps can use the Azure Power BI Embedded service to avoid registering users twice and benefit from its per-session licensing model. Power BI Embedded offers three APIs. Call the Azure API to provision new workspaces and upload content. The Power BI APIs are for enumerating reports and generating access tokens on behalf of the user. Finally, the JavaScript APIs expose a report object model that you can manipulate programmatically on the client side to customize your app even further.

Besides report-enabling custom applications, the Power BI APIs allow web developers to extend Power BI's visualization capabilities. You can read about custom visuals in the next chapter!

Chapter 14

Creating Custom Visuals

The Power BI visualizations can take you far when it comes to presenting data in a visually compelling and engaging way, but there is still room for the occasional requirement that simply cannot be met with the built-in visuals. For example, suppose you want to convey information graphically using a graph that Power BI does not support. Or, you might need a feature that Microsoft currently doesn't have, such as drilling through a chart data point to another report. Fortunately, web developers can extend the Power BI data visualization capabilities by implementing custom visuals. They can do this with open source JavaScript-based visualization frameworks, such as D3.js, WebGL, Canvas, or SVG.

In this chapter, I'll introduce you to this exciting extensibility area of Power BI. I'll start by explaining what a custom visual is and the developer toolset that Microsoft provides for implementing visuals. Then, I'll walk you through the steps of implementing a sparkline visual (this visual is also published to the Power BI visuals gallery) for showing data trends. Finally, I'll show you how to deploy the custom visual and use it in Power BI.

14.1 Understanding Custom Visuals

In Chapter 3, I introduced you to custom visuals from an end user standpoint. You saw that you can click the ellipsis (…) button in the Visualizations pane (both in Power BI Service and Power BI Desktop) and import a custom visual that you've previously downloaded from the Power BI visuals gallery. Now let's dig deeper and understand the anatomy of a custom visual before you learn how to implement your own.

14.1.1 What is a Custom Visual?

A custom visual is a JavaScript plug-in that extends the Power BI visualization capabilities. Because the custom visual is dynamically rendered in the Web browser, it's not limited to static content and images. Instead, a custom visual can do anything that client-side JavaScript code and JavaScript-based presentation frameworks can do. As you can imagine, custom visuals open a new world of possibilities for presenting data and new visuals are posted to the Power BI visuals gallery every week!

 NOTE BI developers might remember that SSRS has been supporting .NET-based custom report items. They might also recall that SSRS custom report items render on the server as static images with limited interactivity. By contrast, Power BI runs the custom visual JavaScript code on the client side. Because of this, custom visuals can be more interactive. To emphasize this, the sparkline visual (whose implantation I discuss in this chapter) demonstrates animated features, although this might not be necessarily a good visualization practice.

Understanding the custom visual framework

To allow developers to implement and distribute custom visuals, Microsoft provides the following toolset:

1. Support of custom visuals in Power BI reports – Users can use custom visuals in both Power BI Service and Power BI Desktop.

2. Power BI visuals gallery – A community site (http://visuals.powerbi.com) that allows developers to upload new Power BI visuals and users to discover and download these visuals. Both Microsoft and the community have provided custom visuals.

3. Power BI custom visual developer tools – Custom Visual Developer Tools (https://github.com/Microsoft/PowerBI-Visuals/) that integrate with Power BI to assist developers in debugging and testing the visual code.

Understanding host integration

Power BI has different hosting environments where visuals can be used, including dashboards, reports, Q&A, native mobile applications, and Power BI Desktop. From an end user standpoint, once the user imports a custom visual, the user can use it on a report just like the visualizations that ship with Power BI. In **Figure 14.1**, the last icon in the Visualizations pane shows that I've imported the Sparkline visual and then added it to the report.

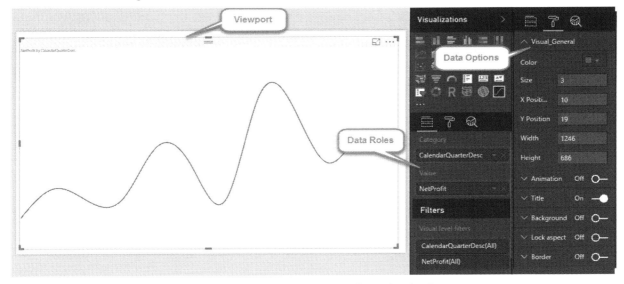

Figure 14.1   The host takes care of the plumbing work required to configure the visual.

When a custom visual is added to a report, the user can specify the size of the visual by dragging its resize handles. The resulting area determines the boundaries of the canvas (also called a viewport) that is available to the visual to draw whatever visualization it creates. When you create a visual, you need to adhere to a specification that determines how the visual interacts with the host environment.

The hosting environment takes care of most of the plumbing work required for configuring the visual. It is the host that takes care of configuring the Fields and Format tabs of the Visualizations pane. The visual simply advertises what capabilities it supports. For example, the Sparkline visual tells the host that it supports one category field and one value field. Once the host discovers this information, it configures the Fields tab of the Visualizations pane accordingly.

The Format tab (shown expanded on the right of the Fields tab in **Figure 14.1**) works in the same way. The visual advertises the formatting options it supports and how they should be presented. However, it is the host that configures the UI (the Format tab). For example, the Sparkline visual tells the host that it supports two properties for formatting the graph: line color and line width. It also supports an optional animation behavior that controls the delay of each redraw and the duration of how fast the graph is drawn. Given this information, the host configures the Format pane accordingly.

The host integration adds a slew of additional features that don't require any coding on your part. The host gets the data based on how the Fields tab is configured, and passes the data to the visual. Interactive highlighting, that cross filters the rest of visualizations on the page (when the user selects an element in one visual), also works without any coding. The host also takes care of report-level, page-level and visual-level filters, and adds Tile and Background settings in the Format pane.

14.1.2 Understanding the IVisual Interface

As I noted, a custom visual must adhere to a design specification. This specification defines an IVisual interface, which every custom visual must implement. The specification is documented and available at https://github.com/Microsoft/PowerBI-visuals/wiki. The IVisual interface defines four key methods, as follows:

- *constructor (options: VisualConstructorOptions)* – when you place a visual on a report, the host calls the *constructor()* method to give the visual a chance to perform some initialization tasks. The host passes an options argument, which among other things includes the viewport height and width. Microsoft recommends that you don't draw the visual in the *constructor* method. Instead, use this method to execute one-time code for initializing the visual, such as to class and style the visual div container.

- *update (options: VisualUpdateOptions): void* – This is the workhorse of the visual. The *update()* method is responsible for drawing the visual presentation. Every time the host determines that the visual needs to be refreshed, such as a result of configuration changes or resizing, the host will call the *update()* method. Similar to the *init()* method, the host passes an options parameter.

- *enumerateObjectInstances (options: EnumerateVisualObjectInstancesOptions): VisualObjectInstancesEnumeration* – As I mentioned, the visual is responsible to advertise its capabilities. You can use the *enumerateObjectInstances()* method to return objects that the host will use to populate the Fields and Formats pane. This method is called for each object defined in the visual capabilities. The host won't display the property if it's not enumerated.

- *destroy(): void* – The host calls this method when the visual is about to be disposed. This typically happens when the visual is removed from the report or the report is closed. The code in *destroy()* should release any resources that might result in memory leaks, such as unsubscribing event handlers.

I'll walk you through the IVisual interface and its implementation details when I discuss the implementation of the Sparkline visual.

14.2 Custom Visual Programming

How do you implement custom visuals and what development tools are available to code and test custom visuals? Microsoft provided a comprehensive toolset to assist web developers to implement custom visuals. In addition, Microsoft published the code of all the Power BI visualization and custom visualizations contributed by Microsoft as open source, so there is plenty of reference material to get you started.

Creating custom visuals is not that difficult but as with any coding effort, it requires a specific skillset. First, you need to know TypeScript and JavaScript to code custom visuals. You should also have experience in Data-Driven Documents (D3.js) because this is the visualization framework that Microsoft decided to adopt for the Power BI visuals. However, you can also use other JavaScript-based frameworks if you prefer something else than D3.js. Finally, you need to have web developer experience, including experience with HTML, browser Document Object Model (DOM), and Cascading Style Sheets (CSS). If you prefer to use an integrated development environment (IDE) for coding custom visuals, some experience with Visual Studio is desired.

To get you started with custom visual programming, let me introduce you to TypeScript – the programming language for coding custom visuals.

14.2.1 Introducing TypeScript

So that they work across platforms and devices, custom visuals are compiled and distributed in JavaScript. But writing and testing lots of code straight in JavaScript is difficult. Instead, for the convenience of the developer, custom visuals are implemented in TypeScript.

What is TypeScript?
When you implement custom visuals, you use TypeScript to define the visual logic and interaction with the host. TypeScript is a free and open source (http://www.typescriptlang.org) programming language developed and maintained by Microsoft for coding client-side and server-side (Node.js) applications. Its specification (bit.ly/1xH1m5Bl) describes TypeScript as "a syntactic sugar for JavaSript". Because TypeScript is a typed superset of JavaScript, when you compile TypeScript code you get plain JavaScript. So, why not write directly in JavaScript? Here are the most compelling reasons that favor TypeScript:

■ Static typing – TypeScript extend tools, such as Visual Studio, to provide a richer environment for helping you code and spotting common errors as you type. For example, when you use Visual Studio and Power BI Developer Tools you get IntelliSense as you type. And when you build the code, you get compile errors if there are any syntax issues.

■ Object-oriented – TypeScript is not only data-typed but it's also object-oriented. As such, it supports classes, interfaces, and inheritance.

Figure 14.2 The TypeScript Playground allows you to compare TypeScript and JavaScript side by side.

To learn more about what led to TypeScript and its benefits, watch the video "Introducing TypeScript" by Anders Hejlsberg at https://channel9.msdn.com/posts/Anders-Hejlsberg-Introducing-TypeScript. Although he doesn't need an introduction, Anders Hejlsberg is a Microsoft Technical Fellow, the lead architect of C#, and creator of Delphi and Turbo Pascal. Anders has worked on the development of TypeScript.

Comparing TypeScript and JavaScript

To compare TypeScript and JavaScript, here's a short sample from the Typescript Playground site (http://www.typescriptlang.org/Playground), which is shown in **Figure 14.2**.

The TypeScript code on the left defines a Greeter class that has a member variable, a constructor, and a *greet()* method. Notice that the TypeScript window supports IntelliSense. This is possible because TypeScript defines the type of member variables and method parameters. These types are removed when the code is compiled to JavaScript, but can be used by the IDE and the compiler to spot errors and help you code. TypeScript is also capable of inferring types that aren't explicitly declared. For example, it would determine that the *greet()* method returns a string, so you can write code like this:

```
someMethodThatTakesString(greeter.greet());
```

14.2.2 Introducing D3.js

Coding the application flow in TypeScript is one thing but visualizing the data is quite another. Again, using plain JavaScript and CSS to draw graphs would be a daunting experience. Fortunately, there are open-source visualization frameworks that are layered on top of JavaScript. Microsoft decided to adopt the Data-driven Documents (D3.js) framework to implement all the Power BI visualizations, but you are not limited to it if you prefer other JavaScript-based visualization frameworks.

What is D3.js?

As you know, JavaScript is the de facto standard language as a client-side browser language. But JavaScript was originally designed for limited interactivity, such as clicking a button or handling some input validation. As Internet evolved, developers were looking for tools that would enable them to visually present data within Web pages without requiring reposting the page and generating visuals on the server side. There were multiple projects sharing this goal but the one that gained the most acceptance is D3.js.

According to its site (http://d3js.org), "D3.js is a JavaScript library for manipulating documents based on data". Documents in this context refer to the Document Object Model (DOM) that all Web browsers use to manipulate client-side HTML in an object-oriented way. D3 uses other web standards, such as HTML, CSS, and Scalable Vector Graphics (SVG) to bind data to DOM, and then to apply data-driven transformations to visualize the data. The D3.js source code and a gallery with sample visualizations are available on GitHub (https://github.com/mbostock/d3).

Automating visualization tasks with D3.js

To give you an idea about the value that D3.js brings to client-side visualization, consider the bar chart shown in **Figure 14.3**.

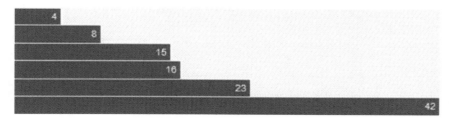

Figure 14.3 Although simple, this bar chart is not easy to manipulate dynamically in JavaScript and CSS.

The left section in **Figure 14.4** shows how a web developer would implement the same chart using HTML and CSS. The code has one div element for a container, and one child div for each bar. The child div elements have a blue background color and a white foreground color.

```
.chart div {
  font: 10px sans-serif;
  background-color: steelblue;
  text-align: right;
  padding: 3px;
  margin: 1px;
  color: white;
}

</style>
<div class="chart">
  <div style="width: 40px;">4</div>
  <div style="width: 80px;">8</div>          d3.select(".chart")
  <div style="width: 150px;">15</div>           .selectAll("div")
  <div style="width: 160px;">16</div>             .data(data)
  <div style="width: 230px;">23</div>           .enter().append("div")
  <div style="width: 420px;">42</div>             .style("width", function(d) { return d * 10 + "px"; })
</div>                                             .text(function(d) { return d; });
```

Figure 14.4   The left section shows the chart definition in HTML/CSS while the right section shows the D3 code.

So far so good. But what if you want to bind this chart dynamically to data, such as when the report is re-freshed or new fields are added? This would require JavaScript code that manipulates DOM in order to put the right values in the right div element. By contrast, the right section shows how you can do this in D3.js. Let's break it down one line at a time.

First, the code selects the chart element using its class selector (.chart). The second line creates a data join by defining the selection to which you'll join data. The third line binds the data to the selection. The actual data could be supplied by the application as a JavaScript array, which may look like this:

var data = [4, 8, 15, 16, 23, 42];

The fourth line outputs a div element for each data point. The fifth line sets the width of each div according to the data point value. The last line uses a function to set the bar label. Note that you'd still need the CSS styles (shown on the left code section) so that the chart has the same appearance. If you have experi-ence with data-driven programming, such as using ADO.NET, you might find that D3.js is conceptually similar, but it binds data to DOM and runs in the Web browser on the client side. It greatly simplifies vis-ualizing client-side data with JavaScript!

14.2.3 Understanding the Power BI Visualization Framework

Curious about how the Microsoft-provided Power BI visuals are implemented? Microsoft contributed the Power BI visualization framework and its complete library of visuals to the open source community. The framework code is available on GitHub (https://github.com/Microsoft/PowerBI-visuals-core). Please note that while it could be useful to explore the inner workings of the core visuals, this visualization framework is now deprecated because the custom visuals are developed using the old interfaces and tools. If your goal is to implement a custom visual, I suggest you start from scratch and use the Custom Visual Developer Tools (discussed in the next section).

 NOTE   As its name suggests, the visualization framework has a lot of plumbing code that all Microsoft visuals share. While code sharing and refactoring are good practices, this common code makes it very difficult to decouple the code for a specific visual so that you can add your own features, such as to extend the built-in Column Cart with markers. The task becomes even more diffi-cult when you have to deal with legacy code and API. This is why I don't spend much time discussing the visualization framework.

Getting started with the visualization framework

The visualization framework includes the following components:

- The source code of all the visuals used in Power BI. Microsoft also published the source code of all custom visuals that Microsoft contributed to the Power BI visuals gallery.

- A playground application to help you test the existing visuals, and experiment with the ones you have created.

Microsoft provided the necessary steps to get you started with the visualization framework on GitHub. I recommend you use Visual Studio 2015 for two reasons. First, the setup steps and walkthroughs on GitHub refer to the Visual Studio 2015 IDE. Second, Visual Studio 2015 integrates with GitHub. If you don't have Visual Studio 2015, you can install the free community edition from https://www.visualstudio.com/vs-2015-product-editions.

Exploring visual code

Once you install the project, the first thing you'd probably want to do is browse the code of the Microsoft Power BI visuals:

1. In the Visual Studio Solution Explorer, expand the Visuals project.
2. Expand the visuals folder, as shown in **Figure 14.5**.

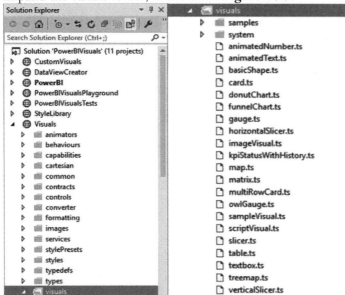

Figure 14.5 Most of the Power BI visuals are located in the visuals folder.

The samples folder includes most of the Power BI visuals. As you can see, the files have a *.ts file extension because visuals are written in TypeScript. Most of the Power BI charts are located in the cartesian folder. The capabilities folder includes files that are used by the visuals to advertise their capabilities to the host. Please feel free to explore and learn from the open source code!

14.2.4 Understanding Developer Tools

If you're a veteran custom visual developer, you'd probably recall the original Developer Tools that were available in Power BI Service (powerbi.com). This toolset is also deprecated and superseded with the Custom Visual Developer Tools (https://github.com/Microsoft/PowerBI-visuals), which I'll discuss next.

 NOTE This section is intended to get you introduced and get started with Custom Visual Developer Tools. For more in-depth information, see the reference documentation within the Power BI Visuals repo at https://github.com/Microsoft/PowerBI-visuals. While you're there, take a look at the tool roadmap at https://github.com/Microsoft/PowerBI-visuals/tree/master/Roadmap.

Getting started with Developer Tools

The Developer Tools consists of a command-line tool (pbiviz) and integration hooks to Power BI Service. The toolset brings the following benefits to developers interested in implementing Power BI visuals:

- Ability to use external libraries – Because the Developer Tools use the standard typescript compiler, you can bring any external library and use it within your visual. Moreover, a custom visual runs in a sandboxed iframe. This allows you to use particular versions of libraries and global styles, without worrying that you'll break other visuals.

- Your choice of IDE – The Developer Tools doesn't force you into a particular coding environment. It's implemented as a command-line tool that works across platforms with any IDE of your choice, including Visual Studio, Visual Studio Code, CATS, Eclipse, and so on.

- Integration with Power BI Service – You can add your visual on a report so that you can test and debug it as you code to see how it'll work when a Power BI user decides to use it. You can also turn on a special live preview mode where the visual automatically updates when you make changes and save the source file.

Configuring the Developer Tools involves the following high-level steps:

1. Follow the installation steps at https://github.com/Microsoft/PowerBI-visuals/tree/master/tools to install NodeJS, the command-line tool (pbiviz), and server certificate. The server certificate is needed to enable the live preview mode for testing the visual in Power BI Service. In this mode, the visual code runs in a trusted https server so you need to install an SSL certificate (included with the tool) to allow the visual to load in your browser.

2. To view and test your visual, you need to enable this feature in Power BI Service. To do so, log in to powerbi.com, then click the Settings menu in the top-right corner. In the Developer section (General tab), check "Enable developer visual for testing" (see **Figure 14.6**). When checked, this setting adds a special Developer Tools icon to the Visualizations pane.

Figure 14.6 Check the "Enable developer visual for testing" checkbox to view and test custom visuals in Power BI Service.

TIP If you use Chrome and you find that the "Enable developer visual for testing" setting doesn't stay enabled after you check it, try running Chrome in incognito mode or clear the browser cookies.

Creating a new visual

The Developer Tools is capable of generating the folder structure and required dependencies for new visuals. You can create a new project by opening the command prompt, navigating to the folder where you want the project to be created, and typing the following command (replace VisualName with the name of your visual):

pbiviz new VisualName

This command will create a new project folder with the same name as the VisualName you provided and will then add some files organized in subfolders. **Table 14.1** shows the structure of the project folder:

Table 14.1 **This table shows the structure of the project folder.**

Item	Description	Item	Description
.api/	Power BI libraries and interfaces	.npmignore	Lists files to ignore when packaging your visual
.vscode/	Settings for launching and debugging custom visuals	capabilities.json	Defines the capabilities of your visual
assets/	Stores additional information to distribute, such as icon, image, screenshot	package.json	Used by package manager for JavaScript (npm) to manage modules
src/	The TypeScript code of your visual goes here	pbiviz.json	Main configuration file
style/	CSS styles	tsconfig.json	pbiviz.json (see bit.ly/2gdlbuv) for more info

Once the project is created, the next step is to open the src/visual.ts file in your favorite editor and start coding your visual.

Installing type definitions for D3.js

Recall that Power BI custom visuals are coded in TypeScript - a typed superset of JavaScript. But where do you get the actual type definitions (also known as *typings*) from? If you target D3.js, you can use the following command to add the D3 type definitions to your project.

npm install typings -g

This command will add a typings folder to your project. In it you'll find an index.d.ts file with the D3 typings. The command also updates the tsconfig.json file to reference the index.d.ts file. The type definitions are provided by Microsoft.

 NOTE Microsoft has indicated that they might discontinue providing type definitions. When I upgraded the sparkline visual to new toolset, I've found that the Microsoft-provided typings are incomplete and missing some D3 interfaces. As a result, the visual failed to build. To resolve this, I had to use the Boris Yankov's D3 typings from https://github.com/borisyankov.

Testing custom visuals

To test the visual, you need to build it and then add it to a report in Power BI Service. Use the pbiviz command-line to build the visual (open the command prompt, navigate to the project folder, then type the command and press Enter).

pbiviz start

First, the command-line tool builds the visual and notifies you of any errors. If all is well, it packages the visual for testing. Next, it launches an https server that will serve your visual for testing. If there are no errors, the command window should show the following output:

info   Building visual...
done   build complete
info   Starting server...

info   Server listening on port 8080.

Next, go to underbi.com. Find a test dataset that will supply the data to the visual and click it to create a new report. Notice that a Developer Tools icon is added to the Visualizations Pane (see **Figure 14.7**).

Figure 14.7 Use the Developer Tools icon to test your custom visual in Power BI Service.

When you click this icon, Power BI Service will add a frame to the report canvas and connect it to the visual you're testing (make sure to execute "pbiviz start" before you click the Developer Tools icon. A toolbar appears on top of the frame. **Table 14.2** describes the toolbar buttons.

Table 14.2 **This table describes the toolbar buttons for testing custom visuals in Power BI Service starting from left.**

Button	Purpose
Reload Visual Code	Manually refresh the visual if auto reload is disabled.
Toggle Auto Reload	When turned on, the visual will automatically update every time you make changes and save the visual file.
Show Dataview	Shows the dataview (actual data) that is passed to the visual's update method.
Export Dataview	Exports the dataview to a JSON format if you want to inspect it further or send it to someone else.
Get Help	Navigates to the tool documentation on GitHub.
Send Feedback	Navigates to GitHub where you can leave feedback.

Debugging custom visuals
You can use the browser debugging capabilities to step through the visual code in Power BI Service.

1. Start your visual test session as explained in the "Testing custom visuals" section.
2. Assuming you use Chrome, press F12 to open its developer environment.
3. In the Chrome Sources tab, right-click the top node and then click "Search in all files", enter some text that appears in your visual, such as *sparkline*, and press enter to search in all script files.

    NOTE   In Microsoft Edge, you can locate the visual script under the "app.powerbi.com/visualSandbox/Dynamic scripts/Unknown script code" folder in the Documents pane under the Debugger tab.

4. You should see a match in the Search results. Click the matching line to load the source file.
5. Put a breakpoint somewhere in your code and then trigger a change that uses this code. For example, if you put a breakpoint in the update method, simply resize the visual on the report (this will invoke the update method). If your code is reachable, code execution should stop at the breakpoint (see **Figure 14.8**).

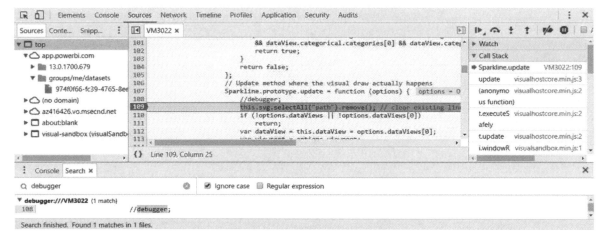

Figure 14.8 Use the browser debugging capabilities to step through your visual code in Developer Tools.

6. Step through the code and examine it. For example, in Chrome you can press F10 to step over to the next line and hover over a variable to examine its value.

While you can change variable values while debugging your code, you won't be able to make changes to the visual source in the browser. You need to do so in your IDE. However, if Auto Reload is turned on, the visual will update in Power BI Service automatically when you save the source file.

 TIP Because the visuals script is entirely reloaded every time the visual is updated, any breakpoints you add will be lost when the debug visual is refreshed. Instead of searching the new debug session, add *debugger* statements in your code.

Upgrading the Developer Tools
Overtime, Microsoft will upgrade both the Developer Tools and scripts. For example, as of this time, the tool doesn't support tooltips (they expect to appear in API Version 1.4 according to the Developer Tools roadmap). The roadmap (https://github.com/Microsoft/PowerBI-visuals/blob/master/Roadmap) informs you when a new version is available. You can upgrade your visual by executing these commands:

```
#Update the command-line tool (pbiviz)
npm install -g powerbi-visuals-tools
```

```
#run update from the root of your visual project, where pbiviz.json is located
pbiviz update
```

The first command will download the latest command-line tool from npm, including the updated type definitions and schemas. The second command will overwrite the apiVersion property in your pbiviz.json.

Now that you've learned about programming and testing custom visuals, let me walk you through the implementation steps of the Sparkline visual.

14.3 Implementing Custom Visuals

A sparkline is a miniature graph, typically drawn without axes or coordinates. The term sparkline was introduced by Edward Tufte for "small, high resolution graphics embedded in a context of words, numbers, images". Tufte describes sparklines as "data-intense, design-simple, word-sized graphics". Sparklines are typically used to visualize trends over time, such as to show profit over the past several years. Although other Microsoft reporting tools, such as Excel and Reporting Services include sparkline elements, Power BI doesn't have a sparkline visual. Yet, sparklines are commonly used on dashboards so I hope you'll find my sparkline implementation useful not only for learning custom visuals but also for your real-life projects.

14.3.1 Understanding the Sparkline Visual

Sparklines come in different shapes and forms. To keep things simple, I decided to implement a "classic" smooth line sparkline that is shown in **Figure 14.9**.

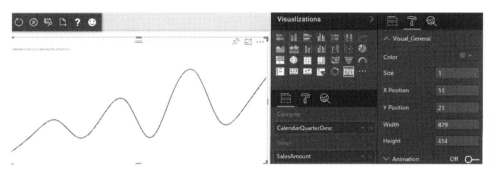

Figure 14.9 You can configure the sparkline using the Data and Format tabs.

Understanding capabilities

Once you import and add the sparkline to a report, you bind the sparkline to data using the Data tab of the Visualization pane. **Figure 14.9** shows that I'm aggregating a SalesAmount field added the Value area by the CalendarQuarterDesc field, which is added to the Category area. The resulting graph shows how sales fluctuate over quarters. You can use any field to group the data, not just a field from the Date table.

The sparkline supports several formatting options to customize its appearance. The General section lets you change the line color and width. The default properties are "steelblue" as a color and one pixel for the line width. The Animation section lets you turn on an animation effect that draws the line gradually from left to right. Although in general I advise against animations and other visual distractors in real-life reports, I wanted to emphasize the fact that Power BI visuals can support anything clients-side JavaScript can do. If you expand the Animation section, you'll see that you can specify two settings: Duration and Delay. The Duration setting controls how fast the line draws (the default setting is 1,000 milliseconds) and the Delay setting controls the interval between redraws (the default is 3,000 milliseconds).

Understanding limitations

The main limitation of the current implementation is that the sparkline doesn't render multiple times in the same visualization, such as for each product category. This limitation also applies to Microsoft-provided visuals, such as the Gauge visual. Preferably, at some point Power BI would support a repeater visual, similar to the SSRS Tablix region. This would allow nesting the sparkline into other visualizations, such as a table, that could repeat the sparkline for each row. As Power BI stands now, the only way to implement this feature is to draw the visual for each category value. Although the sparkline doesn't repeat, it could be used to display multiple measures arranged either horizontally or vertically by adding it multiple times on the report.

Another limitation related to the one I've just discussed is that the sparkline supports only a single field in the Category area and a single field in the Value area. In other words, the sparkline is limited to one measure and one group. Continuing on the list of limitations, the sparkline doesn't support tooltips (it supported them previously) because the new Developer Tools doesn't support them yet. Tooltips are expected to be supported in API Version 1.4 of the Developer Tools.

14.3.2 Implementing the IVisual Interface

I coded the sparkline using Microsoft Visual Studio Code. Visual Studio Code (https://code.visualstudio.com) is a free source code editor developed by Microsoft for Windows, Linux and macOS. Think of Visual Studio Code as a light-weight version of Visual Studio, which is specifically useful if you spend most of your time writing client-side JavaScript code. Visual Studio Code includes support for debugging, embedded Git control, syntax highlighting, intelligent code completion, snippets, and code refactoring.

Let's start its implementation with the IVisual interface. Remember that IVisual has four key methods: *constructor()*, *update()*, *enumerateObjectInstances()* and *destroy()*. You can find the project code in the /Source/Ch13/sparkline folder. The sparkline visual code is in the src/sparkline.ts file.

Implementing the constructor() method

Power BI calls the *constructor()* method to give a chance to the visual to initialize itself. **Figure 14.10** shows its implementation.

```
109  public constructor(options: VisualConstructorOptions) {
110      this.selectionManager = options.host.createSelectionManager();
111      this.root = d3.select(options.element);
112
113      this.svg = this.root
114          .append('svg')
115          .classed('sparkline', true)
116          .attr('height', options.element.clientHeight)
117          .attr('width', options.element.clientWidth);
118  }
```

Figure 14.10 The constructor() method initializes the visual.

First, the code creates an instance of the SelectionManager, which the host uses to communicate to the visual user interactions, such as clicking the graph. The sparkline doesn't do anything with user selection events but it's possible to extend it, such as to navigate to another page or highlight a line segment. Line 111 initializes the D3.js framework with the DOM element that the visual owns, which is passed to the *constructor()* method as a property of the VisualConstructorOptions parameter.

Line 113 creates a *svg* HTML element and classes it as "sparkline". It's a good practice to create another element instead of using the root in case you need to draw more elements in future. The code also sizes the *svg* element so that it occupies the entire viewport.

Implementing the update() method

The *update()* method is where the actual work of drawing the graph happens (see **Figure 14.11**). Line 123 removes the existing graph so that redrawing the sparkline doesn't overlay what's already plotted on the canvas and to avoid drawing new lines when the visual is resized.

When the host calls the *update()* method, it passes the data as a dataView object. For example, if you add the CalendarQuarter field to the Category area and SalesAmount field to the Value area, the host will aggregate SalesAmount by quarter and pass the corresponding data representation and the metadata describing the columns under the *options.DataView* object.

The definition of the *DataView* object is documented at https://github.com/Microsoft/PowerBI-visuals/blob/master/Capabilities/DataViewMappings.md. In our case, the DataView object might look like the example shown in **Figure 14.12**. Since the sparkline visual supports only one field in the Category area, there is only one element in the *DataView.categorical.categories* array. The values property returns the actual category values, such as Q1 2015. The *identity* property returns system-generated unique identifiers for each category value. The *DataView.categorical.values* property contains the values of the field added to the Value area. Because the sparkline visual supports only one field in the Value area, the values array has only one element.

```
121 public update(options: VisualUpdateOptions) {
122     //debugger;
123     this.svg.selectAll("path").remove(); // clear existing line
124     if (!options.dataViews || !options.dataViews[0]) return;
125     var dataView = this.dataView = options.dataViews[0];
126     var viewport = options.viewport;
127     var viewModel: SparklineModel = Sparkline.converter(dataView);
128     if (!viewModel) return;
129     if (viewport.height < 0 || viewport.width < 0) return;
130     var graph = this.svg;
131
132     // stop animation if graph is animating for update changes to take effect
133     this.stopAnimation();
134     // resize draw area to fit visualization frame
135     this.svg.attr({
136         'height': viewport.height,
137         'width': viewport.width
138     });
139
140 var data = viewModel.data;
141 // X scale fits values for all data elements; domain property will scale the graph width
142 var x = d3.scale.linear().domain([0, data.length-1]).range([0, viewport.width]);
143 // Y scale will fit values from min to max calibrated to the graph higth
144 var y = d3.scale.linear().domain([Math.min.apply(Math, data), Math.max.apply(Math, data)]).range([0, viewport.height]);
145 // create a line
146 var line = d3.svg.line()
147     .interpolate("basis") // smooth line
148     // assign the X function to plot on X axis
149     .x(function(d,i) {
150         // enable the next line when debugging to output X coordinate
151         // console.log('Plotting X value for data point: ' + d + ' using index: ' + i + ' to be at: ' + x(i) + ' using xScale.');
152         return x(i);
153     })
154     .y(function(d) {
155         // enable the next line when debugging to output X coordinate
156         // console.log('Plotting Y value for data point: ' + d + ' to be at: ' + y(d) + " using yScale.");
157         return viewport.height-y(d); // values are plotted from the top so reverse the scale
158     })
159
160     // display the line by appending an svg:path element with the data line we created above
161     var path = this.svg.append("svg:path")
162         .attr("d", line(data))
163         .attr('stroke-width', function(d) { return viewModel.size })
164         .attr('stroke', function(d) { return viewModel.color});
```

Figure 14.11   The update() method draws the graph.

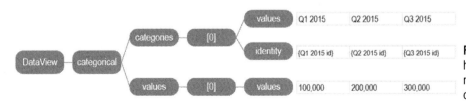

Figure 14.12   When the host calls the update() method it passes a DataView object with the actual data.

Working directly with the DataView object is impractical. This is why line 127 calls a converter object, which converts the DataView object into a custom object for working with the data in a more suitable format. Using a converter is a recommended pattern since it allows you to organize the data just as you are to draw it, which makes your code focused on the task at hand and not on manipulating the data. For example, in our case the *converter.data* property on line 140 returns the data points as a JavaScript array.

The D3.js code starts at line 142. First, the code calibrates the X axis to plot the number of data points. Conveniently, D3.js supports quantitative scaling and the *d3.scale.linear.domain* property scales the

X axis to fit the data points. Next, the code calibrates the Y axis to fit the values given the minimum and maximum data point values. Lines 146-158 plot the line. One cautionary note here is that the zero coordinate of the Y axis starts at the top of the viewport. Therefore, line 157 inverts the data point Y coordinate. Line 161 draws the line using the user-specified line width and color.

Animating the graph

If the user turns on the Animate setting, the line constantly redraws itself using a configurable delay and redrawing speed. The code that animates the graph is shown in **Figure 14.13**. Line 180 checks if the animation effect is turned on. If so, it uses the JavaScript *setInterval()* function to call periodically the *redrawWithAnimation()* function.

```
167  function redrawWithAnimation() {
168      var totalLength = (<SVGPathElement>path.node()).getTotalLength();
169      graph.selectAll("path")
170          .data([data]) // set the new data
171          .attr("d", line)
172          .attr("stroke-dasharray", totalLength + " " + totalLength)
173          .attr("stroke-dashoffset", totalLength)
174          .transition()
175              .duration(viewModel.duration)
176              .ease("linear")
177              .attr("stroke-dashoffset", 0);
178  }
179
180  if (viewModel.animate)
181  {
182      this.timer = setInterval(function() {
183              redrawWithAnimation();
184      }, viewModel.delay);
185  }
```

Figure 14.13 The graph supports animated line redrawing by calling repeatedly the redrawWithAnimation function.

D3.js and SVG make the task of animating the graph easy. Line 168 calls the SVG *getTotalLength()* function to calculate the length of the graph. The *stroke-dasharray* attribute lets you specify the length of the rendered part of the line. The *stroke-dashoffset* attribute lets you change where the *dasharray* behavior starts. Then the SVG *transition()* function is used to animate the path.

Implementing the destroy() method

Remember that the host calls the *destroy() method* to give the visual a chance to release any resources that might result in memory leaks. Our implementation releases the D3.js graph elements. It also releases the timer variable that holds a reference to the timer identifier when the animation effect is used.

```
public destroy(): void {
   this.svg = null;
   this.root = null;
   this.timer = nulll;}
```

14.3.3 Implementing Capabilities

Power BI hosts enumerate the visual's capabilities to provide various extensions. For example, the report host uses this information to populate the Field and Format tabs in the Visualizations pane. For this to work, the custom visual needs to tell Power BI what data and formatting capabilities it supports.

Advertising data capabilities

Figure 14.14 shows how the Sparkline visual advertises its data capabilities. This code is located in the capabilities.json file. The *dataRoles* property informs the host about the field areas the visual is expecting, while the *dataViewMappings* property describes how these fields relate to one another, and informs Power BI how it should construct the Fields tab areas. It can also inform the host about special conditions, such as that only one category value is supported.

```
1   {
2       "dataRoles": [
3           {
4               "name": "Category",
5               "kind": 0,
6               "displayName": "Category"
7           },
8           {
9               "name": "Value",
10              "kind": 1,
11              "displayName": "Value"
12          }
13      ],
14      "dataViewMappings": [
15          {
16              "conditions": [
17                  {
18                      "Category": { "max": 1 },
19                      "Value": { "max": 1 }
20                  }
21              ],
22              "categorical": {
23                  "categories": {
24                      "for": { "in": "Category" },
25                      "dataReductionAlgorithm": { "bottom": { "count": 100 } }
26                  },
27                  "values": {
28                      "group": {
29                          "by": "Series",
30                          "select": [ { "bind": { "to": "Value" } } ]
31                      }
32                  }
33              }
34      "objects": {
35          "general": {
36              "displayName": "Visual_General",
37              "properties": {
38                  "fill": {
39                      "type": { "fill": { "solid": { "color": true } } },
40                      "displayName": "Color"
41                  },
42                  "size": {
43                      "type": { "numeric": true },
44                      "displayName": "Size"
45                  }
46              }
47          },
48          "labels": {
49              "displayName": "Animation",
50              "properties": {
51                  "show": {
52                      "type": { "bool": true },
53                      "displayName": "Visual_Show"
54                  },
55                  "delay": {
56                      "type": { "numeric": true },
57                      "displayName": "Delay"
58                  },
59                  "duration": {
60                      "type": { "numeric": true },
61                      "displayName": "Duration"
62                  }
63              }
64          }
65      }
66  }
```

Figure 14.14   The visual describes its data capabilities in the capabilities.jscon file.

On line 2, the Sparkline custom visual uses *dataRoles* to tell Power BI that it needs a Category area for grouping the data and a Value area for the measure. When the host interrogates the visual capabilities, it'll add these two areas to the Fields tab of the Visualizations pane. On line 14, the custom visual uses *dataViewMappings* to instruct the host that the Category and Value areas can have only one field. To avoid performance degradation caused by plotting too many data points, line 25 specifies a bottom 100 data reduction condition to plot only the last 100 categorical values. So if the user adds the Date field from the Date table, only the last 100 dates will be displayed.

Advertising formatting capabilities

Custom visuals are not responsible for implementing any user interface for formatting the visual. Instead, they declare the formatting options they support and the host creates the UI for them. As it stands, Power BI supports three types of objects:

- Statically bound – These are formatting options that don't depend on the actual data, such as the line color.

- Data bound – These objects are bound to the number of data points. For example, the funnel chart allows you to specify the color of the individual data points.

- Metadata bound – These objects are bound to actual data fields, such as if you want to color all the bars in a series of a bar chart in a particular color.

The Sparkline supports additional settings that allow the user to customize its appearance and animation behavior (shown in the right pane in **Figure 14.14**). All the sparkline formatting settings are static. They are grouped in two sections: General and Animation (it might be beneficial to refer to **Figure 14.1** again). The fill property (line 40) allows the user to specify the line color. The type of this property is color. This will cause the host to show a color picker. The *displayName* property defines the name the user will see ("Color" in this case). The *Size* property is for the line width and has a numeric data type.

The labels section defines the animation settings. The *show* property (line 53) is a special Boolean property that allows the user to turn on or off the entire section. The *delay* property controls how often the line is redrawn, while the *duration* property controls the speed of redrawing the line.

Enumerating capabilities

Here is something important you need to know. The host won't create UI for a capability until you write a code to let the host enumerate that capability! When the host discovers the visual capabilities, it calls the *IVisual.enumerateObjectInstances()* method to obtain the values for each setting. And when the user changes a setting, the host calls this method again to push the new property values. **Figure 14.15** shows the implementation of this method.

```
270  public enumerateObjectInstances(options: EnumerateVisualObjectInstancesOptions): VisualObjectInstance[] {
271      var instances: VisualObjectInstance[] = [];
272      var dataView = this.dataView;
273      switch (options.objectName) {
274          case 'general':
275              var general: VisualObjectInstance = {
276                  objectName: 'general',
277                  displayName: 'General',
278                  selector: null,
279                  properties: {
280                      fill: Sparkline.getFill(dataView),
281                      size: Sparkline.getSize(dataView),
282                  }
283              };
284              instances.push(general);
285              break;
286          case 'labels':
287              var labels: VisualObjectInstance = {
288                  objectName: 'labels',
289                  displayName: 'Animation',
290                  selector: null,
291                  properties: {
292                      show: Sparkline.getAnimate(dataView),
293                      duration: Sparkline.getDuration(dataView),
294                      delay: Sparkline.getDelay(dataView)
295                  }
296              };
297              instances.push(labels);
298              break;
299      }
300      return instances;
301  }
```

Figure 14.15 The host calls enumerateObjectInstances to get and set the visual capabilities.

The implementation of *enumerateObjectInstances* is straightforward. The host passes an options parameter and the *objectName* property tells us which object the host wants to enumerate. The code calls the appropriate *get* helper method to return the object value. When the user changes a setting the code calls the *instances.push* method to save the user selection. After the host calls *enumerateObjectInstances*, the host calls the *IVisual.update()* method so that the custom visual is redrawn with the new settings.

14.4 Deploying Custom Visuals

Once you test the custom visual, it's time to package and deploy it, so that your users can start using it to visualize data in new ways. If you want to make the visual publicly available, consider also submitting it to the Power BI visuals gallery so it's available to the community at https://app.powerbi.com/visuals.

14.4.1 Packaging Custom Visuals

Sot that end users can import your custom visual in Power BI Service and Power BI Desktop, you need to package the visual as a *.pbiviz file.

Understanding visual packages

A pbiviz file is a standard zip archive. If you rename the file to have a zip extension and double-click it, you'll see the structure shown in **Figure 14.16**.

resources	File folder
package.json	JSON File

Figure 14.16 A *.pbiviz file a zip archive file that packages the visual code and resources.

The package.json file is the visual manifest which indicates which files are included and what properties you specified when you exported the visual. The resources folder includes another JSON file. This file bundles the visual code and all additional resources, such as the visual icon.

Packaging custom visuals

The Custom Visual Developer Tools make it easy to export and package the visual.

1. In Visual Studio Code, open the pbiviz.json file.

2. Fill in the visual properties. **Figure 14.17** shows the settings that I specified for the Sparkline visual.

```
1  {
2      "visual": {
3          "name": "Sparkline",
4          "displayName": "Sparkline",
5          "guid": "PBI_CV_194E31A3_85C3_452F_B8C0_A04C34CFC015",
6          "visualClassName": "Sparkline",
7          "version": "1.0.2",
8          "description": "A sparkline is a small graph for showing a trend, usually over tir
             single measure, such as Sales. You can configure the line color, width, and even
9          "supportUrl": "http://prologika.com/contact/",
0          "gitHubUrl": ""
1      },
2      "apiVersion": "1.1.0",
3      "author": {
4          "name": "Prologika LLC",
5          "email": "info@prologika.com"
6      },
7      "assets": {
8          "icon": "assets/icon.png"
9      },
0      "externalJS": [],
1      "style": "style/visual.less",
2      "capabilities": "capabilities.json"
3  }
```

Figure 14.17 Enter information that you want to distribute with the visual in the pbiviz.json file.

3. (Optional) Create a visual icon (20x20 pixels) and save it as an icon.png file under the assets/ folder.

4. Open the Command Prompt, navigate to your project and execute the *pbiviz package* command. The last four lines represent the output the command generates and they are for your reference only.

```
pbiviz package

info   Building visual...
done   build complete
info   Building visual...
done   packaging complete
```

This command-line tool packages the visual and saves the pbiviz file under the dist/ folder. If only users within your organization will use the visual, you are done! You just need to distribute the *.pbiviz file to your users so they can import it in Power BI Desktop or Power BI Service.

Publishing to Power BI visuals gallery

If you would like to make your visual publicly available, consider submitting it to the Power BI visuals gallery. To learn more about how to do so:

1. Open your web browser and navigate to the Power BI visuals gallery (https://app.powerbi.com/visuals).
2. Click the "Learn how to submit visuals" button.
3. On the next page, scroll all the way down and then click the "Submit a visual" button. This will create a new mail in your email client

As of the time of writing this book, you can submit a visual by sending an e-mail to pbivizsubmit@microsoft.com and attaching your *.pbiviz file. Microsoft will review your visual for any issues and the Power BI team will let you know if and when your visual will be published.

 NOTE Is your organization concerned about quality and security of visuals published to the gallery? From a personal experience I can tell you that Microsoft follows a strict process to validate submissions. They'll check the custom visual thoroughly for bugs and best practices. Be patient because it will probably take a few cycles for your visual to appear in the gallery.

14.4.2 Using Custom Visuals

Once downloaded, custom visuals can be added to a report in Power BI Service or Power BI Desktop. As I explained in Chapter 5, you add a custom visual to a report by clicking the ellipsis (…) button in the Visualizations pane.

Understanding import limitations

As it stands, Power BI imports the custom visual code into the report. Therefore, the visual exists only within the hosting report that imports the visual. If you create a new report, you'll find that the Visualizations pane doesn't show custom visuals. You must re-import the custom visuals that the new report needs.

 NOTE As a best practice, you should test a custom visual for privacy and security vulnerabilities by using the Microsoft recommendations at https://powerbi.microsoft.com/en-us/documentation/powerbi-custom-visuals-review-for-security-and-privacy. I recommend you compare the TypeScript and JavaScript files to make sure they have the same code and test the JavaScript code with an anti-virus software.

Removing custom visuals

As you can see, users can easily add custom visuals to reports. Fortunately, Power BI makes it easy to remove visuals from a report if you no longer need them. To do so, edit the report, right-click the visual in the Visualizations pane (works in both Power BI Service and Power BI Desktop) and then click "Delete custom visual" (see **Figure 14.18**).

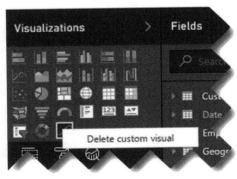

Figure 14.18 Right-click the custom visual to remove it if you no longer need it on the report.

14.5 Summary

The Microsoft presentation framework is open source to let web developers extend the Power BI visualization capabilities and to create their own visuals. Consider implementing a custom visual when your presentation requirements go beyond the capabilities of the Microsoft-provided visuals or the visuals contributed by the community. Custom visuals help you convey information as graphics and images. Any data insights that can be coded and rendered with JavaScript and client-side presentation frameworks, such as D3.js and SVG, can be implemented as a custom visual and used on Power BI reports.

You create custom visuals by writing TypeScript code that implements the Power BI IVisual interface. You can code a custom visual in your IDE of choice. The custom visual advertises its capabilities to the host. The host is responsible for configuring the Visualizations pane to let end users configure the visual. Once the visual is ready and tested, you can export it to a *.pbiviz file, and then import it in Power BI Service or Power BI Desktop. You can also share your custom visuals with the community by submitting them to the Power BI visuals gallery.

With this chapter, we've reached the last stop of our Power BI journey. I sincerely hope that this book has helped you understand how Power BI can be a powerful platform for delivering pervasive data analytics. As you've seen, Power BI has plenty to offer to all types of users who are interested in BI:

- Information worker – You can use content packs and the Power BI Service Get Data feature to gain immediate insights without modeling.

- Data analyst – You can build sophisticated BI models for self-service data exploration with Power BI Desktop or Excel. And then you can share these models with your coworkers by publishing these models to Power BI.

- BI or IT pro – You can establish a trustworthy environment that promotes team collaboration. And you can implement versatile solutions that integrate with Power BI, such as solutions for descriptive, predictive and real-time BI.

- Developer – Thanks to the Power BI open architecture, you can extend the Power BI visualization capabilities with custom visuals and integrate your custom apps with Power BI.

Of course, that's not all! Remember that Power BI is a part of a holistic vision that Microsoft has for delivering cloud and on-premises data analytics. When planning your on-premises BI solutions, consider the Microsoft public reporting roadmap at http://bit.ly/msreportingroadmap. Keep in mind that you can use both Power BI (cloud-based data analytics) and the SQL Server box product on-premises to implement synergetic solutions that bring your data to life!

Don't forget to download the source code from http://bit.ly/powerbibook and stay in touch with me on the book discussion list. Happy data analyzing with Power BI!

Appendix A

Glossary of Terms

The following table lists the most common BI-related terms and acronyms used in this book.

Term	Acronym	Description
Analysis Services Connector (super-seded by On-premises Data Gateway)		Connectivity software that allows Power BI to connect to on-premises SSAS models.
Analysis Services Tabular		An instance of SQL Server 2012 Analysis Services that's configured in Tabular mode and is capable of hosting tabular models for organizational use.
Application Programming Interface	API	Connectivity mechanism for programmatically accessing application features
Azure Marketplace		The Windows Azure Marketplace is an online market buying, and selling finished software as a Service (SaaS) applications and premium datasets.
Azure Machine Learning	AzureML	An Azure cloud service to creating predictive experiments
Business Intelligence Semantic Model	BISM	A unifying name that includes both multidimensional (OLAP) and tabular (relational) features of Microsoft SQL Server 2012 Analysis Services.
Content pack		A packaged set of dashboards, reports, and datasets from popular cloud services or from Power BI content (see organizational content pack)
Custom visual		A visualization that a web developer can create to plug in to Power BI or Power BI Desktop
Corporate BI		Same as Organizational BI.
Cube		An OLAP structure organized in a way that facilitates data aggregation, such as to answer queries for historical and trend analysis.
D3.js		A JavaScript-based visualization framework
Dashboard		A Power BI page that can combine visualizations from multiple reports to provide a summary view.
Data Analysis Expressions	DAX	An Excel-like formula language for defining custom calculations and for querying tabular models.
Data model		A BI model designed with Power BI Desktop or Analysis Services.
Dataset		The definition of the data that you connect to in Power BI, such as a dataset that represents the data you import from an Excel file.
Descriptive analytics		A type of analytics that is concerned about analyzing past history.
DirectQuery		A data connectivity configuration that allows Power BI to generate and send queries to the data source without importing the data.
Dimension (lookup) table		A table that represents a business subject area and provides contextual information to each row in a fact table, such as Product, Customer, and Date.

Extraction, transformation, loading	ETL	Processes extract from data sources, clean the data, and load the data into a target database, such as data warehouse.
Fact table		A table that keeps a historical record of numeric measurements (facts), such as the Re-sellerSales in the Adventure Works model.
Group		A Power BI group is a security mechanism to simplify access to content.
HTML5		A markup language used for structuring and presenting content on the World Wide Web.
Key Performance Indicator	KPI	A key performance indicator (KPI) is a quantifiable measure that is used to measure the company performance, such as Profit or Return On Investment (ROI).
Measure		A business calculation that is typically used to aggregate data, such as SalesAmount, Tax, OrderQuantity.
Multidimensional		The OLAP path of BISM that allows BI professionals to implement multidimensional cubes.
Multidimensional Expressions	MDX	A query language for Multidimensional for defining custom calculations and querying OLAP cubes.
Office 365		A cloud-hosted platform of Microsoft services and products, such as SharePoint Online and Exchange Online.
OneDrive and OneDrive for Business		Cloud storage for individuals or businesses to upload files.
Online Analytical Processing	OLAP	A system that is designed to quickly answer multidimensional analytical queries in order to facilitate data exploration and data mining.
On-premises Data Gateway		Connectivity software that allows Power BI to refresh and query directly on-premises data.
OAuthentication	OAuth	Security protocol for authentication users on the Internet
Personal BI		Targets business users and provides tools for implementing BI solutions for personal use, such as PowerPivot models, by importing and analyzing data without requiring specialized skills.
Personal Gateway		Connectivity software that allows business users to automate refresh data from on-premises data sources.
Power BI		A data analytics platform for self-service, team, and organizational BI that consists of Power BI Service, Power BI Mobile and Power BI Desktop products.
Power BI Desktop		A free desktop tool for creating self-service data models and upload them to Power BI Service.
Power BI Embedded		An Azure cloud service that lets developers embed Power BI reports in custom apps.
Power BI Mobile		Native mobile applications for viewing and annotating Power BI content on mobile devices.
Power BI Portal		The user interface of Power BI Service that you see when you go to powerbi.com.
Power BI Service		The cloud-based service of Power BI (powerbi.com). The terms Power BI and Power BI Service are used interchangeably.
Power Map		An Excel add-in for 3D geospatial reporting.
Power View		A SharePoint-based reporting tool that allows business users to author interactive reports from PowerPivot models and from organizational tabular models.
Power Pivot for Excel		A free add-in that extends the Excel capabilities to allow business users to implement personal BI models.
Power Pivot for SharePoint		Included in SQL Server 2012, PowerPivot for SharePoint extends the SharePoint capabilities to support PowerPivot models.
Power Query		An Excel add-in for transforming and shaping data.
Predictive analytics		Type of analytics that is concerned with discovering patterns that aren't easily discernible

Questions & Answers	Q&A	A Power BI feature that allows users to type natural questions to get data insights.
Representational State Transfer	REST	Web service communication standard
Self-service BI		Same as Personal BI.
SharePoint Products and Technologies	SharePoint	A server-based platform for document management and collaboration that includes BI capabilities, such as hosting and managing PowerPivot models, reports, and dashboards.
SQL Server Analysis Services	SSAS	A SQL Server add-on, Analysis Services provides analytical and data mining services. The Business Intelligence Semantic Model represents the analytical services.
SQL Server Integration Services	SSIS	A SQL Server add-on, Integration Services is a platform for implementing extraction, transformation, and loading (ETL) processes.
SQL Server Management Studio	SSMS	A management tool that's bundled with SQL Server that allows administrators to manage Database Engine, Analysis Services, Reporting Services and Integration Services instances.
SQL Server Reporting Services	SSRS	A SQL Server add-on, Reporting Services is a server-based reporting platform for the creation, management, and delivery of standard and ad hoc reports.
Snowflake schema		Unlike a star schema, a snowflake schema has some dimension tables that relate to other dimension tables and not directly to the fact table.
Star schema		A model schema where a fact table is surrounded by dimension tables and these dimension tables reference directly the fact table.
StreamInsight		An Azure cloud service for streaming
Tabular		Tabular is the relational side of BISM that allows business users and BI professionals to implement relational-like (tabular) models.
Team BI		Provides tools to allow business users to share BI solutions that they create with co-workers.
Tile		A dashboard section that can be pinned from an existing report or produced with Q&A.
TypeScript		A typed superset of JavaScript
Visualization		A visual representation of data on a Power BI report, such as a chart or map.
Workspace		A Power BI content area that is allocated for either an individual (My Workspace) or a team
xVelocity		xVelocity is a columnar data engine that compresses and stores data in memory.

index

Also by Teo Lachev

Applied Microsoft SQL Server 2012 Analysis Services (Tabular Modeling)

An insightful tour that provides an authoritative yet independent view of this exciting technology, this guide introduces the Tabular side of the innovative Business Intelligence Semantic Model (BISM) that promotes rapid professional and self-service BI application development. Business analysts and power users will learn how to integrate data from multiple data sources, implement self-service BI applications with Excel, and deploy them to Share-Point. Business intelligence professionals and database administrators will discover how to build corporate solutions powered by BISM Tabular, delivering supreme performance with large data volumes, and how to implement a wide range of solutions for the entire spectrum of personal-team-organizational BI needs.

Ideal for experienced BI professionals or beginners, this book features step-by-step instructions and demos for building reports and dashboards, deploying and managing BISM, and integrating data from various sources.

ISBN 978-0976635352
Publisher website: http://bit.ly/thebismbook
Amazon: http://amzn.to/21wd3J8
B&N: http://bit.ly/1PwXWeV

The book is available in bookstores worldwide.
Prices and availability may be subject to change.

Also, check out our online and onsite BI training classes at
http://prologika.com/training/training.aspx

- ✓ Analysis Services
- ✓ Reporting Services
- ✓ Power BI
- ✓ Excel data analytics
- ✓ … and much more!

73765934R00209

Made in the USA
Lexington, KY
12 December 2017